Reinventing the State

Development and Inequality in the Market Economy

The purpose of this series is to encourage and foster analytical and policy-oriented work on market-based reform in developing and postsocialist countries. Special attention will be devoted in the series to exploring the effects of free market policies on social inequality and sustainable growth and development.

Editor:
Andrés Solimano

Editorial Board:

Alice Amsden	Patricio Meller
François Bourguignon	Vito Tanzi
William Easterly	Lance Taylor

Titles in the Series:

Andrés Solimano, Editor. *Road Maps to Prosperity: Essays on Growth and Development*

Andrés Solimano, Editor. *Social Inequality: Values, Growth, and the State*

Lance Taylor, Editor. *After Neoliberalism: What Next for Latin America?*

Andrés Solimano, Eduardo Aninat, and Nancy Birdsall, Editors. *Distributive Justice and Economic Development: The Case of Chile and Developing Countries*

Jaime Ros. *Development Theory and the Economics of Growth*

Felipe Larraín B., Editor. *Capital Flows, Capital Controls, and Currency Crises: Latin America in the 1990s*

Mitchell A. Orenstein. *Out of the Red: Building Capitalism and Democracy in Postcommunist Europe*

Ricardo Ffrench-Davis. *Economic Reforms in Chile: From Dictatorship to Democracy*

Stephany Griffith-Jones, Ricardo Gottschalk, and Jacques Cailloux, Editors. *International Capital Flows in Calm and Turbulent Times: The Need for New International Architecture*

Carol Wise. *Reinventing the State: Economic Strategy and Institutional Change in Peru*

Reinventing the State

*Economic Strategy and
Institutional Change
in Peru*

Carol Wise

THE UNIVERSITY OF MICHIGAN PRESS
Ann Arbor

FOR ALL MY PARENTS
Jean, Dick, Sam,
& the memory of Irene

Copyright © by the University of Michigan 2003
All rights reserved
Published in the United States of America by
The University of Michigan Press
Manufactured in the United States of America
⊛ Printed on acid-free paper

2006   2005   2004   2003   4   3   2   1

A CIP catalog record for this book is available from the British Library.

Library of Congress Cataloging-in-Publication Data

Wise, Carol.
    Reinventing the state : economic strategy and institutional change
in Peru / Carol Wise.
       p. cm. — (Development and inequality in the market economy)
    Includes bibliographical references and index.
    ISBN 0-472-11316-X (cloth : alk. paper)
       1. Peru—Economic policy. 2. Peru—Economic conditions—1968–
3. Peru—Politics and government—1980– I. Title. II. Series.
HC227 .W56   2002
338.985—dc21   2002012330

Contents

Tables

Abbreviations and Acronyms

ADEX	Industrialists' exporting association
ANCOM	Andean Common Market
AP	Popular Action party
APRA	American Popular Revolutionary Alliance
BCRP	Central Reserve Bank of Peru
BNDES	Brazilian Development Bank
CADE	Annual business executive meeting
CAEM	National war college
CCD	Democratic Constitutional Congress
CD	Certificate of deposit
CERTEX	Tax-rebate program for nontraditional exports
CGTP	General Confederation of Peruvian Workers
CIAEF	Council of Economic and Financial Cabinet Ministers
COAP	Council of Presidential Advisors
COFIDE	Financial development corporation
CONADE	National development corporation
CONAMYPE	Confederation of small businesses
CONFIEP	Umbrella organization of private-sector firms
CONITE	National Commission for Foreign Investment and Technology
COPRI	Commission for the Promotion of Private Investment
CORFO	State development corporation of Chile
CTP	Confederation of Peruvian Workers
DC	Christian Democrats
ECLAC	Economic Commission for Latin America and the Caribbean
EPF	State Petroleum Company
ESAN	Graduate School of Business Administration (Lima)
FDI	Foreign direct investment
FONAFE	National Fund for Financing Entrepreneurial Activity of the State
FONCODES	National Fund for Development and Social Compensation
FREDEMO	Democratic Front
GDP	Gross domestic product
GFI	Gross fixed investment

ICSA   COFIDE's investment group
IDB   Inter-American Development Bank
IMF   International Monetary Fund
INADE   National Development Institute
INDECOPI   National Institute for the Defense of Competition and the
                Protection of Intellectual Property Rights
INFES   School building program
INP   National Planning Institute
IPC   International Petroleum Company
IPE   Private-sector think tank in Peru
ISI   Import-substituting industrialization
IU   United Left coalition
LIBOR   London Inter-Bank Offer Rate
MEF   Ministry of Economy and Finance
MERCOSUR   Southern Cone Common Market
MITINCI   Ministry of Industry and Trade
NAFINSA   Mexico's state development bank
NAFTA   North American Free Trade Agreement
OAS   Organization of American States
OECD   Organisation for Economic Cooperation and Development
                (industrial bloc countries)
OPEC   Organization of Petroleum Exporting Countries
PAIT   Temporary Income Support Program
PCP   Peruvian Communist Party
PPC   Popular Christian Party
PRI   Institutional Revolutionary Party of Mexico
RGAF   Revolutionary Government of the Armed Forces
SBS   Superintendency of Banking and Insurance
SIN   National Intelligence Service
SINAMOS   National System for the Support of Social Mobilization
SOE   State-owned enterprise
SUNAD   National Superintendency for Customs Administration
SUNAT   National Superintendency of Tax Administration
UNO   National Union Party
UPP   Union for Peru
USAID   U.S. Agency for International Development
VAT   Value-added tax
WTO   World Trade Organization

Acknowledgments

This project began with a Fulbright-Hays grant that I received while completing a Master's degree in Columbia University's School of International and Public Affairs. As a Master's student, my original research question had been the extent to which public policy and capital outlays under Peru's "Revolutionary Government of the Armed Forces" (1968–1980) had shifted in line with this regime's expressed commitment to decentralize and redistribute the country's heavily concentrated investment and income structures. The answer, although obvious in retrospect, caught me off guard: despite the lofty reformist goals of this particular military regime, its legacy was just the opposite. If anything, patterns of state investment and capital accumulation were more highly aggregated by sector, region, and income group when the military finally returned to the barracks in 1980. Like so many students of Peru, I was hooked by the complexities of a situation that had appeared at first glance to be so straightforward.

For this first phase of my research I would like to acknowledge the Fulbright Commission in Lima for its financial support, as well as the Centro de Investigacíon at the Universidad del Pacífico (CIUP), also in Lima. As a visiting researcher at CIUP, I benefited from the dynamic and collegial atmosphere there and in particular from my numerous conversations with Folke Kafka, Guido Penano, Bruno Podestà, and Jurgen Schuldt. While at CIUP, I also had the opportunity to collaborate with another Fulbright researcher at that time, Prof. Patricia Wilson from the University of Texas at Austin. I want to thank Pat Wilson for sharing the first available database on policy outcomes under the military regime, and for encouraging me to coauthor a paper with her on our respective Fulbright projects that was eventually published in the *Latin American Research Review*.

It was the conceptual loose ends from this Fulbright year, and the fact that my project had raised so many more questions than it had answered, that prompted me to enter the doctoral program in political science at Columbia University. There, I quickly joined on to a Latin American doctoral study group that Doug Chalmers had recently launched, and this set the intellectual context for the development of the broader political economy themes on which this book is based. Within that group, I am especially grateful to Marc Chernick, Margaret Keck, and Kathryn Sikkink, for their insights and camaraderie. At Columbia, I also want to thank Doug Chalmers, Bob Kaufman, and Mark Kesselman, who read every word of every draft, and then some. Perhaps the high point of this period was Carlos Díaz-Alejandro's course—

my very first on Latin American political economy—which set a standard that I continue to strive for in my own teaching and research.

For the second fieldwork stint, I returned to Peru armed with the theoretical and methodological foundations of comparative politics, international political economy, and development economics. Even then, I was hardly prepared for the new round of challenges facing the country, including a guerrilla-inspired civil war, hyperinflation, and Latin America's first official debt default in the wake of the 1982 financial crisis. My host this time around was Lima's premier think tank, the Instituto de Estudios Peruanos (IEP), and I especially want to acknowledge Cecilia Blondet, Julio Cotler, Marisol de la Cadena, Efrían Gonzáles, and Oscar Ugarteche for their encouragement and support during my time at IEP. As IEP's lead economist, Efrían Gonzáles was instrumental in hashing over the contours of the explanatory framework presented here. This second phase of my research was also funded generously by the John D. and Catherine T. MacArthur Fellowship in Peace, Conflict, and Security; the Institute for the Study of World Politics; the Organization of American States; the Ploughshares Award; and, the Kellogg Institute for International Studies at the University of Notre Dame.

At the very point when it appeared that Peru had lost its political economic footing once and for all, the country shifted onto a turnaround course that would constitute one of the region's most dramatic comebacks in the 1990s. As with the story of the complete collapse of the political economy in the 1980s, I approach this remarkable recovery from the standpoint of institutional analysis. That is, I disaggregate those state and societal institutions that underpinned Peru's turnaround, and I examine the interplay between international and domestic variables in shaping constructive institutional change over time. For this last phase of the research I want to acknowledge another Lima think tank that hosted me, GRADE, and especially Javier Escobal and Alberto Pascó-Font for their insights and feedback on my research. Funding for this last leg of the project was provided by the John Randolph Haynes and Dora Haynes Foundation; the North-South Center at the University of Miami; and the Fletcher-Jones Foundation.

For support with the finalization of the manuscript I am grateful to Claudia Leo, Ellen McCarthy, and Marcia LaBrenz at the University of Michigan Press, and to my former home department, the Program on Western Hemisphere Studies at Johns Hopkins University's School of Advanced International Studies (SAIS) in Washington, DC. Several former research assistants, including Monica Garaitonandia, Julia Holman, Pablo Montes, Walter Weaver, and Christiane West, provided invaluable support in tending to every last detail. I also want to thank my former colleagues at SAIS, Chuck Doran, Riordan Roett, and Steve Szabo, for their steady support and encouragement.

At SAIS, I am especially indebted to Fouad Ajami for his careful reading of the entire manuscript, and for his incredible commitment and loyalty as both a colleague and a mentor.

Finally, there is a miscellaneous list of colleagues and friends whom I want to mention for their patience, assistance, and good will over the course of this project: Augusto Alvarez, Nancy Anderson, Liz Bauch, Sally Bowen, Deborah Brautigam, Alison Brysk, Max Cameron, Jeanne Cervantes, Javier Corrales, Barbara Durr, Jeff Frieden, Carol Graham, Carlos Iván Degregori, Steph Haggard, Peter Lewis, Cynthia McClintock, Mary Morris, Felipe Ortíz de Zevallos, Olga Samanez, Cindi Sanborn, Martin Scurrah, Sandra Seymour, Michael Shifter, Andrés Solimano, Sue Stokes, and Richard Webb. Manuel Pastor, whom I quite fortuitously met in Lima while we were both conducting fieldwork research, has been a steady source of support and collegial friendship. John Hipp, a sociology doctoral student at the University of North Carolina at Chapel Hill, did a fabulous job in compiling the database and tables for this project. My mother, Jean Anderson, edited numerous drafts and formatted the original tables; and my husband, Glen Steer, while knowing virtually nothing about Peru, did know enough to convince me that a good manuscript is one that can withstand the test of time. He was the main force behind the completion of this book—for this and so much more, I thank him.

Introduction

Throughout most of the post–World War Two era Latin America was perhaps best known for its erratic swings in political regimes and economic strategies and for a decidedly mediocre development record that failed to productively tap the region's rich resource base or buoyant international trade opportunities. While the East Asian region had spawned numerous cases of economic transformation based on high growth and dynamic trade, investment, and distributional gains over this same time period, Latin America could boast of virtually none. Through the "lost decade" that followed the 1982 debt crisis, some pessimists saw an underdeveloping Africa, rather than a newly industrializing Asia, as a more appropriate point of political-economic comparison for the region. The negative growth rates of the 1980s, not to mention the appalling outbreaks of hyperinflation in middle-income countries like Argentina, Brazil, and Peru, did little to dispel such pessimism.

However, with the advent of the 1990s, this all changed. In 1997, Latin American growth rates averaged more than 5 percent of gross domestic product (GDP) for the first time in twenty-five years, and inflation—long the scourge of the region—was heading toward single digits.[1] The region's fiscal deficit had been reduced from an average of more than 9 percent of GDP in the 1985–89 period to less than 1 percent a decade later. Latin American trade with the rest of the world had doubled, and private investment had rebounded from the depths of the 1980s. Because of lingering weaknesses in competitiveness, slack labor markets, and the tenacious hold of poverty and income inequality in the region, these advances still fell short of an Asian-style transformation. Nevertheless, when Latin America's corresponding transition to democracy is factored in, they qualify as a healthy turnaround by anyone's measure.

What explains this turnaround in the region? The answer to this question calls up long-standing debates over what actually drives political and economic development. Political scientists, for example, have long concerned themselves with the extent to which international or domestic variables should be more heavily weighted in the explanation. Economists, on the other hand, have approached this same question according to whether policies sponsored by the state or those that rely on the market deserve credit for triggering a turnaround such as this one. Since the late 1980s an impressive

---

1. These data are cited from the Economic Commission for Latin America and the Caribbean (ECLAC) Web page <www.eclac.org>.

body of policy research has attempted to operationalize such political and economic variables in ways that render them useful as reform prescriptions. John Williamson's (1990, 405) "Washington Consensus"—an ambitious set of proposals for restructuring Latin American economies along staunch market lines—falls solidly in this category, as do numerous policy analyses that have offered specific road maps for the reform of the state (Keefer 1995; Naím 1995; Burki and Perry 1998).[2]

In this book, I seek to answer this same question from the angle of the changing role of the Latin American state in the development process, which includes an in-depth case study of how these themes have played out in Peru. In doing so, I borrow from all three of these research approaches. For example, the political science literature offers compelling arguments about the force of such domestic variables as institutions (state agencies, congresses, political parties), interest coalitions, and executive leadership in explaining political-economic change. While some international relations theorists might insist that such change is rooted in a given country's position within the global system, or in any number of other international influences, I side with a rich tradition of comparativists who have declared this systemic variable an important contextual backdrop that must be taken into account but that falls short of offering a full explanation.

The trends in table 1, which charts the performance of those five Latin American countries that have gone the furthest in implementing market reforms, support this claim. For example, while the 1982 debt shocks constituted a critical juncture for Latin America in that the prevailing state-led strategy literally imploded under the force of rampant fiscal deficits and exorbitant levels of government-backed debt, the response of the respective countries in table 1 was quite variable. The general trend was toward sound macroeconomic recovery, although the five countries in the table can be broken down between fast growers in the 1990s (Argentina, Chile, Peru) and those with much slower growth rates like Brazil and Mexico.

At the same time, the most aggressive traders, Chile and Mexico, emerged from each of these two groups, as these are the only countries that experienced export growth rates that surpassed 22 percent of GDP over the past decade. Nuances and puzzles like these demand further reflection as to the sources and nature of political-economic change, but they also elude international explanations such as those based on external shocks, a given country's

---

2. With its emphasis on fiscal discipline, tax reform, financial liberalization, trade opening, deregulation, and privatization, the Washington Consensus became a "neoliberal" recipe for presidents like Carlos Andrés Pérez in Venezuela, Carlos Menem in Argentina, and Alberto Fujimori in Peru—all of whom ran on gradualist platforms, only to find their respective economies completely unmanageable by the time they were inaugurated.

TABLE 1. Macroeconomic and External Indicators in Argentina, Brazil, Chile, Mexico, and Peru: 1970–2000

	Argentina			Brazil			Chile			Mexico			Peru		
	1970–81	1982–90	1991–2000	1970–81	1982–90	1991–2000	1970–81	1982–90	1991–2000	1970–81	1982–90	1991–2000	1970–81	1982–90	1991–2000
GDPGRO	2.3	−0.6	4.7	7.5	2.3	2.7	3.1	3.9	6.6	7.2	0.7	3.5	4.1	−1.6	4.7
GNPPCGRO[a]	0.8	−2.6	5.0	4.8	−0.0	1.3	0.6	2.1	6.7	3.6	0.6	1.3	1.3	−4.0	4.3
INF	127.9	862.8	21.4	44.6	670.7	579.0	150.0	20.5	9.5	16.8	73.7	18.7	33.3	1,351.1	60.1
PRIVGDP[a]	14.4	13.7	16.5	14.9	16.0	15.5	7.9	12.7	18.8	12.9	12.8	15.4	10.2	14.2	16.7
PUBIGDP[a]	8.6	4.6	1.6	7.0	5.9	4.4	7.5	5.0	4.9	8.2	6.3	3.5	7.1	5.7	3.7
INVEST[a]	22.9	18.4	18.1	22.0	21.9	19.9	15.4	17.6	23.7	21.1	19.0	18.9	17.2	19.9	20.4
RER	97.9	142.7	57.1	109.8	169.3	91.3	51.6	99.4	78.9	85.9	123.4	83.5	226.7	214.7	75.4
TRADEBAL	759.2	4,153.6	−283	−1,395.3	10,920.9	2,718.5	−256.6	1,074.7	−19.0	−2,020.4	6,519.7	−6,045.7	9.5	336.5	1,142.4
CURACCT	−633.7	−1,517.2	−8,701.3	6,210.8	−3,202.9	−15,223.0	−933.8	−1,141.9	−2,000.2	−4,304.8	−868.9	−14,848.9	−483.6	−1,094.7	2,613.9
FDI	186.7	681.9	6,347.5	1,583.6	1,665.8	12,517.6	33.6	5,415.8	2,079.7	931.9	2,020.4	8,793.1	67.7	19.81	1,533.3
PORT	121.6	−397.0	6,952.2	337.3	−220.8	13,752.1	4.8	41.1	565.0	276.8	−271.4	9,312.5	−4.2	NA	140.1
DEBT	13,264.3	54,110.2	106,642.6	36,080.0	108,949.2	179,496.8	6,680.0	19,426.6	27,995.7	27,876.9	97,612.2	147,070.2	6,578.1	15,147.9	27,365.4

Source: GDP, GNP, and debt are from the World Bank, *World Tables, CD-ROM,* 2000 and 2001; GDP growth and debt are from Economist Intelligence Unit Country Reports (March and April 2001); and GNP per capita data are from the Inter-American Development Bank Web site (<www.iadb.org>) 2001. Data on investment from Bouton and Sumlinski 2001 (<www.ifc.org/economics/pubs/discuss.html>). Inflation, exchange rates, and payments are calculated from the IMF's *International Financial Statistics, CD-ROM,* 2001, except for the following: trade balance and current account data for Brazil and Chile prior to 1975, Argentina prior to 1976, Peru prior to 1977, and Mexico prior to 1979 are from IMF 1984; FDI and portfolio investment data for Brazil and Chile prior to 1975, Argentina prior to 1976, Peru prior to 1977, and Mexico prior to 1979 are from IMF 1994.

Note: GDPGRO = growth of real GDP; GNPPCGRO = growth of real per capita GNP; INF = Dec.–Dec. inflation; PRIVGDP = private investment as percentage of GDP based on data through 1998; PUBIGDP = public investment as percentage of GDP based on data through 1998; INVEST = total domestic investment as percentage of GDP based on data through 1998; RER = real exchange rate (1990 = 100), calculated using period average exchange rates, U.S. WPI and domestic CPI; TRADEBAL = trade balance (mil$) = merchandise exports − merchandise imports; CURACCT = current account (mil$); FDI = foreign direct investment (mil$); PORT = foreign portfolio investment (mil$); DEBT = total external debt (mil$).

[a]Data on investment and real per capita GNP are through 1998.

ranking in the global economy, or multilateral policy advice. Given that all five countries in table 1 faced the same external opportunities and constraints in the 1990s, domestic variables and the policy choices they have spawned become essential for specifying the causes of differential outcomes within this general turnaround scenario.

At least one strand of the economics literature—the "new institutionalism"—offers insights that enrich explanations based on domestic variables. While acknowledging the importance that their neoliberal colleagues have placed on market forces, institutional analysts simultaneously insist that the market alone cannot be counted on to foster constructive patterns of development. Rather, Douglass North (1990), Oliver Williamson (1985), and others have argued that favorable economic performance also requires that the market be grounded in a sound set of domestic institutions. This includes formal rules such as the statutes, common laws, regulations, and property rights embodied in the judicial system; informal rules in the way of conventions, norms, and self-imposed codes of conduct; and a wide range of state (e.g., central banks, planning entities, regulatory commissions) and societal (e.g., labor unions, business associations) organizations (Franko 1998, 149). For the new institutionalists, it is the combination of market restructuring and far-reaching institutional reform that would best account for the turnaround in table 1. And it is the variation in institutional structures, broadly defined, that would shed the most light on those differential reform outcomes that have occurred under the thrust of the same market paradigm.

The policy-research literature on Latin American economic reform in the post-debt-crisis era has taken this notion of a market tamed by formal and informal institutions several steps further. First, in light of the many stalled adjustment efforts in the 1980s, this literature came to identify market failure and the profound weaknesses of the Latin American state as two sides of the same coin (Naím 1994). Second, as state reform was gradually cast as a necessary condition for the ultimate success of a market strategy (Haggard 1995; World Bank 1997), this literature challenged the neoliberal notion that privatization and state shrinking were synonymous with such reform (Manzetti 1999). Institutions, as defined earlier, were posited as important, but so too was the reconstruction, renovation, and internal renewal of the state. Third, as the healthy growth rates of the mid-1990s began to give way to a series of external shocks and nagging recession, earlier calls for institutional reform began to shift in favor of a more active state policy (Rodrik 1998; Birdsall and de la Torre 2001). This does not refer to the kinds of reckless interventions that marked the region's past, but instead to the need for a cohesive set of public policies to better combat market failure, to soften the blows of liberalization, and to foster economic dynamism along more equitable lines.

In drawing on these three main political-economic approaches that focus on domestic institutional variables and the best of the policy-reform prescriptions that have emerged over the past decade, chapter 1 sets out to accomplish three main tasks. First, I analyze patterns of economic strategy and institutional change in post–World War Two Latin America from the standpoint of the changing role that the state has played in shaping development outcomes. Three main phases of state intervention are examined: (1) the developmentalist phase that prevailed from the early postwar years up until the 1982 debt shocks, an era in which import-substituting industrialization (ISI), protectionism, and government regulation flourished; (2) the period following the 1982 debt crisis, during which chronic financial insolvency and fiscal retrenchment prompted a retreat from statist strategies and in some cases a virtual collapse of public finances; and (3) the revival of the state's economic presence in the 1990s in a more arm's-length manner, as opposed to the direct modes of participation that had prevailed up through the 1980s.

Second, in order to better specify the ways in which the region has turned the corner, from an all-encompassing statist model to one in which the state has assumed a more market-supporting role in the economy, I construct a time-series database on state participation and economic performance in Latin America from 1960 to 2000. The database confirms that, although deemed problematic by market enthusiasts and multilateral lenders in the wake of the debt shocks (World Bank 1983; Balassa, Bueno, Kuczynski, and Simonsen, 1986), the size of the Latin American state still lagged far behind that of the industrialized countries (Slemrod 1995). Moreover, until the crisis-ridden 1980s, public-sector outlays moved in an upward secular pattern across the five countries, regardless of the different development strategies that may have prevailed over this time period. Although state participation rebounded in the 1990s after the precarious collapse of the 1980s, today's trends are now on par with those of the 1970s. Thus, when all is said and done, a supposedly streamlined Latin American state of the 1990s basically captured the same share of GDP as the grandiose developmentalist state of the 1970s. What to make of these trends?

Given that arguments based on the size of the public sector or the weight of the state in the economy have us literally running in circles, chapter 1 seeks to refine such arguments by identifying the ways in which state intervention became problematic over time. From the time-series database, I extract a cluster of state-related variables that accumulated over the post–World War Two period in the region and that largely account for the severity and duration of the crisis that exploded in 1982. In hindsight, the problem was less the economic scope of the state than it was the quality and nature of state participation across the region. Briefly, the cluster of problems surrounding the latter consisted of an excessive reliance on external borrowing to finance the state; the chronic neglect of fiscal and monetary policy; the placing of too much faith in inefficient state-owned enterprises (SOEs); a perpetual standoff between the state and private investors; and the persistence of dismal patterns of inequality despite a good deal of rhetoric about poverty reduction and the imperative to improve income distribution.

In large part I attribute the turnaround in table 1 to the resolution of this cluster of state-related problems (persistent poverty and inequality notwithstanding), which had become a necessary condition for achieving economic stabilization and recovery in the wake of the debt crisis. Yet, as the 1980s wore on, the track record also showed that the rationalization of the state sector was not an entirely sufficient condition for triggering a sustainable reactivation or anywhere near the levels of growth that would be necessary to revive regional economies. Institutions, regulations, and the state's overall organizational culture would also have to be reformed. Hence, a third task of chapter 1 is to identify those institutional variables that capture the changes that have occurred over the past two decades in Latin America.

In this study I treat institutions in both the classic sense, as articulated by Oliver Williamson (1985) and Douglass North (1990), and in more concrete terms that take into account the coherence of the bureaucracy, the delegation of decisional and operational authority, and the kinds of instruments that policy makers have at their disposal (Willis 1986; Ikenberry 1988; Sikkink 1991; Keefer 1995; Graham and Naím 1998). From the political-economy literature and the actual experiences of the five countries in table 1, four key institutional variables stand out as essential. These include the creation of autonomous agencies within the public bureaucracy; the consolidation of state economic and planning institutions; the stability and character of the leadership coalition; and the nature of the state's ties to organized interests in civil society.

As concerns for institutional reform took center stage in the early 1990s, these state and societal institutions emerged as intervening variables in a couple of ways. First, institutional renovation became the main conduit through which the countries considered here were able to address the cluster of state-led problems identified earlier. I attribute this to the considerable headway that has been made in modernizing institutions along all four of the variables just mentioned. Within state bureaucracies, for example, autonomy has come to mean much more than simply insulating technical staff to pursue specific policy mandates; increasingly, this also refers to the creation of more output-oriented autonomous agencies that are responsible for the delivery of public services according to performance-based criteria (Bresser Pereira 1999, 6–8; Wilkins 1999; Marcel 1999).

Across the five countries, economic ministries and central banks have also been overhauled, and the latter have been granted more leeway in executing monetary policy without political interference (Velasco 1994; Kim 1999; Corrales 2000b; Boylan 2001). Similarly, the old-style planning ministries have been either jettisoned altogether or completely reoriented away from populist sectoral strategies and toward multisectoral policies that support competitiveness and structural adjustment in a more neutral manner. At the executive level, while never entirely free from clientelist pressures, presidential leadership has generally assumed a more managerial and professional stance. For the most part, interest intermediation has become more pragmatic, as representatives on both sides of the negotiating table—state and societal—have settled their differences in a more strategic and levelheaded manner.

Apart from addressing the numerous problems that had accumulated from the past, institutional reforms also emerged as intervening variables in the sense that they were essential for pushing forward an ambitious market-oriented policy agenda. But this involved much more than the implementation of the neoliberal prescriptions (e.g., liberalization, privatization, and deregulation) offered up by the Washington Consensus. Rather, reform of the state in the post-1982 period also involved the redefinition of what it is the state should actually be doing (Przeworski 1999), as well as the revival and concentration of the state's presence in those areas that have traditionally been regarded as crucial for defending the public good. These include, for example, the regulation of natural monopolies; the protection of property rights; the correction of externalities; and the more careful targeting of investments in education, health, and various other endeavors that directly promote more productive and equitable human-capital development.

In essence, deep institutional reforms were instrumental for bringing the state back to life, both quantitatively and qualitatively, and for instilling an ethos of constructive state action in a region where the state had long been regarded as a predatory intruder. Having said all this, it is important to keep these gains in perspective. While the turn-of-the-century prognosis on the capabilities of the Latin American state is certainly more favorable than it was a decade ago, the bar has also been gradually raised on definitions of state effectiveness. In the initial stage of reform post-1982, public policy was considered a success if it met the formidable goals of macroeconomic stabilization. This crucial task having been accomplished by the end of that decade, the benchmark for effective intervention shifted to the state's ability to foster a sound economic recovery. As continued macroeconomic stability laid the groundwork for higher levels of growth and investment in the 1990s, measures of state effectiveness have come to focus increasingly on a number of unresolved microeconomic challenges in the areas of income distribution, efficiency, and competitiveness.

In sum, although I argue throughout this study that the Latin American state has largely reinvented itself over the past two decades, these lingering microeconomic weaknesses suggest that policy makers have been perhaps too literal in following neoliberal dictums for a minimalist state. The microeconomic data presented throughout the book confirm that rather than doing too much, the state still must do considerably more to rectify these microlevel problems. Again, the challenge now is not one of further minimalizing state intervention but rather of finding the proper interaction between state institutions and particular market situations (Amsden 1989; Wade 1990).

The Case of Peru

The remainder of this book focuses on the case of Peru, which stands out among this group of reformers as a dramatic example of a "turnaround" state in the 1990s, defined in terms of growth, investment, and overall macroeconomic stability. The case study seeks to explain this turnaround by analyzing the various economic strategies and patterns of institutional reform that have been embraced by Peruvian policy makers across the three main development phases mentioned earlier. As the title of this book suggests, these long-run development patterns will be examined from the standpoint of the changing economic role of the Peruvian state. While a sizable segment of Peru's established elite continue to attribute the country's economic transformation in the 1990s to the triumph of market over state (Boloña 1996; Gonzáles 1998), this study reveals much stronger parallels with Chile's quiet process of state reconstruction post-1982—itself a reaction to the failure of ideologically driven market reforms implemented during the decade prior to the debt crisis (Schurman 1996; Eduardo Silva 1996; Kurtz 2000).

By drawing strongly on the resources and mentorship of public-sector reform specialists within the multilateral institutions (Keefer 1995; Shepherd 2000), not to mention the determination of former president Alberto Fujimori (1990–2000) to assume the role of a managerial executive advocated along the lines of the "New Public Management" (Pollitt 1990; Bresser Pereira 1999), the Peruvian state has now traded its longstanding predatory image for one that is more market promoting. However, the analysis will also show that, like Chile's, Peru's economic revival has depended disproportionately on autocratic decision-making practices and insulated state agencies

(Guerra-Garciá 1999). Peru now stands at the same critical juncture that Chile reached in the late 1980s, whereby the sustainability and ultimate success of market reforms hinge on the capacity and willingness of bureaucrats and politicians to subject the policy-making process to much broader standards of accountability and societal input (Haggard 1995; Przeworski 1999); and on policy makers' commitment to work more aggressively so that a wider segment of the population can gain access to the benefits of the new market economy (Pastor and Wise 1999a; Birdsall and de la Torre 2001).

Why focus a study of state reconstruction and economic recovery on the Peruvian case, as opposed to other market reformers, like Chile or Mexico, that have also relied on state leadership and the renovation of public institutions as a springboard for economic recovery? In light of the data presented in table 1, the experiences of all five countries clearly offer valuable lessons for other emerging-market economies that are still struggling to overcome the political, economic, and institutional challenges intrinsic to market reform. Peru, however, stands out among its peers in three curious ways.

First is the sheer extremities in the country's economic performance over the past two decades, during which Peru was the absolute worst performer for the 1980s but in macroeconomic terms succeeded in joining the ranks of the Latin American emerging economies over the following decade. By the turn of the millennium, Peru had steadily outpaced its neighbors within the Andean Community (Bolivia, Colombia, Ecuador, and Venezuela) in terms of growth, investment, and overall macroeconomic stability.[3] Even on global competitiveness indicators (e.g., economic openness, quality of government institutions, finance, infrastructure, and labor markets), Peru ranked thirty-sixth out of a total of sixty-two developing countries, compared to the other four Andean countries, which all placed in the fifty-first to fifty-eighth range (Vial and Sachs 2000, 9). Until recently, only Chile had been able to make this same claim to fame in Latin America, and Mexico is now clipping at Chile's heels. Thus, given the rich body of research and policy insights that Chile's turnaround has already inspired (Velasco 1994; Edwards 1995; Schurman 1996; Eduardo Silva 1996; Marcel 1999; Kurtz 2000), and so too Mexico's (Kessler 2000; Chand 2001; Levy and Bruhn 2001; Pastor and Wise 2002), the timing seems propitious for an in-depth examination of those factors that account for another turnaround case in Latin America.

Second, underpinning Peru's radical swings in economic performance since the demise of the country's liberal primary-exporter model in the late 1950s has been an equally erratic pattern of shifting and contradictory development strategies. While other countries in the region have flirted alterna-

---

3. Andean Development Corporation 2000.

tively with state-led and market-oriented development models, as can be seen in table 2, Peru did so with a vengeance. The combination of a severe institutional deficit, frequent and chaotic policy shifts, and drastic dips in economic performance helps to explain why Peru exhibited a barrage of problems—a violent twelve-year guerrilla insurgency that began in 1980, a formal break with the international financial community from 1985 to 1991, the complete collapse of traditional political parties, and the outright abandonment of democracy from 1992 to 1995—that ordinarily strike any given state one at a time. The country's ability to overcome this seemingly insurmountable array of challenges also renders an explanation of the subsequent turnaround all the more pressing.

While I argue throughout the first two parts of the book that the region's notorious development shortcomings are intricately tied to the political, economic, and societal institutions that framed the various strategies that have been adopted, recent empirical evidence and the comparative case analysis developed in part 3 also confirm that the process of economic recovery over the past decade can be attributed to the renovation of these same state and societal institutions. Thus far, I have depicted the Peruvian case as one where the process of institutional reform in the 1990s has been both uneven and incomplete. Yet, even with its cup half empty in this respect, the country has made tremendous economic inroads.

This gives rise to the third compelling reason for the Peruvian case study: while economic success has correlated with a higher quality of state intervention and a partial revival of the country's main institutions, some of these reforms were modest. In other words, minor changes, such as the relocation of a policy to a new office with a new staff (e.g., Peru's privatization strategy, banking-sector regulation) or the overhaul of existing entities (e.g., the tax-collection and customs agencies, the Central Reserve Bank of Peru [BCRP]), went a long way toward promoting the overall reform effort. The implication here is that, even under the direst of economic circumstances, policy makers may not have as far to go as they think in accomplishing certain goals. Conversely, in the event that these same policy makers are able to deepen the process of institutional reform, the possibilities for approximating the dynamic economic gains witnessed in the Chilean and Mexican cases become all the more tenable.

Despite a good deal of ideological posturing and overly stylized facts that credit the various turnarounds reflected in table 1 to the role of market forces, this study argues for a broader explanatory framework based on the intricate and changing ties among state, society, and market. In constructing such a framework, the methodological approach adapted here is distinctly eclectic. The first and final chapters of the book rely on Przeworski and Teune's (1970,

31–46) "most similar systems" approach, in that the five selected cases are as similar as possible on the independent variable (the implementation of deep market reforms) but vary widely on the dependent variables (political-economic outcomes in the postreform era). As Peter Smith (1995, 4) has pointed out, similar system designs "lend themselves especially well to intraregional comparisons . . . since location within a single region can operate as a 'control' for the effects of a substantial range of potential independent variables." The remainder of the book relies on within-case analysis (George 1979; Ragin 1987; Collier 1993, 115–16), which shifts the research design from a cross-country comparison to one that probes the patterns of economic strategy and institutional change that have played out over time within the Peruvian case. In both instances—a broader similar-systems comparison or a more detailed case analysis—institutions emerge as intervening variables that work to shape the diverse range of political-economic outcomes that emerge in this study.

Plan of the Book

The plan of the book is as follows. In line with the within-case method employed here, chapters 2 through 6 encompass the five separate episodes of political-economic development in Peru that are outlined in table 2. Chapters 2 and 3 constitute part 1 of the book, which examines Peru's developmentalist heyday that began with the first phase of ISI in the early 1960s and ended with the virtual meltdown of state capitalism in the late 1970s. The story begins at the very point at which the country's outward-looking strategy based on primary exports ran up against the same volatile price fluctuations and unfavorable shifts in the terms of trade that had prompted Argentina, Brazil, Chile, and Mexico to pursue ISI more intently and much earlier on. Yet, whereas powerful interests within the state and the private sector drove a state-sponsored industrial strategy in these other countries, Peru's ISI strategy in the 1960s unfolded almost as a policy by default. Given the incipient nature of state institutions at this time, and the lack of cohesive organizational ties between the state and key groups in civil society, chapter 2 shows how fairly moderate intentions to launch an ISI strategy in Peru quickly escalated into a much more encompassing role for the state.

The outright incoherence of economic policy and the unraveling of the country's political coalitions prompted a 1968 military coup and the installation of a twelve-year reformist military experiment that departed radically from other South American military regimes emerging at the time. For example, in contrast to the avid free-market authoritarian governments that were erupting simultaneously in the Southern Cone, the Peruvian military

TABLE 2. Presidential Administrations and Development Models in Peru: 1963–2000

	Presidential Administration	Economic Policy	Development Model
1963–68	Fernando Belaúnde	Developmentalism	• Infant industry protection • Large-scale public infrastructure investments • Fiscal expansion • Redistributive rhetoric • Pegged exchange rate • Loose monetary policy • Increased public borrowing
1968–80	Revolutionary Government of the Armed Forces (RGAF) Phase I Juan Velasco (1968–75)	State capitalism (expansion phase)	• Secondary import substitution • Large-scale public infrastructure investments • Widespread nationalization • Agrarian land reform • Redistributive policy • Pegged exchange rate • Erratic monetary policy • Increased public borrowing
	Phase II Morales Bermúdez (1975–80)	(Adjustment phase)	• Promotion of nontraditional exports • Trade liberalization • Crawling peg exchange rate • Fiscal and monetary tightening • Debt renegotiation and increased public borrowing
1980–85	Fernando Belaúnde	Orthodox stabilization with populist overtones	• Promotion of primary exports • Large-scale public infrastructure investments • Fiscal expansion • Crawling peg exchange rate

			• Erratic monetary management
			• Debt renegotiation and increased public borrowing
			• Trickle-down social policy
1985–90	Alan García	Neostructuralism	• Wage and price controls
			• Consumer-led economic reactivation
			• Trade protection
			• Redistributive rhetoric
			• Multitiered exchange rate
			• Expansionary fiscal and monetary policy
			• Neglect of infrastructure
			• Unilateral debt moratorium
1990–2000	Alberto Fujimori	Neoliberalism and the "Washington Consensus"	• Tax and banking reform
			• Privatization
			• Financial liberalization
			• Deregulated labor markets
			• Liberalization of land holdings
			• Trade liberalization
			• Floating exchange rate
			• Tight monetary policy
			• Resumption of debt-service payments and debt renegotiation
			• FONCODES safety net

launched an ambitious state-led development program that sought to strengthen the country's position in international markets and to reverse longstanding patterns of poverty and inequality. Chapter 3 details the ways in which this full-blown state capitalist strategy was hampered by the fact that those crucial bureaucratic, institutional, and administrative supports that would be mandatory for its effective implementation were being built up simultaneously with the launching of the program. Thus, for all its attempts at institutional reform at the level of the state and civil society, the military regime was not able to carve out an effective role for the state as the motor of development or as an effective mediator of pivotal societal interests. In the end, a main legacy of this period was the solidification in Peru of the cluster of problems related to state-led development mentioned earlier, a theme that would plague policy makers and dominate domestic policy debates long after the military's return to the barracks.

Part 2 encompasses chapters 4 and 5, which span the purposive attempt in the early 1980s to turn back the clock to the pre-1960s era of a "small" state, balanced budget, and low inflation, as well as the heterodox backlash and complete collapse of the state that followed. Chapter 4 analyzes the efforts of newly installed civilian policy makers in 1980 to rationalize public spending and to restore the state to its previous ancillary role as a backup for private initiative. However, in the absence of any effort at authentic institutional reform, and under the thrust of severe external financial restraints, this effort quickly stalled. In their rejection of state-led management approaches, civilian politicians and policy makers tended to work around those bureaucratic, institutional, and administrative structures that would have been crucial for the successful implementation of any development program. In essence, rather than a return to the market, this brief spurt of orthodoxy was more a reflection of the animosity that political and economic elites now held toward the state. Meanwhile, as the impact of the 1982 debt shocks intermingled with these institutional weaknesses, the cluster of state-led problems (excessive debt, macroeconomic incoherence, a fickle private sector, predatory SOEs, deepening inequality) spun out of control.

Despite the collapse early on of any semblance of an orthodox adjustment strategy in the early 1980s, Peru's 1985 elections provoked yet another backlash—this time against the market and in favor of a platform that promised to pursue a supposedly more fine-tuned state-led strategy. Examined in chapter 5, this heterodox venture consisted of both a short-term anti-inflation shock program based on wage and price controls and a longer-term program of state-led industrialization that basically embraced its own version of ISI. In hindsight, this particular policy episode proved to be a grand finale of sorts, as institutional reform was completely eclipsed by populist politics, and the

Peruvian state could not begin to rise to the new set of demands that were placed on it. The state literally collapsed under its own weight, rendering hyperinflation and an unprecedented explosion in the country's poverty levels as the most glaring legacies of this period. At this point, the resolution of the numerous state-led problems mentioned earlier could no longer be circumvented or ignored, nor could the reform of the state itself.

Part 3 analyzes Peru's economic turnaround in the 1990s from these very standpoints: the determination of the Fujimori administration to resolve these state-led problems once and for all and its resort to partial institutional reform as the means for doing so. While there was in fact little consensus in the region over the implementation of Washington's sweeping prescriptions for market reform at the outset of the 1990s, the exigencies of hyperinflation and a decade-long recession compelled all five countries in table 1 to adopt this package, each in its own way. For example, while the launching of market reforms in Chile, Mexico, and Peru was largely a state-centered phenomenon, Argentina and Brazil relied more on interest intermediation and the transformation of institutional ties among the executive, political parties, and other civic organizations.

With Chile's transition to democracy in 1990, and Mexico's in 2000, the past decade has seen a shift in those countries toward greater civic participation and intermediation between the state and society over the content and direction of the reform process. Again, in line with its tendency for being slightly out of step in terms of regional development patterns, Peru carried its strategy of using the state as the main locus for reform to extremes—as witnessed in its 1992 civilian coup and the suspension of formal democratic procedures from 1992 to 1995. With Fujimori's bizarre and unexpected resignation under a cloud of corruption in late 2000, and the truly democratic election of President Alejandro Toledo in June 2001, the country is just now embarking on a badly needed microlevel economic-reform strategy based on broadening and deepening the overhaul of domestic institutions and on the initiation of Chilean-style dialogues, or *concertación,* between the state and a wide range of groups in civil society (Kuczynski and Ortíz de Zevallos 2001).[4]

Nevertheless, despite the collapse of political parties since the 1990 election, and the emergence of a decidedly dysfunctional leadership coalition composed of the fiercely independent Fujimori, the military, and considerable segments of the private sector, even partial institutional renovation (as described earlier) took the country all the way through the first phase of market reforms. Thus, chapter 6 analyzes the impressive inroads that were indeed

4. I thank Eduardo Ballón for sharing these insights during a January 2002 fieldwork visit to Peru.

made in the realm of macroeconomic stabilization, the modernization of public finances, and the restoration of growth and investment in Peru. For better or worse, and barring the still tenacious hold of poverty on the country, the decade-long Fujimori government did succeed in resolving the cluster of state-related problems that had completely overwhelmed policy makers by the late 1980s.

As an exercise in assessing the inroads that Peru has made in reforming the political economy and the institutional framework that surrounds it, chapter 6 also identifies those tasks that remain on the reform agenda. This assessment draws partly from my own fieldwork observations but also from a rich body of local research and debate that blossomed in the context of a transition government led by former congressional leader and interim president Valentín Paniagua from 2000 to 2001. Similar to Argentine president Carlos Menem in the late 1990s and Brazilian president Fernando Henrique Cardoso in their second terms, Fujimori was unable to fulfill the mandate that supposedly justified a constitutional amendment to allow him to run for a second term. That is, rather than expanding the reform process into the tough microeconomic areas that still must be addressed in order for Peruvian workers and smaller firms to benefit from a market economy, Fujimori squandered the resources available on sporadic social spending geared toward promoting his candidacy for yet a third term. Moreover, when the electorate and the congress resisted this quest for reelection, badly needed institutional reforms in the areas of justice, the central government ministries, and the country's long-neglected regional governments were completely ignored. If anything, institutional integrity in these areas actually declined.

The completion of these tasks—devising a dynamic microeconomic strategy that will promote competitiveness and greater equality and deepen the processes of institutional reform—has now fallen to the Toledo administration. Yet, in contrast to the outset of the reform period in the 1980s, when Peruvian policy makers were at a considerable loss as to what the proper policy mix should be for stabilizing inflation and promoting sustainable growth, the current reform agenda is highly articulate and very much in the realm of what's possible for Peru. And to its credit, the Toledo administration succeeded early on in bringing together perhaps the most talented cohort of policy makers and administrators that the country has ever seen. Politics, however, are still unwieldy, as the handful of new political parties that have arisen over the past decade still amounts to little more than social groupings that band together at election time and then fragment once in office. Civil society, moreover, has again begun to flex its muscle, with labor unions and any number of civic protestors taking to the streets in ways not possible during Fujimori's heavy-handed reign.

Thus, while Peru has finally turned the corner, such that the tasks of economic and institutional reform are widely agreed upon and broad segments of civil society have accepted the *concertación* strategy as the most appropriate venue for pursuing these goals, party politics have yet to follow suit. Despite the inroads that have clearly been made, without a more cohesive institutionalization of politics itself, the country risks sinking back into the same underachiever niche that it has heretofore occupied. Conversely, with strong political leadership and a little fortitude, the economic track record over the past decade readily shows that Peru is capable of breaking into the ranks of the high achievers. The present juncture is one of the right time and the right place for pursuing the ambitious reform agenda that Toledo identified during his campaign (see Kuczynski and Ortíz de Zevallos 2001). Already, after just a year in office, the presidential cabinet has seen one major changeover.[5] This rotation is far from fatal, given that the new appointments spring from the same mold as the former team. But this does up the ante for Toledo, as it is time for the president and this new team to show that they are the right ones to finally get the job done.

During its first year in government, the Toledo administration made much progress in terms of rectifying the errors of the recent past. At least four special congressional commissions are at work investigating the corruption of the Fujimori era—including money laundering, flagrant interference in the judicial system, and possible abuses that occurred in the privatization process. The military, Fujimori's most prominent partner in crime, has seen a sharp reduction of personnel and the retirement of nearly 500 officials. "Transparency," previously a foreign concept in Peru's public discourse, has become an everyday fact of political life in the post-Fujimori era. In sum, there exists little doubt as to the commitment of the current administration to set the country back on course. The task now is for the Toledo team to look forward and to more assertively advance its own project, one that deepens the political inroads made by the Paniagua transition team, and completes the process of market restructuring necessary to sustain higher and more equitable patterns of economic growth.

---

5. Juan Forero, "Top Peruvian Ministers Forced Out in Cabinet Shakeup," *New York Times,* July 12, 2002, p. A3.

CHAPTER 1

Latin America and the State-Market Debate: Beyond Stylized Facts

The literature on the political economy of development is rich with descriptions of government action over time and in-depth analyses of the causal relationship among state intervention, public policy, and development outcomes. In broad strokes, the story of the post–World War Two Latin American state has been portrayed in this literature as follows.[1] During the heyday of ISI in the 1960s and 1970s, the state was cast favorably as the main protagonist in high-growth "miracles" such as those underway in Brazil and Mexico (Gereffi and Evans 1981). However, as Latin America fell on hard times during the debt-ridden 1980s, the state quickly became the culprit in explaining this downturn. Any notable economic turn-arounds during the 1980s—say, in Chile—were attributed to the "miracle of the market" (Schurman 1996; Kurtz 2000).

Although the affinity for market reform had spread quickly through the region by the early 1990s, by the end of that decade its limits had also become apparent. The state's stock rose again, as the regressive outcomes of unbridled economic liberalization prompted calls for a more cohesive set of public policies to facilitate adjustment and correct for the many instances of market failure. As common wisdom would have it, the state appears to have come full circle: from its market-supporting role under a primary-export-led development model prior to the Great Depression; to its more encompassing "developmentalist" role during the post–World War Two era of ISI; to its widely hailed post-debt-crisis retreat from playing a direct role in the economy; and finally, back to the pre-ISI liberal state meant to bolster private initiative through the enforcement of property rights and the provision of basic public goods.

When this same phenomenon is examined empirically, there is some evidence to support this notion of the Latin American state having come full circle. Having peaked at an average of 24.3 percent of GDP for the region as a whole in the mid-1980s, public expenditure for the 1995–2000 period stood at about 16.6 percent of GDP—right on par with the 17 percent average reg-

---

1. The state is defined here as "more than the 'government.' It is the continuous administrative, legal, bureaucratic and coercive systems that attempt not only to structure relationships between civil society and public authority in a polity but also to structure many crucial relationships within civil society as well" (Stepan 1978, xii).

istered during the 1970s (see table 3). There has been a similar convergence in public investment as a percentage of Latin American GDP (see table 4), which averaged 6.8 percent in the 1970s, compared to 5.4 percent in the second half of the 1990s. These patterns of holding the line on state expansion contrast with those of the industrial bloc countries, where public outlays continue to rise and are now easily 15 to 20 percent higher than those of Latin America (World Bank 1988, 44; World Bank 1997, 22). While one could surmise from the Latin American trends that policy makers finally came to their senses and reined in state expansion, these data also raise some intriguing questions.

First, if public-spending and investment levels in Latin America have circled back to their levels of two decades ago, and if these coefficients have been consistently lower than those in the industrial bloc, what was so problematic about these trends in the first place? Obviously, there is more to measuring the economic presence of the state than the figures just cited; for instance, the overall regulatory framework and the share of GDP captured by SOEs must also be included in any such assessment. Nevertheless, time-series data on the Latin American public sector from 1960 to 2000 seem to throw cold water on the "weight-of-the-state" argument that has underpinned so much of the market-reform drive in the 1990s. These trends also raise the possibility that the state has taken too much of the blame for the policy failures that erupted in the wake of the 1982 debt shocks.

A second question concerns the loose correlation between espoused development strategies and empirical trends in the Latin American state sector. How is it that public spending and investment as a percentage of Latin American GDP are roughly equivalent for two periods that could not be more different qualitatively—that is, the heavy-handed developmental state of the early 1970s versus the reticent, streamlined state of the late 1990s? Not only are these continuities counterintuitive, but they also suggest the extent to which the state-market debate has fallen prey to ideological posturing and stylized facts. The Chilean case, where high growth rates and deep market reforms have coexisted quite compatibly with a strong state presence, underlines the need for more flexible thinking on this subject.

A third question has to do with policy outcomes. In the face of fairly uniform approaches to market reform, how do we explain the diverse political-economic outcomes that have emerged since the revival of growth and investment flows to Latin America in the 1990s? How is it, for example, that Chile has grown twice as fast as Mexico—the country with the second-longest market-reform track record in the region—over the past decade? Or how is that Peru, a country devastated by guerrilla insurgencies, debt default, and natural disasters as recently as a decade ago, outpaced Argentina and Brazil in terms of its GDP share of exports and investment during the 1990s? Such variables as the

TABLE 3. Public-Sector Trends in Latin America (all data as % of GDP)

		Developmental State		State in Retreat		Streamlined State	
		1960–69	1970–79	1980–84	1985–89	1990–94	1995–2000
Argentina	Expend	12.92	14.80	8.74	5.38	6.13	15.85
Argentina	Revenue	10.11	12.96	4.49	4.67	5.65	14.20
Argentina	GovDeficit	–2.81	–1.83	–4.25	–0.71	–0.47	–1.66
Argentina	GovDebt	.88	7.62	20.97	44.20	22.66	24.67
Brazil	Expend	10.52	17.52	21.54	39.30	33.89	
Brazil	Revenue	8.46	20.25	25.14	25.25	30.97	
Brazil	GovDeficit	–2.00	–0.30	–4.53	–18.24	–6.21	–5.00
Brazil	GovDebt	0.05	11.85	22.63	26.92	20.05	12.59
Chile	Expend	18.97	31.79	31.44	24.48	20.95	21.87
Chile	Revenue	17.35	29.61	29.82	24.17	22.56	22.92
Chile	GovDeficit	–1.62	–1.84	–0.26	0.68	1.75	1.02
Chile	GovDebt	14.26	27.84	25.63	63.54	23.70	7.75
Mexico	Expend	8.74	12.28	23.50	23.56	15.20	15.15
Mexico	Revenue	7.82	9.15	15.86	15.58	15.05	13.94
Mexico	GovDeficit	–0.92	–2.90	–7.79	–8.05	1.13	–1.10
Mexico	GovDebt	0.79	12.52	25.23	45.29	21.51	25.10
Peru	Expend	16.72	18.73	18.64	12.85	18.19	18.41
Peru	Revenue	14.82	15.46	13.76	7.27	15.44	17.26
Peru	GovDeficit	–1.88	–3.27	–4.88	–5.58	–1.05	–0.05
Peru	GovDebt	9.94	22.17	33.53	62.35	47.44	36.26
Latin America	Expend		17.07	20.00	24.39	23.60	16.61
Latin America	Revenue		13.64	19.19	20.01	19.32	15.62
Latin America	GovDeficit		–3.42	–4.17	–9.28	–2.25	–0.99
Latin America	GovDebt		12.97	25.85	41.25	27.25	21.29

Source: The IMF's *International Financial Statistics CD-ROM*, March 1999, and the World Bank's *World Development Indicators*, CD-ROM, 2001. Argentina public expenditure, revenue, and deficits from 1960 to 1979; debt for Argentina, Chile, Colombia, and Mexico from 1960 to 1969; and expenditure, revenue, and deficits for Mexico and Colombia from 1960 to 1969 are from *United Nations Yearbook*. Brazil revenue and expenditure data from 1995 to 1998 are from BNDES (Brazilian Development Bank) database 2001, (<www.bndes.gov.br>). Data on the Latin American public deficit from 1995 to 2000 are from ECLAC web site, 2001 (<www.eclac.org>). Total Latin American expenditures, revenue, and deficit during the 1970s and from 1995 to 2000 calculated by summing available country data, weighted by GDP.

Note: Expend = public expenditure as % of GDP; Revenue = public revenue as % of GDP; GovDeficit = Government budget deficit as % of GDP; GovDebt = Public and publicly guaranteed debt as % of GDP.

TABLE 4. Investment Trends in Latin America (all data as % of GDP)

		Developmental State		State in Retreat		Streamlined State	
		1960–69	1970–79	1980–84	1985–89	1990–94	1995–2000
Argentina	PRIINV		13.62	16.48	13.57	14.03	16.63
Argentina	PUBINV		9.11	5.63	4.18	2.67	2.01
Argentina	TOTINV	16.23	22.73	22.11	17.75	16.70	18.64
Brazil	PRIINV		14.58	15.41	16.62	15.45	16.12
Brazil	PUBINV		6.99	6.53	5.85	5.20	3.47
Brazil	TOTINV	18.80	21.57	21.94	22.48	20.65	19.59
Chile	PRIINV		6.98	9.60	14.66	18.07	18.73
Chile	PUBINV		7.92	5.18	4.69	5.27	5.43
Chile	TOTINV	20.97	14.90	14.78	19.35	23.34	24.15
Mexico	PRIINV		12.66	12.67	13.19	15.34	16.17
Mexico	PUBINV		7.60	9.27	5.41	4.36	2.92
Mexico	TOTINV	15.62	20.26	21.94	18.60	19.70	19.09
Peru	PRIINV		7.76	15.84	13.43	13.29	18.73
Peru	PUBINV		7.49	8.00	4.74	3.13	4.53
Peru	TOTINV	18.21	15.25	23.85	18.17	16.42	23.26
Latin America	PRIINV		12.45	12.61	12.23	13.04	14.38
Latin America	PUBINV		6.80	6.94	5.63	5.67	5.40
Latin America	TOTINV	18.21	19.25	19.54	17.86	18.71	19.78

Economic activity of state-owned enterprises as % of GDP

	1978–80	1981–83	1984–86	1987–89	1990–92	1993–96
Argentina				2.70	1.97	0.63
Brazil	6.50	3.51	5.20	8.77	9.51	6.23
Chile	12.40	13.00	15.99	14.03	9.80	7.10
Mexico				6.70	5.52	4.24
Peru	6.85	8.45	10.11	4.40	5.97	5.41

Source: Bouton and Sumlinski 2001 <www.ifc.org/economics/pubs/discuss.html>. Data on public and private investment from 1970 to 2000 are from National Bureau of Economic Research 2001 <www.nber.org.pwt56.html>. Data on state-owned enterprises are from World Bank, *World Tables, CD-ROM,* 1999, 2000, and 2001.

shadow of the past, differences in the pace and timing of market reforms, and a country's ties to the international economy must all be taken into account.

But the one set of variables that differs most across these cases is the institutional dimensions of the state and the nature of the state's ties to civil society. As a number of authors have pointed out, the gaps between expressed policy preferences, concrete government action, and actual development outcomes are best understood by studying the broader institutional and societal context that frames the reform process (Evans, Rueschemeyer, and Skocpol 1985; Sikkink 1991; Evans 1995; Tendler 1997; Bresser Pereira 2000). Despite the apparent continuities over time in the levels of government economic presence, when viewed through this institutional lens, the state-societal dynamics that underpin the Latin American public sector of the late 1990s are worlds apart from those of the pre-1982 era.

Together, these questions form the basis for this chapter. In exploring them I draw, first, on empirical data that track state-sector trends and economic performance in Argentina, Brazil, Chile, Mexico, and Peru during the three development phases mentioned earlier: (1) the ISI/developmentalist era, which for reasons of data availability I treat here as the time period from 1960 to 1980; (2) the decade of economic retrenchment and state retreat that marked the 1980s; and (3) the era of market reform and state streamlining that was well underway by 1990 in all five countries. Second, I rely on institutional analysis as a means for understanding differences in economic performance among these five countries in the prereform period (prior to the 1982 debt shocks) and in the wake of implementing ambitious market reforms.

In this chapter, and throughout the book, institutions are treated in the classic sense, as those formal and informal rules that shape the behavior of individuals and organizations in civil society (Oliver Williamson 1985; North 1990; Burki and Perry 1997). At the same time, I take a more concrete approach to institutional analysis that considers the coherence of the bureaucracy, the delegation of decisional and operational authority, and the kinds of instruments that policy makers have at their disposal (Ikenberry 1988; Keefer 1995; Graham and Naím 1998). From the standpoint of institutional change the bottom line, as aptly summarized by Adam Przeworski (1999, 15), is to encourage "the state apparatus to do what it should while impeding it from doing what it should not."

The Latin American State: From Developmentalism to Debt Shocks

The Political Economy of State Intervention, 1960–80

With the advent of the 1982 debt shocks, the debate over economic development and structural reform in Latin America suddenly centered on the numerous shortcomings of statism as it had evolved over the post–World War Two period. One line of criticism pointed to the bloating of the public sector under the impulse of foreign borrowing in the 1970s and to the erosive effects of rampant state participation on economic growth and income distribution (Balassa, Bueno, Kuczynski, and Simonsen 1986; Edwards 1995). A second criticism stemmed from the comparative success of the East Asian states, as the multilateral institutions were particularly insistent that Asia had effectively avoided the debt crisis through its reliance on a market-led development model over this same period (World Bank 1983).[2] While the crucial role of the state in fostering a high-growth export-led model and more equitable patterns of income distribution in East Asia was subsequently acknowledged (Amsden 1989; Wade 1990; World Bank 1993a), the notion that Latin America's problems stemmed from the weight of the state in the economy remained firmly embedded in ongoing policy debates. The result: a growing chorus of doubters who held that the Latin American state should step back and assign the task of economic development to the private sector and to market forces (Glade 1986; John Williamson 1990).

What light do the time-series data on the Latin American state sector shed on these debates? Ideally, in answering this question we would want to measure the presence of the state sector over time in terms of the extent to which government activities have transformed the political economy and altered the behavior and economic status of individuals and firms. On this count, public expenditures and investment levels tell only part of the story. The rest has to do with the effect of state regulations, patterns of macroeconomic policy making, and other indirect ways in which the state intervenes. For the lack of any single measure that captures these direct and indirect influences, each will be reviewed in turn.

Direct state intervention

Tables 3 and 4 present various measures of direct state intervention: public expenditures and revenues, the public-sector deficit, government debt, public and private investment, and the SOEs' contribution to GDP. As table 3 shows, the link between state largesse and the region's external borrowing spree of the 1970s is less robust than the critics would have us believe. For example, the first column in table 3 confirms that the public sector had asserted its economic presence well before the 1970s (Fishlow 1990). For four of the five countries in table 3, the period from 1960 to 1980 includes the first

---

2. It was impossible to overlook East Asia's average weighted growth rate of nearly 8 percent during this same period, not to mention an average annual inflation rate that was well below 10 percent.

ISI phase of producing light manufactures behind high tariff walls, as well as a second developmentalist phase based on a combination of import substitution and the promotion of heavy industries (autos, steel, petrochemicals) geared toward exports. Chile was the one exception to this trend. Upon the installation of a military regime in 1973, Chilean policy makers jettisoned ISI and embraced a staunch market strategy for the duration of the military's seventeen-year reign. While the Chilean state still maintained its strong presence in the economy, this redirection of public resources into market-supporting endeavors was the harbinger of a more generalized regional trend that took root post-1982.

As private loans on international capital markets became increasingly available to these middle-income borrowers through the 1970s, there was indeed a tendency toward higher public spending. In relative terms, public-spending levels rose in varying degrees in all five countries from 1960 on; yet, in absolute terms, Latin America's average level of public spending as a percentage of GDP still paled next to that of the industrial bloc countries. Take the example of the United States, a country widely considered to be the least interventionist of this group: U.S. public spending as a percentage of GDP stood at 28 percent in 1960, compared to 16 to19 percent in Chile or Peru—those countries with the highest levels of state spending at this time. In 1985, this same figure for the United States was 37 percent, versus Latin America's average of around 24 percent (World Bank 1988, 44). Thus, it appears that state expansion per se was less the problem in Latin America during this period than was the tendency to rely on debt financing to cover a growing public-sector revenue gap.

The universal increase in government-held debt after 1970 reflects two key developments. First was the deterioration of public finances. Although state budgets were generally in deficit throughout the post–World War Two period in Latin America, these deficits accelerated sharply after 1970 (Stallings 1987, 362–63). While tax collections did not collapse entirely, external borrowing made it all the easier for most states to avoid the political conflicts commonly associated with fiscal reform. Second was the way in which these borrowed funds were put to use. Individual country experiences indicate a variety of destinations, including some combination of government consumption (the costs of the state bureaucracy), social transfers, fixed investment, and the financing of capital flight from the region.

As table 4 shows, the link between public investment and governments' ability to borrow was a direct one. In every country but Chile, public investment as a percentage of GDP peaked during the late 1970s or early 1980s, then gradually declined during the following decade of capital scarcity. Chile differed only to the extent that this same cycle occurred earlier, as public investment reached a high during the statist administration of President Salvador Allende (1970–73) and contracted in the period following the debt crisis. Apart from these continuities, individual country experiences indicate considerable differences in how borrowed funds were invested (Larraín and Selowsky 1991, 309–10).

For instance, in Brazil, Mexico, and Peru, governments borrowed to support manufacturing and infrastructure investments; in Argentina and Chile the private sector borrowed to participate more strongly in finance-related activities. In Argentina, Chile, and to a lesser extent Mexico, the explosion of government-held debt post-1982 reflects the degree to which the public sector was called upon to rescue private investors in the throes of the debt crisis. Nevertheless, in the end, Brazil, Chile, and Mexico are considered to have invested these borrowed funds fairly well, while Argentina and Peru did not (Frieden 1991, 74–80). As the following chapters will show, the lost opportunities from debt-backed consumption, versus borrowing for productive investments, emerge as a major theme in the Peruvian case.

The SOEs constitute the final measure of direct intervention and an essential component for understanding the changing economic role of the Latin American state during the developmentalist era. While the SOEs have frequently been singled out as the prime institutional outback for rent-seekers and venal bureaucrats, the disparate trends concerning the SOE share of GDP that appear in table 4 make it difficult to fully pin the blame on the SOEs for the region's economic disappointments. Two interlocking explanations account for the erratic pattern of SOE presence in the Latin American state sector.

First is the genuinely productive role that the SOEs have played in some countries in areas such as transportation, energy, and mining, where economies of scale and overhead costs simply surpass the resources of private entrepreneurs (Hirschman 1967; Glade 1986). For example, Chile's disproportionately higher share of SOE activity can be accounted for largely by state dominance of all aspects of copper production. There are also cases like Brazil, where SOE-sponsored infrastructure and other productive investments have succeeded in fostering the growth of downstream private enterprises (Trebat 1983).

The second explanation brings us closer to understanding how the evolution of the state-enterprise sector has been problematic. Along with the oft-cited inefficiencies related to subsidies and the pricing policies of SOEs (Glade 1986), greater access to foreign loans encouraged states to haphazardly assume a more entrepreneurial role through the creation of public companies. For example, debt data show that SOEs in Latin America consumed some US$80–100 billion in foreign loans from 1972 to 1982, but information is scarce on the ultimate use of these funds (Stallings 1987, 128). Thus, the data in table 4 suggest that, at the height of SOE activity in the 1972–86 period, some of these public entities did indeed serve as slush funds for central governments.

Indirect state intervention

Despite the considerable variation across countries in patterns of state regulation and macroeconomic policy making during this developmentalist era, there were some clear continuities with regard to indirect forms of intervention. Among those regulatory laws that private actors pointed to as most prevalent and distorting of domestic markets were price controls, interest-rate ceilings, onerous corporate tax rates, profit sharing, and high tariffs on trade (Balassa, Bueno, Kuczynski, and Simonsen, 1986; Burki and Perry 1997). It was these regulatory distortions, combined with the rising levels of public investment in the pre-debt-crisis period, that fueled antistatist claims about the public sector "crowding out" private initiative. However, this matter is not so simple. A closer look at the regionwide investment trends portrayed in table 4 suggests that, at least up until the widespread privatization programs of the early 1990s, public and private investment trends moved in tandem and were thus more complementary than adversarial (Pastor 1991, 16). Nevertheless, as amenable as the state may have been to enabling the private sector to knit itself into the public-investment portfolio in most countries, regulations such as those mentioned earlier also sent very mixed signals to domestic entrepreneurs.

Discussions of macroeconomic management in Latin America prior to the 1980s focused on trade, fiscal, and monetary policies, as well as the interplay of these policies with external borrowing by governments in the region. As former Panamanian president Nicolás Ardito-Barletta (1994, 183–84) has pointed out, up until the debt crisis most Latin American governments paid little attention to the technicalities of macroeconomic policy management:

> Exchange rates were fixed relative to several of the main hard currencies. Import controls were part of the import substitution policies. Reserves were normally kept low and were not built up with favorable movements in the terms of trade. Fiscal policy consisted in deciding how much of the government deficit would be financed domestically because this would determine the increase in the quantity of money and inflation. Monetary policy was used mainly to keep interest rates low, producing excess demand for credit and allowing governments to direct credit to priority sectors, which they defined.

In general, the leeway created by foreign borrowing throughout the 1970s permitted most governments to postpone the necessary macroeconomic adjustments in the face of oil-price hikes and international interest-rate shocks. At least temporarily, political leaders were also able to avoid confrontation with domestic capitalists and organized labor by delaying any larger economic policy reforms. As seen in table 1, by 1982 the basic pattern of nonadjustment had generated external imbalances in the form of erratic patterns of foreign direct investment (FDI), burgeoning current account deficits, and an explosion in the debt overhang as the U.S. Federal Reserve Bank turned in 1978 to a combination of high interest rates and a strong dollar as its main anti-inflationary strategy. At this point, internal macroeconomic imbalances took the shape of rising inflation and budget shortfalls within the central government and the SOEs.

In hindsight, the broader outcomes under a developmentalist model present a mixed record for the state. On the one hand, as consumption tripled and investment quadrupled from 1960 on, Latin American GDP grew at an annual average rate of 5 to 6 percent until 1982 (Inter-American Development Bank [IDB] 1986, 430). On the other hand, the state-led development strategy fell short of promoting more productive and equitable patterns of growth. While exports expanded two and a half times during these two decades, the increased levels of investment did little to diversify the composition of trade (IDB 1988, 541). Aside from the 40 percent level of manufactured exports achieved by Brazil and Mexico, by 1982 traditional primary exports still accounted for 80 percent of all exports from the region (Sheahan 1987, 90). Moreover, social spending and human-capital investments registered the least impressive performance of all. On the eve of the debt crisis, Latin America had long surpassed the rest of the developing world in terms of income inequality.[3]

From this mixed record, it is now possible to refine the weight-of-the-state argument by specifying those trends within the Latin American public sector that helped shape much of today's market mind-set. While it turns out that indirect modes of government action have been just as problematic as direct state participation, the preceding analysis shows how the two worked together to tarnish the overall image of the state by 1982. The institutional backdrop pre-1982 was clearly a contributing factor, a point I return to in much more detail later in this chapter. For now, this problematic state-led

---

3. It is important to keep in mind the distributional effects of capital flight. By shifting their assets abroad during this period, domestic capitalists protected their wealth from taxes, devaluation, and inflation. Workers and the poor who were unable to evade these price erosions, or to avoid the additional costs of stabilization, suffered harsh drops in real wages (Pastor 1990).

dynamic, which had crystallized to varying degrees in all five of the cases considered here, can be summarized as:

- an over-reliance on external borrowing, which allowed for the chronic mismanagement of key macroeconomic policies;

- an increasing dependence on public enterprises to carry out the state's development tasks, against the backdrop of weak administrative structures;

- the cultivation of an ambiguous relationship with the domestic private sector, which claimed to lack confidence due to the state's regulatory intrusions and poor macroeconomic skills, while admittedly benefiting from debt-backed public-investment drives and government bailouts; and

- heightened poverty and inequality, as developmentalist policy makers failed to bridge the gap between distributional rhetoric and social policies that were in fact inefficient, poorly targeted, and regressive in practice.

The following section examines Latin America's track record in attempting to rectify this pattern with a more market-oriented management strategy over the course of the 1980s.

The State-in-Retreat, 1982–90

It took the remainder of the decade for policy makers to grasp fully the implications of the price, commodity, and capital shocks that had hit Latin America in the early 1980s. In the wake of the debt crisis, the lax macroeconomic scenario described earlier was simply no longer an option; public and private lending to the region had turned to a net negative outflow, and official aid flows were negligible. Suddenly, the main sources of foreign exchange were export earnings, FDI, and portfolio investment (primarily stocks and bonds), all of which required a more stable and convincing set of market signals. Given the context of severe balance-of-payment crises and these more limited and competitive options for obtaining foreign exchange, policy makers gradually realized that they had little choice but to launch the kinds of market-oriented stabilization and adjustment measures that would appeal to private investors (Schneider 1998; Remmer, forthcoming, 2003).

In the initial phases of stabilization and adjustment, crisis managers generally turned to the orthodox prescriptions that had long been advocated by the International Monetary Fund (IMF) and the World Bank (Kaufman and

Stallings 1989; Sachs 1989). Yet, by 1985, attempts at fiscal and monetary tightening had produced mixed results at best. Of the five countries discussed here, only Chile had succeeded in charting a sustainable path of solid economic recovery, largely because of the progress that had been made with trade and fiscal reform prior to the debt crisis—which, in turn, reflected a rigorous process of internal state reform then underway (Velasco 1994; Marcel 1999). In the other four countries, growth rates were erratic, inflation continued unabated, and the debt burden mushroomed.

Argentina, Brazil, and Mexico sought to service their debt by running massive trade surpluses achieved through competitive exchange-rate devaluations and high import tariffs. However, as inflation hit triple digits in Argentina, Brazil, and Peru by 1985, policy makers lost faith in IMF remedies. All three countries launched "heterodox" anti-inflation shock programs that relied on fixed exchange rates and wage and price controls (Crabtree 1992; Pastor 1992; Edwards 1995). The outcome in each case was disastrous, consisting of four-digit inflation and huge losses in GDP from 1987 to 1990. These results provided yet another reality check on the steep costs of reckless policy interventions in the new age of deeper international financial integration and higher capital mobility.

As for the state's widely acclaimed retreat from the economy during the 1980s, there are two ways of assessing this trend, one quantitative and the other qualitative. On the quantitative front, tables 3 and 4 show that in every country but Brazil there was a clear downward trend in government expenditures, tax revenues, and the SOE share of GDP. It was, however, public investment that bore most of the brunt of state retrenchment in the 1980s, as the prolonged recession forced most governments to cancel their earlier commitments toward infrastructure spending. Cuts in public investment, which are easier to execute than more politically controversial reductions in government consumption, became the prime means for financing the explosive interest payments on the public sector's mounting external debt (Dornbusch 1986, 68). Although more expedient in the short term, these public-investment cuts slowed the recovery process in Latin America, as governments failed to lay sufficient groundwork for the development of future productive capacity.

Privatization became perhaps the biggest catchword for the state's economic retreat in the 1980s. Defining privatization in broad terms as the removal of assets from the public sector and their placement under private control, the data in table 4 suggest that this process did not get seriously underway until the early 1990s. Apart from the reticence of the private sector to come forward without the promise of state protection and guarantees for lucrative returns on liquidated state assets, progress with privatization was slow for other reasons (Glade 1986; World Bank 1995). First was the tension between short-term stabilization and adjustment goals and the longer time horizon needed for the effective curbing of the SOE sector. Second was a misplaced faith in privatization as a quick fix for bolstering public finances or increasing the state's financial liquidity in the context of a decade-long economic crisis. As essential as privatization may have been for modernizing the state sector in the aftermath of the 1982 debt shocks, country-specific efforts were impeded by intense political and bureaucratic conflict (Schneider 1991).

As for a more qualitative assessment of the state's retreat post-1982, this period has subsequently been portrayed in the literature as a "first phase" in the implementation of market reforms (Naím 1994)—a process that was cemented by the end of the decade by a "Washington Consensus" over both the efficacy of the market and the role of macroeconomic stabilization as a necessary condition for the success of market reforms (John Williamson 1990). Yet, in retrospect, rather than a purposive set of short- and medium-term strategies geared toward easing the state out of the economy, what stands out in the individual country experiences is the erratic and crisis-driven nature of state retreat. In Argentina and Peru the state had literally collapsed by 1989, while in democratizing Brazil the state actually reasserted itself with a vengeance. In Mexico, despite the apparent success in implementing market reforms based on liberalization, privatization, and deregulation, policy makers were still struggling by the end of the decade to accomplish basic macroeconomic stabilization goals that had been established back in 1982.

Also of note here is the lack of progress in resolving elements of the problematic state-led dynamic described in the previous section. Despite the abrupt halt in external capital flows to the region, government debt exploded across the board in 1985–89. In some cases, such as Brazil and Peru, the pre-1982 reliance on "foreign savings" translated into a de facto moratorium on debt service payments, which allowed for further profligacy on the part of the central government. Moreover, in all five countries examined here, inflation was still running at two to four digits by 1990. Some measured progress had been made with the reform of the SOE sector; however, outside of Chile, private investors showed no signs of rushing back in. The least progress of all had been made on the distributional front, as social-expenditure cuts fell on the poor and revenue generation shifted sharply toward more regressive value-added taxes on goods and services.

Finally, how do we explain the diverse outcomes that emerge from the data? Chile was unique in its ability to sustain economic growth after the 1982 shocks, although a harsh military regime had provided policy makers with ample political leeway to experiment with market reform until the desired results were obtained. Yet policy makers within Mexico's semiauthoritarian single-party regime were similarly obstinate and heavy-handed about pursuing market reform at any social cost, but economic recovery proved elusive. Some of these differences have to do with the uneven pace and timing of market reforms and with the array of seemingly interminable pressures that each country faced on the international front. However, other puzzles, such as Brazil's stubborn resistance to economic stabilization well into the 1990s, demand further explanation.

Throughout this book I seek answers to these diverse and sometimes counterintuitive outcomes by examining the interplay between ongoing international economic trends and those domestic institutional structures that shape the choice of policy and its implementation (Skocpol 1985; Haggard and Kaufman 1989; Evans 1995). Institutional analysis is certainly not alone in tackling this research question. In fact, it has competed with, and been bolstered by, those approaches that emphasize some combination of societal influences and rational choice (Ames 1987; Frieden 1991; Geddes 1994), as well as those that place analytical weight on the nature of the prevailing political regime (Remmer 1990; Haggard and Kaufman 1995). Before an analysis and interpretation of the data on the "streamlining" of the Latin American state in the 1990s, the next section briefly elaborates on the usefulness of institutional variables for explaining the cross-country diversity in political-economic outcomes under the impulse of market reform.

The Institutional Setting: Four Working Hypotheses

From the standpoint of institutional analysis, the 1982 debt shocks marked the critical point where prolonged economic volatility threw the region's institutional weaknesses into sharp relief, so much so that in the 1990s institutional renovation emerged as a necessary condition for economic recovery and the completion of market reforms (Burki and Perry 1998). In table 5 I have sketched the main institutional variables that stand out in the literature on the political economy of policy reform, and in the following sections I treat each of the four variables situated on the lefthand vertical axis of table 5 as a working hypothesis. In doing so I trace the ways in which analytical weight considering the nature and importance of each variable has shifted across the prereform (1960–80) and postreform (1980–2000) periods, and I highlight the increasing role these variables have been assigned for successfully sustaining market reforms.

TABLE 5. The Institutional Backdrop for Economic Policy Making

	Prereform Period	Reform Period
Bureaucratic autonomy	• Loosely linked administrative structures permeated by special interests	• Insulated political structures with regulated access
	• Clientelism main form of exchange	• Clientelistic exchanges minimized
	• State goals not clearly defined	• State goals not easily subverted
State economic and planning institutions	• Lack of major planning or economic institution; existing agencies marginalized or made ineffectual for political reasons	• A few powerful economic and planning institutions
	• Narrow decisional leeway with policy making ad hoc and dispersed	• Decisional and operational authority linked to strategic policy areas
	• Hiring and promotion within state bureaucracy	• Technically skilled civil service governed by merit procedure
	• Governed primarily by personalistic ties	
Leadership coalition	• Frequent changes of government and/or regime with unpredictable swings in policy	• At the level of the state, stable leadership in the executive able to legitimate itself through skillful use of incentives and disincentives
	• Undisciplined internal bureaucratic structures easily captured by private actors	• A sophisticated network of public-private ties capable of steering policy without directly interfering in it
Interest intermediation	• Fragmented and competing interest group organizations	• Policy mediated through peak organizations (industry associations, trade unions) that are recognized and respected by the state
	• Attempts by the state to forge policy circumventing key societal interests or through haphazard mediation	• Ongoing state-societal consultation and predictable rules of the game with regard to negotiation of new policy initiatives

Bureaucratic Autonomy

> *Working hypothesis:* Economic performance is enhanced by political struc-
> tures that insulate technocrats and economic decision makers from out-
> side pressures, enabling them to maintain organizational integrity while
> pursuing their own goals. The access of popular-sector groups, and even
> political elites, is reduced in order to avoid the vagaries of populist politics.
> These insulated agencies are not entirely cut off from outside influence or
> from party politics, but intrusions and clientelistic exchanges are mini-
> mized, and state goals are not easily subverted.

Discussion

Up through the 1970s, "autonomy" was generally interpreted from the
dependency or neo-Marxist viewpoint that focused on the ability of the state
to intervene against the immediate interests of domestic capitalists in pursuing policies that worked to reproduce a dependent capitalist model (Franko
1998). Such analyses held that state autonomy was enhanced when elites were
divided or when threats from below induced the dominant class to grant the
state wider leeway in the policy-making process. The drawbacks to this
dependency approach as an explanatory framework became all too apparent
when the 1982 debt shocks hit: abstract debates over the "relative autonomy"
of the state offered few insights into the sources of policy success or failure
(Skocpol 1985, 5; Conaghan and Malloy 1994, 14) and hence into the diverse
reform outcomes that began to emerge in the post-1982 period.

A second approach to autonomy concerns itself directly with the question
of economic performance and turns to certain characteristics of the bureaucracy as explanatory departure points. Contrary to the dependency view, this
basically Weberian position holds that policy success stems not from divisions within the dominant classes but rather from the varying degrees of collaboration among state managers, political elites, and the representatives of
powerful interests (Rueschemeyer and Evans 1985). For example, Evans
(1989, 581; 1995, 12) argues convincingly that sound economic performance
derives from the ability of state policy makers to join well-developed bureaucratic internal organizations with a sophisticated network of public-private
ties. Under less successful scenarios, undisciplined internal bureaucratic
structures are controlled by the same public-private network, but chaotically,
leading to the kinds of erratic policy shifts that ultimately undermine reform
programs meant to attract private productive investment.

In further disaggregating this term, Eliza Willis (1986) distinguishes
among three main types of bureaucratic autonomy: the ability of politicians
and bureaucrats to make decisions independently of dominant social groups;

the freedom of the state bureaucracy from the control of patron-client networks; and the level of managerial discretion afforded government bureaucrats, especially those working within the main economic institutions and state enterprises. Obviously, there is no set measure for the extent to which these features exist or can be cultivated within the state bureaucracy. A more likely scenario is one where strategic sectors of the state bureaucracy are "depoliticized" and managed as if they were private. As in Brazil under the Vargas (1930s) and Kubitschek (1950s) administrations (Nuñes and Geddes 1987; Schneider 1991; Sikkink 1991), or in Peru under a reformist military regime in the 1970s (Stepan 1978; Wise 1994), the bureaucracy-at-large can be plagued by clientelism; however, the creation of pockets of efficiency within certain key sectors can also serve as a crucial countervailing force for accomplishing the development tasks at hand.

The need to professionalize Latin American bureaucracies, and to expand on these otherwise sporadic efforts at cultivating strategic units of efficiency within the main state institutions, came clearly into focus in the post-1982 period. As states subsequently advanced on the market-reform agenda, the need to extend these enclaves of expertise within the general structure of government, and to ground them more constructively in broader reform coalitions (Haggard 1995, 57), became all the more urgent. Within this more recent regional context, political-economic debates over the role of bureaucratic autonomy in the promotion of market reforms have become quite literal. Especially since the early 1990s, the general trend in the five emerging-market countries discussed here has been to tackle the broader tasks of administrative reform in the bureaucracy at large (e.g., strategic planning, performance-based management, integrated budget systems, a modernized civil service), while simultaneously creating a range of autonomous agencies to streamline reform efforts in areas like regulation and service delivery where the state's capacity has traditionally been weak (Burki and Perry 1998, 131–35; Bresser Pereira 1999).

This more recent brand of bureaucratic autonomy differs from that of the pre-1982 period in Latin America in that today's enclave agencies tend to sit outside of the central government and are linked not to the line ministries or the congress but directly to the office of the executive.[4] In Chile and Peru, and to a lesser extent Argentina and Brazil, the benefits of this almost strictly vertical arrangement have been the rapid completion of urgent reform goals—for example, in tax and customs administration, banking and insurance oversight, competition policy, and the provision of key public goods (Wilkins

---

4. I thank Kwang Kim for his comments and for sharing his insights on this more recent literature on bureaucratic autonomy.

1999). In most of these instances, the autonomous agencies are self-financed through user fees or their equivalent, and personnel selection and compensation are based more on private-sector standards and contractual performance indicators (Shepherd 2000, 5–6). As healthy electoral competition has clearly heightened over the past decade, and consumers and voters have come to expect concrete results from market restructuring, the channeling of reforms through truly autonomous agencies has allowed for a powerful demonstration effect.

However, as successful as some of these agencies have been in "getting the job done," there is also a downside to this phenomenon of circumventing the public bureaucracy altogether. First, although autonomous agencies in the 1990s were typically self-financed through user fees or other service charges, this has not always translated into financial accountability (Keefer 1995). Second, while heavily dependent on autonomous agencies to make good on their policy goals, Latin American executives have been reluctant to relinquish control in ways that would more firmly institutionalize these agencies. For these reasons, there is a growing consensus that it will be difficult to sustain the integrity of autonomous agencies without integrating them more effectively into the state's legal and administrative apparatus (Burki and Perry 1998; Shepherd 2000)—a feat that only Chile has thus far accomplished (Marcel 1999).

State Economic and Planning Institutions

Working hypothesis: Effective policy outcomes also depend on the consolidation of a few powerful economic and planning institutions that closely link decisional and operational authority in strategic policy areas and have access to a broad range of instruments for implementing policy. Institutional continuity and efficacy rest on a technically skilled civil service governed by merit procedures and bolstered by a network of other public-sector agencies—for example, research institutions, regulatory commissions, and judicial oversight.

Discussion

While the integrity of a certain policy course depends to some extent on the ability of frontline decision makers to distance themselves from the clamor of societal pressures, policy outcomes also hinge on the overall cohesion of state economic and planning institutions (Graham and Naím 1998). Interestingly, however, for all the recent emphasis on institutions as independent variables within political science circles (the "new institutionalism") and the economics discipline (the "new institutional economics"), in both instances institutional definitions remain somewhat removed from the phenomena that they seek to explain. Classic statements from Oliver Williamson (1985) and North (1990) have held the strongest sway. Each posits institutions as those formal and informal rules that shape the behavior of individuals and organizations in civil society (Burki and Perry 1998, 2). Formal rules refer to constitutions, laws, regulations, and internal procedures that guide the conduct of certain organizations; informal rules are the norms and values that guide state-society relations. Underpinning these definitions is mainly a concern for economic efficiency, as Moe's (1984, 759) view on institutions reveals: "Given transaction costs . . . rational actors find them more efficient than markets or alternative organizational arrangements."[5]

But what about the role of these same institutions as a prime locus for political-economic change? Even the Washington Consensus, for all its boldness in ascribing a basically multilateral agenda to the collective policy goals of Latin American reformers, had little to say about the institutional setting that would be most conducive for the realization of such reforms (Birdsall and de la Torre 2001). This is doubly surprising, given that the ultimate success of these reforms would directly depend on the initiation of considerable institutional change in order to sustain them. The region's cumulative experience with globalization over the past three decades has both revealed the weaknesses of national institutions in guiding this process and given rise to new demands for institutional reform.

Throughout this book, my focus will be on the roles that state planning and economic institutions, in particular, have played in the reform process over time. For most of the post–World War Two era in Latin America, the traditional institutional scenario was one where these state institutions were frequently divided, both ideologically and according to levels of expertise. Central banks and ministries of finance generally embodied the more monetarist views of the IMF and were staffed with economists and accountants; planning and other sectoral ministries were more likely to house the dependency or developmentalist views associated with the Economic Commission for Latin America and the Caribbean (ECLAC) and ISI and were staffed with lawyers, engineers, sociologists, and to a lesser extent, economists. Despite the isolated instances of bureaucratic modernization mentioned earlier, these crosscutting policy preferences rarely took root in any constructive manner. Rather, they were subject to constant interference and frequent coalition shifts and hence helped to perpetuate the haphazard macroeconomic patterns that prevailed in the region up through the 1980s.

Yet, in spite of Latin America's serious institutional constraints, the impact

---

5. Quoted in Heredia and Schneider 1998, 2.

of a decade-long economic crisis in the 1980s also created intense pressures and new opportunities for institutional reform (Grindle 1996, 31–34). Some general trends have included the outright elimination of those state institutions that had become relics of a protectionist past, such as Mexico's former Ministry of Industrial Development or Peru's National Planning Institute; the creation of numerous new state agencies across the region to enforce the complicated mass of regulations that have been passed to ensure greater transparency and competition in the provision of infrastructure and public services (Burki and Perry 1998, 4); and, in Chile, Mexico, and Peru, the passing of legislation that grants central banks independence from executive interference and from the fray of congressional and legislative politics.

For the sake of parsimony, in this study I approach this complex process of institutional change from two angles. First, institutions are treated as a set of administrative, legislative, and regulatory rules that guide the adjudication of conflict; and second, they are analyzed in terms of the coherence of the bureaucracy, the centralization of decisional and operational authority, and the kinds of instruments policy makers have at their disposal (Ikenberry 1988, 226–27). On the first count, the extent to which market-oriented rules and norms have been generated in Latin America post-1982 is truly remarkable. All five reformers considered here have offered numerous guarantees in the areas of trade (e.g., market access, dispute-resolution panels), investment (e.g., national treatment for FDI, competition policy to uphold antitrust guidelines), and property rights.

Furthermore, all five have also sought to bolster these new rules and norms and to bind their commitment into the future through participation in the World Trade Organization (WTO) and other regional trade and investment schemes such as the North American Free Trade Agreement (NAFTA), the Andean Community, and the Southern Cone Common Market (MERCOSUR). The consistent enforcement of these rules and norms still lags, however, as judicial systems in the region have proved to be the most resistant to internal change; moreover, some powerful private-sector actors have been much more enthusiastic about benefiting from market-based rules than they have been about adhering to them (Glade 1986). Nevertheless, the generation of such rules is clearly an essential step, as well as a necessary institutional condition for the long-run success of market reforms.

On the second count, it has also been recognized that issues of bureaucratic efficacy and decisional and operational authority are equally important, so much so that this subject has inspired a whole cottage industry of literature on the intricacies of bureaucratic and administrative reform in the region (Rauch and Evans 2000). The two main strands within this literature are those analyses that approach the subject from the standpoint of the "New

Public Management" and those that examine the broader political-economic context within which such reforms must be finessed. The former, unfortunately, tends to rely on normative policy prescriptions and public-administration platitudes (World Bank 1997), while the latter recognizes that bureaucratic and administrative change digs into much deeper institutional tissue than the kinds of rule-based reforms discussed earlier (Haggard 1995; Centeno and Silva 1998; Heredia and Schneider 1998).[6] Indeed, across the region, the generation of "first-phase" institutional rules to support liberalization, privatization, and deregulation was done mostly by executive decree; although the pain of adjustment was widely dispersed, so were the gains in terms of macroeconomic stabilization and the restoration of growth (Naím 1994; Pastor and Wise 1999a).

In contrast, bureaucratic and administrative reform inflicts more concentrated pain (loss of power and access to patronage), while the benefits (greater public accountability, increased efficiency in the delivery of key public services) are far less tangible—hence, the relegation of this brand of institutional change to the category of "second-phase" market reform, that is, policies that are also necessary for the successful sustainability of a market-based development model but that are not as easily implemented due to their potential for generating opposition and political conflict (Naím 1995; Pastor and Wise 1999a). To put this another way, it is one thing to shut down a set of defunct institutions plagued by some combination of backward thinking and fiscal crisis or to create new economic institutions; however, the lasting change of internal rules *within* existing institutions has turned out to be quite another matter and one of the most challenging second-phase tasks of all.

Those who analyze institutional reform from this political-economy perspective identify three main challenges (Haggard 1995, 17; Heredia and Schneider 1998): (1) the need for more penetrating civil-service reform, which entails the reduction of favoritism and politicization of the state bureaucracy through greater reliance on merit criteria in recruitment, promotion, and tenure decisions (Chaudry, Reid, and Malik 1994); (2) the need to strike the right balance between bureaucratic autonomy, as discussed earlier, and the grounding of key administrative agencies in broader reform coalitions; and (3) the need to democratize the reform process, such that greater legislative oversight and citizen input can better offset the excessive power that has been concentrated in the office of the executive since the onset

---

6. The goals of the New Public Management (devolution of decision making, performance and market orientation, and client focus) are sound, but in borrowing heavily from the private sector and the Organisation for Economic Cooperation and Development (OECD) experience, they beg the question of the politics of implementing these strategies in a much different bureaucratic setting, like that of Latin America (see Burki and Perry 1998, 125).

of market reforms. These are also the guidelines that will direct my analysis of Peruvian institutional reform in the chapters that follow.

The Leadership Coalition

Working hypothesis: Effective modes of economic reform are furthered by stable leadership that enjoys the support of dominant groups that can legitimate, through the skillful use of incentives and disincentives, the policy changes they initiate. It is the coherence of this group, backed by autonomous segments of the bureaucracy and the state's sound economic institutions, that accounts for effective negotiations with external actors, as well as the relatively successful shifts in development strategy when the economic need has arisen.

Discussion

Theories of coalition formation commonly presume that political ties are forged around market positions and that the participation of all the various partners is a reflection of sectoral interests and what they hope to gain (Olson 1968; Frieden 1991). For the most part, however, these theories treat coalition formation in an analytical vacuum, with insufficient regard for the broader institutional context. In understanding the two main coalition patterns that have prevailed in Latin America—the populist movements of the early ISI era and the "triple alliance" among the state, foreign capital, and domestic entrepreneurs that followed in the 1960s and 1970s—this interest-driven model provides a useful starting point for analyzing how coalitions are formed but not for explaining the policy outcomes that have emerged. For this, the state's institutional backdrop must also be considered, as it bears strongly on how interests are formulated and then put into action.[7]

The constellation of interests that pushed for the continuation of ISI dates back to the broad, multiclass, populist coalitions that sprang up around this development model at its inception in the 1930s and 1940s.[8] Over time, entrenched ISI interests succeeded in maintaining the model long after it had proved ineffective. Beginning in the 1960s, recurrent balance-of-payment crises and the consistently low returns on the state's wide range of economic endeavors forced a shift to a second, "developmental" phase of ISI. In

---

7. As John Zysman (1983, 295) has argued, "Institutions help determine which political issues emerge as subjects of debate, which groups become allies in the ensuing fight, and how capable of acting on its interests a given coalition will be." Up until the late 1980s in Latin America, policy outcomes under both coalition patterns readily illustrate this point.

8. The Vargas administration in Brazil (1938–45), the Cárdenas era in Mexico (1930s), and the first Peronist government in Argentina (1940s) all exemplify this populist coalition pattern.

Argentina, Brazil, and Mexico, for example, political and economic elites regrouped to promote a more sophisticated industrial pattern of vertical production based on private investment, capital-goods exports, and the staking out of new niches in the international economy (Sikkink 1991). But despite the emergence of the famous triple alliance among the state, foreign capital, and domestic entrepreneurs around this developmentalist strategy (Evans 1979; Gereffi and Evans 1981), it turned out to be no more stable, coherent, or skillful than the unruly multiclass populist coalitions that preceded it.

In the post-1982 period, the incentives for devising more cohesive and skilled leadership coalitions, and for launching more penetrating institutional reform, changed dramatically. As the debt shocks of the early 1980s marked the unraveling of authoritarian military regimes everywhere but Chile, newly elected civilian politicians and bureaucrats were at once challenged to leverage new private investment from the ruins of ISI and to appease their constituents within an increasingly vocal and competitive political market. This confluence of political liberalization and a virtual capital drought gave rise to two distinct coalition patterns post-1982. The first was a regrouping of state-business relations, as intense pressures to raise both domestic and foreign investment induced government policy makers to devise a more targeted and sophisticated range of incentives to attract private capital. Given the context of state retrenchment, stabilization shocks, and deep structural reform, domestic private actors were drawn in to market-reform coalitions through a combination of direct and indirect compensatory policies (Edwards and Lederman 1998, 28–31).[9] As a way of further signaling their commitment to private investors, political leaders across the region also stacked their cabinets with highly trained promarket technocrats (Schneider 1998, 84–90).

The second coalition pattern post-1982 reflected the efforts of civilian leaders to maintain broad political support in the midst of implementing sweeping programs of market reform. Having basically cast their loyalties with the private sector, the corresponding trend of democratization meant that politicians and technocrats still had to find credible ways to accommodate recently enfranchised groups within civil society. In Argentina and Mexico, for example, leadership coalitions were able to survive politically and retain support for market reform by selectively accommodating those factions that were best positioned to thwart the ruling coalition's chance for reelection (Geddes 1994; Corrales 2000a). In all five countries considered here, executive leaders also reached out to appease their poorer constituents

---

9. Direct compensation includes the transfer of cash or financial securities, while indirect compensation implies compensating affected groups through policies that either raise their revenues or reduce their costs (Edwards and Lederman 1998).

by offering short-term social-adjustment relief in the form of safety-net programs and support for emergency employment efforts (Graham 1994).

Interest Intermediation

Working hypothesis: State policy making is enhanced by the organization of
societal interests along tripartite lines, where policy is mediated through
peak organizations (business and industry associations, trade union feder-
ations) that are sanctioned by the state. Such organizations serve as
"strategic levers" that facilitate a consultative relationship with the private
sector and allow government officials wide leeway in the filtering of social
demands onto the political agenda.

Discussion

Whereas the question of interest intermediation in the advanced capitalist
countries has long been dominated by pluralist analyses of the role of voters,
political parties, and congressional coalitions as the main determinants of
policy, in post–World War Two Latin America the numerous interludes of
authoritarian rule rendered such explanations less relevant. Rather, with the
expansion of the developmentalist state, and with it more centralized and
politicized trade unions and producer associations, interest intermediation in
Latin America was conducted along more corporatist lines. At its most
benign, corporatism can be defined as a political order based on functional
socioeconomic organizations in civil society, operating independently but
united with each other and the state in sectoral and national decision-making
bodies (Stepan 1978, 46).

However, critics rightfully contend that such parallel corporatist arrangements in Latin America have rarely conformed to this ideal type of tripartite
exchange (O'Donnell 1988). Corporatist practices in the region have varied
according to the degree of centralization and inclusiveness in the bargaining
process and the extent to which the state was a benevolent or more forceful
sponsor. Although corporatist strategies spanned civilian and military
regimes alike prior to the 1980s, the track record suggests that corporatist
intermediation succumbed most frequently to state coercion and selective
exclusion in the resolution of conflict between competing interests. This was
certainly the case in authoritarian Brazil post-1964; in Chile post-1973; and in
Mexico, where a single ruling party went uncontested until the late 1980s.
Nevertheless, on the eve of the debt crisis in all three countries, even this
heavy-handed mode of corporatism resulted less in a coherent set of policies
formulated via state-societal consultation and more in the subordination of
public policy to private interests.

With the advent of the 1982 debt crisis, and the concomitant collapse of authoritarian rule in most of the region, patterns of interest intermediation moved along two main axes. The first was the state-capital-labor axis, which began to shift from the more clientelistic and inefficient "prereform" column in table 5 to the more effective modes of interaction detailed in the "reform" column. With the hardening of the external sector in terms of aid, trade, and lending to Latin America, domestic groups found themselves face-to-face on their own in search of solutions for the first time since the period following the Great Depression. Suddenly, the success or failure of ongoing reform efforts depended more than ever before on the presence or absence of "responsible" workers' organizations and employers' associations and on levelheaded leadership from within the state. As discussed earlier, newly elected political leaders responded, first, by resurrecting the kinds of state-capital alliances that had long been recognized as essential for signaling a serious commitment to private investment; and second, by offering a much more sophisticated mix of incentives and compensatory schemes in order to successfully carry out the reform tasks at hand.

The second venue for interest intermediation was the political party–congress-executive axis, which came to life during the widespread transition to civilian rule in the 1980s. Operating within Latin America's highly presidentialist political systems, executives across the region relied initially on legislative decrees and the advice of insulated technocratic teams in the implementation of the first-phase reform measures. The fact that the bulk of these reforms were generated outside of congress and the political-party structure was due both to the conditions of economic urgency that prevailed and to the fragmentation and ideological polarization that plagued political parties in many of these countries. Yet, against this backdrop of strong executive leadership and increasingly coherent governing coalitions, political-party systems in some countries—for example, Argentina and Chile—gradually regrouped along more centrist and pragmatic lines (Mainwaring and Scully 1995).

Whereas greater compromise and participation on the part of congress and political parties have been recognized as essential elements for economic success over the past decade, political incentives in some countries have simply not stacked up in favor of greater reliance on the party-congress-executive axis.[10] In Brazil, historically low levels of party organization and weak internal discipline have hindered the development of more constructive patterns of legislative oversight and greater citizen influence over executive-level deci-

---

10. The Achilles heel for each reformer—Brazil's continued struggle with fiscal restraint, Mexico's prolonged banking crisis, or Argentina's decade-long stalemate over labor-market deregulation—can easily be traced to the weakest links in the institutional bases for interest intermediation.

sions (Mainwaring 1995). In Mexico, despite explicit promises to fully liberalize politics on the part of the executive and powerful elite coalitions within the longstanding Institutional Revolutionary Party (PRI), these ruling-party faithful repeatedly proved incapable of managing this transition (Pastor and Wise 2002).[11] Peru, the only country in the region to suspend democratic rule in the 1990s, confirms that there is indeed more than one path to economic recovery. However, the full consolidation and ultimate success of Peru's reform program will depend on the ability of leadership coalitions to forge more reciprocal and cohesive ties with broader segments of civil society along this party-congress-executive axis.

Summarizing the Argument from an Institutional Perspective

Despite the obvious role of international factors in shaping the economic fate of these countries, these external variables fall short of explaining the wide diversity in economic performance over the long run. I have argued here that a more complete explanation lies in the nature of state and societal structures and in the quality of the ties between the two. To summarize the cases, the countries examined here have followed two distinct institutional paths (see table 6). The launching of market reforms in Chile, Mexico, and Peru was largely a state-centered phenomenon, although Chile since the transition to democratic rule in 1990 has also made important inroads in the modernization of state-society relations (Scully 1995). Mexico is in the midst of a similar transition, as reflected in the democratic defeat of the ruling PRI party in the July 2000 presidential elections (Pastor and Wise 2002). Argentina has relied largely on interest intermediation and the transformation of institu-

TABLE 6.   Different Institutional Paths to Market Reform

	State Initiated (bureaucratic autonomy, modernization of economic institutions)	Societal Based (intermediation between the state and organized interests in civil society)
Reform implemented	• Chile • Mexico • Peru	• Chile • Argentina
Reform in progress	• Brazil • Argentina	• Brazil • Mexico
Reform recently initiated		• Peru (2001)

11. This led to the PRI's loss of the executive office in the July 2000 presidential election.

tional ties among the executive, political parties, and other civic organizations (Corrales 2000a). Brazil, as the table shows, has a foot on each reform path, which perhaps explains the difficulties that policy makers have faced in quickening the pace of market reform.

In the following section, and the next five chapters on Peru, these four institutional dimensions of state-society relations become intervening variables, as they shape a given country's response to exogenous trends and set the parameters for policy choice, implementation, and outcome. While this explanatory framework expands considerably on the gray territory between policy input and development outcome, it is not set in stone: because these institutional variables can change over time and across a broad range of tasks, the framework is best viewed as a continuum that allows for a more nuanced assessment of a given state's ability to formulate and follow through on a designated policy course. In line with the preceding analysis of state-society relations over the post–World War Two era in Latin America, there is every reason to expect that more favorable policy performance will correlate with reforms that promote more cohesive state institutions and more coherent ties between the state and civil society.[12] At least thus far, this has been the regional trend since the early 1990s.

The Streamlined State of the 1990s: Reconstruction and Economic Recovery

The sheer magnitude of the crises that erupted in the late 1980s in Argentina, Brazil, and Peru sent policy makers back to the drawing board in launching another set of macroeconomic stabilization and structural adjustment measures. While there was anything but agreement within these civil societies over the pursuit of the larger set of market reforms embodied in the Washington Consensus, a newly elected group of political leaders realistically assessed that they had few other options at the time. Given the very tenacity of these reform-minded executive coalitions, a first round of crisis-driven market restructuring had more or less been completed by the mid-1990s. The initial goals of macroeconomic stabilization and balance-of-payments adjustment had basically been met, and incentives and relative prices had been restructured according to more competitive criteria.

These advances are confirmed by the data, which show that economic

---

12. The most recent empirical studies on the relationship between institutional development, broadly defined, and sustainable growth in the emerging-market economies state unequivocally that the correlation is a positive one. For a review of these empirical studies see Burki and Perry 1998, 17–24.

recovery for the decade peaked in 1997: average regional growth surpassed 5 percent of GDP for the first time in twenty-five years, and the average inflation rate had been reduced to single digits. While portfolio flows remained volatile, net annual flows of FDI in the 1990s were running eight times higher than in the 1980s (Naím 1995, 2).[13] The extent to which these Latin American economies had been reoriented toward the external sector was reflected in the trade figures, which showed that commercial exchange between the region and the rest of the world had doubled since 1990 (Wise 1999, 118). These trends suggest that progress had finally been made in implementing policies based on liberalization, privatization, and deregulation and that, with the exception of deepening income inequality, the worst excesses of the problematic state-led dynamic identified earlier had been tamed.

Perhaps most remarkable from the standpoint of this analysis was the drop in global patterns of government expenditure and public investment to those levels that had prevailed in the early 1970s. The Latin American state's newfound reputation as "streamlined" in the 1990s was based on three main trends. First, as table 3 shows, government deficits had been reduced dramatically by 1995–2000, down from an average of 9.3 percent of GDP in 1985–89 to less than 1 percent of regional GDP (Brazil is the outlier here). While still high, aggregate levels of government-held debt as a percentage of GDP had also been cut in half over these same time periods. Second, across the board, public investment as a percentage of GDP had been reduced to a historical low over the course of the 1990s. Finally, as can be seen in table 4, the SOEs' share of GDP had shrunk considerably from the peak levels that had persisted through the 1980s. Outside of Brazil, this reduction in public expenditure, investment, and SOE presence ran against the grain of longstanding arguments concerning the secular tendency for state spending to rise the world over (David Cameron 1978; Larkey, Stolp, and Winer 1981; Iversen and Cusack 2000).

Despite any outward quantitative similarities between the developmentalist state of an earlier era and this most recent rendition of the Latin American state, the two could be distinguished by the latter's fiscal advances alone. A second distinction, reviewed in the previous section, was the steady if uneven momentum toward institutional renovation, both within the state and at the level of state-society relations. Yet, while these achievements in the way of fiscal and institutional modernization were indisputable, the highly varied economic performance of the five countries summarized in table 1 suggested that there was more to state reform than widespread privatization and fiscal

---

13. These figures are cited from the ECLAC Web page <www.eclac.org>.

retrenchment. Both had perhaps been necessary conditions for the restoration of growth at the macroeconomic level; yet dismal microeconomic indicators, including falling real wages, high unemployment, low productivity, and rising income inequality, suggested that, far from doing too much, the streamlined Latin American state was doing too little in the way of providing public goods and facilitating the adjustments associated with market reform (Stiglitz 1997; Przeworski 1999).

In large part, it was this gap between macroeconomic dynamism and stagnation at the microeconomic level that triggered debates about the need to launch a second phase of market reform to help correct for these shortcomings. As for the state's role in prompting a call for a second reform phase, Moisés Naím (1995, 2) has observed that by the mid-1990s, even in those countries that had gone the furthest with market reform, "the state continued to perform functions better suited to the private sector while exhibiting an appalling incompetence in discharging core public functions." It was insights such as these that caused a metamorphosis of the Washington Consensus, as even its original author acknowledged that there had indeed been some important blind spots with regard to the crucial role that the state still must play in the economy (John Williamson 1996). First was the need to translate the gains from fiscal restructuring into much higher savings rates, while simultaneously targeting public expenditure toward more productive and equity-enhancing endeavors such as health and education. Second was the need to harness institutional reform in ways that promoted efficiency, competition, and transparency (Tineo 1997).

How do these realizations apply to the five countries considered here? A brief review of where these countries stand along both dimensions of institutional reform (state and societal) and the relationship between institutional reform and economic performance in the 1990s is in order. Of the five, Chile easily surpasses the other four on every microeconomic variable mentioned earlier but income distribution. Despite the tendency for antistatists within the Chilean military government and the multilateral institutions to claim this impressive record as a victory of market over state, it is now widely held that the country's success lies in the complementary and mutually enhancing ties that have been forged over time among state, society, and market (Velasco 1994; Schurman 1996; Marcel 1999; Kurtz 2000). It is thus no coincidence that Chile is the only country that ranks highly on economic performance; the implementation of deep market-based structural reforms; *and* the renovation of state and societal institutions, broadly defined.

Especially since the return to civilian rule in 1990, Chile has maintained the strongest state presence in terms of public spending, investment, and SOE activity, but also the lowest levels of government debt and public employment (ECLAC 1998, 111). And, in contrast to the other four countries, Chile has run a fiscal surplus throughout the 1990s (see table 3). This confluence of high economic growth and dynamism and a comparatively higher state presence underlines the need to redefine the streamlined state of the 1990s along more qualitative lines (Tanzi 2000). In Chile, for example, these qualitative institutional differences range from the government's advances on administrative and civil-service reform (Burki and Perry 1998, 132; Heredia and Schneider 1998); to the credible enforcement of property rights and rules around fair business play; to the increased accountability of policy making via greater oversight by political parties, congress, and the judiciary (Haggard and Kaufman 1995; Scully 1995; Patricio Silva 1998; Weyland 1999). Partly as a result of this broad institutional change, and in response to the failures of a purist authoritarian market model that was pursued from 1975 to 1982, Chile has developed a more competitive strategy that recognizes an active role for public policy and greater citizen input in the face of adjustment stress or outright market failure.

Whereas the Chilean case personifies the streamlined state of the 1990s—that is, the efficient use of public resources to foster productive growth and target social spending (e.g., health, primary education) in ways that directly bolster microeconomic development—Brazil still lies at the other end of this continuum. The long-term neglect of state financial institutions under an extended period of military rule (1964–85) and the disproportionate influence of a sorely divided congress have clearly slowed the reform process. With the election of President Fernando Henrique Cardoso in 1994, and the implementation of a highly professional Master Plan for Reform of the State Apparatus (Bresser Pereira 1999), the Brazilian state is quickly modernizing. In fact, Brazil now ranks second only to Chile in terms of the quality of its elite civil service and state bureaucracy (Edwards 1998, 28–29).

However, given a broader institutional context of a weak executive, fragmented political parties, and an unwieldy congress, economic policy is still too subject to clientelism and the political aspirations of regional and party bosses (Heredia and Schneider 1998). This is evident, first, in Brazil's comparatively poor progress in rationalizing public finances in the 1990s. In fact, it was Brazil's failure to put its fiscal house in order that triggered the dramatic currency crisis of January 1999 (Cardoso 2000). Second, Brazil's economic performance for the 1990–2000 period is the worst of the five-country sample, most notably on the distributional front. Underpinning these regressive trends is a pattern of asset concentration that surpasses Chile's by as much as 65 percent (Burki and Perry 1998, 80) and a comparatively weak record on government transparency and the protection of property rights (Edwards 1998, 28–29). Despite the successful inroads that have been made in the way of internal state reform, a concomitant modernization of state-society relations is still in order.

If Brazil and Chile lie at opposite institutional ends of the reform continuum, Argentina, Mexico, and Peru lie somewhere in between. In all three countries, policy makers have forged ahead with sweeping market-reform strategies, while institutional development has been uneven. In all three, the state sector rebounded in the 1990s in ways that partially follow the Chilean pattern of streamlining: public expenditures recuperated from the steep cuts of the late 1980s/early 1990s with a much stronger emphasis on social spending, and fiscal deficits were well below the regional average. Moreover, private investment in all three countries was notably higher in the 1990s, a trend tied directly to the privatization of SOEs. Nevertheless, public investment in Argentina was just half the regional average for the 1990s, and government-held debt was still far above the current average for the region. This second group of trends, combined with each country's decidedly mediocre performance at the microeconomic level, suggests that the state could, indeed, be doing more to address these shortcomings.

Argentina, for example, scores the highest of all five countries on a recently compiled market-reform index (Morley, Machado, and Pettinato 1998), and the country ranks close to Chile on such crucial institutional variables as the quality of the judiciary and elite civil-service corps and the protection of property rights (Edwards 1998, 28–29). At the same time, however, Argentina ranks even lower than Brazil on the degree of transparency in economic transactions and the ability of the state to project an image free from corruption. In line with these less favorable trends, Argentina's concentration of private-asset holdings is 45 percent higher than Chile's (Burki and Perry 1998, 80), and the poorest 40 percent of the country's working population has suffered the steepest distributional losses of the five countries considered here. If we return briefly to the working hypotheses introduced earlier, what is still missing in the Argentine reform effort is significant progress in the overhaul and renovation of the larger public bureaucracy and of those various state economic and planning agencies that house it.

This lopsidedness can be at least partially attributed to the distinct nature of the economic strategy that prevailed from 1991 to 2001 in Argentina, whereby the exchange rate was fixed one-to-one to the U.S. dollar and the responsibility for monetary policy was placed in the hands of a currency board (Pastor and Wise 1999b; 2001). This greatly reduced the policy role of the central bank, and while the Ministry of Economics was transformed into a super-agency and prime champion of market reform, the overall reform effort still lacked the far-reaching institutional innovations within the state bureaucracy that have provided a more stable base for economic dynamism elsewhere.

With the launching of the currency board in 1991, accompanying efforts at state reform were driven by textbook remedies for freeing markets through downsizing and tight fiscal austerity (Ghio 1998). As a result, key economic decisions and policy implementation have been relegated to an autocratic executive, a handful of elite economic policy makers, and representatives acting on behalf of the country's largest producers and conglomerates (Wise 2000). It is no wonder, then, that a centrist coalition swept the late-1999 presidential election on a platform that advocated a more aggressive approach to correcting the market's numerous shortcomings through the reform and strengthening of state institutions. The utter failure of that coalition, including the December 2001 resignation of President Fernando De la Rúa amid violent social protests just two years into his term and the unraveling of the currency board in early 2002, is further testimony that market reform represents just one side of the coin, and state reform the other.[14] In the absence of the latter, De la Rúa and his coalition of center-left parties never gained the footing they needed to truly advance the second-phase reform agenda on which they had been elected.

Whereas state streamlining in Argentina has relied too heavily on fiscal retrenchment and the circumvention of public institutions in the pursuit of private interests, the pattern in Mexico and Peru has been the reverse. In both countries, state economic and planning institutions have been the main locus for market reform, while questions of a concomitant transformation in state-society relations have been continually pushed onto the back burner. Even Argentina and Brazil, despite the many challenges they still face with regard to internal state reform, are following more of a Chilean pattern where deep market restructuring has prompted civic demands for greater participation, accountability, and responsiveness from state agencies. In contrast, such demands have been muted until very recently in Mexico and Peru, where the pace of democratization and the shift to more representative forms of governance have been more halting. This is evident, for example, in each country's comparatively low ranking on the quality of the judiciary and the degree of transparency and honesty in government (Edwards 1998, 28–29).

In both countries, the launching of market reforms within more narrow institutional parameters helps explain the impressive advances that have been made with the modernization of public finances and the recovery of growth

---

14. Hannah Baldock, "Desperate Argentina Seeks IMF Aid," *The Business* (London), Jan. 20/21, 2002, 17.

and private investment in the 1990s. But in both cases, the isolation of the leadership coalition and the reliance on bureaucratic autonomy at the expense of public debate and interest mediation over key policy initiatives have also detracted from these gains. In Mexico, this overly autocratic approach to policy reform accounts for the reckless errors that gave rise to the 1994 peso crisis and to a massive bailout of the domestic banking system, both of which have undermined Mexico's ability to achieve the same levels of macro- and microeconomic dynamism that Chile and even Peru have registered in the 1990s. Mexico's full economic recovery from these financial setbacks has been further prevented by a startling upward concentration of wealth stemming from the combination of low educational achievement, a pattern of oligopolistic asset holdings that surpasses even Brazil's, and the government's failure to credibly enforce a sophisticated body of antitrust legislation that was passed in 1992. These failures at social and economic inclusion were not lost on the Mexico electorate, which in July 2000 handed the ruling PRI party its first presidential defeat in more than seven decades.

In Peru, the extremities of executive authority and the heavy reliance on an entire array of new autonomous state agencies have resulted in a decade-long pursuit of the same purist version of market restructuring that dominated the Chilean reform program from 1975 to 1982. This is not to take away from the enormous inroads that have been made at the level of internal state reform; but the prevailing strategy precluded the kinds of policy flexibility and give-and-take between the state and representatives of civil society that will be essential for shifting the economy onto a higher-wage, higher-productivity, higher-growth track. This is most evident in Peru's surprisingly low ratio of exports to GDP, itself a reflection of market failure in light of the small, open nature of the economy, as well as the government's espoused commitment to an export-led development model.

Underpinning this lackluster trade performance is an investment portfolio composed largely of commodities and privatized services, neither of which has provided the necessary stimulus for the kinds of high value-added exports that have proven most conducive to employment expansion and productivity gains in Chile (Edwards 1995; Meller 1997; Marcel 1999). The current juncture in the Peruvian economic-reform program reflects the need for a deeper level of institutional reform, one where public policy encourages stronger linkages among higher value-added investments, trade-related activities, and human-capital development. Just as similar reform shortcomings in Argentina, Brazil, and Mexico catalyzed voter demands for public policies to stimulate jobs, growth, and more productive investment, in Peru citizens have followed suit in articulating such "second-phase" demands. Especially with the abrupt 2000 resignation of President Fujimori amid a complicated web of corruption charges, Peru's electorate has displayed a more markedly distributional response in national opinion polls. The remainder of this book examines the potential for state institutions, public-policy makers, elected representatives, and interest-group leaders to rise more fully to this develop-ment challenge in Peru.

Conclusion

In light of the trends reviewed in this chapter, it would be difficult to dispute that the Latin American state has indeed come a very long way: from the indiscriminate interventions of the developmentalist era, to the collapse of the 1980s, and now to the revival and redefinition of the state since the 1990s. A main purpose here has been to specify how the state's economic role has changed and to define what constitutes effective state action in today's markedly different political and economic environment. The analysis showed, first, that to varying degrees past problems related to reckless state intervention—excessive borrowing, macroeconomic incoherence, a fickle private sector, and predatory SOEs—have been solved. The main exception to this trend is the persistence of abysmal poverty rates across the region and the worsening of distributional trends in the 1990s—a theme that I explore in more detail through the Peruvian case study.

Second, the analysis challenged the still prevalent view that the advances that have been made are due primarily to the implementation of deep mar-ket-based structural reforms. While the resolution of the larger macroeco-nomic problems was definitely related to the streamlining of the state through privatization and fiscal modernization, the comparative analysis in this chapter confirmed that the reactivation of regional economies and the basically sound political-economic performance over the past decade also stemmed from the renovation of state and societal institutions, broadly defined. In fact, state reform and the success of market policies consistently stand out as two sides of the same coin. However, with the exception of Chile, the one country where high growth, market reforms, and penetrating institu-tional renovation have gone hand in hand, the current juncture in the region is one in which the prospects for sustained economic recovery are still fragile.

This raises a third and final point of the chapter, which is to identify the reform tasks that remain on the institutional agenda. Taking into account the chain of external shocks that hit the region beginning with the Asian crises of 1997–98, I argue nevertheless that the continued vulnerability of the coun-tries examined here has mainly to do with the uneven and incomplete nature of institutional reform over the past decade. As these countries are now hard-pressed to pursue policies that more aggressively promote greater productivity, efficiency, and equity, the answers lie in the realm of deeper institutional reform. This includes everything from advances on administrative and civil-service reform; to the credible enforcement of property rights and rules around fair business play; to the increased accountability of policy making via greater oversight by political parties, congress, and the judiciary. In short, as witnessed in the implosion of the Argentine political economy in late 2001, those countries that relied heavily on a societal-based reform path (see table 6) can no longer avoid the tough tasks of internal state reform. The same goes for the state-centered reformers, Mexico and Peru in particular, where civil society's insistence on greater inclusion and a voice in the reform process can no longer be ignored. The extent to which a sustained economic turnaround for these countries lies increasingly at the core of stronger institutional ties between state and society is well exemplified in the Peruvian case.

PART 1

From Developmentalism to Debt Shocks

CHAPTER 2

The Rise of the Peruvian State and the Quest to Industrialize

Latin America in the Early Postwar Period: From ISI to Developmentalism

From the standpoint of twentieth-century Latin America, the response of individual countries to two world wars and the Great Depression was basically twofold.[1] Early on, a first group of countries that included Argentina, Brazil, Chile, and Mexico explicitly embraced state-sponsored inward-looking industrial policies (ISI) in hopes of cushioning themselves from further external shocks. For a second group of countries, including Bolivia, Paraguay, Peru, and others, the ISI trajectory was nowhere near as viable—first, because this second group's historical status as small, open primary exporters left them ill-prepared for such a venture and hence any pre–World War Two efforts at fostering an industrial base had quickly faltered; and second, because social infrastructure, factors of production, and overall economic activity were so tightly tied to just a few commodity exports in each of these countries that the costs of diversifying into manufacturing industries were deemed to be too high. Thus, although some incipient ISI strategies were maintained in the light durable-goods sectors, this second group of countries basically cast their fate with the sale of commodity goods on foreign markets.

Obviously, neither of these two strategies was without pitfalls. For example, the first group of ISI countries had succeeded in reducing their imported share of finished consumer goods to well below 20 percent by 1950 (Bulmer-Thomas 1994, 276–78). This meant that the "first phase" of substituting imports for domestic production based on local demand had been completed over roughly two decades in these countries. Yet, despite the demonstrated ability of ISI to spur growth and employment in light manufacturing, mounting macroeconomic and balance-of-payment pressures also underlined the need to deepen the industrialization process into more sophisticated sectors that could generate foreign exchange and compete abroad.

In the economic-development literature this attempted shift from light manufacturing (textiles, foodstuffs, hand tools) to heavy industrial produc-

---

1. This first section borrows from Bulmer-Thomas 1994; Franko 1998; and Thorp 1998.

tion (autos, steel, petrochemicals) has been broadly referred to as "developmentalism" (Hirschman 1968; Sikkink 1991; Franko 1998). In terms of economic policy, developmentalism marked a transition from the blanket subsidies and protection granted by the state to a more targeted and selective set of government incentives geared toward the promotion of heavy industry and manufactured exports. By definition, the private sector—both domestic and foreign—was expected to play a more prominent role by investing in this "second phase" of ISI, and some countries went so far as to grant foreigners the same tax treatment that national investors received (Gereffi and Evans 1981).

As for the advisability of pursuing the outward-looking strategy based on primary exports, this approach remained vulnerable to the same volatile price fluctuations and unfavorable shifts in the terms of trade that the ISI group had sought to avoid; moreover, in political terms, the social structures and political coalitions that had evolved around these "enclave" primary-export economies were far too rigid and narrow to properly navigate the political economy into calmer waters when such shocks inevitably occurred (Cotler 1975). Comparatively speaking, developmentalism signaled an effort to modernize domestic politics, as it brought an end to the unwieldy multiclass social coalitions that had underpinned populist governments and ISI programs in these countries. In their quest to industrialize, political and economic elites regrouped to forge smaller and more manageable alliances, invariably with the backing of the armed forces. In Argentina, Brazil, and Chile, hyperinflationary crises and consequent efforts at fiscal streamlining and private-sector accommodation ultimately led to military rule. Although leaders in the ISI countries embellished their development plans with promises of greater equity and social spending, in fact, hindsight shows this policy shift to have been highly exclusive in economic terms and thus anything but distributive (O'Donnell 1988; Cardoso 2000; Pastor and Wise 2002).

As early post–World War Two economic history would have it, the ISI/developmentalist group opted for an inward-looking industrial strategy at the very moment when East Asian reformers were gearing up to make their fortunes as exporters of manufactured goods on an incredibly buoyant international market. As developmentalist policy makers failed to meet their ambitious export targets in the 1960s and 1970s, it is difficult to exaggerate the lost export opportunities for Latin American industrializers during this period. At the same time, those countries that pursued an outward strategy with commodity exports met with a more erratic set of price trends and a slower pattern of growth than those witnessed in world markets for industrial goods. The upshot: erstwhile developmentalist countries in Latin America saw their share of world trade plummet from 8.9 percent in 1946 to 3.5 percent in 1960. The decline of world share for Latin American primary exporters over this same time frame was more modest; nevertheless, they accounted for the same meager share of world trade in 1960 as did the first group (Bulmer-Thomas 1994, 290–91).

Thus, for similar but different reasons, both groups found themselves coping with increasingly difficult challenges in the way of macroeconomic instability and an inhospitable external environment. When domestic politics were factored in to the equation, the tasks of economic management were further complicated. Turning more specifically to the case of Peru, this chapter details the efforts of politicians and policy makers there to launch a catch-up ISI strategy once the primary-export-led model ran up against seemingly insurmountable bottlenecks. Even though the administration of President José Luis Bustamante had failed miserably in its efforts to shift economic activity inward toward manufacturing production in the mid-1940s (Thorp and Bertram 1978; Bulmer-Thomas 1994, 290), the apparent exhaustion of primary-export-led growth by the early 1960s prompted another try. As in the first group of countries mentioned earlier, Peru found itself relying ever more on government spending and public investment in order to accomplish these goals.

The following sections analyze the renewed attempt at salvaging primary-export production and diversifying into manufacturing and other nontraditional economic activities from the standpoint of state sponsorship. After briefly reviewing the broader political-economic backdrop to state intervention, the chapter draws on the institutional framework developed in chapter 1 as the main frame of explanatory reference. Given the incipient nature of state institutions at this time, and the lack of cohesive organizational ties between the state and key groups in civil society, the chapter shows how fairly moderate intentions to launch an ISI strategy in Peru quickly escalated into a more encompassing and developmentalist role for the state. Although equivalent levels of state sponsorship had evolved gradually over the first half of the twentieth century in countries like Argentina, Brazil, and Mexico, in Peru this same trend was compressed into a decade. While even the most optimistic observer would be hard-pressed to declare this first bout of full-fledged statism a success, it is all the more remarkable that policy makers in the 1970s sought to redress these early missteps through a strategy that would basically amount to much more of the same.

The Political-Economic Backdrop to State Intervention in Peru

Perhaps the most striking feature of early postwar Peruvian development is the country's late start in terms of industrialization and the resort to statist policy approaches. Peru's historical registering of low rates of industrialization, and a passive role for government, particularly in comparison to the other leading Latin American economies, stand out in the data on this period. The country's share of manufactured products was just 1 percent of all exports, and its average tariff on imports was by far the lowest in South America (Sheahan 1987, 87, 91). Apart from the adverse economies of scale and high entry barriers mentioned earlier, the two most common explanations for Peru's status as a late industrializer focus on the country's relatively diverse natural resource base, which helped to postpone any pressing need for a state-sponsored industrial strategy until the 1960s, and the overriding influence of transnational economic linkages.[2] The latter consisted of a steady flow of U.S. FDI into the primary-export sectors and the greater success of U.S. policy advisors in prescribing liberal economic measures in Peru (Hunt 1975).

Thus, like many of the countries in the second group of primary-commodity exporters discussed earlier, Peru conformed to the dependency stereotype of a dominant-export oligarchy on the domestic front that joined effectively with foreign investors in imposing a liberal economic policy regime.[3] Much has been made of the influence of the Alliance for Progress and the developmentalist programs simultaneously underway in Argentina and Brazil in swaying policy toward manufacturing and higher levels of state intervention during the 1960s (Levinson and de Onis 1970, 148; Fitzgerald 1979, 43). Certainly each played a role in the policy shift that occurred at this time, but it is also important to examine how such factors worked to reinforce subtle interventionist tendencies that had already been set in motion. The brief spurts of interventionist policy that had occurred prior to the 1960s reveal that a number of complex trends had evolved over time to contribute to an increasing economic and political presence of the Peruvian state by the 1960s.

In economic terms, the Peruvian state's first significant role was underwritten during the Leguía administration, which ruled from 1919 to 1930. Although Leguía's foreign-financed program of public spending became best known for its corruption, it did represent the initial attempt in Peru to promote capital accumulation with massive state backing (Stallings 1987, 249–58). With its emphasis on providing traditional infrastructure support for private capital and attracting foreign investment and loans, the orienta-

---

2. Thorp and Bertram 1978 remains the best full economic historical account of Peru, along with Fitzgerald 1979 and Sheahan 1999 for the post–World War Two period. This first section draws broadly from these sources.

3. Hernando De Soto's (1989, xvi) historical characterization of the Peruvian state as "mercantilist" does not rule out the successful maintenance of a liberal economic policy regime. Underpinning De Soto's account of a burdensome bureaucratic state, which granted favored status to a small domestic elite, was the triumph of that elite in preventing macropolicy and government economic regulation from being turned against it.

tion of this first statist program was that of bolstering the primary-export-led model. Subsequent interventionist phases, as under the Prado and Busta-mante administrations, which reigned consecutively from 1939 to 1948, fol-lowed this same basic pattern.[4] Up until World War Two, the sporadic but growing economic presence of the state was still that of an indirect backup for the private sector and was geared mainly toward promoting and defending the position of Peru's primary exports on world commodity markets.

Public expenditure had also been put to fairly wide political and social uses by the post–World War Two period—first, to fend off what domestic elites perceived as the "socialist" threat of the mass-based American Popular Revo-lutionary Alliance party (APRA); and second, to address Peru's highly skewed patterns of income distribution and dualistic economic structures, which had become implacable by the 1940s. Dualism refers to the rift between modern industry and traditional agriculture, whereby the former contributed nearly 50 percent of GDP by 1950 but only employed 20 percent of the workforce, while the reverse pattern held for the latter (Webb 1975). Over time, this polarization of national production and income became a glaring factor in the country's rising patterns of inequality (Fitzgerald 1979, 91). Thus, social and political spending prior to the 1960s in Peru was tied not to an ISI-type populist coalition but to the effort to maintain political harmony in the face of these extreme disparities that had been fostered and aggravated over time by the primary-export-led model.

Up until the late 1950s, each interventionist spurt had been followed by the successful reconstruction of a liberal economic policy regime. For exam-ple, after the interventionist experiments of the early 1940s, a 1957 report by the U.S. Department of Commerce boasted of Peru's offering the most open and favorable investment conditions in the region. The report referred to the policies undertaken by the Odría administration, which had seized office in 1948. These consisted of the adoption of a freely convertible exchange-rate regime; the elimination of licenses on imports; and the enactment of new pro-foreign-capital laws in mining and petroleum, the latter of which had been enshrouded in conflict and uncertainty over the direction of govern-ment policy. The strongest calling card for foreign capital, according to the report, was the Peruvian government's rapid reduction of public expendi-tures, subsidies, and price controls in 1953–54 and its ability to put the brakes on inflationary credit expansion (U.S. Department of Commerce 1957, 3).

Toward the end of the 1950s, declining opportunities in primary exports,

---

4. An Industrial Promotion Law of 1940 was passed, authorizing a more direct and discre-tionary role for government in granting incentives. But Thorp and Bertram (1978, 390) note, "Despite its title, the law was not specifically designed to promote industry, and was in fact used to benefit enterprises in commerce and agriculture as well as manufacturing."

particularly mining and petroleum, along with a drop in FDI in these sectors, made the liberal economic policy mix less appealing and more difficult
to maintain. The changing composition of the export economy (see table 7)
called up, for the first time during this century, a stronger imperative to
industrialize and with this more direct forms of state support. Although
social demands from the working classes and popular sectors had heretofore
been too weak to extract substantial subsidies from the state, increasing
urban migration and the transformation of the economy toward manufac-

TABLE 7.   Sectoral Composition and Growth of GDP in Peru: 1950–70

	Sectoral Composition (%)			
	1950	1955	1960	1965
Agriculture	20.4	19.3	18.5	15.3
Fishing	0.4	0.6	1.4	2.1
Mining	6.8	7.5	10.4	8.5
Manufacturing	16.7	18.0	20.0	22.2
Construction	6.3	7.5	5.0	5.2
Utilities	0.6	0.6	0.8	1.0
Government	9.1	3.2	8.0	8.3
Finance	2.3	2.6	2.8	3.0
Transport	3.9	4.6	4.3	4.5
Commerce	11.4	11.1	12.1	15.1
Services	22.1	20.0	16.7	14.8
Total GDP	100.0	100.0[a]	100.0	100.0

	Rate of Sectoral Growth (%)			
	1955–60	1960–65	1965–70	
Agriculture	3.6	2.7	4.0	
Fishing	25.5	15.9	10.4	
Mining	11.4	2.4	3.8	
Total primary sector	6.6	3.4	4.5	
Manufacturing	6.7	8.9	5.9	
Construction	−3.7	7.7	−0.3	
Utilities	13.8	9.7	6.7	
Total secondary sector	4.3	8.7	4.8	
Total tertiary sector	3.3	7.6	4.0	
Total growth of GDP	4.5	6.7	4.4	

Source: Fitzgerald 1979, 69. All data are based on BCRP, "Cuentas Nacionales" and "Memorias,"
various years.
   [a]Rounding errors.

turing industry converged to create further pressures for state spending on this front.

Although it would take more than three decades before Peru would see another liberal economic regime characteristic of the Odría era (1948–56), domestic elites and policy makers by the late 1950s were far from ready to embrace a full-fledged statist program. Vestiges of the developmentalist influence from other parts of the region began to crystallize in Peru under the second Prado administration, which was elected in 1956. That influence, which prevailed in Peru up through the military coup of 1968, still favored a leading role for private initiative but accepted a moderate increase in state support and planning (Sikkink 1991). A 1962 quarterly analysis from Lima's Banco Continental summed up the attitude toward development as Peru entered that decade:

> Within the context of a market economy, the principal objective of capital formation by the government is to create the basic conditions under which private enterprise can best fulfill its productive role to the benefit of the community-at-large. This implies that public works are not necessarily an end in themselves but rather perform the function of a structural corner-stone. . . . [I]t is to be hoped that the next government will pursue a course of action consistent with [these] foregoing financial principles.[5]

The "next government" referred to Fernando Belaúnde and his Popular Action party (AP), which won the civilian elections in 1963. With its strong emphasis on modern infrastructure and generous incentives to both foreign and domestic private capital in promoting industry, the Belaúnde government brought Peru more closely into step with the regional developmentalist trend. Yet this period in Peru was also reminiscent of the broad-based middle-class industrializing coalitions that had emerged in Latin America during the 1930s. Whereas other states such as Brazil and Mexico had moved into an intermediate capital-goods stage of industrialization by now, Peru was still in a primary (consumer-durable) stage of ISI and applying protection and other industrial perks indiscriminately across sectors (Beaulne 1975). And, contrary to these other developmentalist efforts, income distribution and long-overdue reforms in health, education, and the agrarian sector now ranked near the top of the development agenda in Peru.

This intense period of catching up during the 1960s was accompanied by fairly sound performance of the major exports listed in table 7, with the result

---

5. "The Economic Situation of Peru," *Peruvian Times*, Aug. 3, 1962, 9.

that annual average GDP grew at about 4.5 percent over Belaúnde's five-year term (Paredes and Pascó-Font 1987, 4). But there were mounting disputes between the government and foreign investors in the major minerals sectors, and the attraction of both local and foreign private capital toward manufacturing required generous subsidies and tax concessions. Thus, Peru's first phase of ISI became rapidly swept up in a well-intentioned but misdirected nationalism, as the state increasingly took on the massive infrastructure and industrial drive with insufficient regard for the sources and supply of financing. While economic liberalism remained the dominant ideology throughout this period, state expenditure ultimately tipped over into much higher levels than had been expected or intended. As table 8 shows, the total investment coefficient steadily declined over this time period, but the private sector's share fell disproportionately.

These trends were aggravated, furthermore, by the highly disarticulate and competing coalitions surrounding the executive and by the outright inability of the state sector to rise to the tasks that were chaotically set for it—which is to say, Peru's resort to statism in the 1960s was ultimately not the result of a broad-based ISI coalition, as in Argentina, Brazil, or Chile, but rather of the absence of one. It is, then, the structure of the economy and society, as much as the intentions of the relevant political actors, that most explains the Peruvian state's mounting presence at this time (Topik 1987, 23). These themes are elaborated on in the following sections. By examining the institutional setting and the attempts at coalition building that framed the development effort of the 1960s, the remainder of this chapter traces the haphazard nature of state intervention and how, toward the end of the 1960s, a state-led strategy had evolved mainly as a matter of policy by default.

TABLE 8.   Peru's Public and Private Sectors: Current and Capital Expenditure: 1950–68 (% of GNP at current prices)

	1950–55	1956–57	1958–59	1960–64	1965–68
Private sector's gross capital formation	15.0	19.6	17.7	14.6	10.7
Public sector's gross capital formation	3.7	4.5	2.6	3.6	4.6
Total gross capital formation	18.7	24.1	20.3	18.2	15.3
Public sector's current expenditure	10.5	12.7	12.6	13.6 (1960–63)	20.8 (1966–68)
Public sector's current surplus	2.6	1.2	1.7	2.0 (1960–63)	–3.0 (1966–68)

Source: Thorp and Bertram 1978, 288–91; BCRP, "Cuentas Nacionales," various years.

The Institutional Setting

The themes of foreign influence and ad hoc interventions by the Peruvian state underpin the ways in which some of the major government institutions came about. Of the four institutions most responsible for economic policy in the 1960s—the Ministry of Economy and Finance (MEF), the Development and Public Works Ministry, the National Planning Institute (INP), and the Central Reserve Bank (BCRP)—the INP and the BCRP were explicitly created in response to outside pressures. Kindleberger (1985, 278) notes the establishment of the central bank in the 1920s as a condition set by Peru's foreign creditors for the further issuance of private loans (Stallings 1987, 255). Similarly, the INP was made the organizational foundation of the planning system installed by the military junta that ruled from 1962 to 1963, as this was required in order for Peru to become eligible for the large amounts of Alliance for Progress funding it had hoped to attract at the time. At the request of the government, ECLAC designed a series of ISI blueprints that the INP took up in line with its new mission (Rossini and Paredes 1991, 277).

This pattern of letting the state sector passively evolve, as opposed to the purposive institution building characteristic of Brazil under Vargas and Kubitschek (Nuñes and Geddes 1987), for example, signaled a deeper problem for the Belaúnde administration: Peru marched into its first major modernization effort without any one planning or financial entity capable of taking the lead in generating and realizing the state's policy goals.[6] With the creation of the INP and the launching of this development effort simultaneously, the former failed to come into its own during the 1960s. The INP staff took some steps toward overhauling the national budget, and they produced two mammoth studies that critiqued the dualistic structures of the Peruvian economy in terms of the related social and economic problems (Cornejo 1985, 34–42). In the end, President Belaúnde's insistence on involving himself personally in almost every aspect of the infrastructure program, and the unwillingness of technocrats within the more established MEF to permit newcomers into their policy network, left the INP isolated from the planning process.

It was the BCRP that produced the government's first formal development plan in 1962 (BCRP 1962). While the task departed from the bank's usual

---

6. Victor Bulmer-Thomas (1987), in analyzing the Central American experience, suggests that export-led growth based on primary products led to the neglect of state financial institutions. Yet Kindleberger (1985, chap. 18) points to numerous historical instances of similar neglect where primary products did not dominate the composition of trade. The explanation for institutional neglect in Peru lies somewhere in between the natural resource–endowment argument and the preferences of domestic elites.

mandate of coordinating macroeconomic policy, the development plan represented another funding stipulation laid out by the Alliance for Progress. The BCRP, at the time, was the only institution capable of generating a development plan proper. In his colorful insider account of this period, Pedro-Pablo Kuczynski points to the BCRP as Peru's one "fairly autonomous institution" (Kuczynski 1977, 16). This assessment rests on the fact that the bank, with the help of a program set up by the Ford Foundation in the early 1960s, had established a relatively sophisticated recruitment and hiring system based on merit.[7] Policy making, however, still centered in the MEF, where no comparable accumulation of talent or sound recruitment practices had been established. The bank, while embodying the orthodox policy current that appealed to Peruvian elites, held less operational sway than the MEF, whose director tended to change frequently with the whims of congress and the executive.[8]

Historically, the lack of interest on the part of domestic elites and a distrust of economic decisions made outside of private hands suffice as explanations for these comparatively meager efforts at state building.[9] These observations apply as well to the broader institutional context that had evolved by the 1960s, which included the executive, the central government, and state bureaucracy at large, as well as an array of independent and semiautonomous state entities. In hindsight, as problematic as the major economic and planning institutions proved to be in executing state policy, the design of the balance of power between congress and the national executive emerged as an equally debilitating factor. Still operating under Peru's 1933 constitution, congress was basically empowered to go about its business irrespective of the wishes of the president. In the event that the political opposition won a majority, the president's hands were virtually tied in the legislature.[10] At the same time, outside access to the executive went virtually unregulated. This setup reinforced the circumvention of established state channels, the penetra-

7. Each year the best economic students within the country were selected and put through an intense training course taught by U.S. economists.

8. The BCRP, furthermore, lacked ultimate authority until the 1970s in such matters as reserve requirements, foreign-exchange policy, and monetary and credit affairs. See U.S. Department of Commerce 1957, 15.

9. Perhaps the most telling aspect of this pro-private-sector bias was the delay until 1963 in creating the Banco de la Nación, which acted as revenue collector and treasurer for the state. These responsibilities had heretofore been in the hands of a private agency controlled by the commercial banks.

10. In the epilogue to his detailed history of this period, Kuczynski (1977) suggests two reforms that could have equalized the balance of power between congress and the executive, thereby strengthening the latter. These are the adoption of staggered midterm elections for congress to place some reliability check on the opposition and reform of the electoral system from one based on proportional representation by party to one based on geographical representation by district.

tion of executive decision making by private parties, and the tendency toward widespread political patronage.

The "small-state," pro-private-sector ethos that prevailed up to this point is evident in the institutional evolution of the Peruvian central government. Though small in the 1960s, the central government was theoretically the hub of the state sector. On paper, each ministry (there were seventeen in all) was linked to the INP through a sectoral planning office and an increasing number of decentralized public agencies (universities, social security offices, etc.) that depended on the flow of funds from the central government. In practice, with its many overlapping mandates and fierce competition between ministries, the central government still conformed heavily to a black-box metaphor (Cleaves and Scurrah 1980, 68–69). Most notorious was the Ministry of Development and Public Works, which became a main entry point for private parties seeking the lucrative construction contracts that marked the early Belaúnde years.

Much of the blame for the chaos within the central government during this time has been placed on the state bureaucracy itself. As in many Latin American countries, state bureaucrats had been cast as unproductive parasites who gained their positions through nepotism (Topik 1987, 21–22). With a fragmented and confused budgetary process that facilitated the use of public funds for private purposes, these images of favoritism and corruption are not far off. Peru was further hampered by the fact that it had never had a strong tradition of public service, in contrast to Chile, Colombia, or Brazil pre-1964. At best, the state sector was considered an unprestigious and low-paid place to be. While there is no doubt about the lack of "modern administrators" in the Weberian sense, profiles of the upper echelons of the Peruvian bureaucracy at this time suggest that there were certain pockets of strength that could have been much better tapped by the Belaúnde administration.[11]

Of the small central government workforce in existence in 1961 (around 120,000 employees out of a total national population of about 10.5 million), a tiny elite corps of senior functionaries spanned positions at the general-director and subdirector levels of the bureaucracy. Though technically recruited by competitive examinations according to Peru's civil-service code of 1950, it was widely recognized in the 1960s that the code was not being fully implemented. Although political patronage and family connections may have taken precedence in the making of official appointments, a survey taken in 1965 of 380 of these top government executives working across the civilian

---

11. In their analysis of the conditions underlying effective state intervention, Rueschemeyer and Evans (1985) place most stress on the importance of a well-developed bureaucratic apparatus and collectivities of career officials carefully cultivated over time.

ministries indicates that a fairly capable group was in place (Hopkins 1967, 46). Over 36 percent of those surveyed had completed some postgraduate studies, 75 percent were college graduates with degrees primarily in law or engineering, and 91 percent had undertaken some college training. More than 80 percent of top management within the ministries of justice, education, and public health—and even within the unwieldy Ministry of Development and Public Works—held college degrees.

Given the existence of a comparatively well-educated "policy-making segment" within the state bureaucracy (over 40 percent of Peru's adult population was illiterate in 1961), the question remains as to why the Belaúnde administration failed to harness this talent to the development tasks at hand. The most obvious explanation rests on financial incentives and the substantial salary differential that had built up between executives working in the public and private sectors.[12] But the privileged social and educational status of this group also implies that they had other alternatives and thus were there, to some extent, by choice. The rampant inefficiency appeared to stem partly from the much less qualified group of bureaucrats working at the lower rungs of the central government and from Belaúnde's heavy reliance on party faithfuls, who were not necessarily a part of this elite corps. The determination to keep strategic posts filled with loyal party sympathizers is reflected in the frequent changeover in high-level staff. From 1963 to 1965 alone, the Ministry of Development and Public Works saw four ministers, each with an average tenure of six months (Hopkins 1967, 64).

The independent and semiautonomous state entities represent the last major aspect of the institutional backdrop of the 1960s. Listed technically in the national budget as the Independent Public Subsector, this category encompassed a whole group of agencies that ranged from the regional-development corporations to the national universities (Rothrock 1969, 110). By the 1960s, as many as 250 entities existed in this legally separate subsector, which also included Peru's state enterprises. Although each entity was formally tied to a ministry, these institutions depended on specially marked taxes and other direct transfers from the central government. Analysis of this sector of independent entities, and its role in the policy process, is difficult because of its very diversity and its vague organizational ties to the central government.[13] The state enterprises, because they went on to play such a

---

12. Hurtado and Robles (1985, 37, 56) note, for example, that the public/private salary ratio in 1961 ranged from 147 for top state technocrats to 138 for government managers and administrators.

13. In his 1964 budget message, the treasury minister complained of having received only 20 percent of the budget proposals from these 250 entities, mainly because it was not clear where the proposals should be submitted (Hopkins 1967, 27).

strong role in public-sector capital formation in subsequent periods, are of most interest here.

Although the state firms suffered from equal definitional vagueness during this period, Saulniers (1988, 204–9) has made headway in distinguishing between two groups. Using the most basic criteria of legal autonomy—a level of government equity sufficient to guarantee control and sales accounting for more than 50 percent of current income—he estimates that seventeen of these entities in the Independent Public Subsector qualified as public enterprises by the end of the first Belaúnde era.[14] Using a more expansive definition, which assigns state-enterprise status to firms operating in productive activities with 50 percent public ownership, he estimates that Peru's public portfolio could have surpassed seventy-five separate entities by 1968. Working from either definition, it is safe to say that, at least in institutional terms, Peru's state-enterprise sector had begun to take off well before 1968.

By the post–World War Two period, Peru's public firms had expanded in fits and starts, in response to the economic needs and political demands of both foreign and domestic capital and to fill the revenue requirements of the state itself. For example, the Corporación Peruana de Vapores began in 1944 as a joint shipping venture that merged public and private interests in an attempt to bolster state income.[15] Development banks in housing, agriculture, mining, and industry had been created a decade earlier. Together, these entities reflected the continued need for state support in the productive sectors, the thrust toward urbanization, and the increasing demands for industrial goods and modern services. The Empresa Petrolera Fiscal (EPF), reorganized for the third time in 1948, was mainly a symbolic exertion of national sovereignty in the petroleum sector. Lacking explicit bylaws until 1968, the circumstances surrounding the creation of EPF proved to be a precursor to the more ideological motives that would come to dominate policy making in the state-enterprise sector post-1968 (Saulniers 1988, 16).

The gulf between development theory and managerial practice was more frequently the rule than the exception in the state-enterprise sector, and the vague budget-appropriation process made the public firms susceptible escape valves for hidden revenues and expenditures (Rothrock 1969, 106). Of note here is the fairly steady trajectory of state intervention that had already been established in this independent subsector by the 1960s. In retrospect, the more explicitly statist policy shift that would occur with the military coup of

---

14. These firms consisted, for example, of the port and air authorities; the BCRP; development banks in agriculture, housing, and industry; and a range of miscellaneous state-held companies in petroleum, fertilizer, food-supply, and coca-leaf production (Saulniers 1988, 206).

15. Rothrock (1969, 188–98) provides a detailed account of the ups and downs of this endeavor.

1968 was more a deepening of than a departure from this trend. Already by the late 1960s, one of the government's main dilemmas was shaping local elite opinion to conform to the increasing necessity of state intervention, as exemplified by this sector.[16]

Overall, in institutional terms, although this brief introduction points to a more prevalent state presence than usually recognized for Peru, when compared to the periods analyzed in subsequent chapters of this book, the 1960s still stand out as an early phase of state formation. As such, the institutional setting did not add up to a coherent springboard for state action. Three separate dynamics served to steer policy off course. First was the making of policy almost independently of institutional life, and not necessarily by those most capable of doing so; second was an almost self-perpetuating instability brought on by the many changes in ministers and personnel; and finally was the ineffectual position of the executive vis-à-vis congress, making it even more difficult to deliver on political promises through those institutional routes that had been established. What basis may have existed to begin cultivating a more autonomous and far-sighted bureaucracy and a cohesive set of state institutions was lost in this shuffle. Into the void stepped an array of competing groups and actors, to which the analysis now turns.

The Development Coalition, or Lack Thereof

While Peru's predominant alliance between domestic elites and foreign capital in the primary-export sectors remained unshaken until the 1960s, the rapid growth and economic transformations over the entire post–World War Two period had converged to create a more socially stratified and complex set of groups and subclasses. The dualistic economic structures that the INP had begun to critique in its early reports remained largely intact, but class lines could no longer be cast in simple terms. With industrialization, a small domestic bourgeoisie had splintered from the oligarchic elite, and a more visible middle class had emerged in the form of bureaucrats, technical managers, and some military professionals (Jaquette 1971, 44–46). The "traditional sector" still referred largely to peasants and agricultural workers, although the intense migration of this group into urban informal employment forced a redefinition of the term to include this growing contingent. Finally, as industrialization proceeded under the thrust of ISI in the 1960s, the blue-collar

---

16. Interestingly, the very first locally published report on state enterprises in Peru was an indictment against the encroachment of the state and an early call for the reduction and reform of the public firms (Centro de Documentación Económico-Social 1965).

workforce expanded proportionately. Although technically a notch above the traditional sector in social position, at least wage-wise, these workers were holding their own next to white-collar workers (Hurtado and Robles 1985, 37, 56).

In short, class lines were being quickly redrawn in Peru. These rapid socioeconomic changes crystallized in the 1962 and 1963 elections, where the major political parties sought to win over these emerging groups without entirely alienating the old oligarchic guard. The participation of seven parties in the turbulent 1962 presidential campaign reflected the more pluralistic nature of the Peruvian electorate; the controversial presidential victory of APRA party boss Victor Raúl Haya de la Torre, and the subsequent decision by the military to nullify the elections, indicated that elite consensus was becoming increasingly fragile.[17] This was confirmed in the elections rescheduled for the following year: as the candidate preferred by the military, Belaúnde captured the presidency through a coalition of his AP party and the Christian Democrats (DC).[18] But the congressional seats divided three ways between the AP-DC coalition, the APRA, and former president Manuel Odría's National Union Party (UNO).

At face value, the platforms of these three main factions were not particularly distinguishable, and because the country's large illiterate underclass was still denied the vote, the following of each was just slightly more so. It was mainly through the UNO party that traditional elites still maintained their foothold. Haya de la Torre had by now abandoned most of the left-wing anticapitalist positions upon which he had founded the APRA in 1924 and that had for so long aggravated Peru's ruling civilian and military groups. The APRA party image had been recast into a middle-of-the-road, pro-free-enterprise, fervently anti-Communist mold by the early 1960s. In his campaign, Odría had capitalized on the prosperity and long-term economic expansion that had characterized his administration in the 1950s. Setting ideology aside, the UNO program pushed foreign investment, a fair deal for both business and labor, and further extension of the impressive public-works effort that Odría had sponsored earlier on.[19] All of the candidates and parties agreed on the need to geographically decentralize the nation's resources away from the wealthy power bloc that prevailed on the coast and the need for the closer integration of the sierra and jungle regions into national life.

---

17. The historical enmity among the APRA, the military, and Peruvian elites is dealt with in Sanborn 1991 and Graham 1992.

18. "Government and Politics: President-Elect Belaunde Terry Negotiating Pact with Opposition," *Peruvian Times,* July 12, 1963, 1.

19. "Biographical Sketches of Leading Presidential Candidates," *Peruvian Times,* June 3, 1962, 1.

The Belaúnde program offered the overlapping goals of allowing greater representation for Peru's middle classes and promoting the socioeconomic status of the traditional sectors and working classes. An architect by profession, Belaúnde also emphasized public works and advocated an extension of the various housing and construction programs he had successfully legislated during his tenure as a congressman in the 1940s. Upon election, the AP-DC coalition immediately sought to cement this apparent convergence of interests and goals into a formal political pact with one or both of the other opposition parties. Although the offer included the prospect of incorporating representatives from all three parties into the president's cabinet, the pact was rejected out of hand by the APRA and the UNO on the grounds that this would compromise the political independence of the opposition. Even before Belaúnde's inauguration, Odría and Haya de la Torre—both clearly with an eye toward the slated 1969 presidential race—had formed a separate APRA-UNO pact, setting up a formidable opposition in congress from day one.

Thus, it was the shadow of the past and opportunistic considerations for the future that sorely divided elites in the 1960s, as opposed to any substantive differences over development ideology or programmatic strategy. The combination of having been put so quickly on the political defensive and the president's own inability to clearly articulate the AP-DC program fostered a general mood for promoting economic progress and social welfare, but no concrete strategy for achieving these goals. In this respect, the first Belaúnde period resembled the early policy phase of the Alliance for Progress, prior to the death of President Kennedy, which was long on well-meaning development platitudes but short on the ways to finance and execute the ambitious goals of the alliance (Levinson and de Onis 1970).

In this context of highly polarized party politics and weak executive authority, the development program more or less lurched forward. An elaborate agrarian reform law was passed in 1964, and the government expanded tax exonerations and investment subsidies for industry, placing special emphasis on the automobile industry and its related components.[20] The president also launched a massive construction program and put forth his "road philosophy," which sought to unite the country from north to south by creating a highway to span the entire eastern slope of the Andes. A companion scheme was the jungle-colonization program. Despite its shortage of arable land and ecological vulnerability, Belaúnde insisted that the Amazon basin could be Peru's next frontier. The last major feature of the program was

---

20. The agrarian-reform law was one of the first major battles between the AP-DC and the APRA-UNO factions in the legislature. As each side tacked on its own biases, the final law was virtually impossible to implement. Astiz (1969, 105) and Cleaves and Scurrah (1980, 40–41), in particular, note the bias in favor of landowners.

Cooperación Popular, the main organization designed to promote administrative decentralization and the absorption of marginal labor.

The absence of a winning coalition in congress, and the AP-DC's definition of policy along such broad lines, fostered the familiar populist dynamic of groups stampeding the state in pursuit of narrow economic interests. As the president moved to meet these conflicting claims, policy tended to "happen." In the discussion on interest mediation in chapter 1, it was suggested that the political economy can still perform reasonably well on all of the major indicators, even in the midst of a large number of competing groups and parties, as long as some stable framework is in place for mediating the interests of the state, capital, and labor. Implicit in this analysis of Peru in the 1960s is the lack of such a framework to help counteract the destabilizing political and economic trends that were set in motion almost immediately. From the standpoint of the state, the reasons are evident from the foregoing discussion. The organization of business and labor in the 1960s, and the relationship of each to the state, require brief elaboration.

From the business angle, interests had reached a fairly sophisticated level of articulation. Some long-standing groups, such as the National Agrarian Society and the National Industrial Society, represented specific sectoral interests, whereas others, like the Chamber of Commerce, represented clusters of commercial interests at large. Encompassing traditional producers and some more recent entrants, Peru's various business groups had become astute at translating their interests into national policy. In his classic study of Peruvian entrepreneurs, Carlos Astiz (1969, 192) points to their mastery of unofficial channels of influence as the most institutionalized aspect of the policy process in the 1960s:

> These organizations fulfill some of the functions which have become characteristic of interest groups throughout the world: they lobby; they handle public relations on behalf of their members; they try to convince the rest of the population of the righteousness of their positions. . . . What makes these pressure groups—or some of the more effective ones—rather different from their counterparts in the Anglo-American systems and in other advanced European countries is the degree to which they resort to personal and private connections to gain access to policy-makers and their success in obtaining positive responses from them.

Private interests were highly articulated, but mediation between the state and capital amounted to what Astiz (1969, 262) calls a "nonconsensual structure of coercion." In other words, they were not mediated at all. With direct access to the top levels of government and control over most of the media and over certain factions within all three of the major political parties, special interests felt no compulsion to support even the very open-ended political pact that the AP-DC had offered up in the beginning. An official government coalition representing the interests of capital and the state was still not seen as a necessity by the private sector or as something that participants on either side would take all that seriously. Although rapidly increasing its role in the economy, the state was still viewed by the private sector as a passive partner for promoting business as usual among domestic capital and its foreign counterparts.

Labor, on the other hand, was becoming a force to contend with in the 1960s. As mentioned earlier, the structure of the workforce was undergoing rapid differentiation. Although figures on the number of organized workers at the outset of the Belaúnde administration vary, Payne's (1965, 129) estimate of 329,000 is the most widely cited. The number of unions registered with the Ministry of Labor peaked in 1964 at 325 (Sulmont 1980, 212–13), with manufacturing, agriculture (mainly sugar workers), mining, and transportation representing the most highly organized sectors. Most of this organization had advanced during the post–World War Two period of economic expansion, under the auspices of the APRA-dominated Confederation of Peruvian Workers (CTP). Even with the boost of the Korean War price boom, these inroads were significant given the high levels of unemployment still present in the economy, as well as the challenges from the burgeoning pool of unorganized labor in the informal sectors.

Though labor was more highly organized by the 1960s, labor's rights were still closely circumscribed. The broader legal framework had evolved in bits and pieces over the twentieth century. The result was a patchwork of laws concerning collective bargaining, social security, minimum wages, and conflict resolution, but no coherent negotiating processes (Bollinger 1987, 1). The lack of a unified labor code, and the highly successful lobbying by groups such as the National Industrial Society on behalf of management, meant that the law could be easily twisted to favor the employer.[21] The labor movement was further hampered by its fragmented union structure. The law separated locals, working conditions, and social benefits for the white-collar workers (bank employees, public school teachers, commercial and industrial employees) and the blue-collar contingent (mine workers, petroleum workers, and coastal plantation workers), leaving each group with a narrowly defined set of goals (Astiz 1969, 205).

---

21. The Belaúnde administration did attempt to put forth a unified labor code in the mid-1960s, the final product containing over seven hundred articles. The legislation quickly stalled over differences between organized labor and the trade associations representing management (Bollinger 1987, 1).

Organized labor, nevertheless, did throw its weight around in the 1960s. Labor struck 820 times during Belaúnde's first two years alone, compared to 1,200 strikes during the entire six-year Prado presidency (1956–62) that had preceded (Sulmont 1980, 212–13). Since the 1940s, government-labor relations had been marked by the granting of economic concessions along with the simultaneous exercise of severe political repression against labor. But as the economic concessions became more difficult to uphold after a balance-of-payments crisis in 1958–59, the pattern of labor-government interaction became more erratic. The Belaúnde administration fluctuated between brutal tactics against the CTP unions, as employed during the 1964 strike wave, and the granting of extraordinary concessions. The most famous example of the latter was the 100 percent increase awarded the public school teachers in 1964. Although labor strife was just one of many problems facing the Belaúnde government when it fell in 1968, surely the expansion of organized labor in this context of highly conflicting interests and ineffectual mediation helped hasten the fall.

Fiscal Crisis and the End of Civilian Rule

Most accounts of the antecedents to Peru's 1968 military coup focus on Belaúnde's failure to effectively resolve the country's long-standing dispute with the International Petroleum Company (IPC) over taxes and property rights and the destabilizing fiscal imbalances that had reached crisis proportions in 1967. Each explanation was a symptom of two larger interrelated economic trends that had set in during this period and that would prevail well into the 1990s. The first concerned the failure to maintain an adequate rhythm of exploration and investment in the primary-export sectors, mainly mining and petroleum. The second trend was the rapid transformation of the public economy from a small state sector with solid financial backing into a much larger government apparatus that lacked the necessary fiscal supports (Paredes and Pascó-Font 1987, 3). This section examines how these political-economic constraints converged to provoke a military takeover in 1968.

Structural rigidities had been building up in the primary-export sectors since the 1950s. Prior to this, Peru had been able to surmount the usual bottlenecks that have plagued primary-exporting economies because it had ample resources for switching to another crop or mineral when the need arose. By the mid-1960s, Peru's export mix was diversified (sugar, coffee, cotton, silver, lead, zinc, fish meal, and copper), but the economy had become increasingly dependent on fish meal and copper as the big foreign-exchange earners (Kuczynski 1977, 5). Fish-meal production, which had begun to peak during the Belaúnde years, would be depleted by ecological mismanagement within a decade. This left mining as the one remaining dynamic sector, and here the road forward had come to depend on the large-scale exploitation of low-grade copper deposits (Thorp and Bertram 1978, 255). Most of these deposits were held by a handful of large multinational firms that had traditionally made out extremely well in Peru in terms of tax breaks and profit repatriation.

The increasingly nationalistic mood aroused by the 1962 and 1963 presidential campaigns no longer looked favorably on these generous concessions to foreign capital in the primary-export sectors. As the Belaúnde government moved to increase profit taxes on the big mining companies, foreign investors adopted a wait-and-see stance toward any further commitments in Peru. The result was that the Southern Peru Copper Corporation had undertaken no new major projects since the completion of the Toquepala mine in the south in 1960. Although local mining investment had shown some dynamism in the 1950s, the larger economies of scale and capital requirements of this new project phase were prohibitive for domestic capitalists. Buoyant copper prices throughout this period helped obscure the fact that Peru had hit a serious roadblock in the only export sector with any potential for economic expansion. As foreign firms continued to hold back in the face of harder investment terms, it was the state mining bank that began stepping in to fill the investment gap (Thorp and Bertram 1978, 221).

The Peruvian government's dispute with the IPC went back much further, although the repercussions for not resolving this conflict in the 1960s were felt more immediately. At question was the government's claim on some US$600 million in back taxes and its challenging of the right of IPC, a wholly owned subsidiary of Standard Oil of New Jersey, to own the La Brea y Pariñas oil field in the north. While Peruvian law held that all subsoil mineral deposits were the property of the state, IPC retained the deed through a series of property transfers dating back a century. In fact, oil's significance as an export had completely declined at this point, as no new deposits had been located and oil production mainly serviced the local market. But because of strong foreign control and the historically high profit margins, the oil industry had a bad image with the Peruvian public in the 1960s.[22]

The predicament for the president was that a successful agreement with IPC would depend on congressional approval. The opposition had pushed

22. Similar to the pattern in mining, local investors had been squeezed out of the petroleum investment portfolio by this time due to the large economies of scale and high capital costs of project development in this sector. The only successful nonforeign participant by the 1960s was EPF, the state oil company (Thorp and Bertram 1978, 226).

hard to inflame the issue, and the APRA-UNO coalition was not anxious to hand Belaúnde a victory. As the dispute became swept up in petty political infighting and nationalistic rhetoric on the home front, all sides failed to grasp that the disbursement of Alliance for Progress funds to Peru ultimately hinged on the resolution of the IPC problem. From the standpoint of the U.S. State Department, Peru's confrontation with the IPC represented a potential security threat on par with the Cuban uprising of the late 1950s (Levinson and de Onis 1970, 156). Looking back now, there is some consensus that the United States erred in never stating this stipulation more explicitly to the Belaúnde administration. In light of Peru's strong historical reliance on U.S. aid, the oversight was a costly one for the AP-DC.

In the end, having received over US$200 million in loans from the United States and the multilateral agencies from 1950 to 1952 (Stallings 1987, 245), Peru's total aid authorization under the Alliance for Progress from 1962 to 1968 was just US$74.5 million. The figure stands in stark contrast to the amounts of alliance aid allocated for neighboring states such as Chile and Colombia, which received around US$400 million and US$500 million respectively (Levinson and de Onis 1970, 155). Just one of the many ironies of the alliance was its inability to see past the domestic political gridlock surrounding the IPC case and come to the aid of a candidate like Belaúnde who had originally embodied the moderate modernization platform on which the alliance was founded.

The Industrial Promotion Law passed in 1959, which triggered a more determined push toward ISI, was both a response to these increasing export constraints and another manifestation of the nationalist trend. As the figures in table 7 show, manufacturing grew by nearly 8 percent a year from 1950 to1965, and it accounted for over 20 percent of GDP by 1965. Compared to the growth of primary exports during this period, manufacturing was second only to fish meal. Yet Peru's ISI drive had also succumbed rather quickly to all of the classic pitfalls associated with this development model (Hirschman 1968; Rossini and Paredes 1991, 227). While manufacturing output had increased sixfold, over half of this output was under foreign control. Manufacturing jobs did double over this time period, but employment generation certainly did not occur in proportion to the very rapid expansion underway in this sector.

Furthermore, the actual investment dynamic behind the high growth rates was a shallow one. As Fitzgerald (1979, 75) notes, about one-fourth of manufacturing output was related to the processing of primary products for local consumption and export. Such was the case with the processing of paper and chemicals from sugar by the WR Grace Company (Reid 1985, 35), as well as fish-meal processing and mineral concentration. Food, clothing, and the local production of industrial inputs and consumer durables dominated the remainder of the manufacturing sector, which frequently amounted to assembly operations for foreign firms. The infant-industry argument had apparently been lost on policy makers in the 1960s, as the industrial law lavished incentives on all industries, old and new, domestic and foreign (Beaulne 1975).[23]

With the foreign-investment boycott in mining and the aid cuts mentioned earlier, the state's multiple giveaways to the manufacturing sector quickly took a toll on the fiscal balance, which had turned negative by 1964–65. The strains on the current and capital account were twofold. First, though laudable, the much greater commitments to education and health were not sustainable without garnering additional tax revenues. Public school teachers, for example, never saw half of the 100 percent wage increase they had won in 1964. Second, the ambitious public-works program had in some respects become an end in itself. The project portfolio addressed important needs in housing, irrigation, rural development, and road construction. But infrastructure investments were not well linked to the export sector or to the manufacturing drive.

As fiscal pressures mounted in 1966, the government had three not necessarily exclusive choices: cut public expenditures, raise taxes, or borrow. Because the legitimacy of the AP-DC platform rested so heavily on the development program, public-expenditure cuts were considered taboo. Although progressive tax reform had been one of Belaúnde's main redistributive promises during the presidential campaign, the administration's tax proposals met with a fierce uphill battle in congress from the very beginning. Peru's fiscal structure in the 1960s included taxes on international trade, as well as a broad range of indirect taxes on sales, turnover, and value-added. The original AP-DC plan called for more direct taxes on wealth and property and a general overhaul of the tax structure in a more equitable direction.[24] But the first tax measures to get through congress in late 1963 were mainly indirect taxes on sales, import duties, and fish-meal exports (Webb 1972, 22). After conceding on those revenues that were least visible in a political sense, the opposition then took an adamant position against further taxes.

---

23. Exemptions granted to the foreign-dominated auto industry, where protectionist barriers jumped from 13 percent in 1963 to 214 percent in 1965, illustrate the extent to which the law went overboard in its attempt to appease private capital (Thorp and Bertram 1978, 266).

24. Data on the Peruvian tax system at this time varies widely according to source, as do the interpretations on tax incidence. Taylor (1967), who headed an Organization of American States (OAS)–IDB tax mission to Peru in the 1960s, argues unequivocally that the tax structure was regressive, while Webb (1972) argues that because of the dualistic nature of the economy, the pattern of incidence was more ambiguous but also more progressive than other authors have allowed.

The APRA-UNO's tax veto was an extremely effective maneuver for undermining the AP-DC program. It was not until the severe fiscal crunch of 1967 that the opposition relented with more piecemeal levies on trade and some ad hoc corporate property taxes. Rather than risk their 1969 electoral ambitions with further tax hikes, the APRA-UNO congressional bloc delegated special legislative power to the executive for a period of sixty days in mid-1968. During the respite, the president's team was able to push through a wide range of direct taxes, a gasoline tax, and a number of administrative reforms. Though they were mainly progressive in nature, Webb (1972, 27) notes the failure of the 1968 measures to fully compensate for the erosion of the tax burden on the top income groups that had occurred during the previous five years of policy stalemate.[25]

With current expenditures increasing at a rate of about 22 percent annually between 1960 and 1965, the long tax interim and the aid blockade forced the government onto private capital markets to finance its large capital budget. In 1965, the economic team secured US$40 million in loans from a small consortium of U.S. banks, which was renewed in the same amount in 1966 and 1967 (Stallings 1987, 266). The ease with which Belaúnde had been able to obtain external financing was offset by the short terms and high rates attached to these loans. Government borrowing, furthermore, went on in a fairly uncoordinated manner. On the disbursement side, the dilemma of debt control was exemplified by the pattern in project spending, where three-fourths of the loans went toward transportation and the bulk for one project, Belaúnde's Carretera Marginal (or jungle highway). This resort to commercial financing meant that Peru emerged from the 1960s with the most highly privatized debt in the region. Private external loans accounted for 56 percent of all obligations, against a regional average of 49 percent (Devlin 1985, 62).

The need for debt refinancing was one of the highlights of the 1967–68 economic crisis. The entire mix of macroeconomic policies related to ISI had also taken a toll on the balance-of-payments. An overvalued exchange rate, which had been frozen since 1959, encouraged currency speculation, capital flight, and a flooding of imports. The neglect of agriculture over industry prompted an additional rise in food imports. The fiscal and trade deficits together brought a loss of confidence and a further drop in private investment. Finally, recession and inflation each worked their way simultaneously through the financial system. Another main irony of this period is that the core management team at the BCRP had been quite capable of prescribing the necessary macroeconomic adjustments all along. But it was not until

---

25. In 1969 indirect taxes, which are generally considered to be more regressive, accounted for about 60 percent of total revenues as opposed to 40 percent in 1950 (Taylor 1967).

1967–68, when the office of finance minister rotated seven times, that the bank team was admitted to the president's inner policy circle (Kuczynski 1977, 283).

By tapping this talent, Belaúnde was finally able to bypass an intransigent political opposition and rectify some of these problems. By mid-1968, the government had finessed a difficult currency devaluation, and a debt-refinancing agreement had been negotiated with the foreign banks in conjunction with an IMF stabilization plan. Conciliatory talks had also gotten underway with the Southern Peru Copper and Anaconda Copper companies to begin developing the rich deposits at the Cuajone and Cerro Verde mines in the south. And, though belated, the necessary tax measures had finally been instituted more or less along the lines Belaúnde had promised during the electoral campaign. The remaining obstacles were the dispute with IPC and the president's conviction that a mutually satisfactory resolution of the problem would open the door for the large amounts of multilateral and U.S. aid that other countries in the region had been receiving all along (Kuczynski 1977).

It was a hastily put together agreement with the IPC during the sixty-day period of rule by executive decree in mid-1968 that invoked the wrath of the opposition and the military and caused a major split within Belaúnde's own coalition. An attempt earlier the same year to appease the military with the purchase of Mirage supersonic jets from France had backfired in the sense that it prompted the United States to rescind aid before it had actually been reinstated.[26] Once the debt rescheduling came through in late September 1968, it became clear that the military had not been deterred at all. With the economic house in order for the first time since the early 1960s, the military took it upon itself in October 1968 to solve the country's increasingly complex development problems. In the end, while Belaúnde made headway in implementing some of his shorter-term reformist goals, he was simply not able to reconcile his program with Peruvian-style democracy as it had evolved in the 1960s.

Although most Peruvian elites have subsequently held the military reformers who intervened accountable for the flaws related to state intervention in Peru, this analysis confirms that the problematic state-led dynamic identified in chapter 1 had already taken root before 1968.[27] To review, that pattern had to do with an overreliance on external borrowing, which substituted for the tough macropolicy management necessary to garner domestic

---

26. "U.S. Ends Aid to Peru in Censure Move," *Peruvian Times,* May 24, 1968, 1.

27. Manuel Ulloa, "Mensaje al congreso del presidente del consejo de ministros," Lima, Aug. 27, 1980.

resources; the increasing use of state firms as policy instruments, without laying the adequate administrative foundations; the fostering of an approach-
avoidance relationship with private investors, who invariably benefited from
external credit flows and the output from state firms but held back due to
poor macropolicy and administrative management; and a neglect of social
policy in the effort to spur higher levels of capital accumulation.

Peru, in fact, had fallen somewhat neatly into the mold just described.
State policy makers during the 1960s were able to postpone the necessary
fiscal and monetary adjustments by resorting to foreign loans on private capital markets. With this cushion, private investors came to rely increasingly on
direct state intervention in both manufacturing and the primary-export sectors. The latter, particularly mining and petroleum, saw a marked increase in
the role played by public firms. Yet state development banks and public
enterprises embarked on their mission with the most minimal effort at building up the managerial and policy-making capacities within these institutions.
The decline of FDI and the mounting presence of an administratively weak
state reinforced the ambivalence of domestic capitalists. Although quite
receptive to the state's protection and economic support in the 1960s, local
capitalists had become increasingly reticent to put their own investments on
the line.

Despite the Belaúnde administration's greater emphasis on social welfare,
and the new economic opportunities that the program attempted to deliver
for underprivileged groups, Peru's socioeconomic matrix consisted of the
same inequitable structures that had divided Peruvians historically. The
enormous gains in value-added per worker in the modern sectors were
accompanied by a negligible rise in employment; conversely, while employment mushroomed in the urban informal sector, the net value-added contribution of this sector was paltry. At the heart of this scenario was the working
population's inadequate access to the levels of education and skills acquisi-
tion that would allow for greater social mobility. Despite an annual average
growth rate of 11 percent in education expenditures through the 1950s and
1960s, by 1970, 47 percent of the Peruvian workforce had obtained less than
three years of schooling (Sheahan 1999, 21).

These economic trends are both an indictment of the failures of the
reformist effort under Belaúnde and a confirmation that social lines were still
rigidly drawn, by class and by geographic location. That 80 percent of the
population still active in the rural and urban informal sectors by 1970 represented a multiethnic majority largely divorced from official state benefits
(Matos Mar 1984). The social, political, and economic marginalization of this
group became a rallying cry for violent protest with a guerrilla-led insurgency

in the sierra in 1965 (Reid 1985, 40). Although put down readily at the time by the military (Klarén 2000, 330), the outbursts held alarming implications for future patterns of violent popular protest in Peru.

Conclusion

The purpose of this chapter has been to set a baseline for analyzing economic strategy and institutional change from the standpoint of the Peruvian state sector once it began to take off in the early 1960s. In chapter 1, four institutional variables were identified as contributing most to effective state intervention in the developing areas: (1) political structures that insulate technocrats and economic decision makers from outside pressures and clientelistic exchange; (2) the consolidation of a few powerful economic and planning institutions that closely link decisional and operational authority in strategic policy areas, with institutional continuity and efficacy resting on a technically skilled civil service governed by merit procedures; (3) stable leadership with the support of a manageable coalition of dominant groups that can legitimate the policy changes they initiate; and (4) the organization of societal interests such that policy is mediated through peak organizations that are sanctioned by the state.

Using this framework as a broad reference point, it becomes clear that the Peruvian state of the 1960s, with its incipient institutional and bureaucratic structures, was poorly prepared to assume the more active stance it had been almost inadvertently assigned over the course of the decade. In fact, rather than a development tool, it seemed that Belaúnde used statism as a way to compensate for his problems in the legislature and at the executive level. Given the state's inability to act constructively in its own right, the task of forging a more balanced and integrated pattern of economic development was more or less relegated to domestic politics. Here, too, statism backfired: although it was meant to unify an unruly political system, political parties and interest groups further splintered. In essence, the abundance of new political actors and parties that came onto the scene in the 1960s lacked any semblance of organizational cohesion by the end of that decade.

The one organizationally cohesive party, the APRA, set a zero-sum pace for party politics out of historical frustration and future presidential ambitions (Sanborn 1991; Graham 1992). The strategy was, in a sense, too effective. All of the various coalitions—the AP-DC, the internal party apparatus of the AP, and the APRA-UNO itself—had unraveled by mid-1968. Finally, Peru's oldest alliance, that between foreign investors and domestic elites in the primary-export economy, had also been seriously weakened by the events of the 1960s. With the decline of the traditional primary-exporter model and the more conscious effort to industrialize, these groups had begun to lose their grasp over local politics. In other countries in the region, some reconstituted combination of state, domestic, and foreign capital had stepped in at similar junctures to carry the industrial effort forward (Evans 1979; Gereffi and Evans 1981). This chapter has demonstrated the weaknesses of the first two potential actors and the counterproductive role of the third in the Peruvian case.

Not unlike their oligarchic predecessors, those factions of domestic capital most likely to participate in a more sophisticated industrial program preferred to do so with the backing of foreign investors. Although the composition of the latter was diversifying into the manufacturing sector, it had only been willing to back domestic capital under almost classically dependent terms (a high level of imported technology and inputs and low levels of local reinvestment). Politics, the economy, and society had reached an impasse, and given the very weakness of the Peruvian state, no one civilian group or combination of groups was able or willing to take the initiative to break through it (Cotler 1975). It was ostensibly with the goals of social unification and state consolidation that a reform-minded military intervened in 1968. What followed proved to be one of the more anomalous efforts at state building in the region, particularly given its military sponsorship. Ostensibly, the coup of 1968 launched Peru's first explicit attempt at enhancing the capacity of the state to intervene more effectively in the economy along the lines discussed earlier.

CHAPTER 3

A State Capitalist Experiment

Dependency Theory, Peruvian-Style

Peru may have arrived relatively late to a state-led strategy, but once the interventionist wheels had been set in motion there was no turning back, at least not at this point. Apart from the institutional weaknesses within the state and civil society that had overwhelmed policy makers in their efforts to apply the brakes on rampant public-sector expansion in 1967–68, other statist influences had been fermenting through the 1960s. At the international level was the continued ability of middle-income sovereign borrowers to access a seemingly endless supply of private bank loans. Hindsight shows that Euromarket lenders during this time, operating on the assumption that governments could not declare bankruptcy, were not at all selective in their choice of clients (Stallings 1987). Thus, despite the Belaúnde administration's chaotic record of spend-and-borrow in the 1960s, and the vaguely anti-imperialist rhetoric of the military junta that took control in 1968, Peru was able to retain its commercial borrowing privileges and hence its profligate spending habits well into the 1980s.

At the regional level, the more radical tone of the Peruvian military was a reflection of larger intellectual debates that were now flourishing within the dependency school (Fitzgerald 1976; Evans 1979). As the phenomenon of "falling behind" was accentuated by the rising fortunes of once impoverished developing countries like those in East Asia (Balassa 1981; World Bank 1993a), academics and policy makers across Latin America were suddenly intent on more precisely isolating the causes of this delayed development. In the previous chapter, the analysis suggested that the obstacles to achieving higher levels of sustainable and more equitable growth in Peru were largely rooted in the domestic political economy. Particularly liable were the mismanagement of the country's rich factors of endowment over time, the poor choices made with regard to the country's integration into international markets, and a set of political and social relations that could most politely be described as stagnant. While this same diagnosis could be generalized to many Latin American countries at this time, the dependency school focused steadfastly on "systemic" explanations that placed most of the blame on the region's position within the international economy.

No matter that the East Asian bloc had been subjected to the same set of external pressures, development debates in Peru and other parts of the region now focused on Latin America's asymmetrical ties with the industrialized countries. In line with many of the neo-Marxist tenets that underpinned the dependency school, explanations for the region's delayed development were now posed in the language of economic imperialism and capitalist exploitation. Class analysts still located the plight of socioeconomic backwardness in a given country's structures of production, but the dependency school insisted that the perpetuation of backwardness on the periphery was a function of elite alliances between the owners of capital in the north and south. While the policy prescriptions varied considerably, they coincided in advocating even greater state intervention and economic oversight as a means of eradicating feudalistic class relations and enabling delayed developers in Latin America to reposition themselves internationally on much more favorable terms (Franko 1998, 52–53).

Thus, in Peru, international lending opportunities and a new development paradigm induced policy makers to persist all the more with a catch-up strategy based on higher levels of state intervention. However, the possibility of such a strategy emerging from the ranks of the Peruvian military had been unimaginable just a generation earlier. Once the staunch defenders of laissez-faire and avowed backers of the country's oligarchic elite, the Peruvian military experienced a change of heart that was catalyzed by the teaching of courses sponsored by ECLAC on structuralist economics and through exposure to the main writings of the early dependency school in the training programs of the national war college (CAEM). Gradually, the top officers had come to see the country's highly underdeveloped political and economic structures as the main threats to national security and as a result had begun to rethink their domestic and international political allegiances.

As the 1970s got underway, the more developmentalist market-friendly attitudes embodied in the Belaúnde administration gave way to a dependency-inspired strategy that quickly defined the state sector as the main engine of growth. The state itself became an intense object of scrutiny and debate (Quijano 1971), and although the evolving development strategy was a variation on the second-phase ISI policies witnessed much earlier in Brazil and Mexico, the Revolutionary Government of the Armed Forces (RGAF) prided itself in declaring the strategy "neither capitalist nor communist." Yet, as the data and analysis presented in this chapter will show, the strategy was indeed capitalist. Given the serious shortcomings of this fascinating experiment in military reformism, I have adopted the term *state capitalism* here as a description of what was attempted under the RGAF, rather than any indication of a new dynamic role for the Peruvian state.

On this count, the heart of the RGAF's problems lay in the transfer of the investment burden from the private to the public sector, without any improvement in the latter's ability to finance this effort and with amazingly little initiative taken to gain access to the substantial private-sector profits that registered over this time period. Spurred partly by this failure to induce private-sector participation, an unexpectedly large portion of the state's expansion also resulted from rescue operations and from actions frequently undertaken to achieve other goals (Saulniers 1988, 26–27). This chapter ascribes the conflicting policies and contradictory outcomes to two main problems. First, they strongly mirrored the highly conflictual nature of Peru's social, political, and economic structures; and second, they were a realistic gauge of the country's extremely weak position in world markets—hence the difficulty of steering a domestic course of development completely free from the exigencies of the international political economy.

This chapter elaborates on another lost opportunity at the time, which was the rapid expansion of the state sector without an equivalent extension of administrative capacities to support the state's various new functions. As the analysis will show, the first phase of the regime did succeed in temporarily consolidating its own position within the state bureaucracy and its position vis-à-vis the country's complicated constellation of class interests. But it fell short of any lasting effort to strengthen the capacity of the state to intervene more effectively in the economy. In the end, a main legacy of this period for Peru was the deepening of the difficult state-led dynamic identified in chapter 1: excessive external borrowing, reckless SOE expansion, heightened conflict between the state and domestic entrepreneurs, and the worsening of poverty and income distribution.

The analysis is broken down into five parts. The first section briefly elaborates on the political-economic backdrop that prompted the 1968 coup, but this time from the standpoint of the military. The second section looks at the RGAF's state-building efforts and its attempt to use the state more explicitly as an instrument for development. The third section analyzes the policies set forth by the regime, paying careful attention to the state-investment program and resulting patterns of capital formation. The fourth section assesses the new entrepreneurial role of the state through the rise of SOEs and seeks to understand the administrative and institutional intricacies of this sector as one of the major themes of this period. The final section looks at the inability of the state to sponsor the necessary economic adjustments in the second half of the 1970s, when faced with mounting pressures from the external sector and the eruption of a number of internal contradictions intrinsic to the state capitalist experiment itself.

Enter the RGAF: Redefining the Parameters of
National Security

The previous decade of divisive infighting within congress, the local press, and society at large distracted from the fact that the Peruvian military had been undergoing a quiet process of internal renewal during the 1960s. The first indication was the nature of the military's 1962 intervention. The armed forces played its traditional role of acting against the APRA in the latter's bid for the presidency. Yet the military's subsequent support for Belaúnde's reformist coalition broke with its historical pattern of arbitrating almost solely on behalf of the country's oligarchic interests. Both traditional economic elites and foreign capital were regarded more warily by the Peruvian military of the late 1960s. The main reasons were the destabilizing standoff with investors in the extractive sectors and the winner-take-all attitudes of domestic and multinational participants who prospered greatly from state-sponsored ISI without contributing in kind to the development of local industry. The poverty-related guerrilla uprising of the mid-1960s had further reinforced the military's perceptions that a sweeping socioeconomic reform effort had now become essential.

As the main civilian institutions were weakened by the chaotic events of the 1960s, the military, in contrast, stood out as a relatively well-developed and professional state organization. Within this setting a small cadre of enlightened officials, led by General Juan Velasco Alvarado, was able to forge the consensus around goals of development and distribution that had eluded political elites in the civilian sectors since the 1962 elections. After the civilians' half-hearted attempts to launch a state-sponsored industrial strategy and to rectify the country's many distributional inequities, the 1968 intervention marked the first time that these more heterodox development themes found firm institutional roots—both within the Velasco-led faction of the military and in some segments of the state bureaucracy.[1]

As the country's first serious effort at political and economic transformation, the twelve-year reign of the RGAF has been referred to simultaneously in the literature as nationalist-populist and bureaucratic-authoritarian. The latter is an exaggeration, as modes of political control in Peru at this time did not compare with the more extreme forms of coercion that had begun to emerge in the Southern Cone (Foxley 1983; O'Donnell 1988). Part of the con-

---

1. Ironically, these more heterodox approaches had been advocated by the APRA in Haya de la Torre's 1931 "Minimum Program" but never embraced as official government policy. Haya himself had long abandoned them in his unsuccessful attempts to capture the presidency (Reid 1985, 41).

fusion stemmed from the military's own inability to articulate its position beyond the catchwords of "reformist" and "anti-imperialist."[2] Nevertheless, this era broke with the past in important ways, such as a widespread agrarian-reform program and new laws governing private investment (domestic and foreign), worker ownership, and job stability.

During its two separate administrative phases under General Velasco (1968–75) and General Francisco Morales Bermúdez (1975–80), the RGAF launched its multisectoral reforms with more than four thousand legal decrees. With all the reforms taken together, one of the most abrupt departures from the country's liberal economic past was the intentional reorientation of the state sector from its previous ancillary position of facilitating private investment into the prime generator of economic growth (Wilson and Wise 1986, 93). Under the new state capitalist model, public ownership replaced private participation in key branches, and the state stepped up its role in organizing production in the modern sectors of the economy.

The public-investment program became a major tool for redirecting private-investment patterns so as to ameliorate the intensified disparities in income and wealth. The reforms centered on the attainment of national economic autonomy through a more integrated productive structure, according to sector and region, that would promote self-sustaining growth and a greater degree of efficiency in the use of human and natural resources. The decentralization of resources away from the more highly developed coast to the economically marginalized regions, a constant point of national contention, became an even more prominent theme under the RGAF (Salinas, Garzón, and Wise 1983).

This period, particularly the first phase under Velasco, also signified Peru's first full-fledged attempt at constructing an insulated and autonomous policy-making apparatus within the state (Stepan 1978; Wise 1994). Given the baseline for the Peruvian state sector established in the previous chapter, the efforts of a strategically placed military cadre to act quickly in transforming the political economy led, not surprisingly, to immediate structural imbalances and to contradictory development outcomes. Most accounts of the "lost opportunities" during this period center on the failure to reconcile redistributive goals with the chosen model of capital accumulation (McClintock and Lowenthal 1983) and the regime's ambiguous stance toward domestic and foreign capital. In the following section I elaborate on another lost opportunity, the RGAF's failure to sus-

---

2. The regime's timeworn description of its strategy as "neither capitalist nor communist" had become almost a cliché by the late 1970s.

tain an ambitious program of institutional reform to complement and bolster the predominant role that the state had come to assume in the domestic economy.

Building State Autonomy

A More Insulated Executive

Having witnessed all the factions and infighting that had overwhelmed the
president and paralyzed policy up until the 1968 coup, Velasco and his cohort
moved quickly to restructure the channels of access to the executive. The
political vacuum into which the junta had stepped, and the economic cushion provided by the stabilization measures of 1967–68, allowed these new
military policy makers wide discretion. At least during this initial phase, the
regime was able to superimpose on the executive the organizational coherence and discipline that it derived from its base in the military. Just as the
armed forces traditionally insulated officials from most societal pressures,
Velasco sought successfully, at first, to insulate the governing elite around the
executive from these same interferences.

Under these unusual circumstances of executive freedom, the junta stylized its managerial approach into a pattern ranging from "most closed to
most open" (Cleaves and Pease 1983, 224). At the closed end of the spectrum
policy decisions were generated in a highly insulated advisory group known
as the Council of Presidential Advisors (COAP), or generated by the ministries and passed on to the COAP, and then presented to the public as a fait
accompli. In its more open policy-making mode, the regime had the COAP
and the ministries collaborate with other state agencies or even submit a proposed measure to public debate. During the initial period of fostering rapid
change, the regime succeeded in this vein by repressing any opposition that
arose from various social and economic groups. It also proved quite savvy in
coopting local intellectuals and civilian *técnicos,* but without letting these
allies get too close to the center of state power.

The ultimate inability of government elites to realize their policy preferences under these conditions of high state autonomy can be partially attributed to the internal unraveling of the government coalition over strategic policy differences. Some members of the COAP were not entirely comfortable
with the high levels of intervention and radical tone of the structural reforms
and preferred to steer the economy back toward the more developmentalist
course that had been attempted under Belaúnde in the 1960s. Others had
become dubious of the interventions altogether and preferred to turn even

further back toward the market. Because of the utmost secrecy surrounding the junta, these nuances were not apparent until much later.[3]

Once internal disunity did set in within this elite working group, the regime faced a Peruvian polity that again placed more than the usual limits on state autonomy. A social network of state-dominated peak associations (to be discussed later) created by the military to gather support for its program later proved more effective for setting in motion the organized opposition to the regime (Sanborn 1991). As Alfred Stepan (1978, 302) has observed, autonomy can also "be a source of weakness because a state elite is not sustained by constituencies in civil society and therefore is almost exclusively dependent upon its own internal unity and coercive powers. The other side of the coin . . . is isolation and fragility."

But in the regime's loss of unity and support, some attention must also be given to the development of the capacity, outside of this insulated elite executive corps, to carry out its policy preferences. In other words, bureaucratic autonomy not only implies that officials who constitute the state have preferences that are more than the simple reflections of those expressed by powerful societal groups; in order to fully realize these preferences, autonomy also entails the cultivation of organizational cohesion, expertise, and extractive capabilities within strategic sectors of the state bureaucracy (Sikkink 1991; Geddes 1994; Knill 1999). During its installation phase, the regime went overboard on the former and did not go far enough to ensure the latter.

Overhauling the State Bureaucracy

One of the main steps taken toward modernizing the state was the structural reform of the central government ministries, including the creation of some new ministries after 1968 to manage the development program along closer sectoral lines. Holding the Ministry of Development and Public Works up as a symbol of graft and corruption under the civilians, the RGAF's first move was to break this ministry up into the ministries of industry, housing, transport/communications, and energy and mines.[4] In the process of redirecting the ministries and the budget and planning apparatus toward the management of specific economic sectors, the RGAF also acted to clip the wings of the Independent Public Subsector. Superfluous nonenterprise entities were dissolved, while those fulfilling functions still deemed economically worth-

---

3. These comments were made by former president Francisco Morales Bermúdez in a speech given in Lima, April 1983.

4. "Military Junta Announces Plans for Reorganization of the Government Administration," *Peruvian Times,* Nov. 8, 1968, 1.

while were brought under more direct ministerial control (Cleaves and Scurrah 1980, 71).

By the early 1970s the Peruvian bureaucracy was finally beginning to take the more coherent shape that other central governments in the region had assumed since the 1950s.[5] Another aspect of this reshuffling was the emergence of new points of institutional influence. The BCRP, viewed as generally embodying the more orthodox "IMF approach" to economic management, became more peripheral to the policy process. The reorganized finance ministry had regained its composure from the internal upheaval of the late 1960s and, under the direction of Morales Bermúdez as finance minister, moved into center stage in the making of macroeconomic policy. The INP, having been nourished during the 1960s with substantial technical and training assistance from ECLAC, also ascended in the formulation and implementation of policy. The INP's ECLAC-based critiques of Peru's dualistic economic structures had found some favor in the finance ministry, and now the ECLAC line became the guidepost for economic policy making.

The INP brought the planning system to life in several important respects (Fitzgerald 1976, 80–84). For one, the INP had by now acquired a generally well-trained group of technocrats who embraced the more progressive side of the RGAF program concerning the necessity to reconcile economic growth with distributional equity. For this new dedicated corps of midlevel planners at INP (Hopkins 1967), the state sector was considered a socially worthwhile place to work in the early 1970s. Through its sectoral offices within the ministries and the executive branch, the INP came to play a pivotal role in drawing up development plans, prioritizing sectoral projects, and authorizing changes in sectoral investment plans (Klitgaard 1971). However, even though the INP's resources increased substantially until the mid-1970s, it did not come to exert full control over state planning. Predictably, earlier antagonisms between the INP and the MEF again flared up, with the result that the INP never achieved the super-ministry status it sought (Cornejo 1985, 126–27).

Of all the institutions created at this time, the Corporación Financiera de Desarrollo (COFIDE) was set up with perhaps the most fanfare. Hoping to emulate the best features of such state holding companies as Mexico's Nacional Financiera (NAFINSA) or Chile's Corporación de Fomento de la Producción (CORFO), COFIDE was given the mandate of mobilizing and coordinating investment capital for the rapidly expanding state-enterprise

---

5. However, subsequent events do not bear out Fitzgerald's (1976, 90) optimistic observation that "the national planning system in Peru appears to be the most effective in continental Latin America."

sector. The directorship of COFIDE, assigned initially to a Harvard- and MIT-trained economist and civil engineer, represented one of the more highly qualified civilian appointments made during this period.[6] Though it was certainly on the right track in attempting to establish Peru's first super-entity to interface financially between the public and private sectors, the special confluence of easy external credit and a massive project portfolio overwhelmed the new agency in its attempts to properly assign and monitor the distribution of resources.

As for staffing and personnel practices within the public bureaucracy, the overriding difference from the past was the infiltration of military officers into the highest-level posts. Each of the ministries now fell under the administrative domain of one of the three branches of the armed services, and until 1975 all ministers were appointed by the president from the rank of general or admiral (Cleaves and Pease 1983, 222). Although the military presence in the bureaucracy never surpassed more than three hundred officers at any one time, these officers also prevailed over such key appointments as ministerial advisors, vice-ministers, agency heads, and directors of state enterprises.

In and of itself, this increased military influence did not bode poorly for the modernization of the state bureaucracy. For example, comparative studies of the Peruvian armed forces suggest that the Peruvian military's emphasis on education and professional training in the post–World War Two period rendered it one of the most merit-oriented institutions within Peruvian society and the region at large (Enrique Obando 1998; Klarén 2000). However, in the process of simultaneously assuming the role of state bureaucrats, there was a lowering of merit-based standards. Even when these were upheld, the increasingly technical character of the development program did not always imply a good fit between an officer's training and the managerial tasks at hand (Stepan 1978, 314).

Within the civilian ranks of the state bureaucracy, two changes were apparent. First was the sheer magnitude of the public-sector workforce by the late 1970s. As table 9 shows, public employment had nearly doubled over the decade (and quadrupled since 1961).[7] Wage patterns in the table reflect the rise and decline of state employment as an economically appealing endeavor after the 1973 peak. Those working within the highest ranks saw a wage reduction of more than 50 percent by 1977, whereas the bulk of the workforce

---

6. "COFIDE: How Will It Work?" *Peruvian Times,* May 14, 1971, 7.

7. Because of considerable numerical discrepancies among sources on the Peruvian public-sector workforce, the figures cited in table 9 and throughout the text should be taken as rough estimates.

concentrated in the service sectors saw a 40 percent cut. This combination of rapid numerical expansion and deep wage erosion indicates the extent to which state employment had become a social safety net of sorts, particularly for those working at the bottom rungs.

While recruitment, hiring, and promotion practices at the middle and lower bureaucratic levels ostensibly adhered to Peru's 1950 civil-service code, in practice the regime applied the code in the same ineffectual manner as its predecessor. Peter Cleaves and Martin Scurrah (1980, 77) provide one of the few firsthand accounts of the actual operating procedures that governed personnel expansion at these levels. Because this problem persisted as a major barrier to the building up of state capacity, they are worth quoting:

> The rule covering almost all cases is that "recommendations" have preponderant influence. . . . [C]andidates secure positions via recommendations from persons outside the public sector who happen to know the

TABLE 9. Public-Sector Employment and Wages: 1969–78

	Growth of Workforce (numbers)					
	1969	1970	1971	1972	1977	1978
Central government	148,049	176,987	192,026	207,726	245,332	242,453
Independent entities	25,370	33,305	55,749	51,669	37,237	31,639
Public enterprises	23,100[a]	—	—	31,386[b]	92,095	85,016
Social Security	13,969	13,243	5,803	6,029	26,530	26,477
Local government	10,114	12,399	13,953	19,519	27,241	34,902
Public benefit societies	5,112	4,229	3,421	2,852	4,336	4,124
Total	225,714	240,163	270,952	318,821[c]	432,771	424,611

	Wage Trends (based 1973)			
Professional Ranking	12/1973	12/1975	12/1976	12/1977
Grade I (highest)	100.0	71.6	63.3	42.3
Grade II	100.0	72.2	54.5	43.5
Grade III	100.0	73.2	56.1	45.3
Grade IV	100.0	74.5	58.3	47.6
Grade V	100.0	77.0	61.8	53.1
Grade VI (lowest)	100.0	82.3	68.4	63.2

Source: Hurtado and Robles 1985, 65; 1969–72 data from INP; public enterprise figures from Echeverría 1985, 51.

[a]1963–69.

[b]1973.

[c]Rounding errors.

hirer. Previously, such influence came mainly from the legislative branch of government; after 1968, it grew out of personal contacts with military and civilian elites in upper-level posts. Here the influential party visits or telephones the vice-minister or agency head to inform him of the availability of a talented friend or relative. This step, which paves the way for employment, often precedes any direct contact between the interested party and the hiring agency.

The second change was the highly capable corps of technocrats who had been drawn into the top levels of public employment as a result of the state having assumed a more entrepreneurial role in the economy. A 1973 survey of over six thousand public managers and consultants cited by Lima's Escuela de Administración de Negocios para Graduados (ESAN) estimates that around 75 percent of these managers had undertaken university and/or postgraduate studies, 35 percent had been working in the public sector for less than five years, and another 30 percent had been there between five and fifteen years.[8] Cleaves and Scurrah (1980, 87) note that the increasing demand for these more specialized professionals even helped infuse a greater element of competition and merit into hiring practices at this level.

The presence of this group again raises the question of the inability of the government to more fully utilize existing talent. Some of the answers are already apparent from this brief analysis: the haste with which the development effort was launched, the lack of clarity in goals, and the built-in tensions of a strategy that merged military and civilian policy makers into a top-down relationship on the latter's own bureaucratic turf. With congress suspended and political parties closely circumscribed during this time, the question of maximizing on these personnel resources is lent all the more significance by the fact that the state bureaucracy had become the main filter through which policy outcomes were shaped.

In line with some of the cases discussed in chapter 1, the cultivation of a greater degree of autonomy within the bureaucracy itself would have been an important first step in better harnessing this talent to the many new development tasks that had been set for the state. The Brazilian experience is instructive on this front. With Brazil faced with the unrealistic prospect of overhauling an entire public administration plagued by clientelism and inefficiency, studies of the Vargas (1930–45) and Kubitschek (1956–61) governments show that each was able to better implement its industrial-development program through civil-service reform and by creating insulated administrative

---

8. Escuela de Administración de Negocios para Graduados (ESAN) 1985, 11, 16.

pockets within the state apparatus that were tied to specific strategic sectors of the economy (Nuñes and Geddes 1987; Sikkink 1991). Barbara Geddes (1994, 45–51) likens these insulated agencies to semipermeable membranes whereby information and resources flow through the agency, but like a cell, are able to maintain its organizational integrity.

During this early period in Brazil, segments of the bureaucracy were insulated across institutional boundaries (within the public enterprises, the state development banks, state economic agencies, and various executive-level policy councils), such that both patronage and efficiency criteria could prevail simultaneously within the same entity (Nuñes and Geddes 1987). Like Peru's BCRP, some entities were completely governed by merit and competence, while organizational goals in others were preserved through these protected pockets of expertise. While insulation cannot guarantee that the correct mix of policies will be chosen, it can go a long way in securing a single-minded commitment to channeling scarce state resources to the tasks that have been designated.

The conditions that prevailed within the Peruvian techno-bureaucracy during the early 1970s were the most favorable yet for the cultivation of a more sophisticated and effective policy-making segment within the state apparatus. These were: the existence of a larger pool of administrative talent; a more established institutional framework than ever before (taking the BCRP, the INP, and the finance ministry as the bureaucratic core); a historically high level of cohesion in the office of the executive; and a tight rein on political participation. The lack of vision and leadership on this front was costly. As the central government organizational chart continued to expand, and the state-enterprise sector multiplied, so did the number of vying interests and conflicting policy goals. Cornejo (1985, 127) points to the emergence of "cells of competition," versus pockets of competence, which characterized the expanding body of talented public-sector professionals in Peru.

Redefining the State Vis-à-Vis Civil Society

The RGAF's approach to interest mediation during the early 1970s provides some of the most telling insights into the complexity of the program and the ambitiousness of the transformative goals. Rather than seek an explicit alliance with domestic capitalists, the Velasco administration sought to implement the state capitalist model by bringing both labor and capital together into carefully structured groups tied vertically to the state (Cotler 1975). In this quest to "overcome class struggle," mass-based opposition movements were suppressed, as were groups such as the National Industrial

Society and the National Agrarian Society that still represented Peru's dominant classes.[9] Civil society was recast into a corporatist image, the idea being
to eliminate detractors and win support for the massive capital-investment
program that was getting underway.

These new corporatist lines were drawn in three realms. The first was
within the state sector, for example, with the creation of the National System
for the Support of Social Mobilization (SINAMOS) in 1971. SINAMOS was
set up to organize the popular classes by functional groups (labor unions,
youth clubs, professional associations, squatter settlements, etc.) and according to geographic area. The remaining reforms occurred in the private sector.
First, the regime envisioned the enactment of a new social-property sector
where workers would assume ownership of the firms in which they worked.
Second, the regime promoted labor-community reforms in such sectors as
industry, mining, and fishing that combined greater worker participation in
the form of profit sharing and comanagement (Cotler 1975, 60).

Although during the Velasco period the RGAF had succeeded in attracting
a contingent of technocrats and administrators that drew widely from the AP,
the APRA, the DC, and even the Peruvian Communist Party (PCP), in the
end this did not compensate for the regime's total lack of a broad constituency when it assumed power. In spite of following through on a number
of explicitly antioligarchic reforms, and the granting of generous industrial
incentives and salary increases until the 1974 fiscal crunch, the regime faced
perhaps its stiffest confrontation from those members of the working and
middle classes who were the targeted beneficiaries of many of these measures.
If anything, corporatist attempts to divide the opposition and quell any criticism of the government's program fueled the intensity of political protest.

This opposition stemmed at least partially from the internal inconsistencies of the policies being implemented. Some segments of domestic capital,
particularly in the auto, appliance, and fish-meal sectors, had welcomed the
RGAF's strong push for industrialization. In 1969, with the backing of a small
clique of local manufacturers and financiers, Velasco was voted honorary
president of the Second Congress for Industrialists (Bollinger 1987, 9). Recognizing the potential for coopting the labor movement in these sectors,
some local capitalists initially endorsed the industrial communities as representing their own long-run interests. But as other crosscutting legal decrees
began to proliferate from the executive, such as the 1970 Job Stability Law
granting workers virtual job tenure, the enthusiasm of entrepreneurs rapidly
diminished.

---

9. The quotation is from "President Velasco's Message to the Nation," *Peruvian Times,* July 30,
1971, 3.

Having been readily handed numerous import privileges and investment incentives by the state since the late 1950s, private capitalists went into the 1970s with little experience in negotiating or protecting their interests under these more politically adversarial circumstances. This, plus the fiercely statist intentions of those within the more radical faction of the junta, worked against a more collaborative resolution of these differences with the regime. As private capitalists gradually realized that their strengths lay outside of the regime, they embarked on an effort to coordinate their opposition with other politically and economically disenchanted groups. The result was the emergence of a middle-sector bourgeois alliance by the mid-1970s that connected well with the more economically cautious faction within the military that seized power in 1975 (Cleaves and Pease 1983, 234–35; Durand 1994).

Nor did many of the RGAF measures meant to harmonize class relations hold water with the labor movement. It is here that the outcomes of RGAF policy making were perhaps the most paradoxical. RGAF strategies were geared toward cultivating a broad working-class constituency, reducing labor conflict, and thus facilitating the rapid industrialization effort. In this process, labor met with continued repression and blatant techniques of cooptation, but the RGAF also allotted organized labor a considerable degree of freedom. In its attempts to undermine the APRA's foothold with labor, already weakened by the party's economistic sell-out platform of the 1960s, the regime recognized the Communist-controlled General Confederation of Peruvian Workers (CGTP), chartered its own parallel union (Workers Confederation of the Peruvian Revolution), and tried to capitalize on the organizational weaknesses inherent in the Peruvian labor movement (Cotler 1975, 70).

The incorporation of the CGTP into this grand scheme to reorganize civil society along tightly controlled functional lines backfired. Most of the profit-sharing gains and wage benefits were realized in the narrow modern sector of the economy, and the proceeds did not dissuade workers from rebelling against the regime's coercive organizational tactics. The industrial-labor communities, rather than providing a framework for mutual accommodation between labor and management, became outbacks of fierce struggle between workers and their employers (Haworth 1983, 103). The year 1975 was the benchmark for conflict between labor and capital in the economy at large. That year, nearly one-third of Peru's wage earners went out on a total of 779 strikes, costing industry 20.3 million hours of lost labor time (Bollinger 1987, 13).

The increased repression, and the rejection by the popular sectors of the institutional alternatives handed down from the regime, set off an unprecedented flurry of organization outside the official state apparatus. This antigovernment grassroots organizing became apparent in the increased number of solidarity strikes, where whole communities supported striking

miners, teachers, and industrial workers (Sanborn 1991). These greater horizontal links between workers formed the cornerstone for the alliance of new
popular parties that triggered the transition to democratic rule in the late
1970s. The result, then, of RGAF efforts to reorganize society into benign
classless units was to enhance class-consciousness and conflict. Most important, through the entire array of participatory experiences inside and outside
of the state, Peru's poor and oppressed emerged from the 1970s better organized and more capable of defending their interests than ever before (Sanborn 1991).

Any semblance of state corporatist reorganization had largely disappeared
by the end of the Velasco period. SINAMOS, lacking the ideological legitimacy of a political party or the participatory integrity of a civic organization
not dominated by the military, was widely regarded as a failure by 1975. Similarly, other state-chartered groups had become defunct or were dissolved
after the takeover by Morales Bermúdez. In his analysis of this period, Stepan
(1978, 292–96) points to two more general explanations for the failure of the
RGAF to better institutionalize its regime.[10]

The first has to do with the contradictions intrinsic to a model of governance based on an exceptionally high level of autonomy at the installation
stage. Given the regime's self-imposed limits against a Pinochet-style utiliza-
tion of raw power to establish itself, it needed a more secure foothold in existing social formations and in the complex patron-client network that encir-
cled the state bureaucracy. Without this, its functionally and territorially
drawn units became hollow social structures. The second set of undermining
factors was conjunctural and had to do with the rapid erosion of domestic
and international resources and with this the political will of the state elite to
push the development program forward. The following section examines
these factors by focusing on the state-investment program and the interplay
of domestic and international economic trends in determining the outcomes
of state policy under the RGAF.

State Policy and Capital Formation

Beyond the general goals of achieving greater national economic integration
and reducing Peru's dependence on the world economy, the RGAF's development aims were expressed at length in the 1971–75 National Development

---

10. According to Stepan (1978, 292), "Institutionalization implies that a regime has consolidated the new political patterns of succession, control, and participation; has managed to establish
a viable pattern of economic accumulation; has forged extensive constituencies for its rule; and has
created a significant degree of Gramscian 'hegemonic acceptance' in civil society."

Plan.[11] As the country's first development manifesto, the plan critiqued Peru's "disarticulated" social and economic structures and explicitly spelled out the new dimensions for state intervention in rectifying these problems. Reform was to begin with the state itself, in terms of further upgrading administrative and personnel practices. The new state-led course for the economy was then charted out sector by sector, according to growth targets, investment projects, and sources of development financing (Cornejo 1985, 60).

The themes that ran across sectors included an emphasis on faster economic growth and the generation of much higher levels of employment. Because of Peru's obvious comparative advantage in mining and petroleum, these were given top priority, followed by industry, agriculture, and fishing. The idea was that, via "backward and forward linkages," the proceeds from natural resource exploitation could be used to push manufacturing past the import-substitution phase and into heavy industry (Klitgaard 1971, 15). State majority ownership was called for in the key productive areas, with the expectation that more clear-cut investment and taxation laws would entice foreign capital to return in these sectors. Finally, the themes of social economic justice and regional decentralization were tied in with the sectoral surveys. The program, according to the plan, was to be financed through tax reforms, greater export profits, and a more cautious use of external financing than that witnessed in the 1960s.[12]

As can be seen in table 10, the state-led model was well underway by the early 1970s. In accordance with the plan, the state's share of gross fixed investment (GFI) had jumped from 29.5 percent in 1968 to nearly 50 percent in 1975. As the table reveals, 1974 was a peak year, with the public share of GFI surpassing the private sector for the first time. In regional terms, these trends implied that Peru had joined step with its more developed neighbors in two ways. First, the state's economic presence during the 1970s had nearly doubled, as had the percentage of GDP captured by the public enterprises. And second, as with the rest of Latin America, Peru's state-enterprise share surpassed the central government by 1973. Because of its much larger size in the 1970s, and its significance in the public-policy process, Peru's state-enterprise sector is dealt with separately in the following section.

It is important to note from the outset that, as in the 1960s, these dramatic increases in state intervention eventually went beyond the intentional shift in government-planning policy. Placing tighter controls on FDI in the extractive sectors did not lead, as the Velasco government had hoped, to a resurgence in private investment. A number of nationalizations and the worker profit-shar-

---

11. Presidencia de la Republica, *Plan nacional de desarrollo para 1971–1975*, vol. 1, Plan Global.

12. Presidencia de la Republica, *Plan nacional de desarrollo para 1971–1975*, vol. 1, 30–31.

TABLE 10. Public Investment Trends as a Percentage of Gross Fixed Investment: 1968–80 (all figures based on 1970 soles)

	1968	1969	1970	1971	1972	1973	1974	1975	1976	1977	1978	1979	1980
Public investment	29.5	34.1	36.4	38.3	39.9	43.6	52.3	48.7	49.6	45.1	43.0	42.8	45.0
Central government	19.2	20.8	19.7	18.5	20.3	18.5	21.9	15.1	15.8	19.0	20.1	23.0	22.7
Public enterprises	6.2	6.9	13.1	13.9	13.2	20.6	23.9	31.6	31.6	24.7	21.8	17.9	19.4
Others	4.0	6.3	3.7	5.9	5.5	4.4	6.5	2.0	2.1	1.4	1.1	1.9	2.9
Private investment	70.5	65.9	63.6	61.7	61.1	56.4	47.7	51.3	50.4	54.9	57.0	57.2	55.0
Total gross fixed investments	100.0	100.0	100.0	100.0	100.0[a]	100.0	100.0	100.0	100.0	100.0	100.0	100.0	100.0

Source: BCRP, "Memoria," various years; 1977–80 data are unpublished data from BCRP; 1968–76 data are from Portocarrero Maisch 1982, 436.
[a]Rounding errors.

ing measures added to an already uncertain investment climate, one that discouraged foreign (especially U.S.) and local investors. As a percentage of GDP, private investment fell from 10.7 percent in the 1965–68 period to 7.9 percent from 1969 to 1973 (Paredes and Pascó-Font 1987, 19). Given the continued lack of dynamism in the private sector and Peru's increased access to international finance after 1972, by mid-decade public-sector ownership had virtually replaced foreign and domestic capital in mining, oil, fishing, electricity, most of the banking system, and the entire marketing of exports.

Peru's reentry into foreign credit markets in the early 1970s was a function of changes that had occurred on the international lending scene, as well as the increased prospects for foreign exchange due to newly discovered oil reserves in the jungle region. On the international side, Peru was able to circumvent a multilateral-aid boycott related to unresolved nationalization disputes and take advantage of the excess liquidity that had built up in the virtually unregulated Eurocurrency market. By this time, Euromarket loans had overtaken FDI and official lending as the major source of development finance for all of Latin America. The apparent freedom that came with Euromarket borrowing, in terms of quick disbursements and few conditional strings concerning the use of the loans or a country's overall political-economic policy, dovetailed with RGAF goals of seeking autonomous solutions without foreign interference.

Peru's easy times of unmonitored borrowing fell between 1972 and 1974 (Devlin 1985, 75), with the 1974–75 balance-of-payments crisis throwing a damper on bank eagerness to lend. During this easier borrowing phase, approximately 80 percent of all credit was extended in the form of syndicated Eurobank loans, with high interest margins and maturities of no more than five years. The lion's share of financing was captured by the public sector and went toward debt refinancing (18 percent), defense (30 percent), and project investments (50 percent). Given the ultimate destination of the Peruvian debt, patterns of capital formation in public-investment projects held the key to the outcomes of the development program. A complete evaluation of these projects lies beyond the scope of this analysis.[13] What follows is a look at global investment patterns, by sector, project, and region, keeping in mind the stated policy goals of the RGAF and these new opportunities offered up by the international political economy at this time.

---

13. Detailed descriptions and operational analyses of some of the top public-investment projects undertaken during this time can be found in Hugo M. Obando 1977 and in the following case studies from the Universidad del Pacífico's "Gestión Pública" research project: Cruz Saco 1985; Manuel Romero 1984; and Gustavo Romero 1985. For some interesting insights on the role and importance of investment projects in the development process, see Hirschman 1967.

State Investment and Policy Outcomes

The RGAF's bias toward reviving the lagging modern sector stands out in table 11, with the investment of over 50 percent of public funds into productive activities. Within the productive sector, the table reflects the emphasis placed on the major export earners—oil, mining, and large-scale agriculture. Industry, which was more an investment priority under Velasco, absorbed 15 percent of state investment from 1968 to 1975. In response to the overboard spending on roads and other economic infrastructure under Belaúnde, this sector assumed secondary importance. The correspondingly low investment in social infrastructure underlines the unavoidable conflict between distributional goals and the pressing need to generate foreign exchange to spur industrial expansion. Health and education were almost entirely neglected, with urban housing construction consuming most public outlays in the social sector.

TABLE 11. The RGAF and State Capital Formation: Sectoral Investment Percentages (based on 1973 constant soles)

	Phase I 1968–75 (%)	Phase II 1976–79 (%)	Total RGAF 1968–80 (%)	Principal Projects (%)
Productive				
Agriculture	14.3	16.6	15.3	71.1
Industry	14.8	7.1	11.3	65.2
Tourism	0.1	0.9	0.5	—
Fishing	1.7	2.2	1.9	—
Mining	5.7	14.1	9.5	65.3
Oil	15.5	18.6	16.9	76.0
Subtotal	52.0	59.5	55.4	
Economic Infrastructure				
Transportation	21.7	12.7	17.6	
Communications	2.0	3.4	2.6	
Electricity	10.0	12.6	11.2	
Subtotal	33.7	28.7	31.4	
Social Infrastructure				
Education	4.7	2.3	3.6	
Health	1.7	3.0	2.3	
Housing	7.9	6.6	7.3	
Subtotal	14.3	11.9	13.2	
Total	100.0	100.1[a]	100.0	

Source: Rizo Patrón 1982.
[a]Rounding errors.

The last column in table 11 indicates the extent to which large productive-sector projects dominated the state-investment program. The twelve big projects that swamped the country's portfolio during this period displayed some of the following characteristics (Hugo M. Obando 1977; Portocarrero Maisch 1982): delayed start-up periods, due mainly to the state's inexperience in negotiating and executing technical projects of such large undertaking; particularly long gestation periods, averaging nine years in most sectors and up to sixteen years with the major irrigation schemes in agriculture; and a high import content, which can be attributed to the heavy reliance on foreign financing.

Thus, within the productive sector, mining was dominated by just two projects—a zinc refinery and the Cerro Verde copper mine. Three jungle oil projects accounted for 75 percent of the state's petroleum investments, with the TransAndean oil pipeline representing one of the largest commitments of the decade. Industrial expansion saw the construction of three new plants, in steel, cement, and newsprint paper, as well as the maintenance of a high level of imported inputs to feed local production. Finally, agriculture was dominated by four huge irrigation projects located mainly on the coast. The giant among these, the Majes Irrigation scheme located in the south, had become one of Latin America's classic white elephants almost before construction had begun.[14]

The most obvious policy oversights in this period were the kinds of small or medium-sized projects that would be most likely to revive the internal market and synchronize with the maturity schedules of external creditors. On this last point, this period underlines the inefficacy of relying on high-interest finance that is short-term in comparison to the maturation period of most of the major projects. While it is true that certain major projects of national priority in the 1970s, such as the TransAndean oil pipeline and Cerro Verde, may have benefited differentially from the rapid flows of private credit, this cannot be said for the public-investment program as a whole (Devlin 1985, 193–200). In the event of minor disequilibrium in the mid-1970s, the more likely scenario was that of stop-and-go development, with projects literally

---

14. Originally designed as a complex irrigation network to tunnel fresh water through the Andes to the arid coast, Majes was calculated to cost a total of US$144 million ("Estudio de prefactibilidad sobre el aprovechamiento hidroeléctrico del Rio Siguas—proyecto Majes," Ministerio de Energía y Minas, Dirección General de Electricidad, vol. 1, 7–4, n.d.). Despite a number of studies, which concluded that the project was not cost-effective, the government tacked on two giant hydroelectric plants to the original plan. Begun in 1973, the project cost over US$650 million, as the five-nation management consortium—considered to be the largest to have coalesced around any one project in the entire region—continued to collect exorbitant fees and interest payments, even during idle construction time. See Lawrence Wippman, "Blending Five Cultures in One Big Project," International Management, Sept. 1983, 29–34.

left standing until credits could be renegotiated. Under conditions of major disequilibrium, which characterized Peru in the 1976–78 period, the entire investment program ground to a halt, and some important national objectives were sacrificed.

The 1971–75 plan had envisioned a combination of large foreign-exchange-earning projects in mining and petroleum and other more moderate endeavors in industry and agriculture aimed at increasing the supply of domestic goods and employment (Hugo M. Obando 1977, 91). Recognizing that project investments represented the cutting edge of the development program, the planning apparatus had been fairly well mobilized to manage the project portfolio. The project-appraisal system moved according to a newly established flowchart, from ministry or state enterprise, to the appropriate sectoral-planning office of the INP, to the INP's prefeasibility study list. The INP and COFIDE then collaborated in raising the necessary mix of domestic and foreign financing, respectively.

Fitzgerald (1976, 84–86) notes some weaknesses in the INP's cost-benefit calculations and the lack of a formal budget system to properly rank the projects within the various sectors. But the main explanation for the questionable cost-effectiveness and highly aggregated patterns of capital formation has to do with the combination of easy foreign credit and minimal public accountability or debate over the content of the public-investment program. Portocarrero Maisch (1982, 449–50) describes the underlying political dynamic that quickly superseded these newly established planning mechanisms:

> Such projects . . . are typically associated with the formation of powerful pressure groups interested in their implementation. Such groups typically comprise international financial sources, the consulting and contracting firms and their local associated groups, as well as their national and international suppliers. These pressure groups develop close links with the corresponding segment of the local bureaucracy. . . . [A]s a consequence, once a large project has reached the feasibility stage, it is almost impossible to avoid its implementation. . . . [T]hrough its capability to select the projects to be supported, international finance, therefore, constitutes an important filter that determines, to a great extent, the resulting pattern of public investment.

This dynamic surrounding external financing and patterns of public-sector capital formation also worked against the regime's expressed goals of geographically decentralizing state resources. The failures on this front come through in the sum the sierra and jungle regions together captured: less than

25 percent of all public investment during the 1970s. The heavy concentration of productive and social investments on the coast reflects the main dilemma of the RGAF's "unbalanced growth strategy," at least as it was applied here. While the wave of modern-sector industrial reforms sponsored under Velasco was expected to quicken the absorption of the traditional sector into the national economy, instead these groups were put permanently on hold.

Because the Velasco period and the 1971–75 plan represent the height of the thrust to transform the political economy, it would be useful to briefly review the general policy outcomes. In terms of global growth targets this first phase more or less achieved the projected goal (7.5 percent), as growth of GDP averaged 6.2 percent until 1974. But the growth projections across sectors were down. In petroleum, for example, growth expectations were wildly overcalculated (by as much as 800 percent); they were moderately so for copper, sugar, and cotton. Revenue projections from fish meal were also way off, as the fish-meal industry had run up against its ecological limits for the time being. It was the rapid expansion of the domestically oriented industrial sector that accounted for most of the high growth, and this was largely a result of Peru's leadership and participation in the six-member Andean Common Market (Ancom).

Created in 1969 and headquartered in Lima, Ancom liberalized trade among its members and established common external tariffs, joint industrial planning, and common treatment of foreign capital (Rudolph 1992, 57; Edwards 1993). Although Peru saw some expansion of nontraditional exports within the context of Ancom, accounting for 10 percent of all exports in 1974, industrial performance overall was at best mediocre. At the base of the "new" model was the continuing dependence on foreign investment to help finance imported inputs and capital goods (Conaghan and Malloy 1994, 59). In the end, with its generous tax credits and investment subsidies, the RGAF government was supporting the development of the same capital-intensive assembly industries with imported technologies, patents, and brands, and in the same indiscriminate manner as the preceding Belaúnde administration. Relocation incentives offered to those industries considered first priority for a decentralized industrialization strategy were not sufficient to reverse market trends (Wilson and Wise 1986, 101).

The RGAF's agrarian policy was the most ambitious, as the 1971–75 plan envisioned the completion of full land reform by 1975. Land-reform measures were geared toward equalizing the skewed property-ownership structure that existed between the large modern coastal plantations and the traditional sierra farms, most of which were smaller than five hectares. On paper, the RGAF committed itself to promoting "cooperative production" and protecting those private small and medium-scale farmers who constituted about 50 percent of the economically active population. In practice, as with the industrial-community reforms, most of the redistribution took place between landowners and workers within the modern coastal agricultural sector (Webb 1975). Pricing policies that favored urban consumers over rural producers exacerbated the neglect and decapitalization of traditional agriculture. As in the 1960s, economic stagnation in the agricultural sector led to an increase in food imports and intensified migration to the cities.

The remainder of the story is more familiar yet and has to do with policy failures surrounding the financing of the development program. In view of the long downward trend in primary-export revenues, and the rapid rise of public expenditures on social subsidies, the current account and fiscal deficits were both close to 10 percent of GDP by 1975 (Sheahan 1987, 261). Although progressive tax reform had been a constantly repeated policy goal, Webb (1972, 28) assesses the measures taken as "a mixed batch of minor adjustments, with a probable net regressive effect on the pattern of incidence."[15] The government, furthermore, had overshot its planned goal of borrowing around US$1.1 billion abroad to finance its development program (Klitgaard 1971, 16), as the total external debt reached US$6.2 billion over this time period (BCRP 1984). With inflation rising and a full-blown balance-of-payments crisis erupting in 1975, any further borrowing from the foreign banks would clearly require an agreement with the IMF.

Apart from the RGAF's many internal policy inconsistencies and contradictory political tendencies, this analysis of heightened economic disequilibrium and underlying conjunctural causes also sheds more specific light on the precedents to the palace coup that took place in 1975. When all was said and done, the main changes that emerged during this period were the advances in agrarian reform and the expansion of state ownership of the productive sector. The main continuities with the past were the heavy reliance on a primary-export-led model, the failure to adequately mobilize local resources, and hence the deepening of the debt-led pattern of state expansion that had taken hold under Belaúnde. Peru's active participation in Ancom had provided an important source of foreign exchange during the Velasco administration; by mid-decade Ancom had virtually stalled due to ideological differences surrounding Chile's 1973 military coup.

---

15. The other main tax measures were a reduction in two of the more progressive indirect taxes previously initiated on gasoline, tariffs on car parts for local assembly; and the many profit exemptions and other tax holidays designated to woo private investors (Webb 1975, 29–30).

The New Entrepreneurial Role of the State

Because the creation of a large public-enterprise sector during this period went to the heart of the state capitalist model, the purpose here is to lay out the new political-economic role of the SOEs in conceptual terms, rather than attempt an in-depth survey of the entire sector.[16] As table 10 shows, the SOE presence in capital formation had increased fivefold by 1975. As a result of this intensely compressed expansion, which normally occurred over four or five decades in other Latin American countries, the SOE contribution to GDP jumped from 1 percent in 1968 to nearly 20 percent in 1975. In terms of the absolute number of firms, the postcoup estimates seem to be no more certain than those for the pre-1968 baseline discussed in chapter 2. Skirting a gray definitional line between firms held "directly" or "indirectly" by the state, post-1968 estimates range from 135 SOE's (Augusto Alvarez 1992, 124–25) to 140 (World Bank 1982, 1).

The state's increasingly entrepreneurial role came about in three basic ways (Fitzgerald 1979, 192–95). First, some firms were taken over from foreign capital for largely ideological reasons. The first to go was IPC, immediately after the coup, which was merged with the existing state oil company (EPF) to form Petroperu. Other examples in this category include Centromin, the state mining company formed from the former Cerro de Pasco company, and Entelperu, a new state telephone company consolidated from the previous holdings of IT&T and a Swedish multinational operating in Peru (Sánchez 1984, 41–42).

Takeovers in the second category were less intentional, as this category included domestically owned firms that had fallen into economic straits. The most dramatic example was the state's assumption of control over a number of the Prado family's assets in the wake of the fish-meal-industry crisis. Included in this transfer was the Banco Popular, whose thirty-odd holdings brought such entities as a movie theater, a small newspaper, and a textile firm into state hands with virtually no public motive (Saulniers 1988, 25). Finally, some firms that were already present in the public portfolio in 1968 were expanded to form such companies as Mineroperu (refining and export of metals), Siderperu (steelworks), and Electroperu (electrical power).

The legal and administrative framework within which this expansion took place was ambiguous from the start. Peru's 1933 constitution was silent on

---

16. The best in-depth analyses of the public-enterprise sector during this period can be found in Saulniers 1988 and Augusto Alvarez 1992. Ortíz de Zevallos (1986) speaks freely as an insider who worked at the top administrative level within this sector.

the norms and operating procedures for public entities, and the 1936 civil code relegated their regulation to special legislation. While the RGAF did begin circulating a draft version of a public-enterprise law in 1971, a comprehensive code endowing SOEs with a coherent legal and administrative structure was never passed. Oddly, the 1971–75 plan, for all its emphasis on state intervention, devoted just a few lines to SOEs in a buried section on the central government organizational structure. President Velasco's famous "Plan Inca," published in all the major newspapers in mid-1974, addressed the dimensions of state entrepreneurship more directly. But again, these proclamations were mainly descriptions of what the state firms should do, with no concrete strategy set forth for how to structure these activities.[17]

The inability to negotiate and codify an established framework for the SOEs meant that the entire sector was governed by a patchwork of ad hoc, and frequently overlapping, administrative decrees. Though nationalized, some of the previously private firms continued to operate under private law (Ley de Sociedades Mercantiles) and enjoyed considerable operational autonomy in doing so. Other firms that had been created by the state fell under direct public jurisdiction. Different rules could even apply to workers within the same job in a given firm, and for the most part, the SOEs were stripped of authority concerning appointments, contracts, and wages (BCRP 1985a, 34–35). The relevant sectoral ministry generally ran these firms, with the result that the SOEs were subjected to extensive interference in their daily operations (World Bank 1982, 11).

In recognition that the lack of uniformity and the absence of clear operational directives had become a major bottleneck in carrying out the development program, the executive-level Council of Ministers set up a multisectoral commission in 1975 to study these problems. The commission, composed of top-ranking bureaucrats, made a number of recommendations that were never implemented. Among these were a reduction in the number of state firms, the centralization of all SOE activities in COFIDE, and the transfer of decision-making authority over crucial labor practices (recruitment, hiring, promotions, and wages) to SOE managers. The inertia surrounding the first commission led to the creation of a second one in 1976, this time with the specific mandate to increase SOE efficiency and to draft a long-overdue normative law.

Under the leadership of Petroperu's general manager, this second commission brought together prominent representatives from both the public and private sectors. The commission reiterated the call for divesting public entities of no strategic importance and criticized the chaotic relationship

---

17. See "The 'Plan Inca,'" *Andean/Peruvian Times*, Aug. 2, 1974, 10.

between the central government and the SOEs concerning subsidies and pricing policies (Saulniers 1988, 64). The commission also noted the destabilizing effects of ministerial interference in everyday management decisions and the constant turnover in membership on the SOEs' boards of directors. The recommendation here was to leave state managers to their own devices and to halt the chronic and politically motivated changeovers in board members and personnel.

The 1976 commission made some important analytic points regarding the problems that plagued the SOE sector, and it helped stake out a valuable common ground for public and private managers to air their concerns. Yet its recommendations met with the same fate as those of the previous commission. Nearly a decade into the RGAF program, the crucial SOE sector was still governed by an intricate uncodified institutional network encompassing the central government ministries, various oversight committees, the INP, the MEF, and the Banco de la Nación (the national treasury). As different agencies carried different weight over specific issues and policy areas, the sector as a whole was characterized by fierce conflicts. In this respect, Peru's SOE sector embodied the classic standoff, often mentioned in the literature on public enterprises, between managerial autonomy and excessive government control (Augusto Alvarez 1985; Vernon 1981; World Bank 1995).

Meanwhile, the SOEs had come to play a pivotal role in the economy. The two major changes from the pre-1968 SOE portfolio—which had generally been characterized by poor performance and low profits—were the large share of fixed capital expenditures now undertaken by the SOEs and the greater use of the SOEs by the central government in regulating prices on domestic goods and services. Paradoxically, although the SOE sector had greatly expanded, Paredes and Pascó-Font (1987, 26) note that other policy instruments concerning investment and pricing superseded the traditional tax and budgetary policies that usually accompany such expansions. These competing policy thrusts quickly brought to the fore a second main dilemma for countries choosing to rely heavily on SOEs as development tools: the inherent tension between the pursuit of a firm's microeconomic investment goals and the macroeconomic and social objectives of the central government (Saulniers 1988).

In the peak period of capital formation and structural reform from 1968 to 1975, Peru's SOE sector moved on a rapid collision course between these two policy imperatives. Social spending during this time centered mainly on state-financed subsidies for oil and foodstuffs. Although this policy of holding urban prices down on food and gasoline was not at all new to Peru, the percentage share of GDP (1.2 percent) consumed by state subsidies had reached new heights by 1974. Two firms, Petroperu and EPSA (a govern-

ment-merged company responsible for financing and administering all of
Peru's agricultural imports and exports), bore the mainstay of an SOE deficit
that approached 20 percent of GDP by 1975. The more serious deficit burden
that appears abruptly in 1974 reflects the RGAF's determination to battle the
Organization of Petroleum Exporting Countries (OPEC) oil-price hikes and
their inflationary impact through subsidies and direct price controls (Paredes
and Pascó-Font 1987, 27–28).[18] Overall, these profligate price and subsidy
policies represented an integral part of the RGAF's attempts to win popular-
sector groups into its political camp.

The SOEs' microeconomic-investment mandate formed the linchpin of
the strategy, reviewed earlier, designed to kick off heavy industry through the
expansion of primary exports. On this count, the tone of the 1971–75 plan
appeared to emulate the Brazilian model, where SOE-sponsored infrastructure and other investments have been successfully used to foster the growth of
downstream private enterprises (Sánchez 1984, 36). There, the private sector
has benefited greatly from SOE output, and until the 1982 debt crisis, SOEs
had succeeded in generating a financial surplus for reinvestment (Trebat
1983, 236–42). However, for starters, the Brazilian SOE sector had accomplished this by allowing SOE managers a high degree of autonomy in daily
operations and in medium- and long-term planning. Furthermore, Brazilian
SOEs were not burdened with providing the kinds of deficit-inducing social
subsidies witnessed in the Peruvian case.

Clearly, Peru's pricing policies were such as to prevent the SOE sector
from generating the savings necessary to finance the enormous investment
program. The massive increases in fixed investment, plus the fact that social
subsidies were not always adequately financed by central government transfers (Paredes and Pascó-Font 1987, 28), meant that the SOEs were able to pay
for less than one-quarter of their capital outlays. Thus, Petroperu,
Mineroperu, and Electroperu, the three big firms that accounted for the bulk
of public investments (around 75 percent) in the 1970s, also took the lead in
the resort to foreign borrowing (BCRP 1985b, 195). While much of the
1974–75 fiscal crisis culminated in these SOE imbalances, there is perhaps a
tendency to place too much blame on the state firms. The problem was actually a two-way street between the SOEs and the central government, as the latter ordered firms to invest without handing over sufficient capital.

Nevertheless, the weaknesses of Peru's SOE sector at this time cannot be
overstated. The symbiotic managerial and financial relationship with the central government reduced most companies to the status of public institutions,

---

18. Oil subsidies alone represented 55 percent of all state subsidies in 1974 (Paredes and Pascó-
Font 1987, 28).

as opposed to freely operating productive enterprises. At the same time, the SOEs had become a main conduit for the inflow of foreign investment and loans and crucial links for implementing the RGAF's ambitious development program. This disjuncture between the SOE sector's critical importance in the transformation of the political economy and the insufficient effort made to properly nurture it along can probably only be chalked up to inexperience and naivete. Without a more coordinated approach, SOEs were able to provide neither a solid basis for private-sector expansion nor the sound entrepreneurial nucleus necessary for the regime to generate a self-sustaining pattern of accumulation.

The Failure to Adjust

As can be seen from the mounting debts and deficits that appear in table 12, economic adjustment had become inevitable by the time of the Morales Bermúdez takeover in 1975. From the foregoing analysis, the main problems can be summarized as follows: a drop in exports related to currency appreciation and ISI; sluggish progress on new mining projects and the inability to locate additional petroleum reserves; the decline in private investment, only partially offset by the grandiose public-investment program; the chaotic management situation within the SOEs; and, the resort to expensive foreign financing to paper over the mounting deficits in the current and fiscal accounts (Thorp and Bertram 1978; Sheahan 1999). Together, these deficits and mounting structural rigidities combined with the 1973–74 oil-price shocks to produce new rounds of inflation in Peru.

The political backdrop for adjustment was an increasingly divided leadership coalition, by now completely alienated from any pretense of popular-sector support and only backed by the country's dominant groups to the extent that the second phase of the military regime symbolized an end to the statist excesses of the Velasco period. This was the context for Peru's three-year saga of attempted economic stabilization from 1975 to 1978, first under direct supervision from its private creditors and then under an IMF agreement after 1977 (Devlin 1985; Stallings 1987). The IMF's usual orthodox package of expenditure-reducing (cuts in subsidies, public-sector wages, and public investment) and expenditure-switching (currency devaluation, higher taxes) policies was used to tackle the growing macroeconomic imbalances. Yet, in spite of the various reductions in public expenditure and investment (see table 10), the government deficit remained at 10 percent of GDP through 1977.

Part of the explanation for the public sector's failure to adjust lies in the

TABLE 12. Macroeconomic and External Indicators in Peru: 1970–80

	1970	1971	1972	1973	1974	1975	1976	1977	1978	1979	1980
GDPGRO	5.8	4.2	2.9	5.4	9.2	3.4	2.0	0.4	0.3	5.8	3.1
GNPPCGRO	4.1	1.9	0.1	2.1	6.6	0.5	-1.8	-2.9	-4.1	1.5	2.0
INF	5.0	6.8	7.2	9.5	16.9	23.6	33.5	38.1	57.8	66.7	59.1
PRIVGDP					6.9	9.2	8.7	8.3	8.4	8.5	9.7
PUBIGDP					8.2	8.4	8.1	6.3	5.5	5.6	7.3
INVEST					15.1	17.6	16.8	14.6	13.9	14.1	17.0
RER	207.2	200.5	195.2	201.7	205.1	189.0	204.7	237.7	301.3	292.3	269.5
TRADEBAL	335	159	132	15	-403	-1,099	-740	-438	340	1,540	826
CURACCT	202	-34	-31	-262	-725	-1,541	-1,193	-922	-193	730	-101
FDI	-70	-58	24	70	58	316	170	54	25	71	27
PORT	-7	-7	-3	-2	-2						
DEBT	3,211	3,308	3,463	3,891	5,241	6,118	7,576	9,171	9,717	9,269	9,386

Source: GDP, GNP, and debt are from World Bank, *World Development Tables, CD-ROM,* 2000. Data on investment are from Glen and Sumlinski 1998 <www.ifc.org/economics/pubs/discuss.htm>. Inflation, exchange rates, and payments are calculated from the IMF's *International Financial Statistics, CD-ROM,* June 1999, except trade balance prior to 1977 obtained from IMF 1984; FDI and portfolio investment data prior to 1977 obtained from IMF 1994.

Note: GDPGRO = growth of real GDP; GNPPCGRO = growth of real per capita GNP; INF = Dec.–Dec. inflation; PRIVGDP = private investment as % of GDP; PUBIGDP = public investment as % of GDP; INVEST = total domestic investment as % of GDP; RER = real exchange rate (1990 = 100), calculated using period average exchange rate, U.S. WPI, and domestic CPI; TRADEBAL = trade balance (mil$) = merchandise exports − merchandise imports; CURACCT = current account (mil$); FDI = foreign direct investment (mil$); PORT = foreign portfolio investment (mil$); DEBT = total external debt (mil$).

stop-and-go nature of the policies' application. The income-reducing measures had unleashed fierce conflicts over who would bear the brunt of the economic downturn, which culminated in the highly successful national strike of
July 1977. Thus, the regime backed off on some of the austerity measures.
Domestic credit was expanded, and social subsidies were increased to over 5
percent of GDP that same year (Paredes and Pascó-Font 1987, 37). State
spending was also driven by the increasing amount of the budget devoted to
debt-service payments and the explosion of arms imports as defense spending
oscillated between 20 and 36 percent of total government expenditures
between 1970 and 1980 (Dancourt 1985).

The thrust for a defense buildup at this time stemmed from the perceived
threat posed by Chile's General Pinochet, who had begun a large-scale rear-
mament after staging the 1973 coup (Encinas del Pando 1983). Velasco had
initially asked the United States for help, but the Nixon administration
declined, complaining that settlements had yet to be reached on U.S. holdings
nationalized earlier. The Peruvian military then turned to Moscow, which
obliged it with more than half a billion dollars' worth of materiel on quite
favorable terms.[19] There is no doubt that it was military spending that added
to the severity of the 1975–78 crisis. Although the banks and the IMF both
threatened to withhold loans when they discovered "hidden" outlays on
defense in the budget, the end result was little more than a slap on the wrist.
By 1980, only three other underdeveloped countries, all of them in the Middle East, devoted a higher percentage of GDP and central government expenditures to defense than did Peru.[20]

In line with the theme of this chapter, these failures to adjust must also be
seen in the broader sense of paths not taken to preserve any advances that
had been made toward strengthening the capacity of the state to intervene
more effectively in the economy. Here, the two most detrimental trends were
the erratic cuts in public-sector personnel and the thrust toward privatizing
the SOEs before the sector had been properly prepared for sale. Up until
1978, most of the current expenditure cuts had been achieved by simply
holding wages down and not granting increases on par with inflation (Paredes and Pascó-Font 1987, 36). As Peru fell out of compliance with the IMF
agreement that year and a full cutoff in external financing brought the crisis

19. U.S. House of Representatives, "Arms Trade in the Western Hemisphere," hearings before
the Subcommittee on Inter-American Affairs of the Committee on International Relations, 95th
Congress, 2d session, June–Aug. 1978, 19.

20. U.S. Agency for International Development, "Economic Development versus Military
Expenditures in Countries Receiving U.S. Aid: Priorities and the Competition for Resources,"
report submitted to the U.S. House of Representatives, Committee on Foreign Affairs, Dec. 1980,
79–85.

to a head, the wage reductions were followed by substantial layoffs in public-sector personnel.

The majority of these employees were let go during the 1978–79 crisis. In their study of these personnel cuts, Silvia Vallenas and Maria Emma Bolaños (1984) emphasize the propensity to lay off those employees in the highest job grades (I–III; see table 9), with longer civil-service tenures, and in those ministries that were most germane to implementing the development targets that had been set. Thus, of a total of around 20,300 layoffs in the public sector, 36 percent were concentrated in the top professional ranks of the ministries of economy and finance, agriculture, industry, energy and mines, education, and the INP (Vallenas and Bolaños 1984, 140).[21] The cuts meant the shrinking of a considerable corps of talent and expertise that had gradually been cultivated over at least half a generation and the disabling of the state sector to manage the unruly 1980s-style crises that had already begun to surface in Peru.

The effect of the economic crisis on the SOE sector at this time was to speed up the calls for divestment and privatization that had surfaced earlier within the various multisectoral commissions. The policy debate post-1975 centered on improving the financial solvency of the SOEs, and a number of companies were proposed for sale. Yet no bidders came forth. The lack of enthusiasm was due partly to the recessionary atmosphere and to the poor financial terms being offered by the government.[22] The divestment procedure also required the review of yet another commission, which was no doubt a deterrent to potential buyers (Ortíz de Zevallos 1986, 133).

The SOEs were pared down to some extent by the same kinds of personnel cuts that had been carried out in the central government. Although there is less information available about who was laid off in this sector, the SOE workforce was reduced by about 8 percent overall in 1978 (see table 9). Because of the more technical demands inherent in this sector, SOE professional staff were generally more highly paid and in scarce supply from 1968 on (BCRP 1985b, 97). Thus, the lost opportunities here probably had less to do with erratic personnel cuts at the top levels than with the revolving door for man-

---

21. Of those top-level workers let go at this time, 22 percent had been holdovers from the first Belaúnde administration, 34 percent had entered public service during 1968–69, and 34 percent had been hired in 1972–73 during the heyday of the structural reforms under Velasco (Vallenas and Bolaños 1985, 140).

22. As an example of the kinds of divestment options coming forth at this time, Ortíz de Zevallos (1986, 133) describes one of the government's stock-option plans: "The income generated by the sale of stocks held by a public enterprise was to be transferred to the Treasury and matched by a corresponding transfer to the company of ten-year government bonds paying only 10 percent interest with a two-year, no-interest grace period. With inflation running over 70 percent a year, this mechanism was very unattractive." Also see "Peru to Hive Off State Companies," *Latin American Economic Report,* Apr. 9, 1975, 1.

agers and directors that had been in effect all along for almost purely political reasons (World Bank 1982, 5).

With the arrival of a high-power civilian economic team under the leadership of Finance Minister Javier Silva Ruete in 1978, the rationalization of the SOE sector received "top priority" (Saulniers 1988, 67). The civilians submitted what amounted to the fifteenth draft of the normative law of public enterprises to the COAP, where it was once again buried. As policy statements became more concise about the need to reorganize and consolidate the SOEs, the implementation process became more inert.[23] Meanwhile, the propensity toward privatization and the embracement of market-oriented reforms had begun to spread throughout the policy-making apparatus.

This period ended with an upswing in ideological attacks on statism and a general turning away from state-led strategies. The mood among political elites at the close of the RGAF era was one of going back to business as usual. In this sense, the central government ministries regained control of the capital-investment program, the INP's political influence quickly waned, and the BCRP and MEF reasserted themselves institutionally in the policy-making process (Cornejo 1985). The military, discredited and anxious to cut its own losses, called for a Constituent Assembly to draw up a new constitution in 1978, to be followed by national elections in 1980.[24] The way in which this convergence of political liberalization, orthodox stabilization, and the rapid turnaround in the external sector shaped the policy agenda in the 1980s is the subject of the next chapter.

Conclusion

Overall, this chapter has argued that Peruvian-style state capitalism, as a development strategy proper, fell short of generating the intended transformations in growth, savings, investment, and distribution. Furthermore, the strategy was hampered by the fact that those crucial bureaucratic, institutional, and administrative supports that would be mandatory for its effective implementation were being built up simultaneously with the launching of the program. Ultimately, although it is difficult in this case to separate out the choice of faulty policies from their weak implementation, it is clear that the

---

23. The 1975–78 National Development Plan (Instituto Nacional de Planificación, *Plan nacional de desarrollo 1975–1978*, Lima, junio 1975) defined the sectoral objectives and activities of the SOEs more explicitly, although the plan was never actualized as a result of the 1975 coup.

24. National Information Service, *"Tupac Amaru" Government Plan: 1977–1980*, Lima, 1977, 13–14.

state's poor political capacity converged negatively with the internal inconsistencies intrinsic to the strategy itself.

If we step back from the twelve-year experiment and examine this period in the light of trends within the state sector that had been set in motion during the 1960s, two longer-term conclusions can be drawn. First, in line with the interventions of the 1960s, the RGAF's program further hastened the process of political and economic diversification in Peru. With the nationalizations, land reform, and various worker-promotion laws, the country's oligarchic groups met their final demise. Although this had been one of the military's most explicit objectives, much less headway had been made in strengthening Peru's position vis-à-vis foreign investors. Other attempts to redraw class lines met with uneven success. The RGAF's effort to cultivate a buoyant domestic bourgeoisie proved more elusive than ever, and the most dramatic effect of many of the industrial- and labor-community reforms was to bring workers and other popular-sector groups out into the open to an unprecedented extent.

Thus, entrepreneurs certainly emerged no stronger from the experience of the 1970s, and workers emerged much better organized and able to articulate their interests. But the terrain for mediation and consensus was still ill defined. By the end of the 1970s, political and economic elites found themselves united against the military and what was widely perceived as the "crowding-out" effect of state expansion, but not at all unified in the pursuit of a coherent alternative. And although organized labor approached a level of militancy and outward cohesion that had been virtually unthinkable in the 1960s, it was still plagued with internal divisions and sectarian splits from emergent new-left forces that had risen up during the turmoil of the post-1975 period (Haworth 1983, 112). Thus, for all its attempts to do so, the RGAF was not able to carve out an effective role for the state as a mediator of pivotal societal interests.

The second longer-term conclusion concerns the solidification in Peru of the problematic dynamic related to state-led development in Latin America that was identified in chapter 1. As in most of the other countries in the region, Peru's strengthened ties to European and North American private capital markets in the 1970s enabled it to maintain domestic consumption while postponing key decisions concerning monetary, trade, and fiscal policy. In the process, the RGAF employed the state as a means of improving the country's position in the international economy. Ultimately, the analysis showed that the Peruvian state was not able to use foreign loans to accomplish this goal; important sectors of the economy had been nationalized, but because of the ad hoc nature of many of the interventions, Peru found itself, ironically, in an even more adverse position with respect to global markets.

Other problematic aspects of state activity, including the heightened reliance on SOEs as major policy instruments, the state's increasingly ambiguous relationship with domestic entrepreneurs, and the difficulty in coordinating long-overdue social policies with the development program, were also solidified at this time. Regarding the SOEs, after the massive interventions of the early 1970s, Shane Hunt (1975, 348) cautioned that Peru's future economic success or failure would depend on the effectiveness of management practices "in every new sector with every state enterprise." The links among the management failures in the SOEs, reckless Euromarket borrowing, and the drop in private investment are certainly not as cut and dried as subsequent administrations in Peru would have it. Yet it is safe to say that this period represents a critical juncture in the sense that the private sector, both domestic and foreign, had simply not rebounded to anywhere near the investment levels witnessed in Peru prior to the 1960s.

Finally, it would be difficult to overlook the distributional shortcomings of the military's program, including the propensity of social subsidies to favor town over country and the near exclusion of the jungle and sierra regions from the capital-investment program. From the standpoint of the dualistic structures of the Peruvian economy discussed earlier, the cumulative effects of the RGAF's many reforms are also disheartening. The informal sector still constituted 75 percent of all workers, while its value-added contribution to GDP had dropped below 40 percent; modern-sector employment was up slightly to 25 percent, while that sector's share of value-added had risen to 64 percent. While vigorous human-capital investments would have been one of the most powerful tools for countering these adverse distributional trends, these were sharply curtailed after 1975. It was the persistence of almost ancient forms of poverty, and the new avenues of participation inadvertently offered up by the military regime, that set the stage for the continued political and economic volatility that would haunt coastal bureaucrats through the 1980s.

PART 2

The State in Retreat

CHAPTER 4

Orthodox Stabilization with Populist Overtones

Peru's Social-Market Model and Its Southern Cone Counterparts

During the final two years of military rule, from 1978 to 1980, new political and economic events converged to set the country off on another erratic course for the 1980s. Peru's penchant for a more market-based strategy by 1980 can be partly traced to the specifics of this transition and to factors that were discussed earlier, in chapters 2 and 3. First, until the 1960s, the country had a strong bias toward laissez-faire and a historical tendency to revert back to a liberal economic policy regime when attempts at direct state intervention failed. Second, transnational actors had a much greater influence during the last half of the 1970s; for example, the private banks and the IMF were unequivocally promarket in meting out stabilization and adjustment guidelines for Peru. Although these programs had been unduly harsh in distributional terms, political elites went into the 1980s convinced that the orthodox cure had worked. Domestic entrepreneurs shared this perception to a large extent, as ADEX (the industrialists' exporting society) and the more domestically oriented Industrialists' Society pushed hard for future economic policies based more solidly on market signals.

The other obvious influence was the neoconservative management approach underway in various Southern Cone countries in the 1970s (Foxley 1983; Ramos 1986). In Chile, Argentina, and Uruguay, military juntas had intervened in the face of high levels of social conflict and political polarization, blaming most of the domestic turmoil on the state-led development strategies that had been in vogue within each country since the outbreak of the Great Depression. By rallying around a purist free-market banner, these regimes promised to put an end to the slow growth and high inflation that had plagued the Southern Cone throughout the post–World War Two period. These projects were both economic and political. By placing almost limitless faith in the dynamism of the private sector and clamping down on civil society, neoconservative leaders sought nothing less than a complete structural transformation of the political economy along market lines.

The specific policies that stemmed from the neoconservative school included the following: (1) attacking inflation through monetary control and exchange-rate devaluation, then pegging the exchange rate to the U.S. dollar once prices had fallen (Fishlow 1985, 135); (2) privatization and abrupt cut-backs in the public sector's share of GDP; (3) an open door for foreign investors (Fishlow 1985, 134); (4) a rapid reduction in tariffs and the reorientation of trade toward comparative advantage on world markets (Ramos 1986, 10); (5) freeing interest rates and eliminating controls over the allocation of private credit in order to promote domestic capital markets; and (6) the dismantling of any potential opposition, particularly organized societal interests (Ramos 1986, 10).

Peru's comparison with this group goes just so far. As in the Southern Cone, market policies were embraced as part of the ongoing battle against inflation and as a reaction to what was perceived as the excesses of statism. But Peru's social-market model was meant to form an economic corner-stone in the transition to democracy and in this sense lacked the fervor of the Southern Cone for a full-scale transformation of state-society relations through harsh authoritarianism. The question of why the neoconservative strategy was taken up so enthusiastically by Peruvian policy makers, at least in rhetorical terms, when it had clearly failed in Argentina and Uruguay, demands some explanation. Part of the answer lies with the per-formance of the Chilean economy, which, with its relatively higher growth and lower inflation up until late 1980, was still being trumpeted by the banks and the multilaterals as a free-market success (Stallings 1987, 185). As the Belaúnde economic team was gradually assembled from technocrats who had sat out the RGAF years working abroad in these institutions, the Chilean-style promarket mind-set had more or less been instilled from afar (Webb 1987, 30).

The following sections examine Peru's efforts to implement the social-market model in four parts. First is a brief analysis of the political-economic context that framed the choice of this particular economic strategy. Second is a review of the policy goals as they were originally set forth by the Belaúnde administration. Third is a brief look at those institutional vari-ables discussed in chapter 1 and the changes that occurred on this front during the 1980s. In terms of the arguments running throughout this book, this period is pivotal in the sense that it represents a further deterioration of those bureaucratic, institutional, and coalitional variables introduced ear-lier as contributing most to the political capacity of the state to effectively carry out a designated set of policies. This observation is substantiated in a fourth section that analyzes the social-market program in practice. Because the program never came together in a cohesive manner, but rather as a clus-ter of measures applied somewhat sporadically, what follows here is a dis-aggregated look at the main policy initiatives as they unfolded prior to the onset of the debt crisis in 1982.

Peru's Return to the Market: The Political-Economic Context

The results of the June 1978 elections to the Constituent Assembly provided a fairly good barometer reading on the direction that electoral politics would take over the next decade. The APRA, having made its historic peace with the military during this period (Sanborn 1991), won a respectable 35.3 percent of the assembly vote. Although Belaúnde's AP had registered for the 1978 elections, in the end the former president sat out the competition so as to concentrate on the 1980 presidential race. This cleared the way for the Popular Christian Party (PPC), founded from the more conservative bases of the Christian Democrats by former Lima mayor Luis Bedoya, and for the array of leftist parties that had come to the fore since 1975. Bedoya's PPC won 23.7 percent of the 1978 vote, while the left together garnered an unprecedented 30 percent (Reid 1985, 76).

The subsequent assembly debates over the new constitution differed in at least two ways from those that had occurred during Peru's democratic transition in the early 1960s. First, the positions of the three representative blocs in the assembly were not nearly as compatible as before. Second, a much stronger presence and more militant agenda was set forth by the left-wing groups in the assembly. In response to the heightened political and economic repression of the 1970s, the newly elected left-wing representatives of labor and the popular sectors had become more vociferous about demanding their basic civil rights. The strident stance assumed by each side meant that the final draft of the new constitution passed by the assembly in 1979 stood as more of a reflection of what these emergent factions hoped to gain under civilian rule and less of a guideline for resurrecting Peruvian democracy according to any formula based on political consensus.

Those constitutional articles that pertained to economic strategy and administrative reform of the state are of most concern here.[1] Not unexpectedly, those delegates representing the interests of private capital from within the ranks of the PPC joined with the conservative wing of the APRA in setting a free-market tone for the debate. With Haya de la Torre at the helm as president of the assembly, the APRA-PPC alliance prevailed in passing a section on Peru's economic system that reassigned the state its pre-1968 role of strictly complementing, rather than displacing or confronting, private enterprise. On this count, the key constitutional clauses guaranteed a pluralistic or

---

1. *Diario de debates de la asamblea constituyente*, plenario general (Lima: República Peruana, 1978–79), vols. 1–8.

mixed economy organized around a "social-market model." This redefinition of the role of the state in the economy directly overrode the left's call for centralized planning, a strong state presence, and a deepening of the distributive reforms initiated under Velasco.[2]

Other constitutional debates relating to state reform were conducted with an eye toward avoiding the political-economic pitfalls of the 1960s, particularly the need for a stronger executive and a more direct and salient role for the BCRP in economic policy making. Provisions were passed allowing congress to delegate power to the president to rule by legislative decree for set periods of time, and, similar to the intentions underpinning the governance of the U.S. Federal Reserve, the head of the BCRP was to be appointed to a set five-year term, meant to allow him or her to stand above the fray of political influence and infighting. For most of the APRA's opponents, the infusion of greater policy-making freedom into the executive was a thin veil for the party's attempt to usher itself into the presidency with a virtually unrestricted mandate (Graham 1992).

In the end, some of the APRA's more progressive elements did support the left in winning a broader range of constitutional rights and a call for better access to state resources in the areas of health, education, and welfare.[3] In terms of expanding the opportunities for political participation, the major innovation was the enfranchisement of illiterates and of all citizens over the age of eighteen, which would bring an additional two million voters to the polls in 1980 (Reid 1985, 78). Finally, out of this legislative grab bag, the military successfully asserted its claims on state resources by winning continued budgetary autonomy for its ongoing operational expenditures and arms transfers (Graham 1992).

The predominant trend on the economic front during this period was Peru's transformation from rags to riches in a matter of months. Just as Silva Ruete's more technocratic economic team had finally buckled down in its commitment to adhere to the IMF stabilization targets, international prices for Peru's mineral exports saw a dramatic turnaround. Having recently completed the Transandean oil pipeline and the Cuajone copper mine, the country was well positioned to benefit from this rise in the export price index between 1978 and 1980. The volume of oil exports, for example, increased 488 percent, while oil revenues grew at an annual rate of 254 percent. The windfall profits meant a substantial increase in tax payments on corporate income and international trade (Paredes and Pascó-Font 1987, 45). Overall, when export receipts began their unexpected takeoff in May 1978, net foreign

---

2. "Peru: Giving Up the Ghost," *Latin America Political Report*, May 1979, 143.
3. "Poking Holes in the Constitutional Draft," *Andean Report*, May 1979, 64–65.

reserves had hit an all time low of -US\$1.3 billion. By late 1979, this deficit had been turned into a US\$1.6 billion surplus.[4]

The treasury had received an additional boost from nontraditional exports, the annual proceeds of which rose from US\$96 million to US\$845 million between 1975 and 1980 (BCRP 1987, 167). With the 1976 reform of the export-tax-rebate program (CERTEX, or Certificado de Reintegro Tributario a las Exportaciones) that had been initiated under Velasco, and a 50 percent exchange-rate devaluation that had been implemented over the same time period, nontraditional exports grew to account for one-fifth of all exports by 1979. Silva Ruete and BCRP president Manuel Moreyra had made the promotion of primary and nontraditional exports a centerpiece of the civilian recovery strategy in 1978 and had begun to reverse the severe credit squeeze on the private sector that occurred during the worst of the balance-of-payments crisis (Thorp 1977, 57). Industrialists, meanwhile, had lobbied successfully for the modification of the Social Property and Job Stability legislation, and the exporting industrialists' association (ADEX) had been guaranteed a decade of government support under the expanded export-incentive system beginning in 1979 (Schydlowsky 1986b, 229).

Another economic sideshow that began to take off during this time was the cocaine trade. Even the most conservative estimates gauged Peru's exports of illegal coca-based products to be worth US\$500 million by 1980, third only to copper and oil.[5] While the bulk of this revenue went to the top wholesalers, the need to launder the increasing quantity of coca dollars to purchase Peruvian currency to pay off local suppliers drew this cash closer into the domestic financial system in the late 1970s. The government, desperate for foreign exchange in 1977, began encouraging this cash flow through the creation of certificates of deposit (CDs) and by basically looking the other way on any bank deposits under half a million dollars. Thus, clandestine coca dollars also provided an unregistered reserve cushion for Peru.

From the standpoint of top policy makers at the time, inflation was the only remaining economic problem on which no headway had been made. Despite the rigorous orthodox stabilization program that had been in effect since 1978, inflation was still running at about 6 percent a month. Within state financial circles, there was no shortage of diagnoses as to the roots of inflation. Collectively, the economic team pointed to the rapid accumulation of reserves and the upward pressure on prices created from too much money chasing too few goods. The chosen remedies centered on increasing the flow of goods through rapid import liberalization, as the list of items whose import was prohibited

---

4. "Peru—A Survey," *Euromoney,* June 1980, 1.
5. "Agriculture: Who's Doing Better with Coke?" *Andean Report,* Apr. 1980, 69–74.

dropped from 670 to 9, and the launching of a range of financial measures geared toward halting excess liquidity. Still, at the end of his term as BCRP president in mid-1980, Moreyra admitted that "inflation is not coming down as fast as we want. We don't have a real explanation, although we think economic theory is not working as it used to work 10 years ago."[6]

By the time of the 1980 presidential elections, the fortuitous turnaround of the external sector had influenced domestic economic policy perceptions in three major ways. First, the price boom served to bolster an unwarranted optimism over the permanency of positive shocks for prices on Peruvian raw material exports, while adverse trends were still viewed as transitory (Paredes and Pascó-Font 1987, 54). Second, because the rapid comeback enabled the country to initiate another major round of external borrowing (Stallings 1987, 285–87), it served to distract from other warning signals already flashing on international debt markets. Finally, having come on the heels of the stabilization program, the boom served to sway policy preferences in favor of orthodox management approaches, ignoring the fact that much of the IMF's highly touted budget balancing and reduction in the public deficit were due to increased revenues, while state spending actually continued to rise.

It was against this unrealistic political-economic backdrop that the 1980 presidential campaign was conducted. With the exception that the AP had now joined the race, the protagonists in 1980 were the same as 1978. While each side basically reiterated its position from before, the difference this time around was that all but the PPC had been wracked with intense internal conflict. The APRA, by far the more cohesive and well-grounded of the participating parties, found itself torn by a fierce succession battle due to the death of Haya de la Torre in 1979. And the various parties on the left, having glimpsed their potential to assume a major role in Peruvian politics for the first time, quickly splintered over differences concerning ideology and strategy (Haworth 1983). As a result, the barrage of left-wing parties captured just 19 percent of the 1980 vote, and the APRA 27 percent.

Into the void stepped Belaúnde, with a broad platform stressing personality over program and offering something for everybody. Given little noticeable improvement in the AP's organizational stature since the 1960s, its success in capturing 45 percent of the 1980 vote had more to do with the collapse of the opposition; the very low level of debate surrounding the campaign; and the fact that Peru's electorate was now larger, younger, and not entirely cognizant of Belaúnde's previously poor performance. Sixty-three percent of the

6. "Manuel Moreyra, the Tough Negotiator," *Euromoney*, June 1980, 31.

public was voting for the very first time.[7] Also of note was the high percentage of blank votes (15 percent) that had been cast in the Andean departments of Ayacucho, Apurimac, and Huancavelica at the beckoning of Sendero Luminoso, the guerrilla movement that had sprung from the PCP in the late 1970s.[8] Its attack on an Andean polling station in the context of the 1980 presidential elections, although ignored at the time, proved to be an ominous warning of things to come.

While the PPC had received just 10 percent of the 1980 vote, the party ascended in forming a postelection congressional alliance with the AP. Despite the AP's more progressive, or at least centrist, reputation of the 1960s, and its larger presence in the congress vis-à-vis the PPC, it was the latter's free-market stance on economic policy making that prevailed. The following section looks at the attempts of this new center-right AP-PPC alliance to carry out the "social-market" mandate that had been written into the 1979 constitution. Because the first two years of the second Belaúnde administration (1980–82) represent Peru's final phase of financial solvency for the entire decade, the question of what was done with this last bit of economic room to maneuver becomes especially relevant for understanding the country's plight through the remainder of the 1980s.

Market Policies *a la Criolla*

Rather than set forth a comprehensive economic program along the lines of the 1971–75 National Development Plan, the Belaúnde team's strategy was laid out in a more piecemeal manner. Finance Minister Manuel Ulloa stated the initial program most succinctly in a lengthy presentation to congress in August 1980.[9] Other aspects of the strategy were set forth in the 1981–85 public-investment program, and the president himself reiterated some policy goals from the AP campaign platform.[10] Overall, what emerged from these various expressions of state policy was an approach that was considerably

7. "Peru: Six Million Peruvians Can't Be Wrong," *Andean Report*, May 1980, 88.

8. The literature on Peru's Sendero Luminoso is vast; good starting points are McClintock 1984; Reid 1985, chap. 7; Degregori 1989; and Gorriti 1999. Raúl González and José María Salcedo in various issues of a Peruvian magazine, *QueHacer*, provide excellent journalistic accounts throughout the 1980s. Also see Raúl González, José María Salcedo, and Michael Reid, "The Dirty War," *Report on the Americas*, June 20, 1986, 33–45.

9. Manuel Ulloa, "Mensaje al congreso del presidente del consejo de ministros," Lima, Aug. 27, 1980.

10. *Programa de inversiones a mediano plazo, 1981–1985* (Lima: Instituto Nacional de Planificación, June 1982).

softer than the pro-market platform detailed earlier and more a reflection of the different policy influences that had played upon the Peruvian economy since the breakdown of the primary-exporter model in the late 1950s.[11]

The strongest vestiges from the neoconservative experiments came through in the administration's call for the reduction of state enterprise and the stimulation of private investment. The latter included the offering of highly advantageous terms to foreign and local private capital to promote raw-material exports in the oil and mining sectors (Reid 1985, 82); a generous increase in credit to the private sector; lower taxes, with a broadening of the tax base; and the maintenance of the CERTEX tax subsidy for priority-export firms. Other measures were more a continuation of the 1978 IMF program—for example, the elimination of state subsidies and government intervention in pricing, marketing, and the financial system; a further reduction in tariffs and trade barriers; and the maintenance of a crawling-peg exchange-rate regime in order to maximize Peru's comparative advantage on export markets.

Some of the president's own initiatives were a direct throwback to his first term and the developmentalist era of the 1960s. This included a mammoth US$11 billion public-investment program for highways, health, housing, electricity, and agriculture, which envisioned 50 percent foreign financing and was endorsed by the World Bank on the basis of favorable commodity-price projections.[12] The price tag was double Peru's outstanding public debt in 1980. Similar was the administration's commitment to develop the central jungle and to transfer tax proceeds from mining and petroleum to local-level social-emergency programs. Belaúnde also vowed to adjust wages and salaries on a quarterly basis and to create "one million new jobs" through the incorporation of more labor-intensive projects into the development program.

Ironically, despite the strong deflationary underpinnings of the Southern Cone plans, no concrete anti-inflationary shock program was put forth by the incoming team. Ulloa had stressed the need for fiscal restraint, wage controls, and the phasing out of food subsidies as the first steps toward fighting inflation, all of which ran counter to the president's plans. The result was that the battle to stabilize prices was never fought as consistently or coherently as some analysts outside the administration argued it should have been (Schydlowsky 1986b). The program that did begin to come onstream in late 1980 can be broken down into four main lines of policy: the privatization drive, state capital formation, trade liberalization, and ongoing macroeconomic policy approaches. The outcomes of the social-market strategy will be

---

11. Haggard and Kaufman (1989) remind us that development models are not simple packages of policies; rather they are configurations of political, institutional, and historical events.

12. "Peru: Public Investment Program, 1981–85," Consultative Group Presentation, The World Bank, Apr. 27, 1981.

reviewed through a look at each of these policy areas after a short inquiry into the political capacities of the Peruvian state to carry out the program.

The Political Capacity to Implement the Program

Bureaucratic Autonomy

The earlier discussion of bureaucratic autonomy in chapter 1 stressed the importance of insulated political structures within the state apparatus for carrying out a designated set of policies. Three different kinds of autonomy were discussed: the ability of politicians and bureaucrats to make decisions independently of dominant social groups; the freedom of the state bureaucracy from the control of patron-client networks; and the level of managerial discretion afforded government bureaucrats (Willis 1986). Thus far, this study has looked at two separate development phases within the Peruvian state bureaucracy.

The first phase, during the 1960s, stood out as lacking in this regard, even though the research did uncover a well-educated policy-making segment within the state that could have risen to the occasion if properly cultivated. The second phase, under the Velasco administration in the early 1970s, emerged as the country's first attempt at constructing an autonomous policy-making unit within the state. The effort floundered in that it focused too narrowly on the insulation of a small executive-level working group around the president, without nurturing strategic sectors of the bureaucracy to carry out executive policy preferences.

On this last point, Philip Keefer (1995, 16) has observed that "the conditions for autonomy to be advantageous are unlikely to hold where: the policy environment changes rapidly; there is no agreement on appropriate objectives even by trained professionals; the agency lacks expertise; and there is no consensus in the society, or agreement across the spectrum of relevant political organizations, about appropriate agency decisions." This being precisely the situation that Belaúnde had inherited in 1980, the president's efforts to use the office of the executive as the basis for autonomous policy decisions met with predictably disadvantageous results.

Having been granted the power by the 1979 constitution to legislate by special decree on certain issues and for set periods of time, Belaúnde began compensating with a vengeance for the prior weaknesses of the executive office that had plagued him in the 1960s. With regard to state autonomy, the pattern was not far off from that of the RGAF era, whereby the near obsession with the expansion of executive authority took precedence over the need to foster pockets of expertise within the bureaucracy to carry out the executive's will. While much of the erosion in the capacity to successfully execute state policy had already occurred with the massive layoffs of top public-sector personnel in 1978, the Belaúnde administration made no visible effort to reverse this trend. As policy making came to rely almost solely on executive decree, its implementation was of peripheral concern.

State Economic and Planning Institutions

Those institutions that emerged as central to the economic policy-making process in the 1980s included traditional entities such as the MEF, the BCRP, and the national treasury (Banco de la Nación), as well as newer entities like Petroperu and COFIDE that had been created during the military era. One new institutional player to emerge in the 1980s was CONADE (Corporación Nacional de Desarrollo), which was created in mid-1981 when COFIDE was divided up into three parts: CONADE was to set policy, ICSA (COFIDE's investment group) would serve as the state's holding company, and COFIDE S.A. was to monitor policy outcomes (Saulniers 1988, 39).

Two trends marked the institutional setting in the state sector under civilian rule in the early 1980s. The first was the squaring off of the most powerful economic institutions, such as the MEF and the BCRP, along lines described by Richard Webb (1987, 47), BCRP president from 1980 to 1985, as the "balkanization" of economic policy making. The problem was partly historical, representing an ongoing competition and jealousy between the two entities (Cornejo 1985, 131); it also had to do with the return of party politics in 1980 and, despite the AP's claims to the contrary, the tendency to place party faithfuls in strategic posts whenever possible. The BCRP, run historically on a much stricter merit system than any of the other state economic institutions, and now with greater constitutional protection to fight off the exigencies of party politics, became a logical scapegoat for frustrated party dignitaries intent on shaping policy to suit their own needs.

The second trend was the visible neglect of any serious attempt at planning. The INP drops off the earlier list for this very reason. Although the institute's development reports had improved immensely, from newsprint mimeos describing the country's problems in the 1960s to fairly in-depth analyses, it had been increasingly marginalized during the Morales Bermúdez years. In late 1980, the INP was physically relocated from downtown Lima to a remote suburban zone, where transportation, phone lines, and the ability to coordinate with other state agencies on daily policy matters were all reduced to a minimum (Cornejo 1985, 117). The time lines on the development plans had become shorter by the late 1970s, and some plans, such as the 1979–82 plan, did not even correspond with a given administration. The most long-range plan to emerge under the second Belaúnde administration was the 1981–85 public-investment program, which was more a reflection of the president's zeal for building public works and a necessary prerequisite to securing the external financing to do so.

The Leadership Coalition

In chapter 1 different coalitional styles were identified as contributing to the political capacity of the state to intervene in the economy. The first is the "triple alliance" of state, foreign, and domestic capital that served countries such as Brazil and Mexico in their drive to kick off heavy industry (Evans 1979; Gereffi and Evans 1981). The second, which prevailed to some extent in most of the East Asian industrializing states, consists of a strong collaboration between the state and domestic entrepreneurs, without necessarily permitting foreign capital's entry into the development coalition. This study has emphasized the difficulties that Peru has had over time in forging a coherent coalition to push a development program forward (Cotler 1975).

The analysis of the 1960s pointed to the longevity of the old dependency-style coalition between foreign capital and domestic elites in Peru, sustained by an unusually buoyant primary-export economy. The weakening of these ties during the first Belaúnde administration was marked by the rise of middle-class party politics, but in the most chaotic fashion. As the analysis showed, coalitions were broken as easily as they were made, leading ultimately to the end of civilian rule. The military era, rightly, had made the dissolution of this "backward" alliance one of its prime goals. But having dissolved it with excessive and erratic state intervention, the RGAF did little to endear domestic capitalists to its program. Peruvian entrepreneurs thus came out of the 1970s suspicious of the state and uncertain of their future role in the economy.

Yet, although business clearly went into the 1980s poised to catch up from the crisis of representation that it had experienced over the previous decade (Conaghan and Malloy 1994), in fact, the government succeeded in alienating the private sector very early on. Part of the problem was the outdated mind-set of the AP-PPC coalition and its unrealistic goal of turning the country back into a primary exporter spurred by foreign investment and domestic capital. Although some local investors were still active in primary exports, domestic capital overall was no longer just of one mind. The diversification of local private investment into manufacturing, agroindustry, real estate, and banking in the interim since Belaúnde's first term made for a more complex set of policy demands from the private sector, something that the administration failed to grasp.

As in the 1960s, with the lack of any cohesive alliance among domestic actors, party politics again took precedence and produced the same chaotic results. With the heavy reliance on centralized executive authority to carry out its program, the government succeeded in polarizing the policy-making process along three main axes. First was a three-way tug-of-war among Belaúnde and the office of the executive, Ulloa and the economic team, and the congress (Malloy 1982, 8). Along the second axis, the "internationalist" faction in the government (MEF, BCRP), which favored a more orthodox approach to economic management, was pitted against the "nationalists" (INP and the line ministries), who called for a softer developmentalist strategy. As the short-lived mineral price boom kicked into recession by late 1981, the growing distance between the haves and the have-nots represented a third axis, which was increasingly symbolized by the guerrilla insurgency.

The Intermediation of Societal Interests

Peru's first attempt at interest mediation along corporatist lines was analyzed in chapter 3. The analysis showed that the RGAF's efforts to radically restructure the interests of labor and capital vis-à-vis the state had deteriorated into a situation of mutual distrust among all three by late 1975. The question was not taken up explicitly again until the early 1980s. While domestic capital had supported the incoming Belaúnde administration, organized labor made it clear immediately that the AP-PPC lacked a support base with workers. More than one million work hours a month had been lost in September and October 1980 due to strike activity, and by mid-1981, organized labor had staged over 180 strikes. In January 1981, the government initiated a more modest attempt at interest mediation that, in contrast to the RGAF's grandiose corporatist design, sought labor peace through a National Tripartite Commission composed of representatives from industry, government, and the major labor confederations (Malloy 1982, 8; Bollinger 1987, 18).

Initially, the commission's goal was to steer labor and capital away from adversarial relationships, under the guidance of the state, and toward settlements beneficial to both. At the top of the agenda was the need to fight inflation, which the government intended to do by negotiating wage and price targets with the representatives of business and labor. But the government was ultimately not able to persuade workers and employers to accept its income and price proposals, because of the failure of its earlier efforts to actually bring inflation down.[13] As the commission became a forum for reaching agreement on a wide range of economic policy objectives, and the means to

---

13. "Economy: A Hard Lesson in the Psychology of Inflation," *Andean Report*, Aug. 1981, 141.

obtain them, the possibilities for consensus faded. The attempt broke down, mainly because of the lack of confidence in the government's ability to uphold its part of the bargain, and the relationship among the state, capital, and labor proceeded in a highly conflictual fashion.

Throughout its first year in office, the Belaúnde government promulgated 212 executive decrees, while less than twenty laws were passed by congress (Woy-Hazelton and Hazelton 1987, 112). The barrage of executive legislation caught the opposition somewhat off guard, as it interpreted the constitution as granting the executive such powers only under exceptional circumstances. The catch was that it was up to congress to decide when to delegate authority to the president, and with its newfound majority in the congress, the AP-PPC coalition basically granted itself the go-ahead in passing a number of key laws. During 1981, for example, the entire economic program was legislated in this vein, with congress acting mainly as a rubber stamp (Malloy 1982, 7). The president even succeeded in passing a law that expanded executive and ministerial functions in several areas, thereby single-handedly altering the structures of the state.

Meanwhile, the AP's powerful general secretary and second vice president of Peru, Javier Alva Orlandini, had succeeded in reorganizing the legislative committees so as to further circumvent congressional debate and short-circuit the impact of the opposition. In their study of congressional politics under the Belaúnde administration, Woy-Hazleton and Hazleton (1987, 114) aptly summarize the toll taken by these "autonomous" legislative maneuvers: "Instead of being 'taught democracy' through effective participation . . . citizen confidence in a democratic system's ability to produce results declined, while traditional patron/client relations were reinforced at the national level."

Peru's Social-Market Model in Action: Four Policy Currents

The Privatization Drive

In line with its goals of reviving private-sector participation to pre-1968 levels, the administration placed top priority on the reduction of the SOEs and the stimulation of foreign and local private investment. The privatization theme was also applied to other reform measures, such as the Agricultural Promotion and Development Law of 1980, meant to reward efficiency by allowing the agrarian cooperatives inherited from the RGAF to parcel out individual plots for private ownership. Because the reform of the SOE sector and the concern with attracting private direct investment dominated the domestic debate over privatization, these two objectives will be dealt with in turn.

On the privatization front, the government succeeded in passing the long-awaited Law of Entrepreneurial Activity of the State in mid-1981. While the law was in many respects a reiteration of the 1979 constitutional clauses on the new role for state intervention, it finally joined together in one legal document all the norms applicable to public firms. It distinguished between those companies of public and private legal status and between mixed entities and shareholdings of the state. The law also represented the first formal attempt at regulating the SOEs in the areas of labor relations and financial procedures and in specifying the organizational ties with other central government entities (Branch 1982, 7; Ortíz de Zevallos 1986, 136). But the law stopped short of addressing the more controversial issues surrounding the privatization debates in congress, such as concrete guidelines for divestiture and the future objectives for those firms that were to be retained by the state (BCRP 1985a, 14–15).

Other SOE reform measures taken in 1980–81 included the transfer of most firms to limited-liability corporations under private law (Ley de Sociedades Mercantiles) and the passing of a budget resolution stating that those SOEs operating at a deficit would be sold, liquidated, or merged (Branch 1982, 4). The administration had also designated yet another multisectoral commission for the evaluation and reorganization of public enterprises, comprising representatives from the central government ministries and from a cross-section of private-sector associations. Through a combination of these quasi-legal mechanisms, and by setting forth a survival-of-the-fittest standard for SOE performance, presumably the administration intended to better clarify the dimensions of state entrepreneurial activity not addressed by the new law.

The flurry of SOE legislation passed in 1981 also attempted to institutionalize a new flowchart within the central government to facilitate the coordination and consolidation of the SOE sector. Oversight was to begin with the Council of Economic and Financial Cabinet Ministers (CIAEF), with CONADE acting as its technical secretariat. CONADE would monitor and evaluate the performance of the firms, reporting back to the CIAEF and the relevant sectoral ministries (World Bank 1982, 32). In their reform efforts, however, both CONADE and the CIAEF's multisectoral commission quickly ran up against the many unresolved managerial and institutional drawbacks within the SOE sector that were discussed earlier. In the absence of more explicit or forceful policy directives from the top levels of the administration, the privatization drive was informally relegated to the ministerial level. And the ministries, not eager to erode their base of power, made few attempts at large-scale privatization of their own firms (Branch 1982, 4; Yarrow 1999).

Originally, Ulloa had announced that over 80 SOEs would be sold, turned into joint ventures, or liquidated. Shortly thereafter, COFIDE produced two lists. One contained those companies that the state would hold on to, which included Centromin, Electroperu, Petroperu, the railway (Enafer), and other large productive enterprises created during the Velasco era. Later, another list began circulating in top government circles, which included around 40 "nonessential" firms to be sold off through direct purchase, public tender, tax exemptions, or other incentives.[14] To provide an idea of the concrete possibilities for privatization in Peru at the time, the World Bank's fairly cautious estimate was that of some 140 firms existing in 1981, the state held 90 to 100 percent of the assets in nearly 100 of these companies (World Bank 1982, 10).

While opportunities were clearly present, the aspirations for privatization were highly unrealistic. Apart from all the bureaucratic foot-dragging, various estimates of the value of the planned SOE sales ranged from US$200 to 400 million, or 1 to 3 percent of GDP. To put these figures in perspective, Peru's total net private direct investment from 1981 to 1983 hardly surpassed US$200 million (Thorp 1987; BCRP 1987). The estimates meant that local officials had not done their homework in assessing the formidable market constraints to privatization, although they had already begun including the proceeds from the expected sales in short-term state revenue projections (World Bank 1982, 49–50).

The very limited divestment that did occur consisted mainly of the sale of government assets to special interests, facilitated by the fact that many technocrats and politicians close to the administration had moved into top-level jobs as directors and managers of the state corporations (Saulniers 1988, 36). Where special interests could not be called into play, little headway was made in cutting back the state. In the end, just a few insubstantial full liquidations were undertaken, for example, with a supermarket chain, a machine tool and tractor factory, and a fish freezing and canning plant (Reid 1985, 83–84).

The practice of blaming most of Peru's economic ills on the SOEs, while employing them for private benefit, left many of the formidable problems handed down from the 1970s unresolved. First, pricing policy still subjected many firms to the whims of the central government. Second, external borrowing by the firms was still not properly monitored, despite new efforts by COFIDE to more strictly control debt financing (World Bank 1982, 32–34). Third, the sector was still plagued by a high turnover of top personnel and the

---

14. "State Company Sell-Off to Begin," *Andean Report*, Feb. 1981, 21; "Mining and Oil Get Going while Government Streamlines State Companies," *Andean Report*, Nov. 1981, 213; "State Companies for Sale," *Andean Report*, Oct. 1982, 183.

long-term deterioration of public-service salaries. By the end of the Belaúnde term, the debate over these hard issues had degenerated to the level of panel discussions where state functionaries and private-sector representatives each summarized the problems from their own viewpoint and then shelved the findings.[15]

The other major aspect of the privatization drive—the attraction of much higher levels of foreign and local private direct investment—also met with disappointing results. As table 13 shows, private-sector capital formation hit an all-time low in 1985. The figures are especially disheartening when compared with those discussed in chapter 2 (see table 8), which showed Peru's private-investment share of GDP averaging around 17 percent through the 1950s. Furthermore, the dynamic of the 1970s, where the public sector virtually displaced the private sector in leading the economy, had still not been reversed. The economic participation of the two ran neck and neck throughout the 1980–85 period, until the public sector's share of gross fixed investment again outpaced the private in the wake of the 1982 debt crisis.

TABLE 13. Macroeconomic and External Indicators in Peru: 1981–85 (Belaúnde term average growth and investment)

	1981	1982	1983	1984	1985	1981–85 (1)
GDPGRO	7.2	−0.4	−12.6	4.1	2.3	0.1
GNPPCGRO	5.3	−2.8	−16.1	1.0	0.4	−2.44
INF	75.4	64.4	111.2	110.2	163.4	
PRIVGDP	21.5	20.8	15.1	12.1	12.0	16.3
PUBIGDP	7.3	8.7	8.7	8.1	6.1	7.7
INVEST	28.8	29.5	23.8	20.2	18.1	24.0
RER	245.1	251.1	281.2	291.5	348.7	
TRADEBAL	−553	−428	293	1,007	1,219	
CURACCT	−1,733	−1,612	−875	−235	102	
FDI	125	48	38	−89	1	
PORT						
DEBT	8,586	10,709	11,339	12,153	12,879	

Source: GDP, GNP, and debt are from World Bank, *World Tables, CD-ROM,* 2000. Data on investment are from Glen and Sumlinski 1998 <www.ifc.org/economics/pubs /discuss.htm>. Inflation, exchange rates, and payments are calculated from IMF 1999, except trade balance prior to 1977 obtained from IMF 1984; FDI and portfolio investment data prior to 1977 obtained from IMF 1994.

Note: GDPGRO = growth of real GDP; GNPPCGRO = growth of real per capita GNP; INF = Dec.–Dec. inflation; PRIVGDP = private investment as % of GDP; PUBIGDP = public investment as % of GDP; INVEST = total domestic investment as % of GDP; RER = real exchange rate (1990 = 100), calculated using period average exchange rate, U.S. WPI, and domestic CPI; TRADEBAL = trade balance (mil$) = merchandise exports – merchandise imports; CURACCT = current account (mil$); FDI = foreign direct investment (mil$); PORT = foreign portfolio investment (mil$); DEBT = total external debt (mil$).

---

15. See, for example, ESAN 1986.

During the last year of military rule, the Silva Ruete–Moreyra team had begun a high-profile campaign to revive private investment in Peru, and this continued after 1980. For example, in its attempt to create a more favorable investment environment, the Belaúnde government lifted the ceiling on profit remittances from 20 percent to 40 percent, which ran counter to the Andean Pact's Decision 24—a provision that Peru had been instrumental in enforcing during the early 1970s. The CONITE (or Comisión Nacional de Inversiones y Tecnologías Extranjeras), which was the office within the finance ministry responsible for supervising foreign investment, also passed a regulation permitting subsidiaries of foreign companies operating in Peru to buy into Peruvian firms.[16] Foreign mining and petroleum companies received particularly generous treatment, as they were given greater access for exploration and substantial breaks on export and other taxes (Reid 1985, 84).

But investors from abroad still complained that Peru's government regulations were confusing and complicated by long administrative delays. Although the local private sector had won some reversals of the job-stability and worker-participation laws, the fact that these still remained on the books acted as a deterrent for foreign investment. Moreover, there were widespread rumors of corruption and of the need to bribe civil servants every step of the way in pushing through a foreign-investment proposal. The result was a brief spurt of FDI, mainly from the United States, which then dropped to historically low levels after the 1982 financial shocks hit. In spite of the very inviting terms offered to the mining and petroleum multinationals, the plunge in world mineral prices and continued failure to locate new reserves in Peru worked against a comeback in these sectors. In the end, Belaúnde's major venture, the Tintaya copper mine near the southern Andean city of Cusco, was financed largely by the state.

State Capital Formation

A second set of policy goals centered on the rerouting of state investments into economic infrastructure to support private enterprise in the productive sectors. As can be seen from the decline in growth and investment rates in table 13, the administration had its work cut out for it in terms of reviving the country's sagging productive sectors. The 1981–85 public-investment program included over eighty projects and estimated an annual average expenditure rate of US$2.3 billion over the five-year period. The program slated the distribution of state funds to be split: 40 percent for productive-sector projects, 35 percent for economic infrastructure, and 25 percent to social-sector

---

16. "Special Report: Foreign Direct Investment," *Andean Report,* Sept. 1983.

projects. More specifically, the stated objectives were: (1) the revival of agriculture; (2) improving the country's physical infrastructure, especially in hydroelectric expansion and highways; (3) increasing investments in water, health, education, and rural and urban development; and (4) as discussed earlier, the leveraging of private investment in mining and petroleum through state support (World Bank 1985, 29–30).

Two trends stand out in the investment portfolio that gradually got underway after 1980. First was an erratic shift from the trajectory that state capital formation had been on during the previous major cycle of project investments under the RGAF. Industry, for example, after averaging 11 percent of all state investments from 1968 to 1980, dropped abruptly down to less than 2 percent after 1980. Similarly, agricultural investments dropped from 15 percent to 10 percent, and petroleum from 17 percent down to 7 percent (Wilson and Wise 1986, 99). The reductions were more than compensated for by a rapid 15 percent jump in electrical-power investment after 1980. In this quick reorientation of state investments, the administration overshot its mark on the earlier projections. Economic infrastructure ended up consuming nearly 50 percent of the state investment budget, while the productive and social-service sectors received only 30 percent and 12 percent, respectively.

The second notable trend had to do with the repetition of the mostly unfavorable patterns surrounding state capital formation that had been established over the previous decade. Peru's brief economic revival from 1979 to 1981 had allowed for a second, albeit shorter, period of relatively unhampered commercial borrowing. As in the 1970s, 60 percent of the external public debt went toward investment projects (BCRP 1984), with the twenty major projects implemented between 1978 and 1982 accounting for nearly 50 percent of investment over these four years (Portocarrero Maisch 1982, 22). By 1982, the state enterprises had regained control of the public-investment program, and the three big SOEs in oil, mining, and electricity undertook 70 percent of all state investments (Portocarrero Maisch 1982, 18). Thus, as before, state capital formation remained highly aggregated—by project and also by sector and region. And the success or failure of the investment program still hinged largely on the outcomes of big project spending.

In agriculture, for example, just four large coastal irrigation projects dominated the portfolio, and these were the same kinds of costly large-scale investments that had done little to reduce the stagnation of agricultural production in Peru during the 1970s. The Majes irrigation project was among these. By now, finance costs alone on the project had hit US$300 million, a staggering figure given the original total estimate on the project of less than US$150 million; a ground feasibility study done very belatedly also showed a less than 10 percent return on agricultural production from the project, with many of the difficulties due to unexpectedly rocky soil on the southern coast where Majes is located.[17]

Belaúnde's jungle-colonization projects from the 1960s were also brought back into the agriculture portfolio. Although the jungle-colonization drive was ostensibly undertaken to produce food for domestic consumption and to facilitate the extraction of petroleum and wood for export, public officials involved in the projects complained that they were doing little to promote the long-term development of the Peruvian Amazon (Wilson and Wise 1986, 109). Rather, the projects were providing a noncoastal outlet for sierra migration related to conflicts over land title and serving as bases for the attempt to eradicate coca production. The future development of the area was being thrown into further question by the lack of any environmental controls to prevent soil depletion.

Both electricity and transportation were also dominated by three or four gigantic projects. The justification for the massive spending on hydroelectric power centered on meeting projected national demand for industrial energy; however, the failure to coordinate power expansion with a coherent industrial policy undermined this goal. As under the first Belaúnde administration in the 1960s, and during the RGAF regime, project spending basically took on a life of its own, propelled by special interests and their international allies. Highways, not surprisingly, represented the second-largest commitment in the program. The bulk of these projects consisted of new link-ups to the Carretera Marginal (jungle highway) of the 1960s and the reconstruction of a section of the Pan American Highway on the coast that feeds into Lima's most popular beach resorts (Wilson and Wise 1986, 110).

In the end, the government did not meet its very ambitious spending targets. By 1982, many projects still lacked financing, with the result that about US$6.9 billion was invested over 1981–84, 40 percent below the amount sought (World Bank 1985, 30). Realized investment in the social sector also fell 40 percent short of the 1981–85 plan, leaving few resources for health, education, and other basic necessities felt most keenly in the traditional sectors (Wilson and Wise 1986, 110). Once the more severe stage of the debt crisis set in post-1983, some projects simply stood still as unpaid contractors and suppliers stopped work. Perhaps the most striking feature of this second investment cycle was the lack of any apparent learning curve. The very large-scale nature and ultimate disarray of many of the inherited ventures meant that the state was ever more burdened by its own investment program, and the private sector weakened by the neglect of macropolicy and institutional reform.

---

17. "Majes: A Test Case," *Andean Report,* Dec. 1980, 221–24; "Special Report on Three White Elephants: Charcani V, Carhuaquero, and Majes," *Andean Report,* June 1983, 109–12.

Trade Liberalization

As noted earlier, the thrust toward trade liberalization had started in earnest during the 1978–80 period under strong pressure from the IMF. Peru's commercial opening also gained momentum at this time as key policy makers came to perceive the high levels of protection as a contributing cause of inflation and the whole set of existing incentives related to ISI as distortionary and detrimental to the country's long-term prospects for industrialization. Under the impulse of competitive exchange-rate devaluations engineered by the Silva Ruete–Moreyra team and the CERTEX subsidy to promote nontraditional exports, Peru's manufactured exports had grown from just 2 percent of total exports in 1970 to 18 percent by 1980 (Sheahan 1999, 50–55). Thus, the mood toward manufactured and nontraditional exports was still very upbeat on the eve of Peru's return to civilian rule, as witnessed in the outgoing government's proposal to maintain the CERTEX subsidy that compensated domestic exporters for tariffs paid on imported inputs.[18]

With the change of administration, however, the critique of the country's existing trade regime came to encompass the structure of both ISI and nontraditional exports. The criticisms waged against Peru's pattern of ISI were valid, and similar to those made in chapters 2 and 3.[19] The first ISI stage of replacing manufactured consumer-good imports was completed during the early 1970s, and the second stage of developing intermediate and capital goods was initiated. The latter concentrated on "heavy" industries such as chemicals and the processing of minerals and metal products, which now accounted for 40 percent of manufactured value-added. Foreign ownership of the manufacturing sector had declined to 15 percent under Velasco, but only a little over half of industry was owned by private nationals.

The complaints centered on the low levels of vertical integration, the high degree of enterprise concentration, and an incentive structure that encouraged capital-intensive industry at the expense of job creation. Profits were still high, wages were high when compared to the rest of the national workforce, and reinvestment was sluggish. The incoming team argued that the country was simply not getting back from industrialists what it had been putting out

---

18. "How to Turn Peru into a New Taiwan," *Latin America Economic Report*, Sept. 21, 1979; "Cofide Plots the Course of Expansion," *Euromoney*, June 1980, 8.

19. This analysis of trade policy under the Belaúnde administration draws largely from a draft memo developed jointly by the World Bank and the United Nations Industrial Development Organization that circulated in Lima. The memo, entitled "Peru: Development and Policy Issues of the Manufacturing Sector" (Jan. 1981), was formulated by a group of consultants, including Roberto Abusada, who later assumed a frontline position on trade policy in the government.

in the way of abundant credit at subsidized interest rates, cheap production inputs, and the protection of imports. The policy remedy on the import side was to introduce competition as a way of forcing the industrial sector to become more lean and efficient. Thus, the average nominal tariff was brought down from 46 percent to 32 percent, and by the end of 1981, 98 percent of all registered items could be imported freely, as opposed to 38 percent in 1978 (World Bank 1985, 48).

Exporting industrialists also fell under attack, despite buoyant returns on nontraditional exports until 1980. Administration insiders advocated liberalization of this sector on two grounds. First, it was argued that the actual manufacturing component of nontraditional exports was too low and that 80 percent of these products (fish, wool, cotton, wood, and minerals) still involved raw-materials processing. And second, it was argued that those nontraditional exports were still too dependent on incentives and domestic market conditions. Those working within the trade secretariat of the finance ministry, such as Commerce Vice-Minister Roberto Abusada, questioned the high fiscal costs and alleged corruption surrounding the CERTEX system. This mounting pessimism over the future of nontraditional exports was also fueled by the 1979 mineral price boom and a lasting conviction that primary exports still represented the main path forward for Peru (Schydlowsky 1986a).

Trade reforms on the export side centered on limiting the amount and raising the price of credit available to industrialists. The CERTEX program was revamped in 1981, as the range of basic deductions was reduced from 15–30 percent to 10–25 percent. Interest rates on credit lines available through the state industrial bank, typically much lower than market rates, were also set according to market trends (World Bank 1985, 49–50). With all the measures taken together, the effects of the trade-liberalization policy were immediate. The lower tariffs brought a flood of foreign products into the domestic market, some of which were necessary industrial inputs, but the import of luxury consumer goods also skyrocketed. Losses stemming from increased competition gave rise to a new level of demand for credit on the part of local industry, which, now more expensive, sent many firms deeply into the red.

As ADEX and the National Industrial Society vehemently protested the government's measures as an attempt to "Chileanize" the economy under pressure from the IMF and the international banks, the administration began backtracking on these measures. At the 1983 annual convention for domestic exporters, members of the economic team reversed the government's earlier position, repudiating the strong reliance on traditional exports and foreign borrowing in effect since 1980, and professed a new faith in the potential for nontraditional exports to lead the economy (Schydlowsky 1986b, 236). Nominal tariffs were brought back up to pre-1978 levels, and the CERTEX subsidy was reinstated on agroindustrial products. The 1984 CERTEX subsidy was about US$180 million, more than 1979's expenditure of US$150 million (World Bank 1985, 49).

As inefficient as Peru's trade regime may have been prior to the liberalization measures, the government received universally poor marks for its handling of the trade reforms. To succeed, it had been acknowledged that trade liberalization would require a downwardly flexible exchange rate in order to promote exports and offset the flood of cheap imports. Yet the real effective exchange rate had been allowed to steadily appreciate. The failure to coordinate tariffs with exchange rates was felt strongly in the agricultural sector. The complete reduction of protective barriers for agriculture and the overvalued exchange rate worked together to prevent a reactivation in the countryside, despite government attempts to direct subsidized credit to the rural areas.

The inability of the private sector to penetrate policy making under Belaúnde through the usual personalistic and party ties led to new attempts at articulating and defending its interests. The ADEX, for example, began turning to sophisticated academic consultants to help bolster its participation in national policy debates and even created its own junior college in 1982 with course offerings in economics and international trade. A new association of private business institutions was also created in 1984, under the acronym CONFIEP (Confederation of Private Sector Firms), to serve as an umbrella for representing the interests of domestic capital as a whole. Looking back on the experience of the early 1980s, one former president of the National Industrial Society was still not completely able to explain the irony of a staunchly pro-private-sector government program that did so much in so short a time to alienate the bulk of the domestic entrepreneurial class:

> We just never got to them. They were very cordial to us. We had access to the ministers. They would listen to us at meetings. But then we would leave and their advisers would come in (and they were very dogmatic) and they would get their point of view across. No matter how many meetings we had where we represented our point of view, the dogmatic técnicos and economists would have more influence.[20]

Macropolicy Trends

Another slant on the inability of the local private sector to influence policy making had to do with the grave internal conflicts within the administration

---

20. The interview is cited in Conaghan 1988, 46.

over which direction to go.[21] Hindsight readily shows that all of the competing views eventually tended to cancel each other out. Much of the conflict centered on controlling the president's populist urges, given the espoused technocratic aspirations of his economic team. This helps to explain an erratic pattern of announcing mutually incompatible targets but not following through convincingly on any of them.

Finance Minister Ulloa and the economic team, nicknamed the "dynamo group" at the outset of Belaúnde's second term, called immediately for wage and price adjustments to reduce inflationary pressures and recommended currency devaluation and the cutting of state subsidies to balance the budget. The president, however, had announced that nationwide municipal elections would be held in November 1980 and was thus reluctant to move too quickly on the reform front. Instead, the public-sector deficit was tolerated, the exchange rate continued to appreciate, and the liberalization of government-controlled prices slowed. Inflation was reduced in 1980, and the AP scored a victory at the polls, but at the expense of much lower public savings. This drop in public savings did not correspond with the needs of the state investment program, not to mention the expectations of the multilaterals.

In recognition of the need to remain on good terms with the banks and the IMF, the economic team upped its orthodox image in early 1981 and took steps to rationalize Peru's borrowing procedures. A new debt law was passed requiring congress to set an annual ceiling on public-sector borrowing, the ratio of which now amounted to 35 percent of GDP, and a committee was set up to review the terms and conditions of possible loans on a case-by-case basis. COFIDE and the Banco de la Nación were to act exclusively as borrowing agents in the regulation of loans to the public sector.[22] In this show of good faith, the government had prepaid US$377 million in previous refinancing credits, with the result that the banks disbursed US$1.7 billion in medium-term credits to Peru during 1981 and 1982 (more than their US$1.5 billion total exposure to the government at the end of 1980 [Webb 1988]).

Caught in a balancing act between financing Belaúnde's spending urges and moving forward with the planned liberalization of the economy, the economic team was periodically able to exert some control. In January 1981, prices on the daily food basket were increased by 30 percent, other public subsidies were slashed, and the trade-liberalization measures mentioned earlier were brought onstream (Paredes and Pascó-Font 1987, 49–50). The government's justification for these and other measures aimed at opening up the

---

21. Statistical trends cited in the next two sections are based on data gathered from the BCRP, the MEF, and the INP.

22. "Peru's Long Haul Back towards Democracy," *Euromoney*, April 1982, 47.

economy was to make Peruvian industry more qualified to compete on world markets and to burn up excess foreign reserves that were believed to be creating inflationary pressures on the economy through an increase in the money supply.

On this last point, concerning the management of domestic inflation, Schydlowsky (1986b) notes that by the time the reins of the economy were handed over to Belaúnde and Ulloa in 1980, there was already a strong conviction on the part of policy makers that inflation stemmed from the balance-of-payments surplus and that it would require a burning-off of reserves, in combination with a tight monetary and fiscal policy, to halt the rise of prices (BCRP 1982). This being the basic IMF policy stance on inflation, Peru followed these prescriptions, even though inflation had actually doubled during 1977–79 when these same policies had been strictly applied (Webb 1987, 29). The early credit repayment and the seeping off of valuable foreign exchange on luxury imports during 1980–81 did quickly reduce Peru's reserves, but so quickly that this itself became the first warning signal in the series of economic shocks that soon followed.

Alternative views on inflation hold that its sources are more complex, stemming from a combination of weak fiscal restraint and supply constraints related to the underdeveloped structures of the economy and, increasingly, to rising international interest rates and the dramatically difficult external circumstances of the 1980s (Foxley 1983; Sheahan 1987, 100–110). In the Peruvian case, Schydlowsky (1986b, 233) argues that inflation was also intrinsic to government policy:

> The circle started with the removal of subsidies on food and gasoline. As the prices of these rose, the cost of living increased, which required a rise in the nominal wage in line with the policy objective of keeping real wages constant. At the same time, however, a higher domestic price level required devaluation in order to prevent the occurrence of overvaluation. The devaluation, in turn, caused an increase in the price of imported food and in the base price of gasoline, which required a further increase in the domestic prices of these goods, which in turn required further wage increases and devaluation. The economic team called the initial steps of this process a "corrective inflation." Unfortunately, however, after a while only the inflation part of the label remained.

Inflation did indeed increase and was approaching 100 percent in 1982. By late 1981, the prices of Peru's main commodity exports had fallen 19 percent in real terms and were to drop another 15 percent in 1982. Rising debt-service payments due to a five-percentage-point jump in the LIBOR (London Inter-

Bank Offer Rate) in 1981, and a government budget deficit approaching 10 percent of GDP, all signaled the need for help. Negotiations with the IMF began for a US$650 million extended fund facility loan and an additional US$200 million from the fund's compensatory-financing facility to offset part of the decline in Peru's commodity-export income. There was considerable disagreement over the pacing of the program, with the IMF pushing for a rapid shock treatment and the economic team for a softer approach. As Peru's international reserves dropped below US$400 million, on par with the depths reached during the 1977 crisis, these differences were momentarily set aside, and Peru gained access to the fund's compensatory-financing facility in June 1982.

The fund's projections for Peru were optimistic and envisioned a rapid recovery in exports by 1983 and a mild comeback for GDP. Such projections, however, overlooked the dire state of public finances and the lack of discipline within the central government. In 1982, total outstanding short-term public and private debt grew to US$2.5 billion, the highest amount of loans contracted in Peru during any given year to date. The major SOEs, furthermore, had somehow managed to borrow around US$500 million in short-term credits on their own in 1982 (Webb 1987, 36). By now, nearly 80 percent of the budget deficit was financed externally, and rising interest rates in the United States had placed an additional US$300 million debt-service burden on this deficit in 1981 (Paredes and Pascó-Font 1987, 52).

Economic Crisis and the Fragmentation of Policy

As domestic policy faltered and international economic contingencies hardened for all of Latin America, Peru had three choices for confronting the crisis of the early 1980s. The first two, not necessarily exclusive, consisted of negotiating with the banks and the IMF to reschedule outstanding debts and/or adjusting by cutting investments and generating large trade surpluses to help service the debt. A third option, unilateral default, was still unthinkable as long as Belaúnde and his party remained intent on completing the massive project portfolio that depended so heavily on external financing. At this early stage of the debt crisis, most states, including Peru, feared any sort of go-it-alone strategy due to the trade and aid sanctions believed to follow such a move.

The trade-surplus option, which was exercised initially by more industrialized and highly indebted states like Mexico and Brazil, was less possible in the Peruvian case—first, because raw-material exports still accounted for 80 percent of trade income, and prices for these goods were plummeting; and second, because besides having to confront the rising protectionism on world markets, Peru's trade liberalization, in effect up until the eve of the crisis, had already led to the deindustrialization of the small uncompetitive manufacturing sector that had been developed. Freak weather conditions stemming from the El Niño current, which simultaneously provoked floods in the north and drought in the south of the country, exerted additional pressure on trade balances in 1983.

The decision, then, was to go straight for debt renegotiation. Peru's relations with the foreign banks became all the more important, and as testimony to this, Belaúnde called in Carlos Rodríguez Pastor, a foreign banker himself, to take over at the MEF. The new finance minister went to the banks, the Paris Club, and the IMF requesting a US$880 million loan to cover 1983 debt payments and the need for a new infusion of cash. What ensued was a complicated patchwork of refinancing and rollovers, with the securing of further credit and the drawing on the IMF's compensatory-financing facility tied ever more strongly to external pressures for fund compliance and increased orthodoxy.

The fund's stabilization parameters widened to include positive real interest rates, higher public tariffs, and supply-side tax cuts.[23] Under the thrust of the program, public consumption dropped by 15 percent in 1983, and the growth of prices on goods freed from government control surpassed that of the regular market by 45 percent (Paredes and Pascó-Font 1987, 59). As local industry sunk under higher interest rates, restricted demand, and the cutoff of credit altogether, the IMF conceded to a temporary increase in trade tariffs. As inflation hit 111 percent in 1983 (see table 13), the prescription of tight monetary and fiscal targets as the main anti-inflationary strategy held sway.

Acting within the bounds of the IMF agreement, Peru was able to reschedule US$1 billion of its 1983 debt service and another half billion for 1984 (nearly double the amount originally sought). As a result of the rescheduling, the public sector was able to service its debt, although at the expense of a 30 percent overall increase in debt-service payments and at high interest costs. The rescheduling brought the promise of an additional US$450 million from a syndicate of banks, contingent upon compliance with the goals agreed on in the IMF plan. Yet, as early as June 1983, Peru's compliance was a matter of question. In particular, the fund's negotiators were dismayed to find that the Peruvians had delayed the public-sector payroll by three days, so as to slip under the quarterly target. The banks then withheld US$220 million of the fresh credits earlier committed, and the IMF agreement was all but dead.

---

23. During the Reaganomic heyday of the early 1980s, there was even some talk in the U.S. Congress of cutting aid to those Latin American countries that failed to implement supply-side tax cuts for domestic capital.

As table 13 shows, 1983's year-end economic indicators were the worst ever. The collapse of Mexico's finances the year before, along with Peru's own increasing risk premium, prompted the banks to abruptly withdraw some US$739 million in trade credits. Chronic inflation had skewed the distribution of national income in favor of the owners of capital, with the result that financial and commercial speculation had exploded.[24] An estimated US$600 million drain in capital flight during this brief time span led to the scrapping of a 1980 regulation requiring that local holders of CDs, financed largely by the cocaine trade, report these holdings for tax purposes. These and other efforts to shore up the central bank's reserves did not reverse the downward trend. Reserves fell by US$700 million, public external debt jumped 21 percent, and there were few doubts as to Peru's new status as a debtor country with a serious inability to pay.

As this is also the critical juncture at which policy makers within government circles began to reject packaged orthodox solutions (Conaghan 1998, 149), it is worth pausing to ask why so little was done so late to properly intervene.[25] There was, of course, the problem of not feeling the shocks until they had fully hit, which was especially the case with Peru's unforeseen natural disasters in 1983. Also, the behavior of international lending institutions, particularly the banks' commitment to some new loans during the low point of 1983, as well as access to the IMF's compensatory-financing facility—geared toward temporary balance-of-payment problems related to export shortfalls—no doubt fostered the perception that the recession would soon pass.[26] On the domestic side, former BCRP president Richard Webb (1987, 36–37) attributes part of the policy paralysis to the trials of "life in the bunker":

> Major programmatic changes are difficult to decide, even as cool academic exercises. Surrounded by daily financial emergencies (road blocks by rice farmers waiting to get paid, banks going under, falling reserves, unpaid contractors threatening to stop work on key projects), and political emergencies (major strikes, military pressures, intense flak from lob-

---

24. Peru's largest private bank, the Banco de Crédito, owned by the powerful Romero-Raffo business empire, cashed in quickly on tax breaks, low interest rates, and high inflation: in 1981 alone its net profits increased by an amazing 78 percent (Reid 1985, 84–88).

25. The difficulty in responding more effectively to the crisis was certainly not due to the qualifications of the economic team. BCRP president Richard Webb and Commerce Vice-Minister Abusada held economics doctorates from Harvard and Cornell, respectively. Ulloa came with polished international banking credentials and Kuczynski with impeccable managerial experience.

26. Both Abusada and Webb, for example, stated that no one on the economic team perceived the shocks of 1981–82 as more than transitory and that a stronger motive for securing the US$1 billion from the fund was to buy fiscal time against Belaúnde's spending spree on public-works projects. (Richard Webb, interview with the author, Sept. 10, 1986, Lima; and Roberto Abusada, interview with the author, Aug. 12, 1987, Lima.)

bies, the media and congressional opposition, including members of the government party), and in the context, furthermore, of a newly recovered and still highly nervous democracy, major programmatic changes begin to appear heroic.

Despite Peru's bleak stabilization track record throughout the period, the IMF offered one more chance in 1984. The new plan pressed harder for a lower budget deficit, a tighter monetary stance, and higher interest rates, and the government agreed. An eighteen-month US$250 million standby loan was approved, and the banks released another US$100 million of the new credit promised the year before (World Bank 1985, 9). Looking back, this was the last fresh money Peru would see from the banks for an entire decade. The sharper external demands for orthodoxy contrasted starkly with the diminishing will to implement such measures within the congress, the executive, and the major state institutions. Additional tensions erupted among Peru, the banks, and the IMF over hidden arms expenditures, averaging US$400–500 million annually since 1980, which led to the termination of all pending agreements.[27]

Looking at the failure of IMF adjustment programs across the region at this time, Fishlow (1986, 79) concludes that "the IMF model, rather than its implementation, seems to be at fault." For Peru, it is impossible to separate the two. In terms of the model, the fund's insistence on the budget deficit as the driving force of inflation overlooked the increasing percentage of that deficit accounted for by servicing the external debt. Moreover, it was the IMF's "stamp of approval" that facilitated 1982's unprecedented rise in commercial short-term credit and hence an extension of Belaúnde's spending binge. However, as much as the IMF may be to blame for perpetuating this moral hazard, and as wrong as its orthodox model may have been for a country with Peru's vulnerabilities, domestic policy makers cannot be let off the hook for the considerable distortions that emerged in the gray area between the model and its implementation.

The Belaúnde administration showed no inclination to reform state institutions that were suffused with biases toward the rich and powerful. And by

---

27. The figures represent the outcome of the military's success in maintaining autonomy over its budget under the Belaúnde administration (Obando 1998). The official rationale was that the external security threat of the 1970s had given way to the internal menace posed by the rise of domestic insurgencies. Yet only a small fraction of the sums went toward counterinsurgency equipment. Instead, the army, navy, and air force appeared to be locked into a contest to outspend each other on costly Mirage fighter jets and Black Hawk helicopters from the United States. Only in early 1985 did the army start purchasing a large amount of rifles and night-vision equipment for the antiguerrilla operations that supposedly prompted the astronomical spending. See *Latin America Regional Report: Andean Group,* Oct. 5, 1984; Dec. 14, 1984; Apr. 5, 1985; and May 17, 1985.

its last year in office, it was no longer even clear who was responsible for government policy. Amid the economic policy vacuum that set in from 1983–85 came a US$4 billion increase in high-penalty refinancing credits (Webb 1988), with the result that Peru had little choice but to quietly halt service payments on its external debt in mid-1984. Although fiscal, monetary, and trade policy wavered post-1983 between the IMF's tighter stance and a more slack approach, there was now a generalized backlash against orthodoxy within all sectors except the very minor political space still occupied by the far-right contingent within the PPC.

The 1983 Municipal Elections: A Critical Political Realignment

At this point in the democratic transition, Peru's democracy was only surface deep. The fallout from nearly a decade of regressive austerity measures had by now provoked a dramatic response from below. A growing number of poverty-related insurgent factions, Sendero Luminoso being the most prominent, completely eschewed all legal forms of political participation. In contrast to the 1965 guerrilla uprising, Sendero proved itself to be much more than a transient phenomenon. While the Belaúnde administration insisted on phrasing the guerrilla problem in Cold War terminology, and tracing its roots to external "communist interference," Sendero made serious inroads in first the southern and then the central Andean provinces.

As Sendero proceeded from low-level political agitation in 1981 and 1982 to violent assassinations of locally elected officials and destruction of major state-investment projects, the government upped the ante by declaring much of the southern Andes an emergency zone and sending in the military. While the political opposition in congress argued that the conflict could only be quelled through a blitzkrieg development effort in the long-neglected sierra region, the administration opted for what it perceived to be the fastest solution to the problem. A full-force military operation was deployed in 1983, and the conflict quickly escalated into an Argentine-style dirty war between the state security forces and Sendero.[28] By the end of Belaúnde's term, unofficial deaths and disappearances related to the conflict were estimated by international human rights groups to be higher than five thousand (Woy-Hazleton and Hazleton 1987, 118).

At the same time, Peru's newly enfranchised poor chose to register their

28. Raúl González, "Gonzalo's Thought, Belaunde's Answer," *Report on the Americas,* June 1986, 34–36.

grave discontent by casting a ballot for the opposition in the 1983 nationwide municipal elections. Not surprisingly, the elections produced what political scientists refer to as a critical political realignment—that is, the electoral emergence of a new hegemonic bloc, in this case consisting of the center-left sections of the APRA led by Alan García and a group of six left-wing parties that had organized into the United Left (IU) coalition. The APRA moved up to capture 33 percent of the vote, and the IU another 29 percent, with the latter winning the municipality of Lima and placing its leader, Alfonso Barrantes, in the office of mayor on a Marxist ticket. The elections highlighted two unfolding political trends related to the democratization process and shaped by the economic crisis.

The first concerns the effects of concentrating greater state power in the executive, promoted by the constitutional reforms and bolstered by the traditional propensity for special interests to seek to influence the executive through direct personal ties. Clearly, constitutional powers to legislate a program did not translate into the autonomy to carry one out, and the executive's ultimate inability to orchestrate policy and exert control over other political and economic actors posed a serious challenge to the formulation of effective solutions to the crisis. The second reality brought home by the 1983 elections concerns the intrinsic weaknesses of the classic primary-export-led model as a viable development option for Peru and the dissolution of those traditional alliances that had held it together.

The vote confirmed that there was no turning back the clock or eradicating the various legacies of the military experiment, as Belaúnde's social-market project had intended. In its attempts to reverse the labor and agricultural reforms of the Velasco period, the administration met with unexpected popular resistance that the reforms themselves had fostered. Similarly, it had misread the interests and needs of domestic capital, which by now had succeeded in reorganizing around a mixed economy, forming more modern groups like the Romero-Raffo consortium, based in the financial system and investing across sectors (Reid 1985, 86–88). The time lost by not formulating a coherent policy had given the political opposition a chance to regroup. The electoral emergence of the APRA and the more leftist IU as credible political machines, able to incorporate the diverse interests of this new constellation of social forces into winning party platforms, marked a turning point in Peruvian politics on par with 1968.

The electoral rise of the IU as the country's second-largest political force was especially striking in view of Peru's basically conservative past and can be explained by a decade of grassroots outreach, the cultivation of organized labor as a core constituency, and the eventual ability of all six parties in the coalition to compromise on the moderately left Barrantes as a candidate. The

APRA's ability to win a victory in a legally contested race was even more remarkable, given the party's unsuccessful attempts to do so since its inception in 1924. Although it is not possible to recount the full story of the APRA's electoral breakthrough to assume its historic role as the country's governing party, the death of Haya de la Torre and the party's negotiated resolution of old enmities with the military helped open it up to intellectual cross-currents more appropriate to the 1980s and to nonaligned voters across classes and income groups (Sanborn 1991; Graham 1992).

This political realignment of 1983 kicked off the presidential campaign, and even though elections would not be held until 1985, García quickly moved to the front of the race. There were few substantive differences in the APRA and IU campaign platforms. Both worked on the theme of constructing a multiclass national alliance and advocated civilian solutions to the guerrilla-military conflict raging in the Andean emergency zone. Both geared their positions to Peru's large, young popular-sector electorate. The economic platform of each centered on the declaration of an official debt moratorium to provide the breathing space for redistributional policies and for a reactivation strategy that would link industrial and agricultural production according to a more integrated and regionally decentralized plan.

The main differences were the IU's status as a recently formed coalition of parties that lacked the internal discipline of a single party and its more extreme position favoring nationalization of the financial sector and raw-material production. In contrast, the APRA proposed to rationalize the state sector through privatization and administrative reform. Also, García recognized that economic reactivation in the wake of the debt crisis would require greater cooperation with domestic business and financial groups and sought a social pact with private industry along these lines. The rise of a more sophisticated and charismatic leader personified by García, a more modern business sector, and the country's brief success with nontraditional exports during 1978–80 provided the vision for a locally financed national-industrial project meant to generate employment and economic dynamism. The fate of this APRA-led national project forms the subject of the next chapter.

Conclusion

In retrospect, Peru's turn to a more market-oriented management model in the early 1980s is best understood as a quest to recapture or reinstate the buoyant economic indicators that prevailed prior to the 1960s. The trend until the 1960s was one of high growth fueled by foreign and domestic private investment, low levels of direct state economic participation, and little need for external borrowing; the budget was basically in balance, and compared to the 1980s, the 1950s stood out as a period of next to zero inflation. The traditional primary-export model, and the liberal economic policy regime that supported it, had not been at all successful in distributional terms, but given the highly unstable economic environment that prevailed throughout the 1960s and 1970s, subsequent policy makers were apparently willing to sacrifice equity over growth if that was what it would take to finally turn the economy around.

However, given these aspirations, the outcomes of the program were highly paradoxical. Rather than eliminating the cumulative distortions from nearly two decades of chaotic state intervention, the social-market strategy (or at least the manner in which it was implemented) actually served to dig Peru deeper into the negative pattern of state-led development identified as having taken root by the late 1960s. As discussed in chapter 1, this consisted of (1) a high level of external financing to support the state's endeavors; (2) heavy reliance on public firms to perform the state's development tasks; (3) the perpetuation of an ambiguous relationship with crucial domestic private investors; and (4) the inability to coordinate the necessary social policies with the chosen development model.

On each of these four points, the track record worsened. The external debt exploded under the thrust of more costly short-term borrowing, and macropolicy trends during the second Belaúnde administration became perhaps more incoherent and erratic than at any other time during the post–World War Two period. The tax structure, after years of piecemeal measures following the major 1968 reform and the AP's heightened reliance on indirect taxes to finance its program, reached its most regressive point yet. The more progressive taxes on income and wealth now accounted for just 25 percent of all state revenue, compared to 60 percent in 1950 (World Bank 1988, 268–69).

Within the context of a highly touted privatization drive, the state firms actually expanded their presence in the economy, as public officials openly employed them for personal gain. In terms of the relationship between the state and private capital, the approach of the Belaúnde team was every bit as damaging to investors' confidence as the nationalizations of the early 1970s; as testimony, private investment hit an all-time historical low. The outright neglect of social policy, under the guise of the belief that the social-market program would prompt a distributive trickle-down, proved more costly than ever imagined. During the five-year Belaúnde term, poverty-related insurgencies proliferated, and the synergistic effect of a regressive income policy and staunch popular resistance exploded into what could best be described as a political economy of violence.

In the end, the social-market model of the early 1980s was not as much a development strategy as it was an attitude toward the state. In its rejection of explicit state-led management approaches, the Belaúnde government tended to work around those bureaucratic, institutional, and administrative structures that would have been crucial for the successful implementation of any development program. In effect, the embracement of a market strategy became an excuse for not drawing on those planning and managerial resources that the state did have to offer. The lesson of this period, particularly in the more severe crisis context that set in post-1982, is that market policies are also "interventions" that demand a basic level of capacity, coordination, and willpower to be carried out (Kahler 1990).

The prevailing attitude toward the state as overly intrusive, yet at the same time weak and ineffectual, served to reinforce these very characteristics of the state (Sikkink 1991). When all else failed, profligate spending on large, poorly planned infrastructure projects came to substitute for any semblance of institution building. The incoming García administration recognized the need for a stronger and more autonomous state apparatus, as well as the importance of cultivating a set of agencies that better represented the general interests of the nation, but it would continue to wrestle with these problems all the same.

CHAPTER 5

The Neostructuralist Backlash

The New Heterodoxy

By the mid-1980s, most Latin American governments had lost what little enthusiasm they may have ever had for orthodox stabilization programs sponsored by the IMF. When the debt crisis first erupted in 1982, most countries had turned to the fund for short-term finance and macroeconomic policy advice. But as stringent domestic adjustment measures had failed to alleviate the recession-inflation spiral, and as new supplies of capital had still not appeared, domestic-policy responses began to branch out in new directions. Argentina and Brazil, each with long histories of high inflation and eclectic approaches to economic adjustment in the post–World War Two era, launched "heterodox" stabilization programs in 1985 and 1986, respectively. Peru, with no comparable history of hyperinflation prior to the debt crisis, and closely wedded to a monetarist management approach since the late 1970s, also announced a heterodox program in July 1985.

At a broad level, the three programs displayed important similarities. Each was designed with the help of domestic economic advisors who had done some training in the United States or Europe and who imparted a more flexible diagnosis of the causes of inflation. Contrary to the IMF's uniform insistence on excess aggregate demand as the driving force of inflation, these "neostructuralist" advisors saw price rises as rooted in the inertial effects of indexing wages and prices and the various shocks emanating from the international economy (Fishlow 1985, 143; Sheahan 1987, 103–10). Policy prescriptions for all three programs centered on monetary reform and the coordination of wage and price controls to break inflationary expectations, yet without the drastic output losses associated with orthodox strategies. All three can also be seen as compromise packages, as recently elected civilian regimes were pressed to juggle the demands of the international financial community with the social and political demands of their domestic constituencies.

This chapter examines Peru's heterodox program—first as an attempt to utilize a more finely tuned set of state-led interventions in light of the disappointments associated with Velasco's ambitious statist strategy and with Belaúnde's social-market model; and then as a way of coping with the many new constraints imposed by the international political economy. The program initiated by Alan García and his economic team differed from the Argentine and Brazilian efforts in three main ways.[1] The first, which received the widest attention, was the official declaration of a partial moratorium limiting debt-service payments to 10 percent of annual export earnings. Second was an explicit policy to redistribute income to the poorest groups, rather than simply stabilizing the drop in income. Finally, Peru's program also articulated a longer-term strategy that blended neostructuralist macropolicy management with more standard structuralist strategies of state-led industrialization (Thorp 1987).

This long-run policy thrust can be explained as a direct outcome of the special mixture of political liberalization and severe economic crisis that characterized the post-1983 period in Peru. As discussed earlier, a critical political realignment had occurred: within sections of business, labor, agriculture, and the internal organizations of the state, new patterns of cooperation and conflict had emerged. Thus, while the debt crisis hit Peru at its most vulnerable point, when economic policy was oriented almost entirely toward a declining external sector and the ability of state elites to respond was quite low, it also had a modernizing effect in terms of promoting a wide debate about the country's overwhelming problems and their possible solutions. The demands of groups, especially within the popular classes and the private sector, became more cohesive and were taken up seriously by those ascendant center-left political parties discussed in the previous chapter.

As a catch-up strategy for economic restructuring, the heterodox program placed rigorous demands on the political capacity of the state to manage this project. Given the preceding analysis of the evolution of the Peruvian state sector, it will be seen that the program faltered rather quickly (Crabtree 1992; Pastor 1992; Sheahan 1999). Apart from the obvious explanation of stringent pressures from the international economy, some of the most basic bureaucratic instruments and institutional supports for such a program were still lacking.[2] The first section of this chapter looks at the structural backdrop for the program, according to the four main institutional variables that have been discussed throughout this book. Following are two sections that analyze

---

1. Economists have used a number of variables to discuss the varying outcomes among the three heterodox programs. Explanations have centered on the differing levels of idle productive capacity present in the economy, price elasticity of exports, size and bargaining leverage on the external debt, incomes policy, fiscal and monetary control, and so on (World Bank 1989; Dornbusch and Edwards 1991; Pastor 1992; Edwards 1995).

2. As John Zysman (1983, 308) has argued: "A broad economic challenge that affects the national position may induce efforts to use the state to promote economic restructuring and competitive adjustments to the market. Yet, unless there exists a state structure that can be used as an instrument of such a policy, the effort is likely to fail."

the rise and fall of Peruvian heterodoxy. The remaining sections address the broader consequences of the García period, the country's desperate search for a viable development coalition in the wake of the program, and the realistic options for Peru's reintegration into the international financial community after five years of a basically autarkic approach to economic management.

State Intervention without State Capacity

Bureaucratic Autonomy

Although the political complexions of the Belaúnde and García administrations were radically different, there was strong continuity in the area of exercising executive authority and the neglect of the state bureaucracy. If anything, García deepened the pattern established by his civilian predecessor of making policy almost solely by executive decree and with little regard for the mechanics of carrying it out. García's resort to an almost purely presidential style quickly overshadowed the earlier campaign promises to modernize and upgrade the state's administrative capacity. Initially, the president did move to improve wages for technical personnel in those state economic agencies that were crucial to the implementation of his program.[3] But this was not accompanied by the delegation of greater decision-making leeway and authority to the relevant ministers or to their top staff. With García's tendency to deal directly with a diverse range of representatives from special interests, it was not long before the political opposition was complaining of an "imperial presidency."

García's propensity toward an autocratic and exclusionary leadership style was bolstered by the very mediocre pool of technical and intellectual talent he had to draw on from the ranks of the APRA party (Graham 1992). Furthermore, the APRA's apparent renovation in bringing the younger and forward-thinking García to office did not hold up under everyday political life. Faced with a local APRA leadership network stacked with conservative and sometimes corrupt caudillo types (Sanborn 1991), the president pursued a double track in the exercise of executive authority. First, to keep the peace, he permitted the widespread infiltration of lower-level party figures who were not likely to present a challenge into the state bureaucracy.[4] Second, while filling

---

3. Wage data from Lima's Institute of Public Administration (INAP) show that wages for technical personnel in the ministries of finance and agriculture and in the INP doubled over the 1985–86 period.

4. By one estimate, patronage appointments in the social security administration ballooned by nearly 100 percent between 1985 and 1990 (Keefer 1995, 2).

the lower-rung posts according to mainly political criteria, García cultivated his own private technical team of independent advisors.

The strong reliance on a presidential advisory team followed in the footsteps of Velasco's COAP and Belaúnde's technocratic "dynamo group" of the early 1980s; in all three cases, the format served to insulate policy making and to deflect challenges from the opposition or from within one's own ranks. But the practice of a highly insulated group of technical advisors basically taking over the state apparatus virtually self-destructed under the García administration. The cumulative toll over the three administrations (the RGAF, Belaúnde, and García) was a situation whereby policy was basically made at the whim of the executive with few reliability checks.

State Economic and Planning Institutions

The tendency for the two main state economic institutions—the finance ministry and the BCRP—to become the focus of fierce conflicts over the content and operationalization of economic policy continued post-1985. On the one hand, the MEF became the bureaucratic fiefdom of APRA finance minister Luis Alva Castro and his own team of *técnicos,* who were frequently at odds with the directives stemming from the executive. On the other hand, as party politicking rapidly pervaded the recruitment, hiring, and promotion process, the central bank's status as the more autonomous of the two institutions was put to an even greater test than during the Belaúnde administration. Despite the stipulation in the 1979 constitution that the bank's executive chair was to be appointed to a five-year uninterrupted term, BCRP chair Leonel Figueroa was effectively forced to resign in mid-1987 in the throes of a dispute over the need to change course on a range of monetary and fiscal targets.[5]

The prime attempt at institutional innovation under the García administration was the revival of the INP as a major force in the policy-making arena. The merits of this move stemmed from the INP's historical bias in favor of the structuralist policy approaches being embraced by the president and his team and from the perceived need to bring Peru's planning system back to life. Yet it turned out that housing the program at the INP was, in fact, the most effective way for the president's special advisory team to circumvent the more economically conservative finance ministry and central bank in pushing its highly experimental policy package through the congress. While the INP was ostensibly responsible for the 1986–90 National Development Plan,

---

5. "Government Puts Economy on Hold but Central Bank Printing Presses Work Overtime," *Andean Report,* June 1987, 97.

and for mapping out the government's overall economic strategy, the plan expressed a range of neostsructuralist ideas and strategies that heretofore had not surfaced at the INP per se.[6]

The plan, for example, rejected the use of the exchange rate as a tool for adjusting the economy; it also expounded on a range of fiscal and monetary issues concerning the relationship between inflation and the fiscal deficit, which typically fell within the domain of the MEF and the BCRP. Some of these ideas had been voiced at the top echelons of the BCRP toward the end of the Belaúnde era and had also been tossed about from time to time within the impressive network of private economic think tanks and research institutes that had sprung up in Lima during the early 1980s. But the INP itself never stood out as a credible institutional base for formulating the much more macroeconomically complex tenets of the heterodox program.

The Leadership Coalition

Once it had made the decision to at least temporarily go it alone on the international front, and had received a massive electoral mandate in 1985, there were a number of possibilities open to the García administration for pursuing a development coalition. On the domestic side, the guerrilla insurgency now cast a long shadow over civil society, and as economically and politically divided as Peruvians had been historically, the threat from Sendero and other violent splinter factions placed unprecedented pressure on national groups to set aside their differences and to seek a consensual solution to the problem (McClintock 1989). Similarly, the severe pressures from the external sector fueled a sense of urgency over facing the economic crisis from a position of national unity.

With almost universal agreement in 1985 that the country's two greatest challenges were the reactivation of the economy along more distributive and self-sufficient lines and the reduction of daily political violence, new coalitional possibilities were present along both the executive-parliament-party and the state-capital-labor axes discussed in chapter 1. On the former, the most logical alliance would have been between the APRA and the IU factions, which together controlled the congress. After all, the strongest constituency of each came from the middle and poor sectors of society, and in the end, much of the IU platform would be adopted by the APRA. While García and Lima mayor Alfonso Barrantes courted each other publicly until the latter's

---

6. See Instituto Nacional de Planificación, *Plan Nacional de Desarrollo, 1986–1990,* Lima, 1986; and the plan's companion volume, entitled *Un modelo económico heterodoxo: El caso peruano* (Carbonetto ed. 1987).

resignation as leader of the IU in 1987, a true alliance between these two main political forces met with firm resistance within the ranks of each.

From the point of view of the IU, there were questions about the possible deals the APRA may have cut with the military and distrust stemming from the belief that the opportunistic style of Haya de la Torre still lay just below the party's surface.[7] García's bravado and omnipresent approach to politics did little to dispel these fears. Finally, it had been the left's initial distrust of the APRA that had enabled it to surmount its own formidable internal rifts in order to participate successfully in the 1983 and 1985 elections (Sanborn 1991). An APRA-IU coalition may have been more palatable to the center-left segments of the APRA, as the two had frequently acted in concert as part of the congressional opposition under the second Belaúnde administration (Woy-Hazleton and Hazleton 1987, 111). But the APRA party as a whole was still seen as having "sold out" ideologically in the 1950s and was thus repugnant to the bulk of the IU.

As for an alliance along the state-capital-labor axis, the difficulties here were threefold. The first difficulty was the division of organized labor and the less organized working poor along party lines, with the former largely in league with the IU and the latter with the APRA. The second was the lack of a cohesive core constituency within the state itself, be it within the planning institute or the main state institutions, with the initiative and vision to play a part in such an alliance. The third, ironically, was that although domestic capital had now come around to accepting the idea of closer collaboration with the state, it was plagued by the president's highly impulsive maneuvers and the paucity of sound administrative follow-up on many of the promised policies. The failure of domestic groups to coalesce around the heterodox program along either of the two axes left the fate of the program up to the vicissitudes of internal party politics and bureaucratic back-biting, which had by now become the most constant features of the Peruvian policy-making process.

The Intermediation of Societal Interests

By 1985, the composition of organized societal interests in Peru, and their position vis-à-vis the state, had joined step with other Latin American countries, such as Argentina. That is, interest representation had become more articulate and assertive, while the state's ability to intermediate had not improved proportionately and had even deteriorated. Thus, García's call for serious tripartite negotiations could not have been more timely as an appro-

---

7. Alfonso Barrantes, interview with the author, Oct. 10, 1986, Lima.

priate approach to the country's problems, but again the state was not able to follow through on its side of the bargain. In the course of trying to please all sides at once, the administration succumbed to the familiar populist pitfall of pleasing no one. Apart from these state-related difficulties in launching García's "social *concertación*" strategy, its implementation was riddled with numerous other contradictions.

Early on, three of the four major labor confederations had signed an agreement with the main national business associations stating their intention to support *concertación* (Bollinger 1987, 20). Yet the president had also made it clear from the start that he favored those poorest and most disenfranchised segments of society, who did benefit briefly from state-sponsored employment programs like the Temporary Income Support Program (PAIT) (Vigier 1986; Graham 1994, 101–2). Although the García administration proved much more skillful than its two predecessors in dealing with organized labor, it missed an important opportunity to harness the energy of this more organized constituency to the development program.

From the standpoint of domestic capital, interest mediation centered almost immediately on whether local investors would actually be willing to step forward and meet the state halfway with the necessary investments in new export-oriented industries—or on the degree to which the Peruvian private sector would continue to squeeze idle industrial capacity without putting up a substantial amount of its own risk capital. The situation remained highly ambiguous through the first year of the program. While private investment during 1986 was up 18 percent over the previous year (BCRP 1987, 25), capital-flight estimates were also running between US$600 million and US$1 billion for the same period.[8] The difficulties of forging ahead with the investment program were aggravated by García's impetuous decision in mid-1987 to nationalize that portion of the financial system that still remained in private hands (ten commercial banks, seventeen insurance companies, and six finance companies). This was a last straw in the sense that whatever business confidence had been mustered quickly faded.[9]

But the interest-mediation process between the state and domestic capitalists was also hampered by organizational weaknesses within the private sector that had still not been resolved. Interest representation in this sector had definitely come a long way from the almost strictly personalistic style that had

---

8. The figures cited here are from MACROCONSULT, a Lima think tank, and were conveyed to me by its former director Claudio Herzka.

9. Barbara Durr, "Peru's Nationalization of Banks Shakes Business Confidence," *Christian Science Monitor*, Oct. 13, 1987, 11.

prevailed through the 1960s via traditional organizations such as the National Industrial Society and the National Agrarian Society (Astiz 1969). It had also emerged from the rut of the early 1980s, which saw any number of private-sector representatives integrated into executive-level consultative commissions meant to tackle a specific problem, only to have their final recommendations buried or ignored (Conaghan 1988, 56–57). The turning point had been the 1983 annual executives' meeting (CADE), where an explicit decision was reached by the private sector to begin "making policy" on its own with the formation of the umbrella organization CONFIEP a year later (Durand 1994, 12–13).

Although CONFIEP's membership included fourteen major business groups by late 1986, Francisco Durand (1994) notes that CONFIEP's internal organization was still too incipient for it to achieve any true clout in the policy-making process. Given the historical tendency of the Peruvian private sector to band together in times of crisis and to otherwise fragment in pursuit of short-term individual gains, CONFIEP still had not made the full transition to a viable institutional entity. Clearly, with the abrupt drop in external capital flows, a state-capital alliance geared toward leveraging local investment, and acted out institutionally through CONFIEP, was the logical path forward for the García administration. The inability to properly pursue this path, for all the reasons discussed earlier, left the task open for García's successors.

García's Policies, 1985–1987: From Emergency Plan to Heterodox Reactivation

When García assumed office in July 1985 the APRA did have an emergency plan for the first one hundred days of government. This, combined with 50 percent of the popular vote and a majority in both houses of congress, enabled García to act quickly. The immediate tasks lay in controlling domestic inflation and currency speculation and in alleviating an explosive current-account deficit. The APRA's earlier calls for a unilateral debt moratorium were substantiated by the fact that service payments on the debt had approached 50 percent of the country's export earnings when Belaúnde stopped paying and that Peruvian debt had already been written down to less than half its value on an emergent secondary-debt market trading out of New York. These steep discounts implied that an imminent return of voluntary lending to Peru was not likely.

García's inaugural announcement of the "10 percent solution," limiting service payments on Peru's medium- and long-term public debt to no more than 10 percent of annual export earnings, differed from Belaúnde's ad hoc moratorium in two ways.[10] First, García won a wide national consensus for his unilateral stance and was therefore able to turn the problem around and make it work for him. Second, with its focus on selectively honoring those obligations necessary to maintain trade and development financing, and on seeking alternative methods of debt repayment (e.g., debt equity swaps), the 10 percent solution represented Peru's first attempt at a coherent debt strategy since the problem originated in the mid-1970s. Stated policy through 1987 was to keep up on payments to the multilaterals and on food imports and regional trade agreements and to punctually service any debt contracted after July 1985.

On the domestic side, the emergency plan sought to halt inflation through direct price administration and the control of imports and foreign exchange. Peru's venturing from conventional orthodox wisdom was a long time coming and obviously a response to past policy failures. The embracement of this experimental mix of policies can be explained, ironically, by the very limited and weak technical expertise within the ranks of the APRA. As García was forced to reach outside of his party, bringing in local consultants from the European Economic Community, the International Labour Office, and academia, neostructuralist policy influences from other settings were quickly put into action by the president's economic team.[11]

This first phase of heterodox shock set a price freeze on all goods and services; the exchange rate was devalued and then fixed at an official rate; all dollar accounts were also frozen on the condition that they could be turned into local currency at the new official rate plus a 3 percent premium. The fixed exchange rate was combined with wage hikes and lower interest rates to encourage a transfer of income from financial and speculative activities to the productive sector. The partial debt moratorium, combined with import controls and long-overdue cuts in arms purchases, did provide a cushion to spur economic reactivation. Treasury reserves were also built up by the BCRP's highly unorthodox decision to purchase dollars, made cheap by a fixed exchange rate, from those regional banks flush with the proceeds from Peru's illicit US$500–800 million annual cocaine trade.

By early 1986, the economic program began to move forward in a series of quarterly packages aimed at taking advantage of the high levels of idle capac-

---

10. "President García Delivers Inaugural Address," Foreign Broadcasting Information Service (FBIS-LAM), July 29, 1985.

11. García's original core team consisted of Argentine economist Daniel Carbonetto and Pierre Vigier, on loan respectively from the International Labour Office and the European Economic Community; Cesar Ferrari, a Ph.D. economist trained at Boston University; and APRA party faithful Javier Tantalean. Both Ferrari and Tantalean headed up the INP during García's first two years. Also influential was Carlos Franco, editor of Lima's prestigious academic journal *Socialismo y Participación*. Franco represented the strongest Velasquista faction among the president's advisors.

ity present in the economy. The medium-term strategy hinged, first, on coordinating the expansion of productive capacity with the expansion of mass consumption; and second, on the need to capture and reinvest the economic surplus in order to sustain a consumer-led economic recovery. García's team also stressed the need to coordinate import substitution with export promotion and to integrate the popular sectors via redistributive reforms.[12] If the Velasco era was the heyday of structuralism in Peru, then the García administration was an attempt to refine this same strategy. However, the differences this time around were considerable. Not only did García lack the breathing room that external borrowing had afforded the RGAF in the early 1970s; he also inherited an exceedingly more volatile macroeconomic scenario than that taken over by Velasco in 1968.

The reactivation strategy deepened throughout 1986 with periodic wage hikes, emergency work programs, and generous subsidies for Peru's depressed agricultural sector. García had begun urging business executives to invest at their 1985 annual meeting (CADE) and offered tax refunds and credit incentives for companies that created new jobs. By year's end, a complex economic superstructure had evolved that combined import controls with multiple exchange and interest rates, with the bulk of the tax breaks and subsidies channeled into manufacturing and agroindustry. The short-term success of the program was tremendous: real wages increased by 30 percent in the countryside, with the average urban correlate up by 20 percent; industry grew an astounding 15 to 20 percent; and the growth of GDP surpassed post–World War Two records at 9.2 percent (see table 14). Inflation, moreover, was reduced from an average rate of 163 percent in 1985 to 78 percent in 1986. The boom made for APRA's clean sweep in the November 1986 municipal elections, and García held his ground as perhaps the most popular president to date.

These immediate gains aside, some predictable longer-range challenges had already surfaced. First was the difficulty of moving out of the price freeze without precipitating a new inflationary spiral, a dilemma that had similarly plagued Argentine and Brazilian policy makers. Second, it was not until early 1987 that the government formed a National Investment Board as the first formal step toward tripartite negotiation, or *concertación*. Third, because of the prolonged freeze on government-controlled prices and a continued world depression for oil and mineral prices, tax collections dipped to their lowest

---

12. As the country's first development treatise since the Velasco period, the plan quickly became much bigger than the economic program it proposed. Many of the objectives worked at cross-purposes, pitting inward growth policies against outward ones and short-term goals against medium- and long-term concerns. For more detail on the nuances between the García and Velasco experiments, see table 2.

TABLE 14. Macroeconomic and External Indicators in Peru: 1981–90 [a]

	1981	1982	1983	1984	1985	1986	1987	1988	1989	1990	1986–90 (1)
GDPGRO	7.2	-0.4	-12.6	4.1	2.3	9.2	8.5	-8.4	-11.6	-5.4	-1.5
GNPPCGRO	5.3	-2.8	-16.1	1.0	0.4	8.7	6.3	-13.4	-11.4	-8.5	-3.66
INF	75.4	64.4	111.2	110.2	163.4	77.9	85.8	667.0	3398.7	7481.7	
PRIVGDP	21.5	20.8	15.1	12.1	12.0	13.2	13.4	15.5	13.1	12.2	13.4
PUBIGDP	7.3	8.7	8.7	8.1	6.1	5.4	4.4	4.2	3.5	2.5	4.0
INVEST	28.8	29.5	23.7	20.2	18.2	18.6	17.8	19.7	16.6	14.7	17.4
RER	245.1	251.1	281.2	291.5	348.7	241.8	161.2	167.3	103.9	100.0	
TRADEBAL	-553	-428	293	1,007	1,219	-73	-500	-134	1,246	399	
CURACCT	-1,733	-1,612	-875	-235	102	-1,393	-2,064	-1,819	-570	-1,384	
FDI	125	48	38	-89	1	22	32	26	59	41	
PORT											
DEBT	8,586	10,709	11,339	12,153	12,879	14,882	17,485	18,240	18,577	20,064	

Source: GDP, GNP, and debt are from World Bank, World Tables, CD-ROM, 2000. Data on investment are from Glen and Sumlinski 1998 <www.ifc.org/economics/pubs/discuss.htm>. Inflation, exchange rates, and payments are calculated from IMF 1999, except trade balance prior to 1977 obtained from IMF 1984; FDI and portfolio investment data prior to 1977 obtained from IMF 1994.

Note: GDPGRO = growth of real GDP; GNPPCGRO = growth of real per capita GNP; INF = Dec.–Dec. inflation; PRIVGDP = private investment as % of GDP; PUBIGDP = public investment as % of GDP; INVEST = total domestic investment as % of GDP; RER = real exchange rate (1990 = 100), calculated using period average exchange rate, U.S. WPI, and domestic CPI; TRADEBAL = trade balance (mil$); merchandise exports – merchandise imports; CURACCT = current account (mil$); FDI = foreign direct investment (mil$); PORT = foreign portfolio investment (mil$); DEBT = total external debt (mil$).

[a] Garcia term average growth and investment

point in a decade. García's tax cuts to the business sector also failed to generate expected new revenues, as many firms evaded taxes by fleeing into the informal economy.[13] The projected income from the sale of thirty to forty public firms was blocked by the lack of interested buyers and by the government's reluctance to take on the complex problem of privatization, despite earlier campaign promises to do so (Ortíz de Zevallos 1986).[14] The partial debt moratorium failed to help as much as expected, as it had been necessary to pay out close to 20 percent of export earnings during García's first year just to maintain the necessary trade financing.[15]

The success of the heterodox reactivation now rested on its medium-term goal of capturing new private-sector savings and investments before foreign reserves were depleted. In 1987 García finally launched a highly touted "national-industrial project" with the country's top twelve business groups.[16] Priority investment projects were defined as those that were decentralized, net savers of foreign exchange, and that promoted employment and intraindustry links. A special employment and investment fund was created to offer bonds to finance-approved projects, and a new foreign-trade institute was set up to promote in-kind debt-payment schemes based on the expected returns from nontraditional exports. With all the generous tax and credit incentives, the APRA government succeeded in taking the *concertación* process up to the letter-of-intent stage. However, most of the US$400 million in new projects never moved forward as planned.

Potential investors had been put off by some of the government's other, less appealing measures, such as a mandatory bond-purchasing scheme for 1986's most profitable firms. And, there remained the confidence gap generated by the guerrilla insurgency and its targeting of local industrial plants for

13. By moving part of their operations into the informal economy, producers had realized their own reactivation by using cheap government-controlled inputs, while evading price controls and taxes on their own output (Thorp 1987).

14. The government did announce a divestiture plan in 1986 that targeted the sale of thirty to forty smaller companies, with the expectation of raising US$400 million within two years. But, similar to the pattern under the previous administration, the two-year period saw a divestiture of just two small shareholdings, plus one physical plant that sold for half a million dollars. These data are reported by Joseph Borgatti, "Divestiture Program of Inversiones COFIDE S.A. (ICSA)," USAID Bureau for Private Enterprise, Washington, D.C., Mar. 21, 1988, 50/2–50/3.

15. The intended debt-for-equity swaps had not materialized—mainly because such arrangements require a certain level of financial sophistication at the negotiating stage, which the administration lacked; and because Peruvian debt, now offered at about 17 percent of its original value on the secondary market, was without buyers.

16. Although minerals still accounted for over 60 percent of national income, mining representatives were excluded from these meetings, and minerals received the worst rates within the new multitiered exchange-rate system. The policy bias was an ideological one, reflecting APRA's ambitions, originally expressed by Haya de la Torre, to move away from enclave development based on primary exports.

expensive physical damage. Peruvian entrepreneurs, though increasingly modern in their outlook, were still not accustomed to investing without the backing of foreign capital, and there were the usual suspicions from abroad about the ability of an inefficient state sector to execute the highly interventionist heterodox program successfully. Policy debates taking place within the government at the time did not help relieve these anxieties, as there was open confusion over the problem of reconciling popular demands and the attempted industrialist pact with the state's rapidly diminishing resources. As the demands of labor and business began bearing down on the executive, the ongoing policy debate within the government erupted into a major dispute among state agencies.

The more fiscally conservative BCRP and MEF pointed to the mounting deficits and the imperative for slowed state spending accompanied by a tax overhaul. On the other side, the fiscal expansionists operating out of the INP favored a deepening of consumer-led growth and a stronger promotion of the export projects being discussed with the private sector. The president announced a major economic package in April 1987 meant to strike a compromise among all the various factions that were emerging. The MEF and BCRP won some tax and exchange-rate adjustments, while the INP secured wage hikes for labor and lower interest rates for the private sector. In order to preserve foreign exchange, García adjusted the debt strategy to a "capacity to pay" stance that further limited debt payments until after domestic growth targets had been met.[17] Though intended to ameliorate conflict and win more time for the program to work, the economic package was the first clear sign that the heterodox policy was in serious trouble and that García had begun to lose control.

Under the capacity-to-pay policy, loan disbursements from the multilaterals began to turn negative, and previously negotiated in-kind debt-payback schemes were thrown into question. It was within this context of an increasingly desperate foreign-exchange situation and the unraveling of any semblance of a cohesive politics of growth that García announced his intention to nationalize all private banks and finance and insurance companies in mid-1987. Although this move contradicted García's earlier campaign pledges, the immediate explanation for it centered on the need to democratize credit and make more working capital available for Peru's small and medium-sized entrepreneurs. The decision is probably best interpreted in light of the gov-

---

17. Groundbreaking countertrade deals had been signed with two banks (Midland Bank and First Interstate of California) in late 1987, but this debt-repayment strategy was plagued by various bottlenecks. The basic problem was Peru's inability to guarantee a steady flow of products contracted in a given agreement, with the investment lag in export-oriented projects adding to this shortage.

ernment's frustration over what it perceived as high levels of capital flight, as up to this point the APRA had assigned small capitalists a marginal role in the national-industrial alliance.[18] With the nationalization, García attempted to coopt a major position of the IU and further consolidate his largely unorganized grassroots political support base. Yet, at the same time, he succeeded in alienating those top economic groups with whom he had been cultivating a working relationship since the early 1980s.

The Antipopulist Backlash and Other Political Implications

With the collapse of public finances in late 1987, and the growing distance among those groups within the state and business community whose cooperation would be essential for any realistic attempt at economic restructuring, another Peruvian experiment had come to an abrupt end. Because the proposed nationalization caught even IU and APRA members of congress off guard, the outcome was the passing of a vague nationalization law that left the government and the private sector to battle out the initiative in the courts. The divisive issue brought Belaúnde's dormant AP-PPC coalition temporarily back to life and gave rise to a conservative opposition Democratic Front (FREDEMO), which championed private-property rights and succeeded in keeping the conflict alive. As the García presidency wore on, time would quickly reveal the huge political and economic costs that the bank nationalization would inflict on the entire country.

Although the issues and actors were quite different, the standoff was similar to the pattern of the previous administration, whereby government policy broke down halfway through the presidential term and the executive became increasingly isolated. The pattern was obviously rooted in the complexities of constructing a constitutional democracy in the midst of ongoing economic crises and in the drawbacks to the executive office discussed in chapter 4. Yet it was also reinforced under García by a combination of political miscalculations and by the way the chosen economic policy interacted with unresolved structural limitations at the level of the state.

As for García's domestic political strategy, a quick injection of populist wage policies and a brief reversal in the terms of trade between industry and agriculture, followed by a retraction, led to an urgent search for other ways of

---

18. Javier Iguiñiz, Catholic University economics professor and chief economist for the IU coalition, pointed out that the professed goal of democratizing credit by way of the nationalizations was greatly hampered by the absence of any prior preparations, such as the establishment of local popular lending programs with clearly defined projects and investment schemes. See *Peru Report*, Sept. 1987.

maintaining alliances with organized labor and the popular sector. Rash actions to solve one problem created problems elsewhere, the ramifications of the bank nationalization law being the strongest case in point. The erratic handling of *concertación,* and the president's insistence on negotiating directly and in private with the major representatives of economic power, as opposed to utilizing institutional channels within the state and the CONFIEP, left both sides vulnerable and with little recourse when personalistic ties began to sour. The exclusion of organized labor altogether from the negotiations made that alliance all the more difficult to maintain.

This inability of base groups to find effective political representation once they have played a key part in supporting candidates and parties in democratic transitions is a paradox common to all democratizing states in the region (Sanborn 1991). In the Peruvian case, even the interests of the influential economic elites who had promoted García were abandoned, as the APRA oscillated between a populist stance and its modernization pact. Apart from leading to the strategic error of pursuing neither course very efficiently, the stalemate underlined the ultimate weakness of representative groups, the difficulty all sides had in exerting their political will, and the challenge this augured for the survival of democracy in Peru.

Similarly, on the external front, one is left to wonder if greater economic breathing space could have been gained from a more consistent political approach. Early on, García won the support of prominent U.S. academic economists for his partial debt moratorium (Fishlow 1986). Moreover, the U.S. government, because it took the guerrilla insurgency seriously and because of the sensitive issue of Peru's first democratic presidential succession in forty years, was treading softly with García.

The U.S. government's Inter-Agency Review Committee did request that the banks downgrade Peru's debt in November 1985, but the country's honoring of its private-sector commercial payments and the banks' low level of exposure to Peru helped delay other commonly feared sanctions such as the freezing of the country's foreign assets and the interruption of trade finance. The APRA also held Peru's commercial and multilateral creditors at bay by presenting the moratorium as temporary and declaring its intention to form a new foreign-debt committee to negotiate directly with the country's creditors.

The space afforded by international political and economic actors, and the astounding growth rates of 1986 and 1987, had the perverse effect of permanently postponing these negotiations on the Peruvian side.[19] The result was

---

19. Peru's delegation to the 1986 annual IMF–World Bank meetings made a particularly poor impression, reiterating the country's debt stance with a lot of anti-imperialist rhetoric. If there had been a propitious time to negotiate with the multilaterals, this was probably it.

the IMF's declaration of Peru as an "ineligible" borrower in August 1986 and the subsequent freezing of around US$900 million in multilateral loan disbursements to Peru. In view of Peru's now precarious financial position (see table 14), the lesson of the partial debt moratorium was twofold. First, even small underdeveloped states with formidable internal security threats would not be let entirely off the hook, particularly when little effort was made to dialogue with international lenders. The paying out of 10 to 30 percent of annual export earnings to service the debt did not deter the usual trade and aid sanctions, although it did help to slow the pace with which they were applied. Second, the fiscal crisis resulting from this one-shot financing based on debt nonpayment confirmed the APRA's original campaign statements on economic policy—that is, in the absence of sufficient quantities of external financing, sustainable growth policies would require a substantial increase in domestic resources, through taxes and private savings.

The double bind, of course, was that rigid limitations from the external sector quickly rendered what had been envisioned as a long-term policy for garnering domestic resources into a short-term crisis-management program, and not a particularly well-managed program at that. Heterodox policy, as nothing more than a short-run inflation-management strategy, had the disastrous effect of holding down those key prices, including interest and exchange rates, necessary to build a strong private-sector economy (Thorp 1987, 5/1). And, having lost its momentum as a long-run force for restructuring the economy, heterodoxy only served to intensify the increasingly inverse relationship between a more interventionist model and the poor capacity of the Peruvian state to intervene effectively.

At the level of the state, the most glaring limit to García's program was the continued failure of any one development institution to take the lead in formulating and carrying out public policy. The reform stalemate in the public-enterprise sector also created a bottleneck in the government's modernization drive, as the SOEs continued to control half of Peru's modern-sector capital stock yet remained in limbo for all the reasons discussed in chapters 3 and 4.[20] The locus of the reactivation program at the INP suited the APRA's desire to project a broad multiclass image, as the planning institute still embodied much of the populist legacy from the Velasco period. But even under Velasco, the INP never came to fruition as a powerful development entity (Cleaves and Scurrah 1980, 74–75). Thus, García's team easily penetrated the INP, making economic policy decisions at the top, with the

---

20. In the wake of García's term it had become apparent that the SOE sector had actually expanded with the nationalization of the Belco petroleum company in 1986 and the creation of nine additional SOEs (Manzetti 1999, 65).

agency's own bureaucrats often informed afterward through the media.[21] The policy-making patterns at the BCRP and the MEF were similar, as the APRA literally battled out intraparty rivalries within the state financial institutions.

Despite García's stated intention to reform Peru's corrupt public administration, the filtering of the APRA party into the state bureaucracy brought out the worst traits in both. With the APRA having taken over with a sixty-year backlog of pent-up political patronage from within the party, the spoils of office augmented the APRA's clientelistic tendencies and enhanced intraparty conflicts that had been temporarily assuaged by the prospects of finally winning the presidency. The older party bosses, not entirely at ease with García's fast pace and independent leadership style, frequently challenged state policy decisions on these grounds alone. The younger APRA generation, with an eye toward permanently maintaining the party's new hegemonic presence as the prime force in Peruvian electoral politics, undermined party cohesion and the overall policy-making process by going to battle early over the crucial question of who would succeed García.

The eruption of the biggest rivalry, between the president and APRA finance minister Luis Alva Castro, resulted in the latter's resignation and a mass firing of his managerial counterparts within the BCRP in mid-1987. This politically motivated personnel overhaul and marginalization of the more economically astute central bank was disheartening, as this was the one state financial institution that had been intentionally cultivated to play a more autonomous and stabilizing role in the policy process.

The Consequences of Heterodox Policy

Through this analysis of Peru's second major attempt at economic restructuring, it is possible to separate out two kinds of outcomes. The first outcomes are rather abstract and have to do with the interplay among economic crisis, state structures, and policy making under the García administration. The second outcomes are more concrete and relate to the dire political-economic situation that followed the heterodox program upon its demise in late 1987. While the latter must be seen as an accumulation of problems that had been festering since the 1960s, this period post-1987 is widely seen as having more firmly cemented a political economy of violence in Peru. On this last

---

21. My interviews with midlevel bureaucrats at the INP during this time revealed that the economic program was weakly rooted there, both as a development model and as a concrete plan of action. Although the INP still housed the ECLAC "heterodox line" upon which it was founded in the 1960s, for these frontline state planners in Peru during the mid-1980s, heterodoxy seemed more a matter of not going back to the IMF.

point, the discussion will focus on the more volatile socioeconomic impacts of García's state-led strategy.

State Structures, Economic Crisis, and Heterodox Policy

On the interplay of these three factors, the similarities between Peru's first attempt at economic restructuring, under Velasco, and the García era are striking. Under both experiments, the purposeful resort to statist policy approaches was preceded by economic crisis and then seriously undermined by the poor political capacity of the state to intervene in fostering higher levels of productive growth. Referring back to two of the institutional preconditions for effective policy reform discussed in chapter 1—political insulation of state policy makers and the consolidation of state economic institutions—the analysis reveals that the contingencies over time in Peru had been just the reverse of what was called for.

Political insulation during this period correlated less with state capacity or autonomy and more with unaccountable and loosely linked administrative structures controlled by special interests. At the highest levels of government—for example, the technocratic team surrounding the president—insulation led to isolation and hence fragility (Stepan 1978, 301). Similarly, the technical discontinuity and entrenched clientelistic norms that prevailed within the economic institutions of the state rendered them almost residual as points of causal analysis in the policy-making process.

Yet, at the same time, the García period shows how state-led expansion and interventionist reforms, while making economic management more chaotic and unruly, also politicized economic issues, thereby setting in motion those organizational bases within civil society that are also essential components for shaping a state's capacity to act. The inability of all groups to find effective representation had to do with the incipient nature of these organizations and, even more so, with the tentative structures of the state. In fact, one of the greatest lessons of García's attempt to form a more cohesive alliance between the state and society was the extent to which the Peruvian state—as a coherent set of administrative, political, and economic structures—was still very much the missing actor.

These observations provide part of the explanation for the outcomes of the program, which, if we were to ignore the "new" heterodox label altogether, looked more like a blueprint of the mid-1950s populist meltdown that marked the end of Juan Perón's first administration in Argentina. There, the use of extended price controls and the expansion of wages and government spending met with brief initial success in terms of income redistribution and the moderation of inflation, only to be quickly followed by accelerating inflation and a backsliding in distributive gains (Foxley 1983, 4). The results, under both Perón and García, stemmed from policy packages plagued with internal inconsistencies and erratic implementation.

Viewing the outcomes of the heterodox experiment from the angle of the economic crisis as another critical juncture for Peru, John Ikenberry (1988, 224) nicely summarizes the ways in which "crisis acts as a solvent, throwing into relief discontinuities between underlying social forces and existing institutions." It is these episodic ruptures that prompt a reshaping of social relations and changes in institutional structure. Critical junctures can help drive institution building and, in turn, revitalize the policy-making process (Grindle 1996). In Peru, domestic responses to the crisis amounted to half of this equation. Political alliances were broken and reconstituted across the various sectors of civil society, as all groups struggled to defend their interests. Even in the wake of the heterodox program, the response within civil society and the private sector, in particular, had been to strengthen representative organizations and to formulate a more cohesive set of policy demands (Durand 1994; Stokes 1991).

But the relationship between this greater social determination to organize and the political will for building up the institutional capacities of the state was an asymmetrical one. Beginning with the Mexican Revolution, Latin American history is full of similar junctures where domestic elites "have seized the political initiative . . . and set down the initial orientations of the state by devising an array of institutions which embody their ideological vision" (Bennett and Sharpe 1980, 183). But each case shows that the internal strengthening of the institutions of the state does not follow naturally from the displacement of the ancien régime, as policy makers in Peru have frequently presumed; rather, this requires a conscious decision and a long-term purposeful effort on the part of a broad alliance of domestic actors.

Political alliances in Peru during the 1980s instead focused on the forging of social pacts between the state and representatives of business, labor, the military, and the rural sector. The resulting policy paralysis can be attributed to a number of political, economic, and institutional factors that have been discussed throughout this study. Yet the paralysis is also testimony to the failure of social pacts to smooth over the political struggles intrinsic to this diverse group of actors or to substitute for the kinds of internal reform and building up of administrative capacities that would be necessary prerequisites for instituting broad structural change. Many of the social pacts made during the democratic transition period in the early 1980s were at best tenuous, upsetting the wishful notion shared by many democratizing societies that the necessary changes can be ushered in free of conflict.

The Institutionalization of Political Violence

As for the socioeconomic impact of the heterodox program, the costs could not have been higher, particularly for those very groups whom the program was supposed to favor. Given the prevalence of poverty-based violence in the sierra region, the government's immediate aim had been to raise the living standard of that region's primarily self-employed agricultural producers. Through massive subsidies and price supports, the strategy succeeded, with a 75 percent improvement in the rural versus urban terms of trade by 1986.[22] As a result of the overall employment and income policy, the formal sector of the economy saw a 10 percent expansion in the rate of employment, and the public-sector wage bill increased from 7.9 percent of GDP in 1985 to 8.7 percent in 1987.

But by late 1987 most of these gains had begun to erode. The rural versus urban terms of trade dropped back to the same low pre-1985 level, and real wages began to descend in the wake of massive inflation (see table 14). In short, the positive gains had only been realized at the expense of large financial and external imbalances. The public-sector deficit reached 11.2 percent of GDP by 1988, due mainly to the collapse of the tax system. While García had followed through on his commitment to initiate a major income-tax reform in 1986, only 4 percent of the economically active population declared personal tax liabilities that year. As Peter Klarén (2000, 389) notes, in 1987 "three times as many Ecuadorians and twelve times as many Chileans (in relation to the total population) filed income tax returns as did Peruvians." And contrary to the previous periods studied here, public investment accounted for little of the deficit. In the absence of foreign financing, state capital formation slumped to the average levels witnessed in the 1950s (4 percent of GDP).

In the end, with the drop in public investment, the shrinking of the tax base, and the overly expansionist budget, the government quickly lost whatever opportunities the partial debt moratorium may have afforded to chart the economy on a course of sustainable and more equitable growth. As economic adjustment became imperative, the government embarked on a series of reform packages throughout 1988 with the stated goal of equally distributing the adjustment burden among all social groups. But the packages, four in all, were mainly erratic and insufficient one-shot fixes based on hikes in publicly controlled prices, currency devaluations, and interest-rate adjustments. As annual inflation approached 2000 percent by late 1988, what had been promised as an orderly adjustment gave way to a chaotic and highly regressive

---

22. Statistical trends and data cited in this section derive from World Bank 1989.

distribution of the costs of stabilization under the thrust of hyperinflation.[23] Spending on human capital was a main casualty of the crisis, as teachers' salaries and current expenditures on education for 1990 were one-fifth lower than in 1975 (Sheahan 1999, 21).

Meanwhile, political violence had now become a permanent fact of everyday life in Peru. On the economic front, guerrilla hostilities had extended to the foreign sector, with major attacks on such local multinational subsidiaries as the Nissan assembly plant and the Lima offices of the Bank of Tokyo. The attacks on state infrastructure, agriculture cooperatives, and technological research centers also heightened, as did the assassinations of those employed in such endeavors. Of the roughly 9,000 official deaths that were registered during the 1980s, some 235 were of ranking government officials. The overall effect was to further weaken the capacity of the state to manage the economy, as qualified managers became increasingly deterred from assuming the responsibility of government service under such high stakes.[24]

On the political front, the insurgency was clearly no longer just an Andean phenomenon. Terrorist actions in Lima were now estimated to account for 50 percent of the total activity, and Sendero had also infiltrated the jungle region, forming an apparent marriage of convenience with local drug traffickers. By 1990, this political violence had become institutionalized across broad segments of civil society. This was apparent, first, from the increasing number of insurgent groups apart from Sendero, such as the Tupac Amaru Revolutionary Movement and the Rodrigo Franco Command, that had so willingly taken up arms against the state; and second, from the role that the armed forces had come to play both in fighting the various guerrilla insurgents and in jumping onto the terrorist bandwagon themselves. Despite García's commitment to reverse the previous administration's policy of fighting terror with terror, the indiscriminate use of force by the military had now become commonplace in the designated emergency zones. Questions about the fate of two thousand to three thousand persons believed to have disappeared at the hands of either the guerrillas or the military since 1980, and numerous other instances of group massacres known to have occurred, simply went unanswered (Obando 1998).[25]

Not surprisingly, in a 1988 survey commissioned by the Peruvian Senate

---

23. Throughout the literature, the usual rule of thumb on measuring hyperinflation is a rate of 40 to 50 percent a month. For a more thorough analysis of these economic technicalities under the García administration, see World Bank 1989.

24. "SL's Urban Political War Indicating Increased Military Presence in Government Anti-Terrorist Decisions," *Andean Report,* June 1988, 140–43; "1988: A Peak Year for Subversion," *Peru Report,* Feb. 1989, 70–72.

25. "Peru in Peril: The Economy and Human Rights, 1985–1987," Washington Office on Latin America, Nov. 1987.

Committee on Violence and National Pacification, the majority of the respondents pointed to the highly deficient security policy and the need to alleviate the plight of the country's economically marginal masses as the two greatest challenges facing Peru in the 1990s.[26] The survey, which involved 8,133 interviews throughout the country, showed that most Peruvians favored social change, the provision of greater economic opportunities for youths, and the pursuit of a national peace accord as the only way to halt the political violence. In other words, the majority of the respondents still endorsed what the García administration had set out to accomplish. The fact that it had failed miserably set the political winds in another direction, as the results of the November 1989 nationwide municipal elections soon showed.

Reconstructing a Development Coalition

In the two-year interim between the 1987 bank nationalization and the November 1989 nationwide municipal elections, the FREDEMO, formed under the leadership of famed Peruvian novelist Mario Vargas Llosa, enabled one last comeback for the dormant sectors of the AP and the PPC. Again espousing the implementation of the social-market model that had been written into the 1979 constitution, the FREDEMO coalition captured 37 percent of the nationwide municipal vote in the November 1989 electoral contest. The IU took another 21 percent of the vote, and the APRA 13 percent.[27] The lack of a significant majority outcome in the November 1989 vote indicated the difficulty that all of the participants would have in capturing the presidency with the same winner-take-all outcomes that had occurred for the AP-PPC in 1980 or the APRA in 1985. This was confirmed by the remarkable outcome of the 1990 presidential race, where Vargas Llosa lost to the relatively unknown Alberto Fujimori, whose backing had come together in a loose coalition (Cambio 90) just a couple of months before the vote.

Putting aside the question of the depth of its support, the FREDEMO did succeed in reviving the liberal economic debate in Peru for the first time in nearly a decade. Drawing on many of the ideas put forth in Hernando de Soto's (1989) regional bestseller *El otro sendero,* Vargas Llosa projected an economic scenario whereby the drastic reduction in government regulation would unleash the country's true entrepreneurial forces and bring a booming informal sector into the legal economy. Grassroots capitalism on the home-

---

26. "National Survey of Attitudes to Violence," *Peru Report,* Aug. 1988, 7–7.

27. "Los otros ganadores," *Caretas,* Nov. 14, 1989, 18–25; "Elecciones en Lima: Cifras testarudas," *QueHacer,* Dec. 1989–Jan. 1990.

front was to be bolstered by the country's reinsertion into the international economy, which would revive private investment. On the surface, this latest turn of political-economic events in Peru resembled the Southern Cone pattern of erratic flip-flops between populism and orthodoxy during the post–World War Two period (Dornbusch and Edwards 1991). Yet, at a more penetrating level, this turn to orthodoxy and its embracement by a politically ascendant "new right" was not such a cut-and-dried matter.

As with the country's social-market endeavor of the early 1980s, the FREDEMO's liberal economic thrust seemed more a reaction against the statist excesses of the García era, rather than a new consensus over how to actually approach the country's formidable problems. This becomes apparent when the coalition is broken down into its component parts. Apart from the economically orthodox Vargas Llosa faction was a more moderate segment of domestic capital that favored a gradual adjustment strategy.[28] There were also populists who had rallied behind Belaúnde and who had already begun haggling with FREDEMO hardliners over the proposed privatization targets.[29] Finally, there was the country's burgeoning mass of small-scale entrepreneurs, who remained apart from the FREDEMO for reasons of ethnicity and socioeconomic position (Brysk and Wise 1997). The basic disaffection of this group, as well as the popular sectors, perhaps best explains the inability of the FREDEMO to prevent the presidency from falling into the hands of independents.

Conclusion

The previous three chapters charted the rise of the Peruvian state sector since the 1960s and along with this the evolution of a problematic pattern related to state expansion that had acted as a political-economic undertow to state-centered and market-oriented development strategies alike. The pattern, as described in chapter 1 and reiterated throughout this book, has to do with a strong dependence on external financing and a neglect of crucial macroeconomic policy variables against the cushion of foreign savings; a heavy reliance on state enterprises to provide employment and cheap inputs and services, with little regard for their productivity and profitability; the perpetuation of a conflictual relationship with domestic capitalists, who have benefited greatly from government largesse but have held back their investments due to all the macroeconomic uncertainties and the state's obvious administrative weaknesses; and finally, social policies that have consistently taken a back seat to the pressing need to shore up the productive structure.

28. "CADE 89," *El Comercio*, Dec. 2, 1989, B9.

29. "Mario Vargas Llosa Edges Ahead in the Presidential Election Race and the Democratic Front Prepares to Divide the Spoils," *Andean Report*, May 1989, 143.

The present chapter finds the country at a particularly painful juncture, whereby the resolution of the worst symptoms of state intervention had become a prerequisite for reestablishing relations with the international financial community, not to mention fending off a full-blown civil war on the domestic front. This was true for each of the four aspects of the pattern mentioned earlier. Although the strong reliance on external borrowing was never the same option for García, he fully exhausted the debt alternative by obtaining de facto financing with the unilateral moratorium on debt payments (World Bank 1989, xxv). The consequent outbreak of hyperinflation demanded that some action be taken in the way of solid macroeconomic policy reforms. Without such reforms, there was zero chance of reducing inflation or attracting foreign loans and increases in multilateral aid. The García recipe, where hyperinflation was left to do the dirty work of economic adjustment, turned out to be political suicide.

As in the 1970s and the early 1980s, the domestic debate over how to proceed with economic adjustment wavered between a draconian shock treatment and a more gradual approach to stabilization (Dornbusch and Edwards 1991, 45–46). The former strategy, which implied rapid increases in real revenue at the expense of short-term output and real wages, would surely throw fire on what had emerged as one of the region's most volatile domestic battles. Pursuit of the latter, more cautious course left policy makers in the same situation that they had faced since 1985—that is, the need to seek a broad support base for adjustment from the country's diverse social, economic, and political groups, as well as to insure that the poorest segments of the population were not left to bear the brunt of the adjustment effort. This very scenario, unfortunately, turned out to be the García era's main legacy: incredibly high human costs, particularly for the very poorest.

In the context of the 1990 presidential campaign, some strands of the development debate directly took on these pressing problems. For example, the FREDEMO coalition emphasized the need for macroeconomic reform and to restore full relations with the foreign sector. Likewise, there was a renewed concern for cleaning up the mess in the SOE sector once and for all. Finally, missing in the electoral dialogue were the two elements most likely to make a future program work: broad consensus over an economic-adjustment strategy and a much deeper commitment to equitably distributing the costs. The increasing polarization between right and left, orthodox and heterodox, indicated that domestic groups were still at a loss over how to face the country's problems head-on—hence the election of a maverick independent candidate who would steer the Peruvian political economy in yet another dramatic direction for the entire decade of the 1990s.

PART 3

Reinventing the State

CHAPTER 6

Neoliberalism and State Reconstruction

Another About-Face: Peru Joins the "Washington Consensus"

With the country having defaulted on service payments for its public and private external debt during the García years, it took President Alberto Fujimori just ten days after his inauguration in July 1990 to realize that he had, in fact, zero room to maneuver in implementing a gradualist reform strategy. Fujimori's campaign platform, for example, had originally called for administered prices, a downsized but activist state, and an economic strategy geared toward fostering labor-intensive microindustries (Stokes 1996a, 61). But like other leaders elected at this time on similar platforms, such as Venezuela's Carlos Andrés Pérez and Argentina's Carlos Menem (Corrales 2000a), both of whom moved immediately in launching market-shock programs, Fujimori followed suit. Hence, Peru quickly adopted the package of stabilization and adjustment measures based on liberalization, privatization, and deregulation that had come to be coined the "Washington Consensus" (Williamson 1990). Seemingly overnight, the country went from rogue state to model reformer.

The president's initial success in conquering inflation and restoring growth under a market strategy went a long way toward securing support for him among voters of all political persuasions. Add to this the capture and imprisonment of Sendero's core leadership by late 1992, and the stage was set early on for Fujimori's election to a second term. However, in contrast to other leaders, such as Argentina's Carlos Menem and Brazil's Fernando Henrique Cardoso, Fujimori went so far as to suspend congress and the constitution in April 1992 rather than negotiate his reform measures through the democratic channels upheld by these other civilian presidents. Although formal democratic rule had been restored by the time of Fujimori's 1995 reelection bid, it was, ironically, these heavy-handed politics, bolstered by the economic recovery of the early 1990s, that won the president his second term.

Throughout his tenure in office, Fujimori resorted to the selective distribution of subsidies and other economic incentives (Graham and Kane 1998) and to the masterful use of public-opinion polls to maintain his following (Conaghan 1995). While military backing, a risk-averse civil society, and the president's own political cunning all go a long way toward explaining the

Fujimori phenomenon, less obvious are the factors that contributed to the comparatively successful economic trends that were discussed in the introduction to this book. As table 1 shows, Peru held its own along with Argentina and Chile during the 1990s in terms of its annual average rates of growth of GDP and gross domestic investment. Similarly, Peru's annual rates of growth in employment and real wages outpaced those of much larger and more developed economies, such as Brazil and Mexico.

As tempting as it may be to attribute this impressive turnaround to free markets and quasi-authoritarian rule, this chapter points to a quiet process of state reconstruction and institutional reform that occurred over the course of the 1990s. This explanation may seem paradoxical, given that Fujimori had become best known for his fierce independence and resistance to institutionalizing his own support base or the state's ties with civil society (Roberts 1995). However, having inherited Latin America's most volatile political economy in 1990, the president had little choice but to overhaul those state institutions that were crucial for economic recovery and hence his own political survival. Included in these renovations, for example, were longstanding financial entities like the BCRP and the MEF, which were essential for the successful completion of the macroeconomic stabilization effort.

Another key aspect of institutional reform in the early 1990s was the reinvention and/or creation of new state entities geared toward achieving the longer-term goals of economic restructuring along market lines. The purposes of these longer-term institutional goals were, first, to modernize and sustain the state's revenue stream at levels that would allow for the proper provision of essential public goods while at the same time reducing the prohibitive levels of government-held debt; and second, to rationalize the new market-based development strategy through the design of institutions that sought to guarantee property rights and to promote a competitive business environment. In essence, Peru's economic turnaround is testimony to a pattern of "autonomous" institutional reform that has entailed the siphoning off of strategic pockets of the public sector and the management of these units as if they were private entities (Nuñes and Geddes 1987; Keefer 1995).

Over time, it was precisely the autonomous nature of these state agencies that would put them at odds with the office of the executive.[1] In other words, the institutional underpinnings of Peru's economic recovery were as much inadvertent as they were a purposive part of the designated economic strategy under Fujimori.[2] Just as the RGAF was directly responsible for organizing

---

1. Having created these agencies, the president was steadfast in resisting further reforms that would diminish his direct control over them—for example, the staggering of agency directorships such that the time line of appointments did not coincide exactly with the executive's own five-year term.

2. I owe this insight to Richard Webb.

those base groups within civil society that later emerged as the main catalyst for the transition to democracy in the late 1970s (Sanborn 1991), so too did the Fujimori administration infuse new technocratic vigor and professional life into state agencies that could carry the reform project forward into the post-Fujimori era. Because this modernization process has yet to fully penetrate the sectoral ministries, the state bureaucracy at large, or the legal-juridical apparatus, the degree of institutional reform achieved thus far constitutes a necessary but not entirely sufficient condition for more dynamic, equitable, and sustainable growth in Peru.

This latter set of challenges goes to the very heart of the reform tasks inherited by the administration of President Alejandro Toledo in June 2001. As economic growth tapered off in 1998 and 1999, Peru arrived at the same crossroads that other emerging-market countries like Argentina, Chile, and Mexico had arrived at somewhat earlier: full economic revival would require deeper institutional reform in numerous areas (tax collection, the financial system, social policy, the administration of justice, and respect for the rule of law), as well as a more inclusive and encompassing development coalition to move these policies forward.

Yet, rather than broaden the reform coalition in ways that would facilitate the wider participation and input demanded by second-phase reforms, the Fujimori cohort closed ranks in the guise of offering apolitical technical solutions to these more recent patterns of economic stress. A deeper problem was that the everyday concerns of political survival and the burden of constantly defending a decade-long incumbency distracted the ruling coalition from articulating a cohesive development strategy for the longer term. Whereas this very coalition was once a source of confidence in the country's improved investment ratings, and a signal to the electorate that things were on track, it increasingly came to be perceived by domestic and international observers alike as a main source of uncertainty.[3]

The following sections of this chapter chart the progress of Peru's political-economic turnaround in the 1990s from three angles: the rise and fall of the Fujimori coalition; the timing and sequencing of market reforms; and the institutional transformations that underpinned the reform process. The analysis will show that, in all but the distributional arena, those most pressing problems related to state-led development inherited from the 1960s, 1970s, and 1980s have basically been resolved. Moreover, Peru's "first phase" of market reform based on liberalization, privatization, and deregulation has been completed. With the inauguration of the Toledo administration in July

---

3. Alfredo Thorne, "Peru after the Presidential Election," *Global Data Watch*, Banco de J. P. Morgan, S.A., June 2, 2000, 17–18.

2001 an essential round of "second-phase" market reforms remained to be tackled, along with a more penetrating effort at institutional modernization. The final sections of this chapter speak directly to these tasks and to the kinds of political coalitions that are now necessary to achieve them.

The Political-Economic Backdrop: Military Resurgence and Market Reforms

Just as the magnitude of the prevailing social violence and economic collapse would have been unthinkable a decade earlier, so too would the election of a candidate like Fujimori who had virtually no ties to the country's established political parties and *criollo* elite. Indeed, the coalition of traditional conservative parties that had rallied around Mario Vargas Llosa was stunned by its defeat at the hands of an outsider who had been outspent by a ratio of more than sixty to one (Marcus-Delgado 1999).[4] The final tally in the second round of voting, which gave Vargas Llosa 37.6 percent to Fujimori's 62.4 percent, suggested an even more profound political realignment than had occurred in 1983. However, the partyless nature of this political shift, Fujimori's lack of clearly stated positions, and the unexpected tenacity of the newly elected president would pose new opportunities and constraints for political-economic management in the 1990s.

At face value, Fujimori drew most of his support from the country's silent majority: low-income voters, small-business owners, workers in the informal economy, and evangelical Protestants. In all, Fujimori captured the majority of the country's poorest districts in both the urban and the rural areas, while Vargas Llosa mainly carried the middle- and upper-class districts within Lima and the other major cities (Roberts and Arce 1998; Marcus-Delgado 1999). Given the trauma of hyperinflation and an all-out civil war, this electoral triumph of poor over rich and countryside over city should perhaps not have been such a surprise. Rather, it was further confirmation of the widening chasm between the state and civil society (Crabtree 1998, 20) and a wake-up call concerning the utter failure of the standing political parties to properly mediate between the two.

In hindsight, the transformation that had occurred within the Peruvian military over the course of the 1980s also lent momentum to the Fujimori phenomenon. By virtue of the increased role that the various branches of the

---

4. In his memoir Vargas Llosa (1994, 434) reflects back on this phenomenon: "I asked who this Alberto Fujimori was, who now, only ten days before the election, seemed to begin to exist as a candidate, and where he came from. Up until then I don't believe I'd given a single thought to him, or ever heard anyone mention him in the analyses and projected results of the election."

armed forces had come to play in combating the country's guerrilla insurgencies and exploding drug trade (Mauceri 1996, 136–41), a new generation of military leaders sought a more active role in domestic politics. Prior to the 1990 presidential race the military had drawn up the "Green Book," its first sweeping plan of action since the early days of the RGAF (Maxwell Cameron 1997, 51). But in contrast to the RGAF's nationalist-reformist project, military leaders of the late 1980s called for the implementation of market reforms with solid backing from business, government, and the military, as well as "a strong government that would last 20 years if necessary" (Crabtree 1998, 21–22; Obando 1998). While Fujimori's last-minute ascendance in the 1990 race took everyone by surprise, including the military, the armed forces could not have found a better candidate to fulfill their newly articulated vision for Peru.

The "First Phase" of Market Reform

As seen in table 14, by 1990 the arrows on growth, investment, and inflation had all moved radically in the wrong direction. Similarly, Peru's current account deficit continued to hover at an all-time high, and the overvaluation of the exchange rate exacerbated this trend. Public finances had literally collapsed under the thrust of the heterodox program, and the assessments on the damage inflicted by the country's various guerrilla insurgencies were now running in the range of US$22 billion (Manzetti 1999, 232). At the outset of the Fujimori administration more than 50 percent of the population was classified as living in poverty, and half of those fell into the category of "chronic and extreme" poverty (Sheahan 1999, 108). With the greater infiltration of patronage appointments from the ranks of the main political parties during the 1980s, Peru's available pool of public-sector expertise had also hit an all-time low.

Thus, similar to the other market reformers discussed in chapter 1, once the decision was made to finally buckle down with a strict stabilization program, the policy package moved forward with little debate and just a handful of advisors. To the extent that a policy debate did occur, it was in the form of a "Plan for Economic Stabilization and Growth" that was generated by a group of the country's most talented economists in conjunction with Professor Jeffrey Sachs of Harvard University (Paredes and Sachs 1991). Although academic economists and private-sector consultants had actively shaped the policy-reform debate in Argentina, Brazil, Chile, and Mexico during the 1990s, in Peru such links between the government and the professional economics community were still comparatively weak (Conaghan 1998). Hence, the Fujimori team paid little heed to these proposals and instead opted for the Washington Consensus blueprint (Gonzáles 1998), as this was deemed the quickest way to reduce inflation and entice desperately needed foreign capital back into Peru. It is interesting to note that the Paredes-Sachs plan also fell firmly within the Washington Consensus camp, but it raised additional issues concerning the exchange-rate regime, the proper sequencing of market-reform measures, and the need to provide an adequate social cushion for adjustment.

On the stabilization front, the main challenge was to rationalize macro-economic policy making after years of haphazard management. The first crucial step was to purge the country of hyperinflation; this was approached by way of a tight monetary policy, draconian spending cuts aimed at reducing public-sector deficits, and the unification of the multitiered exchange rate. Virtually overnight, government-controlled prices and subsidies were lifted on everything from gasoline and utilities to sugar, rice, and medicines. Between August 1990 and February 1991, emergency taxes were introduced, a new managed floating-exchange-rate system was established around the unified rate, domestic credit was tightened, and interest-rate ceilings were basically lifted (Paredes 1991, 301).

While similar measures had brought a swift end to Bolivia's hyperinflation several years earlier (Pastor 1992), table 15 shows that this was not the case with Peruvian hyperinflation. A main difference between Peru's approach and Bolivia's was the Fujimori team's insistence on moving to a floating-exchange-rate system at the outset.[5] Whereas the Bolivian program had relied on devaluation and the initial fixing of the exchange rate to the U.S. dollar in order to provide a nominal anchor for price stabilization, the fate of Peru's stabilization depended on the ability of the financial authorities to properly manage the new floating-exchange-rate regime. As table 15 shows, the combined reliance on a floating exchange rate, tight credit, and market-driven prices and interest rates created further pressures for inflation and exchange-rate appreciation. The BCRP's attempts to reverse these trends through intervention in the foreign-exchange market turned out to be part of the problem: a haphazardly managed "dirty float" greatly increased the recessionary costs of the program without fully rectifying the basic problems.

In order to quicken the pace of economic adjustment Fujimori brought in Carlos Boloña as minister of economy and finance in February 1991. Boloña was a Ph.D. economist with strong neoliberal credentials who forged ahead

5. As Paredes (1991, 309) notes, "The alternative of correcting the initial overvaluation of the currency through a large nominal devaluation and then using a fixed and fully convertible exchange rate as a nominal anchor . . . was disregarded from the start without a consistent and convincing argument."

TABLE 15. Macroeconomic and External Indicators in Peru: 1991–2000 (Fujimori's two terms)

	1991	1992	1993	1994	1995	1996	1997	1998	1999	2000
GDPGRO	7.1	-1.8	6.4	13.1	7.5	2.5	6.8	0.3	1.4	3.6
GNPPCGRO	19.1	-9.0	4.5	11.2	5.8	0.8	5.0	-3.3		3.8
INF	409.5	73.5	48.6	23.7	11.1	11.5	8.6	7.2	3.5	3.8
PRIVGDP	11.7	12.0	13.4	16.8	19.6	18.8	20.8	20.7		
PUBIGDP	2.7	3.1	3.4	4.2	4.3	3.8	3.8	3.8		
INVEST	14.5	15.2	16.8	21.0	23.9	22.6	24.6	24.5		
RER	79.8	75.0	81.6	73.8	70.4	70.3	70.3	70.4	79.2	83.3
TRADEBAL	-188	-341	-605	-999	-2,166	-1,987	-1,723	-2,463	-617	-335
CURACCT	-1,500	-2,087	-2,287	-2,555	-4,117	-3,429	-3,056	-3,638.0	-1,822	-1,648
FDI	-7	150	687	3,108	2,048	3,242	2,697	1,881	1,969	558
PORT			201	492	159	181	156	-348	-372	-423
DEBT	20,716	20,338	23,573	26,528	30,852	29,328	30,523	32,397	29,100	30,300

Source: GDP, GNP, and debt are from World Bank, *World Tables*, CD-ROM, 2000, except 1999 and 2000 GDP growth and debt are from Economist Intelligence Unit Country Reports (March and April 2001) and GNP per capita data are from the Inter-American Development Bank Web site (<www.iadb.org>). Data on investment are from Bouton and Sumlinski 2001 <www.ifc.org/economics/pubs/discuss.htm>. Inflation, exchange rates, and payments are calculated from IMF 2001, 1998 current account data and Peruvian FDI and portfolio investment are from Inter-American Development Bank Web site (<www.iadb.org>).

Note: GDPGRO = growth of real GDP; GNPPCGRO = growth of real per capita GNP; INF = Dec.–Dec. inflation; PRIVGDP = private investment as % of GDP; PUBIGDP = public investment as % of GDP; INVEST = total domestic investment as % of GDP; RER = real exchange rate (1990 = 100), calculated using period average exchange rate, U.S. WPI, and domestic CPI; TRADEBAL = trade balance (mil$) = merchandise exports − merchandise imports; CURACCT = current account (mil$); FDI = foreign direct investment (mil$); PORT = foreign portfolio investment (mil$); DEBT = total external debt (mil$).

with the implementation of deeper structural reforms and the renegotiation of the country's external debt. During the first half of 1991, tariffs on trade were reduced to a maximum of 25 percent; the capital account of the balance of payments was liberalized; numerous labor-market regulations left over from the military regime were eliminated; land-tenure laws were amended to offer a broader scope for private initiative; the tax code was broadened and simplified; and the sale of some twenty-three SOEs was announced (Paredes 1991, 313–15; Boloña 1996). By 1990 there had been a general consensus in the policy community that the adoption of structural reforms of this magnitude in the midst of the initial stabilization plan could detract from achieving the goals of the plan (Edwards 1990). Nevertheless, the economic team proceeded apace, apparently convinced that the benefits of launching the entire range of structural reforms simultaneously, along with mending Peru's relations with its external creditors, would outweigh the potential threat to the stabilization effort.

After unilaterally resuming payments to service the debt, the government initiated negotiations for settling the arrears it had run up with all the main multilateral lenders. This was a hurdle that had to be overcome before Peruvian policy makers could reschedule some US$8 billion in debt with the consortium of Western country debtors known as the Paris Club, not to mention another US$9.2 billion in commercial-bank debt. However, the president's decision to take matters into his own hands in April 1992—by closing the congress, suspending the constitution, and dismantling the judiciary—threw a quick wrench into any of the planned debt rescheduling. The Paris Club, in particular, insisted on a credible timetable for the restoration of democratic rule as a precondition for the rescheduling of Peru's debt.

The Civilian Coup and Its Aftermath

As the economic program moved into its second year, there was still some question as to whether the particular strategy in place would be the one to stabilize inflation and trigger an economic recovery.[6] At the same time, the various guerrilla insurgencies and violent civil-military confrontations that had endured for more than a decade still showed no signs of abating: estimates suggested that more than twenty-six thousand lives had already been claimed. It was ostensibly this security threat that prompted the April 1992 civilian coup and the heightened tensions between the executive and the legislature over the former's effort to further increase the military's role in eradicating the guerril-

---

6. This section draws on Cotler 1995; Stokes 1996a; Maxwell Cameron 1997; Crabtree 1998; and McClintock 1989.

las. But Peru's democratic rupture also had to do with the president's attempt to carve out a role for himself as an almost purely "managerial executive."[7]

Having launched his presidency with a fairly eclectic cabinet and group of advisors, Fujimori switched within the first year to surrounding himself with independents who were nonthreatening and readily amenable to his point of view. This was especially so when it came to ministerial appointments. Simultaneously, the president forged an ever stronger political alliance with the armed forces and with the National Intelligence Service (SIN) in particular. By early 1992, it had become apparent that the president had a low threshold for the usual congressional checks on executive power. Although both Belaúnde and García had taken full advantage of their constitutional privilege to legislate by executive decrees during set periods specified by congress, both also had promoted their policy proposals through the majority party coalitions that each held at the time. Fujimori, in contrast, showed little interest in coalition building, policy debate, or the legislative process.

The president's preference for ruling by executive fiat was confirmed in April 1992, when he issued Legislative Decree 25418, which announced that he would do just that. The decree, which officially dissolved congress, the 1979 constitution, and the court system, also created the "Government of Emergency and National Reconstruction." Although it was a shock to international observers, hindsight shows that the warning lights concerning this radical decision had actually been blinking for several months prior to the coup. In late 1991, for example, congress resisted executive orders that sought to limit the freedom of the press and to greatly extend the military's power in fighting the counterinsurgency effort in the country's numerous emergency zones. These unresolved conflicts, combined with the president's rejection of social-expenditure requests put forward by congress, prompted the latter to pass a February 1992 law geared toward limiting the executive's powers. Thus, with the April 1992 coup the president showed his true political colors: a preference for military cronies and a stronger sense of obligation to the armed forces than to upholding democratic principles.

After turning to the likes of SIN director and former army captain Vladimiro Montesinos and General Nicolás Hermoza Ríos, head of the Joint Command of the Armed Forces, as his closest advisors, Fujimori created a quasi-authoritarian civilian-military regime that would dominate politics throughout the decade. Again, international actors did not take kindly to the notion of a coup, civilian or otherwise, and it was external pressure that most

---

7. Although the New Public Management school uses this phrase in reference to managers who are more public-service and results oriented (Pollitt 1990), the Fujimori rendition of the managerial executive was quickly warped by the 1992 coup. At this point, it became difficult to distinguish between public service and executive maneuvers that privileged management itself.

compelled Fujimori to begin going through the motions of restoring democratic norms. At this point, politics and economics entered into an even more
complicated dance, which entailed three sets of elections between April 1992
and November 1993, as well as a third wave of executive decrees that sought
to deepen the process of structural reform (Boloña 1996; Gonzáles 1998). In
November 1992 delegates were selected for a Democratic Constitutional
Congress (CCD), which produced a new constitution that the country voted
on by referendum exactly a year later. In the midst of the CCD, nationwide
municipal elections were held in January 1993.

Although public opinion echoed resounding support for the president and
his rash actions, the vote in each of these elections was considerably more
cautious. The Fujimori coalition won just over half of the eighty seats that had
been put forth for the CCD, and the 1993 constitution passed by just over 52
percent of the vote. Despite the capture of Sendero's leader and mastermind,
Abimael Guzmán, by a small, elite counterterrorist squad in a Lima hideout
in September 1992, the Fujimori forces received little bounce from this victory in the January municipal elections. In fact, after sinking like a stone in
the public-opinion polls, Fujimori's candidate for mayor of Lima withdrew
from the race just prior to the election.

Thus, the neoliberal strategy was quickly pushed forward against a highly
ambivalent political backdrop. The president garnered broad public support
by hammering away at the moral corruption of the country's traditional legal
and political institutions. But subsequent voting patterns suggest that the
results of his political reform were not entirely embraced. The new constitution itself cast doubts in that it expanded the president's powers to dissolve
congress, to declare national states of exception, and to promote military personnel without congressional oversight (Stokes 1996a, 66; Gonzáles 1998,
44–45). Even more telling, in terms of the president's personal ambitions, was
a new constitutional clause that allowed for the executive's immediate reelection to a consecutive term and then further reelection after the lapse of one
term. Thus, as of late 1993, President Fujimori also became incumbent Fujimori, a turn of events that rendered solid economic performance and favorable public-opinion ratings of the utmost importance for the president's
political survival.

Economic Recovery and the Deepening of
Structural Reforms

As can be seen in table 15, the first convincing signs of economic recovery
appeared in 1993, as growth rates and investment (both private and public)

began to recuperate from the rock-bottom levels to which they had fallen during the García era. Moreover, for the first time in a decade, the annual inflation rate was below 50 percent. On the upside, because of the steep losses in personal income and the high levels of idle capacity that prevailed at the outset of the reform effort, there was considerable room for economic expansion. On the downside, the combination of rapid unilateral trade liberalization, tight monetary policy, and the continued appreciation of the exchange rate threw Peru's external accounts into disequilibrium (Gonzáles 1998).

While capital repatriation and a burst of privatization-related FDI helped to finance the current account deficit, the external gap increased nearly threefold between 1991 and 1995. Peruvian policy makers thus found themselves in similar straits as other market reformers in the region. Policy makers in Chile, and eventually Mexico and Brazil, moved to rectify these problems—for example, by adopting a more flexible and competitive exchange-rate regime and by more aggressively promoting an export-led model of growth (Wise 1999). In contrast, the Fujimori administration stood out for its insistence on a hands-off strategy and chose instead to assign the task of economic adjustment primarily to market forces.

Although this theme holds steady across the main components of the structural-reform program reviewed later, it does not detract from the integrity of this early stage of market restructuring in Peru. Rather, the problem of policy inflexibility reared its head later, when challenges from the external sector demanded a more nuanced or hands-on approach to market reform but policy responses moved in the opposite direction. In other words, although the institutional bases necessary to orchestrate a cohesive and effective economic policy response were finally being laid, an increasingly dominant president and his inner circle apparently came to associate political survival with a strict adherence to the economic laissez-faire that had marked this first phase of market reform in Peru.

Trade Liberalization

In setting the baseline for this study, chapter 2 showed that until 1963 Peru's economy had been far more open than that of the other top countries in the region. By 1990, the reversal of this liberal trade stance was such that the tariff structure had splintered into fifty-six different rates ranging from 10 to 110 percent; within this framework, 539 import items were banned outright (Rossini and Paredes 1991, 284–85). Thus, the trade regime inherited by the Fujimori administration fit the classic Latin American mold under ISI: commercial policy had largely fallen prey to those special interests that stood to lose most from the lowering of tariffs. The damage over the long run was a policy bias that favored industry over agriculture, fostered a distorted and inefficient manufacturing structure, and caused exports to stagnate. Between 1988 and 1990, Peru's industrial production had contracted by 30 percent (Abugattas 1998, 64), and the country's exports per capita were lower overall than they had been in the 1950s (Rossini and Paredes 1991, 285).

Despite steady pressure from the multilaterals to reduce trade barriers, policy makers had departed from this highly protectionist strategy just once—between 1978 and 1982—during the transition to civilian rule. By 1981, the average nominal tariff had been brought down to 32 percent, and 98 percent of all registered items could be imported freely (World Bank 1985, 48). On the export side, under the thrust of a depreciating exchange rate, export incentives applied through the CERTEX system, and increased participation in the Andean Pact, this period saw a fifteenfold increase in manufactured exports (Sheahan 1999, 50). However, with the advent of the 1982 debt shocks and the gradual appreciation of the exchange rate, protectionist interests again prevailed, and this brief experiment in trade liberalization came to an end.

In the wake of 1990s shocking hyperinflation, Peru, having once set the pace for protectionist trade and investment norms within the Andean Pact, now led the way as a champion of liberalization. By March 1991, nontariff barriers had been dismantled, and a dual tariff structure had been established under which 87 percent of tariff items were subject to a 15 percent tariff and the remainder to a 25 percent tariff (Boloña and Illescas 1997). In this sense Peru had quickly joined step with other emerging-market countries in the region, where unilateral trade liberalization had similarly been embraced both as a tool for promoting macroeconomic stabilization and as a means of forcing competitive changes at the microeconomic level (Wise 1998). But unlike these other reformers, who were more aggressive in coordinating macroeconomic policy with export promotion, Peruvian policy makers remained steadfastly committed to a hands-off economic policy.

Fiscal Shock

The data reviewed in chapter 1 on the Latin American state sector showed that by the mid-1990s Peru had recuperated from the outright fiscal collapse that had occurred a decade earlier. The rationalization of public finances was such that tax revenues had doubled from the depths of the García administration, when they had fallen to just 7 percent of GDP, reaching nearly 16 percent by the end of Fujimori's first term. At the same time, public expenditures were brought more realistically in line with tax revenues: the government deficit was less than 1 percent of GDP from 1990 to 1994, and public debt as a percentage of GDP—while still high by regional standards—had been reduced from nearly 50 percent in the mid-1980s to 32 percent in the mid-1990s. Three underlying factors contributed to Peru's fiscal overhaul, which was considered by some to be the most successful component of this first wave of structural reforms under Fujimori (Durand and Thorp 1998).

First, there was a recognition, once and for all, of the essential role that fiscal adjustment plays in sustaining a macroeconomic stabilization program to the extent that it is credible at home and abroad (Baca 2000). In the wake of hyperinflation, fiscal soundness was all the more important, as policy makers and economic agents could no longer hide behind inflation in the setting of completely unrealistic revenue targets. Second, deep institutional changes underpinned the tax reform that was carried out between 1991 and 1994, including a complete revamping of the national tax agency (SUNAT) and a strengthening of its capabilities in all areas of revenue collection (e.g., streamlining of the tax structure, creation and updating of tax rolls, technical-staff training, computerization, etc.).[8] Third, the increase in tax revenues was bolstered by the more stable base for economic recovery and higher growth that had been established as a result of the implementation of the entire package of structural reforms reviewed in this section.

As impressive as these advances have been, few inroads were made in shifting the tax structure toward greater reliance on direct taxation or taxes on income and property. Apart from the fierce political resistance by powerful economic groups to these more progressive tax categories, fiscal reform along these lines was further hampered by the very small percentage of Peruvians who were actually in the habit of paying taxes. To the government's credit, the number of income-tax returns filed rose from fewer than 200,000 in 1991 to more than 423,444 in 1994, yet 85 percent of the revenues collected came from less than three thousand large taxpayers (Durand and Thorp 1998, 221). Thus, while the tax structure had been simplified to just five categories (income tax, assets tax, excise duties, a housing and urban tax, and a value-added tax [VAT]), revenue collection depended disproportionately on indirect taxes and the tax on consumption (VAT) in particular. Peru is not unique in this respect, as the increased reliance on the more regressive VAT tax was a regionwide trend in the 1990s (ECLAC 1998, 67–71). But as the VAT came to account for 44 percent of all taxes collected by 1994, Peru's shift toward greater regressivity was compounded by preexisting inequities that were intrinsic to the tax structure at the outset of the reform.

---

8. See ECLAC 1998 for more detail on the bureaucratic and administrative aspects of the fiscal reform that has taken place in the region over the past decade.

Privatization

The fiscal collapse of the late 1980s also rendered privatization inevitable at this point. With the SOE share of GDP having peaked at more than 10 percent under García, operating losses amounting to more than US$500 million by 1989 could no longer be sustained (Manzetti 1999, 65). While the usual suspects lobbied for the same gradualist approach that had thwarted all earlier attempts at privatization in Peru, this time the executive's assertive elite-level decision-making style prevailed. In late 1991, with strong backing from Finance Minister Boloña and the multilaterals, a new privatization law was passed, and within a year the government's newly created privatization commission (COPRI) had begun to quickly unload state assets. In contrast to the footdragging and political charades that had surrounded previous efforts at privatization, COPRI staff moved forcefully in selling off some US$9.1 billion in state assets by the end of 2000. During Fujimori's first term, for example, seventy-two privatizations had been completed in such sectors as electricity, telecommunications, mining, industry, and banking, and the privatization program had generated commitments for another US$11.3 billion in private project investments (Araoz, Bonifaz, Casas, and González Vigil 2001, 40). What explains this abrupt departure from past practices?

Certainly the liberalization of Peru's foreign-investment regime and the overall economic recovery were important contributing factors, but it was the creation of COPRI and the long-overdue professionalization of the privatization strategy that accounted for these inroads (Franco, Muñoz, Sánchez, and Zavala 2000).[9] First, with the creation of COPRI, the legal guidelines for privatization were finally in place, the most important being an explicit set of instructions for assessing the value of individual firms and concrete procedures for divestiture. Second, the technical and financial expertise of COPRI's staff was such that the agency actively involved itself in the restructuring of companies to make them more attractive to potential buyers. Third, apart from better preparing state firms for sale and assisting in the preparation of proposals for financial backing, COPRI started its sell-off campaign with smaller firms, which are easier to unload; the strategy with the larger firms was to begin by offering stock options in a more piecemeal fashion. This latter approach represented a major difference from past efforts, which hinged on grand privatization schemes that simply stalled.

This is not to say that privatization's enemies had been completely neu-

---

9. These insights are based on my interviews conducted in Lima with two former COPRI directors, Carlos Montoya (interview with the author, May 25, 1992) and Manuel Llosa (interview with the author, July 18, 1995), and with COPRI official Carolina Castillo (interview with the author, Dec. 17, 1998).

tralized or that the strategy was free of problems. Along each step of the legislative way congressional foes sought to exclude key sectors such as mining and petroleum, which set the stage for a bruising fight over the privatization of Petroperu during the 1995 presidential campaign. This, in turn, helped to sour public opinion against the government's plan to sell off every last firm in its portfolio. Other problems, such as the challenge of raising sufficient funds to restructure the large number of SOEs that were in a semiliquid financial position, meant that potential buyers had to be guaranteed lucrative returns for some time to come. This made it all the more difficult to apply the kinds of antitrust criteria that typically prevail in the OECD countries: in the absence of a sufficient competitive policy to guide the process, the lack of transparency and solid financial information eased the way for new private owners to set above-market prices for public goods previously provided by the SOEs (e.g., transportation, electricity, telephones).[10]

Financial Reform

On the foreign front, financial reform meant completing the unfinished business of renegotiating Peru's outstanding debt and interest arrears with the multilaterals, the Paris Club, and the commercial banks. As a result of García's partial debt moratorium, Peru's debt had grown at an average annual rate of 6.8 percent between 1985 and 1989, as opposed to a 2 percent annual rate of increase for the rest of the region during this same period (Larrain and Sachs 1991, 228). Because the statutes of the IMF and the World Bank stipulated that no new credit could be obtained from these institutions by a country that had fallen into arrears on previous loans, policy makers began repairing Peru's damaged borrower status by negotiating with the IMF through its Rights Accumulation Program (Boloña 1996, 216). It took Fujimori's entire first term to restore Peru's good standing with the multilaterals. This, plus the reinstallation of democratic political procedures by 1995, then paved the way for the renegotiation of Peru's Paris Club debt in 1996 and the rescheduling of some US$10.6 billion in arrears and interest on the country's commercial debt under a Brady deal in 1997.

The remainder of the financial reforms involved a complete redefinition of

---

10. In March 1993 the National Institute for the Defense of Competition and Protection of Intellectual Property (INDECOPI) officially opened its doors for business. INDECOPI functions as an umbrella agency that oversees intellectual-property protection, consumer rights, the elimination of barriers to entry, and antitrust matters. Given the magnitude of these tasks, it was decided at the outset that INDECOPI would establish ex-post rather than ex-ante controls on economic activity (Beatriz Boza, INDECOPI director, interview with the author, Dec. 8, 1998, Lima). In the aftermath of privatization, some have questioned the efficacy of this ex-post approach (Barak 2000).

the government's presence in this sector (Paredes 1991, 314; Kisic 1998, 48). A new legal framework was written that simplified the rules of the domestic financial system and deregulated financial markets (e.g., the lowering of marginal-reserve requirements, the liberalization of interest rates, and a reduction of the tax on debits). At the same time, the capital account of the balance of payments was liberalized, and this included the opening of the banking system to foreign interests and the freeing of foreign-exchange transactions. These measures, along with the launching of the privatization program and the Foreign Investment Promotion Act of 1991, contributed to the development of the Lima stock exchange.[11] Having long been hampered by poor transparency and a burdensome regulatory backdrop, the combined effects of financial-sector reform helped to increase the capitalization of the Lima stock exchange from just US$800 million in 1990 to US$19.5 billion in 1997 (Manzetti 1999, 275).

Social Compensation

As noted earlier, the social fallout from the García period was a welfare deficit that had exploded into crisis proportions. The unmet basic needs of the population—including everything from food and housing to education and health care—were such that 55 percent of all households had fallen beneath the poverty line by 1991, compared to 38 percent in 1985 (Sheahan 1999, 108). Given that much of the violence over the preceding decade had been poverty-inspired, the multilaterals strongly encouraged the Fujimori administration to implement a safety-net scheme to help offset the burden of further adjustment.

After a first year of false starts, the president sidestepped the relevant line ministries that had long proved inadequate in delivering basic public goods and created the National Fund for Development and Social Compensation (FONCODES) in August 1991. Similar to compensatory social programs that had been implemented simultaneously with sweeping market reforms in Bolivia, Chile, and Mexico, FONCODES relied on a combination of traditional social-welfare relief and new demand-based criteria requiring that communities generate specific proposals for assistance (Graham 1994). Through FONCODES the administration targeted desperately needed compensatory resources toward poor communities; the bulk of these went toward economic infrastructure (road maintenance projects, irrigation, deforesta-

---

11. Under the new FDI regime, foreigners were allowed to invest in Peru and to repatriate profits and capital equipment as they saw fit. Additional legislation was passed that protected all investors, domestic and foreign, from sudden changes in existing laws and that established procedures for the resolution of disputes over investment (Manzetti 1999, 251).

tion) and social infrastructure (health facilities, schools, basic housing).[12] As with the other safety-net schemes being implemented in Latin America at this time, FONCODES was designed to temporarily alleviate poverty and to provide some political breathing space for sustaining market adjustment. With FONCODES's per capita expenditure averaging just US$12 from 1991 to 1994 (Graham and Kane 1998, 86), the program was never meant to resolve longstanding structural inequities in Peru.

Fujimori's simultaneous accomplishment of two main goals, increased political capital and short-term poverty relief, came through clearly in the process of implementing FONCODES. Especially after the 1993 constitutional referendum, where the president lost in all departments outside of Lima, FONCODES became a main venue for channeling public resources to those regional districts where the government had fared particularly poorly at the polls. As many of these districts had long been neglected by the central government, one result of the president's politically driven allocation of social resources was the direction of scarce funds to regions with extremely weak social indicators. This image of greater inclusion at the local level was bolstered by an overall increase in social expenditures, from 16 percent of government spending in 1990 to 40 percent in 1995 (Sheahan 1999, 125). This, in turn, helped deliver Fujimori's victory in all but one regional department (Loreto) in the 1995 presidential election. However, this fortuitous mix of politics and temporary social relief also distracted from the need to formulate a cohesive long-term strategy for poverty reduction and income distribution in Peru.[13] By 1994, 48 percent of the population was still living below the poverty line (Sheahan 1999, 108), and "for the average household, 1997 incomes were lower than those of 1975" (Webb 2000, 280).

Perhaps the most innovative social policy under Fujimori was the Citizen Participation Program, which sought to increase the participation of low-income groups, especially from the provinces, in the privatization program. Modeled after similar efforts in Bolivia and Chile, and run out of COPRI, Peru's Citizen Participation Program was authorized to sell 20 percent of all state assets. Purchasable shares could be bought in three-year installments during which the government guaranteed the price (Graham 1998, 124–34). The program showed that, when offered the chance to make even a small investment as shareholders, low-income groups responded enthusiastically. Beginning in late 1994 shares were sold, for example, in the state-owned cement company and subsequently in two electric firms and in the remaining

---

12. This information derives from various issues of "FONCODES: Nota Mensual."

13. For example, Fujimori focused on visible projects like school buildings rather then on core institutions, such as the education system itself, with obviously weak results.

portions of the telephone company that were still publicly held. While the very first auction of state shares in the cement firm was expected to last thirty days, more than three thousand bidders had purchased the available shares in a little less than four hours! However, as with FONCODES, the symbolic value of the Citizen Participation Program was much greater than the actual distributive impact (Manzetti 1999).

Reinventing the State

By definition, the sheer magnitude of market measures that had been introduced during Fujimori's first term implied a fundamental shift in the balance of public and private influence over the economy. Public activity, in particular, was restructured along three main institutional lines: the streamlining of the Peruvian state during the Fujimori era; the reconstruction and renovation of the country's main economic institutions; and the increased reliance on bureaucratic autonomy in the 1990s through the creation or overhaul of numerous state agencies involved in revenue collection, regulatory oversight, and the delivery of essential public services. Again, the underlying argument here is that, while laying the necessary groundwork for the impressive economic turnaround of the 1990s, the confinement of institutional reform to the state's internal organizations will not be a sufficient condition for sustaining sound economic performance. Rather, as the recent experiences of Argentina, Chile, and Mexico have shown, reform sustainability requires broader coalitional support and the strengthening of institutional ties between the state and those civic organizations that represent the ultimate stakeholders in the reform process.

The Streamlining of the Peruvian State

In Peru, "streamlining" has entailed both a haphazard retrenchment of the public sector, which began under García's watch, and a more purposeful restructuring of the Peruvian state after 1990 as fiscal reforms and the privatization program were launched. On the side of haphazard cuts was the steep compression of public spending from a peak of US$1,059 per capita in 1975 to just US$178 by 1990, a decline of 83 percent (Webb 1991, 2–3). Between 1987 and 1990 the public payroll shrunk by 75 percent, but the burden of adjustment fell mainly on real wages as very little workforce downsizing actually occurred (see table 16).[14] More than ever before, the public sector offered

---

14. Table 16 shows that public employment stood at 752,688 in 1998, whereas the 1990 figures were basically the same.

TABLE 16. Outline of Peru's Nonfinancial Public Sector: 1998

	No. of Entities	Expenditures S/.billions	Expenditures %	Remuneration S/.billions	Remuneration %	Employees Number	Employees %	Average Remuneration S/.000	Average Remuneration Index
Nonexecutive branches of government									
Constitutional agencies outside the executive	9	814	2	339	4	10,682	1	31.7	252
Executive of the central government									
Central government: 16 ministries and Council of Ministers	17	19,191	47	4,337	46	333,928	44	13.0	103
Decentralized institutions	63	4,210	10	207	2	11,378	2	18.2	145
National universities	28	937	2	356	4	31,092	4	11.5	91
Regional governments (CTARs)	23	3,662	9	2,113	22	301,663	40	7.0	56
Regional bodies (FONAFE)	10	1,043	3	501	5	6,512	1	76.9	612
ESSALUD Health/Social Sec. (FONAFE)	1	2,543	6	760	8	30,177	4	25.2	200
Revenue-generating entities (FONAFE)	78	8,152	20	847	9	27,256	4	31.1	247
Municipalities									
Provincial municipalities	192								
District municipalities	1,825								
Total (excluding municipalities)	229	40,551	99[a]	9,459	100	752,688	100	12.6	100

Source: Ministry of Economy and Finance, Lima.
[a]Rounding errors.

de facto employment relief for a rapidly shrinking middle and lower-middle class. In the meantime, the state's capacity to supply the most basic public services was drastically reduced. Nowhere was this more apparent than within the SOE sector, which on the eve of the privatization drive was running an astonishing US$2.5 billion in annual losses (Manzetti 1999, 248).

Obviously, the more purposeful effort at streamlining in the early 1990s would require the rationalization of the public sector but also the revival of the state's ability to provide an acceptable level of public goods. On the side of rationalization, the greatest strides were made with the SOEs, where close to half of the state's assets had been sold by 1998 (Manzetti 1999, 262–64). Similarly, a handful of state development banks were either sold or closed down, as was the Foreign Trade Institute and the National Planning Institute—the very symbol of populism in Peru. Despite the announcement of further cuts in public-sector employment and the intention to overhaul the central government ministries (Boloña 1996), these other aspects of streamlining never took off. In 1996 the government did propose a new "Program to Modernize the Public Administration," to be run out of the MEF, which ostensibly would have tackled these tasks. Yet in the end the president was not willing to expend the political capital that would be required to simultaneously downsize and reform the public bureaucracy.[15] The program died in less than a year.

Although the SOE workforce was cut from 140,000 to 50,000 between 1991 and 1994 (Manzetti 1999, 262), table 16 shows that over the course of the decade total public-sector employment held steady as hiring at the regional level offset central government layoffs. Likewise, the organizational contours of the central government had changed very little from the structure laid down post-1968. Some minor reforms were initiated, such as the merging of the Ministry of Housing and Construction with the Ministry of Transportation and Communications (Boloña 1996, 243), and the Ministry of Energy and Mines was overhauled, downsized, and made more efficient. In addition, the Ministry of the Presidency was revamped into a super-ministry in 1992, along with the Ministry of Economy and Finance. Throughout the 1990s, these two ministries, plus the Ministry of Defense, accounted for the mainstay of central government expenditures.

A second overriding change was the cultivation of numerous enclave or autonomous agencies involved mainly in revenue generation, service delivery, and regulatory oversight. These public entities stand apart from the

---

15. Leonie Roca and Rosa María Palacios, interview with the author, Dec. 17, 1998, Lima. Roca and Palacios are two consultants who worked on the Program to Modernize the Public Administration before Fujimori canceled it in 1997.

national budget and are instead financed through a separate fund (FONAFE) located within the MEF that the agencies themselves generate through user fees and other service charges. As table 17 shows, these FONAFE-financed entities staff far fewer employees, and the average remuneration is two to six times higher than the salaries paid by the central government ministries. It should come as no surprise, then, that this leaner and more modernized strand of the Peruvian state has been associated with highly professional service delivery in the 1990s (consumer protection, revenue collection, market regulation), while the services provided by the traditional line ministries (education, health, infrastructure) continue to lag far behind.

The Renovation of State Economic Institutions

As seen in the previous chapter, Peru's two main economic institutions, the BCRP and the MEF, had become mere shells of their former selves by 1990. The BCRP had lost all credibility, most obviously because of its failure to fight off hyperinflation but also because the García administration had rotated the bank's supposedly autonomous directorship four times in five years. Once Fujimori and his advisors had made the decision to attack hyperinflation by launching a market-shock program, the renovation of these two key economic policy–making entities quickly became an essential part of this effort. Overall, Peru's public administration suffered from four main shortcomings when the Fujimori team was handed the reins of government, and these two institutions were no exception.[16]

First, the very structure of government, in terms of the degree of centralization, autonomy, and the functions performed across agencies, was completely unproductive and inefficient. Second, there was little financial accountability with regard to how public resources were dispersed and few checks to discourage the diversion of state funds for illicit use. Third, personnel policies worked against the modernization of the public sector, as salaries were far too low to retain employees with the proper skills and civil-service tenure offered few incentives for improved worker performance or career advancement. And fourth, there were no mechanisms to deter officials from engaging in arbitrary or capricious behavior and few significant consequences when they did. From the analysis thus far it is clear that the Fujimori administration's track record in addressing these shortcomings was selective and uneven. But the BCRP and MEF were overhauled in ways that directly addressed these weak spots.

---

16. I borrow here from Keefer 1995 and Shepherd 2000. See both for greater detail on Peru's public administration.

TABLE 17. Peru's Autonomous Agencies: A Select Sample

Financial Oversight

Superintendency of Banking and Insurance (SBS): A preexisting financial oversight entity that exercises control over the banks and insurance companies, SBS was strengthened considerably during the early 1990s. Its director is nominated by the president and ratified by Congress for a five-year renewable term that coincides with that of the president. SBS is fully financed through state-mandated contributions from the banks and insurance companies, and its personnel policy has been placed under the private sector's legal regime.

Superintendency for the Administration of Private Pension Funds (SAFP): Created in 1992 as part of an overall effort to encourage citizen contributions to private pension funds, SAFP regulates those private entities that now manage pension funds in Peru. SAFP is a decentralized agency within the Ministry of Economy and Finance. The president chooses its director for a five-year term that coincides with that of the executive. The agency is self-financed through contributions from the private pension funds that it regulates, and private sector labor law governs its personnel policy.

Tax Administration

Superintendency for National Tax Administration (SUNAT): Although created in 1988 by the García administration, SUNAT has been completely modernized since 1991. SUNAT collects income and sales taxes and assists other public agencies in the collection of employment taxes. The president appoints its director, Congress approves its budget, and personnel policy is set by public sector criteria within the Ministry of Economy and Finance. SUNAT is self-financing, as the law authorizes it to draw on a fixed share of taxes (up to 2 percent) collected to cover all administrative and operating costs.

Superintendency for National Customs (SUNAD): Also created as part of the 1988 effort at tax reform, SUNAD has been similarly professionalized since 1991. As a customs agency, SUNAD is authorized to enforce tariff collection and to sanction illegal trade activity. It is a decentralized agency located in the Ministry of Economy and Finance. The latter nominates SUNAD's director, but the president has the final say in this matter. The agency is fully financed through the use of up to 3 percent of revenues collected for its own budget. SUNAD's personnel policy is governed by private sector labor law.

Miscellaneous Regulatory Bodies

National Institute for the Defense of Competition and the Protection of Intellectual Property (INDECOPI): Created in 1992, this is an omnibus regulatory agency with responsibilities ranging from the registration of intellectual property, to combating anticompetitive behavior, to enforcing newly defined norms of consumer protection. An especially innovative part of its mandate includes the adjudication of conflicts of interest through two different administrative review panels that operate apart from the judiciary system. A board of directors, an advisory council, and an internal control unit manage INDECOPI. It is an autonomous agency located within the Ministry of Industry, and the latter appoints the president of INDECOPI's board. INDECOPI is financed partly through its intellectual property rights registry and partly (about 20 percent) through the national budget. Its personnel are governed by the private sector's labor regime.

Supervisory Board for Private Investment in Telecommunications (OSPITEL): Created in 1994 with the objective of applying demonopolization guidelines and promoting market competition in the recently privatized telecommunications sector. OSPITEL reports to the office of the prime minister and is run by a six-member directive council, with each member serving a three-year term. All disputes are heard before quasi-judicial entities at two levels, with the second level offering the final decision. OSPITEL generates all of its operating budget through services charged to firms that fall under its supervision. Private sector labor law governs its personnel.

Other Independent Agencies

Commission for the Promotion of Private Investment (COPRI): Created in 1991 as an umbrella agency to manage the privatization of state assets. This has been done through the appointment of special expert subcommittees (CEPRIs) that implement the sale of particular companies to private bidders. COPRI reports directly to the president and is funded through its own proceeds from privatization.

Social Security Administration (ESSALUD): Established in 1999 to replace the Peruvian Social Security Institute (IPSS), ESSALUD administers Social Security funds. It is authorized to invest, enforce, and execute the collection of contributions; to formulate social security disbursement guidelines; and to develop disease prevention and other health related programs. ESSALUD is a decentralized entity under the Ministry of Labor and it generates 100 percent of its income through contributions and other nongovernmental sources.

National Fund for Compensation and Social Development (FONCODES): Created in 1991 with the stated objectives of generating employment, helping to alleviate poverty, and improving access to social services. Housed in the Ministry of the Presidency, FONCODES is a grant-making agency that responds directly to requests from local community groups for financing of small infrastructure projects (e.g., potable water, sewage treatment, school buildings). The fund is financed partly from international donors and from the ministry's own budget.

National Institute for Education and Health Infrastructure (INFES): A preexisting program that was revamped by the Fujimori administration in 1991 to address public infrastructure needs in education and health. As a decentralized agency within the Ministry of the Presidency, a five-member Directive Council that includes the president and the vice president of the Republic governs INFES. INFES generates its own income, and private sector law governs its personnel practices.

Source: Keefer 1995; Kim 1999.

With regard to the BCRP, important legal steps were taken to restore the bank's autonomy from domestic political intrusions and to reinforce its overriding mandate to preserve monetary stability (Velarde and Rodríguez 1998; Kim 1999). The 1993 constitution did retain the same seven-member board of directors (three appointed by congress and four by the executive, including the bank's president), as well as the stipulation that the BCRP president serve a five-year term parallel to that of the Peruvian executive. Although the recent historical record suggests that staggered terms between the Peruvian executive and the BCRP president would be more likely to promote central-bank autonomy, Fujimori saw this differently. Nevertheless, according to the new constitution, neither the BCRP president nor the board of directors can be removed at the whim of the executive, as this now requires a two-thirds congressional vote triggered by evidence that the parties concerned had failed to uphold the bank's monetary-policy mandate. Other important BCRP reforms concerned the establishment of a budgeting system separate from the national budget and the application of private-sector labor law to all BCRP personnel (Kim 1999).

The MEF was similarly strengthened in ways that supported the longer-run objective of carving out a new role for government as the facilitator of private initiative. As one of two "super-ministries," the MEF has been staffed with a highly qualified upper cadre of managers since 1991, and it has taken the lead in reforming public financial management in Peru (Shepherd 2000).[17] By 1997, a new budget-framework law was in place, which introduced programmatic spending and greater flexibility and transparency (Peru's national budget is now published on the Internet). A remaining challenge is for the MEF to take a stronger lead in expanding the scope and depth of reform throughout the line ministries. On this count, the MEF's failure to advance the aforementioned Program to Modernize the Public Administration is telling (Ugarte 2000, 421–27). The initial objectives of the program—to rationalize and professionalize the activities of the ministries, to deregulate administrative and procurement rules, and to introduce a performance-measurement system (Shepherd 2000, 6)—are every bit as relevant today as when they were proposed by the government in 1996.

The other designated super-ministry, the Ministry of the Presidency, had been created by the García administration in 1986 as a main venue for promoting miscellaneous APRA projects (e.g., Lima's electric train) and then deactivated as that party exited office in 1990 (Marcenaro 1996). The ministry

---

17. Although central government salaries, including those at the MEF, have remained low compared with those paid by the autonomous agencies, administrative talent has been retained at the MEF through multilateral financial assistance (e.g., the United Nations Development Programme) that supports a more competitive salary structure at the top.

was resurrected by legislative decree immediately following the 1992 civilian coup and went on to quickly capture around 23 percent of the central government budget by 1995 (Graham and Kane 1998, 85). With its revival, the ministry's formal objective was to promote a sweeping set of social programs in three functional areas: social development (health, food assistance), infrastructure (schools, housing, water purification), and regional development. Informally, it served as the much larger vehicle through which the president secured political support by channeling public resources to districts where voters had strayed.

It did not matter that each of these functional areas already occupied budget lines in various other central government ministries when the Ministry of the Presidency was brought back to life. Like his predecessor, Fujimori sought an institutional locus for an ambitious social program that he could personally take credit for at election time and for which there would be little budgetary oversight or procedural accountability. This he clearly found in the Ministry of the Presidency, which even Fujimori's most polite critics referred to as the president's own "mafia." However, this arrangement also worked to postpone debate over the urgent need for a longer-term social policy that would tackle inequality through improved access to much better quality education and healthcare services.[18]

Bureaucratic Autonomy

Ever since the political and economic meltdown of the 1960s, successive administrations in Peru have recognized the need to shield policy makers from undue populist and clientelistic pressures. Until 1990, this realization had been consistently manifested through the insulation of the executive and small elite-level working groups around the president. Except for a brief interlude during the early 1970s, insufficient effort has been made to nurture strategic sectors of the state bureaucracy to carry out executive policy preferences. This changed dramatically during the Fujimori era, as the degree to which autonomous public agencies were established and utilized effectively in Peru has perhaps been unparalleled in the region (Shepherd 2000, 5). The political impetus for this partial transformation of the public sector remains somewhat of a puzzle, particularly in light of Fujimori's avowedly anti-institutional stance on all other matters, not to mention the very half-hearted efforts that have surrounded the reform of the line ministries and bureaucracy at large.

---

18. This is the main theme of a powerful set of essays written by local social-policy analysts and published at the Universidad del Pacífico in Lima (see Portocarrero Súarez 2000).

The literature on bureaucratic delegation, which analyzes this phenomenon from the standpoint of both the OECD bloc and that of the developing countries, offers three insights with regard to this strong reliance on autonomous agencies in Peru.[19] First, this was the first civilian administration since 1963 that did not command a majority vote in the Peruvian congress. This is the opposite scenario from the one that awaited other civilian presidents who inherited similarly daunting reform challenges in the early 1990s, such as President Carlos Salinas in Mexico and President Carlos Menem in Argentina. As they were relatively secure about their support bases and tenure in office, the impulse of these other executives was to delay delegating authority to independent public entities such as central banks (Mexico) or regulatory boards (Argentina) for fear that such bureaucratic reforms would diminish their political control over the policy-making process. In contrast, Fujimori, with no real political party to call his own and no guarantee of a "natural" legislative coalition to back him in congress, pursued the autonomous-agency route as the only certain means for controlling his market-reform agenda.

A second insight from the literature concerns the recognition that market reforms will flounder in the absence of a proper institutional base. As Philip Keefer (1995, 25) has observed, the potential benefit of autonomy is "that it insulates agencies from the influence of different government entities that attempt to use their oversight capacity to distort agency decisions in favor of narrow interests. The agency is relieved of the burden to balance every technical decision against the parochial concerns of a multitude of entities with oversight responsibilities." In a very real sense, then, the cultivation of a cluster of autonomous agencies to act as the standard-bearer for implementing and sustaining market reforms became part and parcel of the reforms themselves.

A third insight on bureaucratic insulation concerns policy efficacy. As voters in Peru had virtually abandoned party affiliation and instead cast their ballots according to the government's ability to visibly improve the delivery of essential public services (Stokes 1997; Graham and Kane 1998), the more efficient outputs from autonomous agencies became a main factor in enhancing Fujimori's electoral prospects. In short, they enabled the president to vastly improve the productivity and efficiency of fiscal spending, while simultaneously attending to the needs of key constituencies. There was, however, a distinct downside to this new link between political survival and the development of autonomous public agencies in Peru.

---

19. See Boylan 2000 for an excellent review of this literature.

For example, in other bureaucratic settings autonomous entities have more commonly been used as the surest way to render policy reforms irreversible (Boylan 2000, 5–7). As such, they tend to be governed by commissions composed of public and private representatives who serve staggered terms and are appointed by congress (Evans 1995; Keefer 1995). This is not so in Peru, where autonomous agencies remain under the direct control of the president, who can hire and fire agency staff at will. Thus, although Fujimori delegated authority to these autonomous agencies as a means of guaranteeing the success of his own policy goals, he did it in such a way as to render them "relatively easy to create and easy to disable" (Shepherd 2000, 7). While tremendous strides have been made in the way of efficiency, transparency, and service delivery, the future viability of this autonomous-agency approach will depend heavily on the extent to which the agencies can be integrated into a broader legislative and managerial framework.

In sum, as table 17 shows, Peru's autonomous agencies can be roughly grouped into four categories: those that deal with financial regulation, those that handle tax administration, other miscellaneous regulatory bodies, and new independent agencies that relate directly to the goals of sustaining market reforms. Despite the diversity of these activities, the independent agencies share the mandate to manage economic change at the point of service delivery (Keefer 1995; Wilkins 1999). As such, they operate with varying degrees of managerial autonomy and are not held to the normal budgetary process through which line ministries obtain resources. In contrast with the central government ministries, these autonomous agencies are subject to clear performance requirements and bottom-line limits. At the end of the day, however, they are still under the president's direct control.

"Second-Phase" Reform, First-Phase Politics

By the end of Fujimori's first term the economic rules of the game had been radically transformed. In other words, a first generation of market reforms had basically been completed against a political-administrative backdrop that resonated with the management strategies adopted by other market reformers in the region during this time: "presidents and technocratic economic cabinets were able to design and implement changes in macroeconomic rules with relatively little interference from the rest of the political system or the public sector" (Naím 1994, 35). Having implemented a somewhat generic Washington Consensus program in the early 1990s, political leaders and policy makers in Latin America began to turn their attention to the consolidation of these reforms from the mid-1990s on. While all market reformers faced continuing challenges in the areas of macroeconomic management, income distribution, and the modernization of state organizations, the more specific content of "second-phase" reforms varied according to a given country's political, social, and institutional legacies.

For example, by the mid-1990s one of Argentina's most pressing second-phase challenges was the deregulation of domestic labor markets, while in Mexico the 1994 peso crisis had driven home the urgent need for a sweeping reform of the banking sector (Pastor and Wise 1999a; Kessler 2000). For Brazil, the rationalization of fiscal policy had been delayed to the point where this was the main trigger in setting off a massive run on the exchange rate in January 1999 (Cardoso 2000). While the specific tasks may vary, they present quite similar challenges in terms of the complexities and difficulties of following through on second-phase reforms. This is the case because, first, the gains from the policies now required (civil-service reform, administration of justice) are much more subtle than the obvious benefits of macroeconomic stabilization, while the pain (downsizing, loss of power and access to patronage) is more concentrated. Second, apart from the need to involve a much larger chunk of the central government in the reform process, the implementation of this next round of reform requires debate and negotiation with those most affected. In other words, second-phase market reforms require a more inclusive and accountable style of politics.

For Peru, it was the failure to shift to a more open and participatory mode of politics that constituted the most glaring reform gap in the 1990s. Again, this contrasts with the political trajectory of those market reformers mentioned earlier, where the patterns of executive autonomy and bureaucratic insulation that characterized the implementation of market reforms have given way to much greater levels of political competition and accountability in the consolidation phase. This is certainly true in the cases of Argentina, Brazil, and Chile, as attested to in the outcome of national elections that took place during 1998–99 in all three countries; even in semiauthoritarian Mexico, the seventy-one-year political grip of the single-ruling PRI party was finally broken by the opposition's victory in the July 2000 presidential elections. There, as elsewhere, the combination of deep market restructuring and internal state reform laid the groundwork for a political opening that not even the power-hungry PRI could prevent. Following, I examine the ways in which state-society relations evolved under Fujimori's long tenure, with an eye toward identifying both the constraints and the possibilities for Peru's transition to the same competitive political mode that has taken root in other countries now in the midst of consolidating second-phase market reforms.

The Leadership Coalition

As the dust began to settle on the mass of market measures that had been implemented during Fujimori's first couple of years, it became apparent that the postreform leadership coalition looked nothing like the elite party-controlled cliques that had ruled the country from 1980 to 1990. While the executive's style of governing Peru continued in the same insulated and autocratic vein, his two main allies—domestic business and the military—had not sustained a presence within the upper echelons of government since the return to civilian rule in 1980. Hindsight shows that the role of each of these allies in the leadership coalition lent credibility to the Fujimori administration at the very moment when public confidence in national leaders had sunk to an all-time low. However, as the 1990s wore on, the president's focus on indefinitely prolonging his own incumbency helped tip the balance of power uncomfortably on the side of the military. Not only did this disproportionate influence of the military puncture any myths about the depth of Peru's democratic transition, but, just as importantly, the lack of accountability and proper legislative oversight did not bode well for the ability of the second Fujimori administration to advance another wave of necessary reforms.

How is it that an executive like Fujimori, with no mentionable ties to the business community at the outset of his presidency, was able to forge a viable partnership with the Peruvian private sector when all of the other attempts reviewed in this study had failed? This remarkable alliance must be understood from the standpoint of Fujimori's own pragmatism, as well as the institutional strengthening and internal reform that occurred within the Peruvian business community during the early 1990s. The trend toward modernization of key state agencies must also be factored in here, as this provided the private sector with unprecedented guarantees in the way of property rights and policy continuity. With regard to the president's role in this alliance, once the decision had been made to proceed with a market-shock program back in 1990, Fujimori quickly grasped the need to bring the domestic private sector on board. In contrast to Belaúnde's constant waffling on market measures, or García's highly erratic behavior when it came to spurring private initiative, Fujimori toed a steady line in the announcement and implementation of market reforms.

Whereas the 1990–92 congress had been put off by this managerial executive style, the private sector found some comfort in it. This is not to say that business was enamored with the entire program, but the consistency and clarity of the new economic rules, and the positive signals from higher growth and lower inflation, helped forge a viable working coalition.[20] Even before his

---

20. Arturo Woodman, former CONFIEP president, interview with the author, July 18, 1995, Lima.

inauguration in 1990, Fujimori began meeting with representatives from CONFIEP, the private sector's umbrella organization, and during his tenure as president he gave the closing speech at the annual conferences of CONFIEP and CADE—the yearly meeting of business executives (Durand 1998, 270–72). Through the course of the 1990s, the president also appointed prominent business leaders to direct FONCODES and to key ministerial posts—for example, at the Ministry of Economics and Finance, the Ministry of Industry, and the Ministry of Foreign Affairs. The Fujimori team was also able to move past the collective-action gridlock that had long plagued government-business relations by offering some compensatory relief (labor-market flexibilization, lower taxes, political access) to domestic entrepreneurs.

For the private sector's part, domestic business had come a very long way from the days when bank owners chained themselves to their desks in protest of García's 1987 attempt to nationalize the country's financial institutions. This, in fact, turned out to be a catalyzing moment for CONFIEP, as it marked the point at which a highly heterogeneous set of domestic business interests began to set aside their differences and unite to become a peak organization proper. Since the García fiasco, CONFIEP has attracted generous external support to the tune of US$2 million annually from the U.S. Agency for International Development (USAID) and the multilaterals, which over the years has financed office space, support staff, conferences, publications, and even a business think tank (IPE).[21] As part of this process, CONFIEP realized the need to bring small businesses into its fold, as this sector generates the bulk of employment and constitutes by far the largest group of firms in Peru. Thus, the Confederation of Small Businesses (CONAMYPE) was formed and officially incorporated into CONFIEP in 1995 (Durand 1998, 268).

As for the military's strong presence in Fujimori's leadership coalition, up until late 1992 the military's high profile in national politics could perhaps be justified by the demands of quelling a long-running guerrilla insurgency and an explosion in drug trafficking (Elena Alvarez 1998, 123–24). But the president's continued reliance on military advisors like Montesinos and Hermoza Ríos for the remainder of the decade was a reflection of both his own unease with the give and take of competitive politics and the utter opportunism of those advising him. Once the guerrilla insurgencies and narcotics trade had been deftly brought under control, both Montesinos and Hermoza Ríos were there for the president at each subsequent critical juncture: the precoup battles with congress and the 1992 coup itself; the president's 1995 reelection

---

21. José Valderráma, IPE director, interview with the author, Dec. 18, 1998, Lima.

campaign; Peru's 1995–98 border conflict with Ecuador; the resolution of the 1996–97 hostage crisis at the Japanese embassy in Lima; and the prompt response to renewed damage from floods caused by El Niño in 1998.

Yet the flip side of this "loyalty" to the president was the increased politicization of the Peruvian military under Joint Chief Commander Hermoza Ríos, with SIN director Montesinos pulling most of the strings behind the scenes. The president had issued a new military law in November 1991 that eliminated the time-honored system of merit-based promotion and rotating appointments that had earned the Peruvian armed forces a reputation as one of the region's more professional military institutions. It was this new perverse system of incentives and disincentives that prompted a failed coup attempt against Fujimori in November 1992. As the 1990s wore on, those military personnel who displayed loyalty to the Fujimori-Montesinos–Hermoza Ríos triumvirate were rewarded with job security, promotions, and pay raises. Those who did not fell prey to threats of dismissal and blackmail, based on wiretaps and other forms of information gathering by Montesinos. The success of Montesinos and Hermoza Ríos in militarizing Peru's civilian regime once again put the country at odds with the rest of the region (Hunter 1997). Ultimately, these unsavory allies would prove to be Fujimori's undoing.

The Intermediation of Societal Interests

Throughout this study, the intermediation of societal interests in Peru has been discussed along two axes—the state-capital-labor axis and the party-congress-executive axis. On the first count, except for the military's anomalous presence in too many facets of everyday life, interest intermediation in the Peru of the 1990s has conformed to a regional trend. Like other elected leaders in Latin America, Fujimori constructed the kinds of state-capital alliances that are essential for signaling a serious commitment to private initiative. At the same time, the president and his advisors offered a sophisticated mix of incentives and compensatory schemes to those who were essential for sustaining market reforms (the private sector) and to those who were key to Fujimori's survival in office (the mass base of popular-sector constituents throughout the country who carried the president to victory in all three national elections after 1990).

The indisputable loser along this axis was labor, both organized and otherwise. In Peru and in the region at large, the combination of a prolonged period of economic restructuring, company downsizing under privatization, and labor-market deregulation has taken the wind out of the unions' sails. Furthermore, like García, Fujimori focused state resources and political attention on the disorganized and poorest segments of the workforce and thereby cultivated a vertical relationship between the executive and the most marginalized sectors of the working population. Against this backdrop, after peaking in 1978, union activity and influence in Peru accounted for just 13 percent of private-sector workers in 1995 (Thomas 1998, 163). Peru having gone from being one of the most regulated Latin American labor markets in 1990 to being one of the most liberalized by 1995 (Burki and Perry 1997, 40–41), this rapid transformation has thus far meant a proliferation of temporary contract work and an urban unemployment rate of close to 9 percent between 1990 and 1999. When the continuingly high levels of informal work and underemployment are factored in, economic uncertainty and fears of job loss have also hampered the formation of those horizontal organizational ties that characterized Peruvian labor during its heyday in the late 1970s.

Although Peru fits the regional mold in terms of interest intermediation along the state-capital-labor axis in the 1990s, the same obviously cannot be said of the relationship among political parties, congress, and the executive. The inability of political parties in Peru to revive themselves and reform from within, or to forge a viable horizontal coalition of the kind that eventually unseated General Pinochet in Chile, is confirmed by the paltry percentage of votes that the standing parties captured during every election in the 1990s. By the time of the 1995 presidential election the three traditional parties (the APRA, the AP, and the PPC) together captured less than 13 percent of the total vote. This reflects the public's disgust with the abysmal performance of all three parties during their time in elected office in the 1980s, but the decline of traditional political parties in Peru also has to do with the adherence to a majority-runoff electoral format for the first time in 1990 and to the design of further rules under the CCD that complicated an electoral system that was already far too complex.

Matthew Shugart and John Carey (1992) have argued that, in contrast to plurality elections as in the United States, majority-runoff systems offer low barriers to entry and hence tend to generate larger candidate lists with much higher levels of uncertainty.[22] Peru's majority-runoff format also discourages alliance building and invites the rise of dark-horse candidates, Fujimori's ascendance being a case in point. Another deterrent to cohesive political brokering along the party-congress-executive axis was the decision of once-major parties like the APRA and the AP to boycott the 1992 elections for the CCD. At the time, potential opposition candidates for the CCD were understandably reacting to Fujimori's threat to require that CCD delegates sit out

---

22. For example, according to Peru's electoral law, any group wishing to field candidates in presidential or legislative races must obtain a minimum of just 120,000 signatures.

two full congressional terms before seeking reelection and to the president's plan to pare down the Peruvian congress into a unicameral body with 120 representatives elected under one single district (Maxwell Cameron 1997, 62–63). Hindsight shows that because these parties abstained from the CCD altogether, most of Fujimori's proposals prevailed while the traditional parties became all the more marginal.

The fact that the opposition parties never even tried to assert a presence in the CCD put them further at odds with a median voter who had emerged from the turmoil of the 1980s with a fierce sense of independence and antipathy toward traditional partisanship (Schmidt 1996; Tanaka 1998). Thus, the CCD marked the turning point where political organizing in Peru shifted toward large eclectic movements that coalesced around election time and then scattered until the next election (Cotler 1995, 349). Such was the case with Fujimori's Cambio 90 or the Union for Peru (UPP), which backed the losing presidential candidate and former U.N. secretary general Javier Peréz de Cuéllar in 1995. Geared almost entirely toward achieving electoral gains, and low on ideological or programmatic content, these movement coalitions were a far cry from demonstrating the internal discipline and institutional cohesion that now characterize political-party structures in countries like Argentina, Chile, and Mexico.

In sum, although the absence of authentic interest intermediation along the party-congress-executive axis is indisputable in the Peru of the 1990s, it is impossible to ignore the favorable economic returns over the past decade. These trends are contradictory, particularly in light of recent work that attributes successful instances of neoliberal reform in other emerging-market countries to the firmer grounding of such reforms along this very axis (Haggard and Kaufman 1995; Corrales 2000a). Similarly, the current thinking on political parties in Latin America implies that an inchoate or collapsed party system such as Peru's would be much less likely to succeed on the economic front (Mainwaring and Scully 1995, 22–23). This gap between political-economic theorizing and concrete outcomes has spawned a rich body of research on Peru in the 1990s, which has focused on two main questions: (1) what drives Peruvian politics in the era of market reform? and (2) what accounts for economic success, given that interest intermediation and policy formulation have circumvented the party-congress-executive axis since the advent of Fujimori?

Most of the literature to date offers society-based answers to these questions. Susan Stokes (1998), for example, analyzes public opinion as a proxy for the president's political support and the perceived success of market reforms. After voicing broad support for the president and his economic program even before it began to pay off, the public shifted from this "intertemporal" posture, based on the expectation of future prosperity, to a "normal economic voting" posture in which government support rose and fell more directly with the performance of the economy (Stokes 1998, 1). Yet the government's mediocre showing in the three elections held during 1992–93 showed that intertemporal responses to public-opinion polls do not always translate into votes. Because Peruvian respondents proved to be quite fickle during this period, others have emphasized the ways in which state resources have been strategically deployed as a way of winning back votes and tying the masses to an executive who has otherwise shunned the institutionalization of such ties (Graham and Kane 1998; Schady 2000).

Coined by some as "neoliberal populism" (Dresser 1991; Roberts 1995; Kay 1997)—the use of inclusive political gestures and targeted material rewards to smooth over the exclusive and regressive impact of neoliberal reforms on the population at large—this strategy definitely helped to extend Fujimori's incumbency beyond all expectations.[23] But precisely because of its shallow roots in civil society, and its failure to tackle the underlying structural roots of poverty and inequality, this neoliberal populist strategy seemed to have run its course by the end of the decade. Despite the continued channeling of generous state resources to those districts and regions where the president sought to lure voters into his camp, he was not able to avoid the lightning-bolt rise of opposition candidate Alejandro Toledo in the first runoff vote for the 2000 presidential elections. For fear that not enough votes could be bought, the president and his cronies resorted to the kinds of balloting fraud and dirty campaign tricks that Mexico's PRI party had long been famous for but that set new unseemly records in post-1980 Peru.[24]

Returning to the earlier questions, my answer is decidedly state-centered and meant to complement these societal explanations. I have argued throughout this chapter that the internal reform and modernization of those state agencies that are essential to the success of a market strategy constituted a necessary condition for sustaining economic reforms and for stabilizing politics. For the first time in the post–World War Two period, at least some quarters of the Peruvian state could be taken seriously. The private sector responded in kind and forged the closest thing to a government-business pact that the country had yet seen (Durand 1998). For better or for worse, a coali-

23. As Bruce Kay (1997, 56) notes: "Fujipopulism seems to depend on executive philanthropy bankrolled by a liberal state. . . . [I]t is anti-elitist and anti-ideological in its orientation, multi-class in its composition, autocratic in its style of management. . . . [It] bypasses, and weakens, intermediary institutions and creates new institutions that permit the president to establish a direct, personalistic relationship with the masses."

24. Clifford Kraus, "Peruvian's Lead in Vote Prompts Charge of Fraud," *New York Times,* Apr. 11, 2000, A1.

tion composed of the state, domestic capital, and the military provided the stability needed to restructure the economy along market lines. But the exhaustion of first-phase market reforms by the mid-1990s, and the contagion from massive external shocks in Asia, Russia, and Brazil from 1997 to 1999, again highlighted the fact that state renovation and stable leadership are necessary but not entirely sufficient conditions for coping with new economic challenges.

Markets without Politics

It was the quest for political stability and continuity in economic policy that enabled the president and his backers to amend the rules surrounding reelection in 1995 and to neutralize political conflict over that decision. Similar concerns had underpinned constitutional amendments to allow for the reelection of the executive to a second consecutive term in Argentina and Brazil in the mid-1990s. Like Fujimori, President Menem of Argentina had also sought to further bend constitutional rules in order to run for a third term. However, it was Menem's own party that reined him in on the grounds that, within a democracy, such fundamental rules as those surrounding presidential succession should not be up for periodic renegotiation.[25] In Peru, obviously, there were no such reliability checks to deter the executive from almost single-handedly reinterpreting these same rules. Even apart from the highly questionable legal justification for a third term, there were at least two other reasons why an extension of Fujimori's stay in office was not in the country's best interests.

First, little that was new had actually been accomplished in the way of deepening market reforms during his second term. As reelection in 1995 afforded Fujimori a much longer time horizon on his tenure in office, the president's appetite for further reform was visibly curbed (Durand and Thorp 1998; Boylan 2000). As a result, privatization slowed considerably, exports were still lackluster and too dependent on raw materials (fish meal, mining, and services related to the processing of primary goods), and social policy had yet to reach sufficiently beyond the executive's concern for political survival and hence his doling out of immediate adjustment relief. Second, the prospect of a third term predictably provoked broad opposition (national opinion polls showed that nearly 70 percent of Peruvians felt that it was time for the president to move on); this prompted Fujimori and his congressional allies to exert their will through direct intervention in the country's legal and

25. Senator Augusto Alasino, leader of the Peronist Party in the Argentine Senate during Menen's second term, interview with the author, May 8, 1998, Buenos Aires.

judicial apparatus. The parties always at odds, the relationship between the country's democratic transition and Fujimori's prolonged incumbency became even more conflictual.

Done in the name of maintaining political stability, the executive's rash legal interventions ultimately provoked a series of political crises (Tanaka, forthcoming, 2003). For example, when the equivalent of Peru's supreme court ruled that a third consecutive term was unconstitutional, congress quickly dismissed the dissenting justices.[26] Various civic organizations then mobilized and gathered 1.2 million signatures in support of a referendum on the matter, only to have congress fabricate a package of questionable laws that killed the referendum. In the period leading up to the 2000 presidential elections, the judicial system, and in particular the main electoral agencies that fell under its jurisdiction (the National Elections Board, the National Registry for Voters, and the National Office for Electoral Procedures), had all been tampered with in ways that favored Fujimori's reelection. Any critical voices within the media were subjected to constant surveillance and harassment by Fujimori's foot soldiers within the SIN.

The 2000 presidential election was a grand finale of sorts, at least in terms of Fujimori's efforts to project a technical, apolitical image in what turned out to be a quintessential show of dirty politics. Whereas debates over second-phase policies regarding such issues as education, health, and the administration of justice had dominated presidential elections in other Latin American countries in the late 1990s, Peru's 2000 contest was notable not for serious debate but for the procedural infractions and venomous attacks that emanated from the Fujimori camp. Like opposition candidates in Argentina, Chile, and Mexico, Peru's leading opposition candidate, Alejandro Toledo, vowed to uphold and strengthen the market program now in place, while also tackling the distributional problems associated with it. Toledo also promised to advance political reforms that would set the country firmly back on a democratic trajectory.[27] Not surprisingly, public-opinion polls in Peru had shown for some time that these were the issues that most concerned the electorate.

But the tone of the election quickly fastened onto the ethnic and racial themes—"El Chino" Fujimori versus "El Cholo" Toledo—that had been so crucial in sinking the candidacies of European-style elites like Vargas Llosa and Peréz de Cuéllar. The difference this time, however, was that there was no front-running *criollo* candidate for Fujimori to scapegoat. Rather, the Stan-

---

26. See Coletta Youngers, "Fujimori's Relentless Pursuit of Re-election," *NACLA: Report on the Americas,* Jan./Feb. 2000, 6–10.

27. Campaign speech by Alejandro Toledo, sponsored by the Inter-American Dialogue and the Brookings Institution, Washington, D.C., Apr. 28, 2000.

ford-educated Toledo infused the race with an Andean ethnic identity and a Horatio Alger–like rise from poverty that topped Fujimori's own image of the struggling Japanese immigrant. Fujimori's dark-horse victory of 1990 also overshadowed any serious debate, as it appeared that Peru's majority-runoff system could again wreak unexpected havoc, this time on the president himself. Indeed, not only did Toledo place second to Fujimori in the first round of voting on April 9 and therefore force a runoff race, but the opinion polls showed that the two would run a virtual dead heat in the second round of voting.

The first-round election had been wrought with accusations of government-sponsored fraud and therefore met with the same international disapproval and threats of sanctions that the 1992 coup had provoked. As the Fujimori administration refused to guarantee a fair and clean runoff race, Toledo bowed out of the second-round election, vowing to reenter only when the electoral playing field had been cleared of all irregularities. In the end, the second-round vote was held on May 28, but Fujimori took just 51 percent of the vote and, after failing to secure a majority bloc in congress, managed to cobble together different independent factions to back him in the legislature. The fact that voters had invalidated 30 percent of the ballots cast in the second-round runoff election left few doubts concerning the lack of legitimacy for a ruling coalition that had served its political and economic purposes but simply refused to rotate out in democratic fashion.

As it turned out, just as international actors and local opposition forces in Peru seemed to have resigned themselves to a third Fujimori term, in September 2000 the president suddenly announced that new elections would be held and that he would not be a candidate. Despite steady demands at home and abroad—for everything from the reinstatement of the constitutional tribunal to the firing of Montesinos—it appears that the impetus for Fujimori's announced withdrawal was mainly an internal crisis. The triggering event was a videotape that fell mysteriously into the hands of the political opposition and that showed Montesinos blatantly bribing a newly elected member of congress to switch his party affiliation over to the legislative coalition that backed Fujimori.[28] This prompted the president to dissolve the SIN and request the resignation of his treacherous security chief and right-hand advisor. Not surprisingly, the military split ranks, with Montesinos and his backers mustering enough incriminating evidence to bring Fujimori down with them but not enough power to invoke a full-fledged military coup.

By November 2000 Fujimori had faxed his resignation to the Peruvian

---

28. David Gonzalez, "Peru Spymaster Stays Out of View as Rumors Swirl," *New York Times,* Sept. 18, 2000, A1.

people from Japan, where he had secured political asylum, and Montesinos had literally gone underground. Congressional president Valentín Paniagua, a former justice minister under the first Belaúnde administration, stepped in as president of a transitional government, and a new set of national elections were scheduled for April 2001. Earlier, I argued that Peru's most glaring second-phase reform gap had been the failure to shift to a more open and participatory mode of politics. And now, almost uncannily, domestic actors were given a second chance to seize this political opportunity structure. In just eight months, Paniagua's transition cabinet proved how much could be accomplished when politicians and policy makers truly committed themselves to rebuilding Peru's public institutions and to governing by consensus according to the preestablished constitutional rules.[29]

As interim president, Paniagua recruited top-notch advisors from quite diverse political backgrounds, all of whom voluntarily refrained from entering their names on the April 2001 ballot so as to focus steadfastly on the reforms at hand.[30] The most immediate tasks taken up by this interim team included purging the government of the thick web of corruption that had finally sent Fujimori and Montesinos into exile and the restoration of fair and competitive elections. On the first count, numerous investigations were launched with regard to allegations of the previous administration's involvement in widespread money laundering, drug trafficking, illicit enrichment, torture, and murder. The armed forces were also restructured, and those top officers who had violated the law were dismissed. At the same time, control over social expenditures was shifted away from the Ministry of the Presidency, and interim leaders introduced new mechanisms for consulting with civic organizations about reform strategies in such crucial areas as education, labor codes, and the country's institutions of justice.

On the second count, the main electoral authorities were completely overhauled, and the Paniagua government invited five international observer missions to oversee the April 2001 election. A quickly reformed National Elections Jury approved the registration petitions of nine presidential candidates for the April race, three of whom forged ahead to dominate the contest. Predictably, Alejandro Toledo took the lead as the candidate who had fought the hardest for the restoration of democratic norms. To the political right of

---

29. Steven Levitsky and Cynthia Sanborn, "A Hard Choice in Peru," *New York Times*, May 9, 2001, A31.

30. For example, Diego García Sayán, one of the country's most prestigious civil-rights lawyers, stepped in as justice minister, and former U.N. secretary general Javier Peréz de Cuéllar took over as prime minister. Equally important, a top academic expert in electoral politics was appointed to direct the highly tainted National Office for Electoral Procedures.

Toledo emerged Congresswoman Lourdes Flores Nano, backed by a coalition composed of remnants of the PPC, some Fujimori defectors, and the Catholic church. From the left-wing flanks sprang another flash candidate in the form of the APRA's Alan García, who had returned from nearly a decade of self-imposed exile just weeks before the election. With the Peruvian courts having ruled that earlier charges of corruption and human-rights abuses against García had expired under the country's statute of limitations, Peru's former president and longstanding persona non grata surged virtually out of nowhere to edge out Flores Nano and capture second place after Toledo in the first-round vote.

Three main themes dominated the first- and second-round elections in April and June 2001—both considered the cleanest the country had yet to sponsor. The first was the vehement anti-Fujimori sentiment, fueled by a steady stream of corruption scandals that were now erupting daily in the media. While the track record confirms that the country had benefited overall from the deep market reforms that had been implemented in the 1990s, the costs of economic restructuring and the lack of sufficient social supports were still keenly felt. This, plus revelations of multimillion-dollar foreign bank accounts and hidden assets that kept cropping up in relation to the Fujimori-Montesinos government, understandably incensed voters. While Montesinos was finally apprehended in Venezuela in June 2001 and incarcerated in Lima to face some 140 different criminal charges, Fujimori continued to lead the good life in Japan protected by that country's political asylum law.[31]

A second theme was the personal mudslinging that went on among all three candidates and that no doubt cut into Toledo's margin of victory. Whereas the election had been Toledo's to lose when Fujimori resigned, he ultimately won the June 2001 runoff with just 52 percent of the valid votes cast, compared to García's truly remarkable comeback at 47 percent.[32] But at least 13 percent of all vote casts were blank, as voters punished the candidates for their irresponsible antics. The shrill banter surely sunk the first-round candidacy of Flores Nano, who, despite being favored by the United States and endorsed by a group of former Latin American Christian Democratic heads of state, had failed to distinguish herself sufficiently from the incumbent Fujimori bloc in congress and therefore could not withstand the hostile anti-Fujimori attacks waged against her. The completely unpredictable emergence of García as a candidate proper was similarly related to the electorate's

---

31. Scott Wilson, "The Stakeout That Snared a Spy," *Washington Post,* June 26, 2001, A1; Calvin Sims, "Fujimori Is Wined and Dined by Tokyo's Powerful," *New York Times,* June 28, 2001, A3.

32. Sebastian Rotella, "Peru's Victor: Happy, but Anxious," *Los Angeles Times,* June 5, 2001, A1.

antipathy toward Fujimori. However, García's ability to rebound from having just an 8 percent approval rating in preelection polls to actually capturing 47 percent of the second-round vote confirmed that he had not lost his touch as a consummate politician. By apologizing to voters for his past errors and casting himself as a reconstructed market-friendly democrat, García was able to remobilize a dormant APRA base and compensate for the negative campaigning in ways that eluded Flores Nano and Toledo.

Finally, following at a distant third was the campaign theme that most concerned Peruvian voters: the kinds of second-phase policies that would better promote sustainable growth and more broadly distribute the benefits of economic reform. While both García and Toledo offered up proposals that were variations on this theme, the latter more firmly committed to the continuation of the ongoing market strategy but in ways that more aggressively addressed its shortcomings to date. More than once during the campaign García sent jitters through regional markets with his proposals to cap utility prices, limit Peru's debt payments, and expand employment through state support in sectors like construction and agriculture.[33] Again, Toledo's inability to steer the campaign away from his own personal peccadilloes and sustain a much higher-level debate about concrete policy options was costly in that he assumed the presidency with a much weaker electoral mandate than had been widely expected. However, the return of competitive politics and the momentum established by the interim Paniagua government certainly placed the entire reform trajectory on much more optimistic footing than the previous option of waiting another five years to breathe new life into the political economy.

Markets without Planning

In spite of these extraordinary political machinations, the Peruvian economy showed strong signs of recovery by mid-2000. It appeared that Peru had finally crossed a major threshold in the sense that sound performance and professional management practices were more credibly grounded in the country's main economic institutions. This was reflected in the response of the external sector, as capital flows and interest-rate spreads remained favorable to Peru and as multiyear lending agreements went forward with the IMF, the IDB, the World Bank, and the Andean Development Corporation. Negotiations were also on track with a German consortium for the construction of a new US$1.2 billion international airport in Lima, and a previously stalled US$3 billion transportation and distribution contract for the Camisea gas project in the south of the country was brought back to life. However, Fuji-

---

33. James Wilson, "Overcoming Fujimori's Shadow," *Latin Finance*, May 2001, 34.

mori's ratings in national public-opinion polls lagged right up until his resignation, despite this more favorable economic news (Schmidt 2000).[34]

The normal economic voting posture described by Stokes (1998) seemed to have run its course by 2000, which could be partially explained by the self-inflicted political shocks described earlier. But a widening gap between macroeconomic dynamism and microeconomic stress had also shaped Peruvian public opinion in ways not well captured by either the normal economic voting or the intertemporal model. According to the latter, economic recovery in the early 1990s had met with a pessimistic response on the part of the population, as higher growth and real wage increases called up painful memories of hyperinflation. Ironically, in the first stage of market reform, pessimism concerning present performance correlated with optimism about the future (Stokes 1996b). Yet, a decade later, the future had arrived, and the gains from market reform still eluded the majority of Peruvians. Household surveys showed that in the average Peruvian household, "income either stagnated or fell slightly between 1985 and 1997" (Webb 2000, 217).

In light of these figures, and given the increasingly cynical political backdrop, the president's lower approval rating in the midst of an economic recovery surely reflected a distributional response on the part of those who had yet to fully benefit from Peru's higher growth rates in the 1990s.[35] Again, it was similar distributional trends that prompted demands for second-phase reform in the other emerging-market countries discussed here and that ultimately helped to elect proreform political coalitions that sought to more aggressively bridge the distributional gap. In Peru, distributional demands were muted by authoritarian politics right up until the very end of Fujimori's tenure. In particular, it was the executive's tight control over social expenditures, which provided short-term relief to the poor but did little to tackle the underlying causes of inequality, that emerged as one of the few points of policy consensus among the leading candidates in the 2001 presidential election.

Across the region, the tenacity of these regressive distributional patterns flies in the face of neoliberal thinking, which holds that market reforms will expand the national pie and enable a wider segment of the population to gain access to this newly found wealth (Balassa, Bueno, Kuczynski, and Simonsen

---

34. Alfredo Thorne, "Presidential Elections Heat Up in Peru and Mexico," *Global Data Watch*, Banco de J. P. Morgan, S.A., Mar. 24, 2000, 8.

35. In an innovative study of social mobility in Peru from 1991 to 1996, Carol Graham (2000, 261) analyzes new panel data that show that nearly 38 percent of the respondents (N = 676) experienced either upward or downward mobility. Between 1991 and 1994, about 20 percent crossed above the poverty line, while about 8 percent dropped below it. But the 1994–96 figures were literally flat: of the 23 percent of respondents who crossed the poverty line, 11.4 percent rose above it and 11.4 percent sunk further into poverty. See Stokes 1997 for a compelling analysis of how such trends have fed back into voting patterns in Peru.

1986; Krueger 1990; Przeworski 1999). Recent research on Latin America's distributional shortcomings in the aftermath of market reforms offers two main explanations for this counterintuitive outcome. First, income inequality has lingered in the region because of the high levels of asset concentration—both productive and human-capital assets—that are still present in these economies (Baer and Maloney 1997; Birdsall and Londoño 1997). And second, the failure of liberalization and privatization to penetrate these entrenched dualistic structures is no longer seen as an adjustment lag but rather as an endogenous feature of market reforms that must be addressed through more assertive public policies (Sheahan 1997). In other words, the region's track record suggests that, over time, microeconomic adjustment will not occur solely at the hand of market forces.

Tellingly, both Fujimori terms passed without the generation of an integrated development plan that reflected the government's policy goals on this very question. Understandably, "planning" had been given a bad name by both the RGAF and the García debacle of the late 1980s; nevertheless, it is sobering to think that the Peruvian military was the only national institution to offer a longer-term vision for the country in the era of market reform, and this more than a decade ago in the form of the "Green Book."[36] The Fujimori administration had succeeded in attracting a higher level of professional expertise than any of the preceding administrations reviewed in this study, so the lack of an integrated development strategy that linked macro- and microeconomic goals into the medium term cannot be laid at the feet of technical incompetence. The failure to better harness the talent of this sophisticated policy segment surely had to do with the peculiar circumstances that led to the vetting of executive access by the likes of Montesinos and to the president's own discomfort with talented technocrats who might upstage him.[37] This situation is worlds apart from that in other emerging-market countries in the region, where executives have purposefully armed themselves with large, high-profile technical teams that have themselves come to signal reform credibility.

36. As a matter of planning by default, the national budget has served as a guideline of sorts, as have the periodic sectoral plans generated by the line ministries. However, Reynaldo Bringas, the director of the national budget at the MEF, admits that in the absence of a larger set of policy guidelines, MEF budgeted mainly according to "estimates" in the Fujimori era. Reynaldo Bringas, interview with the author, Dec. 10, 1998, Lima.

37. This explains Boloña's abrupt dismissal by Fujimori in January 1993 and his replacement by Jorge Camet, an elderly industrialist and former CONFIEP president who had none of Boloña's talent but did not compete with the president for the national spotlight (Bowen 2000, 170). If Boloña was the mastermind of the market-reform program, Camet was the caretaker (Durand 1998). This explains Camet's ability to survive an unprecedented six-year term as minister of economics, but even so, the president kept him on a short leash, offering Camet a series of six-month contracts during his entire tenure at the MEF!

In the final chapter I review the piecemeal steps that have been taken to infuse microeconomic dynamism into the Peruvian political economy and to attack inequality at its roots. In doing so I borrow from the experiences of other market reformers in the region to highlight the ways in which the Peruvian effort could be strengthened. Peru again finds itself at a very critical juncture. Wittingly or not, Fujimori and his small base of advisors reinvented the Peruvian state in ways that make it more capable of steering the economy onto a higher growth–higher productivity track, regardless of who occupies the executive office. To tinker with the impressive array of state agencies that appears in table 17 would be to derail these goals. Thus, the institutional incentives work in favor of executive action to insure the longevity of these agencies (Keefer 1995). While this was never Fujimori's style, the Toledo team would do well to carefully nurture these modernized pockets of the state. They are germane not only to the next administration's political success but also to the promotion of greater economic stability and more widely shared prosperity in the post-Fujimori era.

Conclusion

Up until 1990, the tendency in Peru had been for each successive administration that prevailed from 1963 on to hand over an even bigger bundle of political and economic problems than it had inherited upon taking office. The crisis of the late 1980s finally put an end to these delay tactics, as the combination of state collapse, hyperinflation, and civil war made it virtually impossible for politicians and policy makers to avoid implementing a long-overdue set of reforms. In hindsight, a maverick independent politician such as Fujimori may have seemed the least likely candidate of all to succeed in restructuring the economy along market lines and in reconstructing the Peruvian state. Yet the magnitude and longevity of the 1980s crisis, combined with Fujimori's own fortitude, created a unique set of opportunities for the initiation of sweeping political-economic change.

Already, Peru's transformation in the 1990s stands on par with that of the 1970s: just as the twelve-year nationalist military regime put a final end to the country's longstanding oligarchic class, Fujimori's decade in office marked the demise of traditional political parties controlled by ineffectual *criollo* elites. And as the RGAF had radically redrawn the lines between state and market in favor of the former, Fujimori reversed them just as radically in favor of the latter. While the tasks of fine-tuning Peru's market model in a more dynamic and distributive direction, and of deepening the process of democratic transition, have been left to Fujimori's successor, the country that emerged from the decade of the 1990s is considerably different from the one that entered it. This is so both in regional terms and when Peru is assessed according to the macroeconomic and institutional variables laid out in chapter 1.

When compared with the rest of Latin America, Peru, as the data in this chapter confirm, has as its main reference point for measuring economic performance no longer an Andean bloc still struggling to implement market reforms but rather such emerging-market countries as Argentina, Chile, and Mexico. Furthermore, whereas the previously identified cluster of adverse trends related to state-led development (reckless borrowing, bloated SOEs, a fickle private sector, and regressive income distribution) were still fully intact at the outset of the first Fujimori administration, a decade later all but the distributional challenges had basically been resolved. With regard to institutional reform, the modernization of key entities like the BCRP and a handful of ministries (Economy and Finance, Energy and Mines, Industry and Commerce), as well as the renovation or creation of a range of highly professional and efficient autonomous agencies, has catapulted Peru into the ranks of the top ten developing countries on such competitiveness indicators as the quality of state management and public spending (Vial and Sachs 2000, 10–11).

There is, however, much more to political-economic success than the inroads just mentioned. While I have argued throughout this chapter that Peru's cup is now more than half full on the reform front, progress in eradicating poverty and bridging the distributional gap has not kept pace with the country's impressive growth and investment performance over the past decade. Peru is certainly not alone on this count, but regressive distributional trends have been exacerbated by the politicization of social spending and by the bias toward short-term adjustment relief at the expense of initiatives that target human-capital development over the longer term. These shortcomings in social policy are symptomatic of a larger problem, which is the failure to articulate an integrated trade-led development strategy geared toward the promotion of higher value-added exports, the expansion of local labor markets, and the strengthening of domestic firms. As Brazil, Chile, and Mexico have all ventured down this path, Peru's reticence stems not from a lack of technical expertise but rather from the concentration of economic policy making in an elite executive-level clique that prevents the kinds of policy debate and ideological flexibility that gave rise to more competitive development strategies in these other countries.

Numerous other institutional bottlenecks still need to be tackled. In this chapter I have argued that, of the four institutional variables identified at the outset of this study as most conducive to successful policy outcomes (bureaucratic autonomy, sound economic organizations, stable leadership, and cohesive ties between the state and civil society), Peru has made tremendous strides at the level of internal state reform. Yet even here, there is a need to dig much deeper in overhauling the central government's line ministries, especially those that pertain directly to social-service delivery and human-capital development; and, if the autonomous agencies are to continue as the main anchors of market reform, they must be incorporated into the state apparatus in ways that make them accountable to more than just the whim of the executive.

Similarly, the unraveling from within of a decade-long leadership coalition composed of Fujimori, the military, and the business community now offers the recently elected democratic opposition a vital chance to stake out its leadership claims in a manner that is both more accountable and more inclusive. Although the outgoing coalition was patently successful in launching the first phase of market reforms in Peru, this same coalition emerged as the main bottleneck in the pursuit of second-phase market reforms. This was due to Fujimori's rejection of the kinds of interest intermediation and inclusive politics that underpinned the implementation of second-phase reforms—not to mention the transition to democracy—in other emerging-market countries in the region. At the very moment when Fujimori's leadership coalition became unstable, it collapsed amid a swirl of scandals involving bribery, blackmail, and trafficking in various illicit goods. The moral of the story appears to be that neopopulism, or the doling out of state largesse in ways that endear a leader to the masses without undermining market reforms, can take a politician like Fujimori far, but in the end, the country's disorganized mass of poor cannot save that leader from his own political excesses.

As the Toledo administration seeks to carve out a new leadership coalition, and civic organizations clamor for greater representation and dialogue between the state and society, the economic risks now lie mainly in the political realm. The question is not of which policy course to follow but of whether Fujimori's successors will have the wherewithal and tenacity to restore the administration of justice and to more fully institutionalize the reforms now in place. Albeit brief, the impressive track record of the Paniagua transition government along these very lines suggests that politicians and policy makers may not have as far to go as they think in accomplishing such goals. What is at stake is the difference between settling into a political stalemate that could condemn the country indefinitely to mediocre growth, social instability, and regressive income returns or forging ahead with a Chilean-style broad-based coalition that can craft a pragmatic set of political and economic reforms that would render free markets and liberal politics more compatible in Peru.

CHAPTER 7

In Search of a Competitive Strategy

The Argument Revisited

In this book I have analyzed patterns of economic strategy and institutional change in post–World War Two Latin America from the standpoint of the changing role that the state has played in shaping development outcomes. Three main phases of state intervention were examined: (1) the developmentalist phase that prevailed from the early postwar years up until the 1982 debt shocks, an era in which protectionism and government regulation flourished; (2) the period following the 1982 debt crisis, during which chronic financial insolvency and fiscal retrenchment prompted a retreat from statist strategies over the course of the 1980s; and (3) the revival of the state's economic presence in the 1990s, but in a more arms-length manner, as opposed to the direct modes of participation that had prevailed up through the 1980s. On the basis of this historical analysis I argued that, as much as Latin America's economic doldrums of the 1980s reflected a deep crisis of the state, it was the reform of state institutions that provided the springboard for economic recovery in the 1990s. A main task here has been to specify the ways in which the region has turned this corner, from an all-encompassing statist model to one in which the state has assumed a more market-supporting role in the economy.

On this point, the dramatic external shocks of the early 1980s marked a critical juncture in at least two respects. First, the magnitude and longevity of the crisis forced a rethinking—within the multilateral organizations and the academic community and on the part of Latin American policy makers themselves—about the role of the state in the development process. From the dire fiscal deficits and high levels of government-backed debt that appear in the database presented in chapter 1, there was little doubt that state-led development had gone completely astray by the 1980s. Yet, despite some visible progress at public-sector downsizing, the decade-long recession that ensued also confirmed that it was not enough simply to cut back the state. In fact, by the mid-1980s, Latin America's overall levels of state participation as a percentage of GDP were much lower than those of the OECD bloc and roughly on par with the newly industrializing countries of East Asia (Amsden 1989; Wade 1990; Slemrod 1995). The latter region's higher levels of growth, investment, and real wage gains, as well as its comparatively lower levels of inflation and government debt (World Bank 1993a), suggested that quantitative indicators of public-sector activity revealed little about the remedial measures that would be required to restore growth and investment in Latin America.

At the outset of this study I tackled this question by identifying a cluster of state-related problems that had accumulated over the post–World War Two period in the region and that largely account for the severity and duration of the crisis that exploded in 1982. This pattern consisted of an increasing dependence on foreign loans to support the state's endeavors, which until 1982 allowed for a lax approach to fiscal and monetary policy; a heavy reliance on SOEs to provide infrastructure support and manage the productive sectors of the economy, but with insufficient regard for developing the necessary technical and administrative capabilities to insure the state's entrepreneurial success; the perpetuation of an ambiguous relationship with private investors, who benefited handsomely from the state's debt-backed expansion pre-1982 but who also claimed to lack confidence due to the state's weak administrative structures and the ad hoc nature of public policy making; and the continued neglect of social policies, as concerns about poverty reduction and income distribution consistently took a back seat to the periodic balance-of-payments crises that characterized the developmentalist era.

Through a comparative analysis of the reform record among five emerging-market countries in the region (Argentina, Brazil, Chile, Mexico, Peru) and a more in-depth examination of the Peruvian case, I argued that the resolution of this cluster of state-related problems had become a necessary condition for achieving economic stabilization in the wake of the debt crisis. Again, however, the track record also showed that the rationalization of the state sector was not an entirely sufficient condition for triggering a sustainable reactivation or anywhere near the levels of growth that would be necessary to revive regional economies. As the 1980s wore on, it gradually became evident that institutions, regulations, and the state's overall organizational culture would also have to be reformed. Moreover, as the pillars of corporatism collapsed in the absence of the whole web of subsidies, benefits, and tax preferences that tied civil society to the state under ISI, institutional reform also came to mean a transformation in state-society relations. In short, political leaders, state officials, and the representatives of a wide range of societal interests were forced to mediate their respective concerns in a more transparent and consistent manner.

Thus, a second way in which the 1982 shocks constituted a critical juncture for Latin America was the extent to which the debt crisis underlined the importance of institutional reform as an equally necessary condition for spurring a full economic recovery. In this study I have treated institutions in the classic sense, as those formal and informal rules that shape the behavior of individuals and organizations in civil society (Oliver Williamson 1985; North 1990; Burki and Perry 1998). At the same time, I have relied on a more concrete approach to institutional analysis that considers the coherence of the bureaucracy, the delegation of decisional and operational authority, and the kinds of instruments that policy makers have at their disposal (Ikenberry 1988; Sikkink 1991; Keefer 1995; Graham and Naím 1998). From the political-economy literature and the actual experiences of the five countries at hand, I constructed an analytical framework comprising four key variables that capture the kinds of institutional change that has occurred over the past two decades in Latin America. These include the creation of autonomous agencies within the public bureaucracy, the consolidation of state economic and planning institutions, the stability and character of the leadership coalition, and the nature of the state's ties to organized interests in civil society.

As concerns for institutional reform took center stage in the early 1990s, these state and societal institutions emerged as intervening variables in a couple of ways. First, institutional renovation became the main conduit through which the countries considered here were able to address the cluster of state-led problems identified earlier. I attribute this to the considerable headway that has been made in modernizing institutions along all four of the variables just mentioned. Across the five countries, economic ministries and central banks were overhauled, and the latter have been granted more leeway in executing monetary policy without political interference (Corrales 2000b; Boylan 2001). Within state bureaucracies, autonomy has come to mean much more than simply insulating technical staff to pursue specific policy mandates; increasingly, this also refers to the creation of more output-oriented autonomous agencies that are responsible for the delivery of public services according to performance-based criteria (Bresser Pereira 1999, 6–8). Similarly, while never entirely free from clientelist pressures, executive leadership has assumed a more managerial and professional stance. For the most part, interest intermediation has also become more pragmatic, as representatives on both sides of the negotiating table—state and societal—have settled their differences in a more strategic and levelheaded manner.

Apart from addressing the numerous problems that had accumulated from the past, institutional reforms also emerged as intervening variables in the sense that they were essential for pushing forward an ambitious agenda of market reforms. But this involved much more than the implementation of the neoliberal prescriptions (e.g., liberalization, privatization, and deregulation) offered up by the Washington Consensus. Rather, reform of the state in the post-1982 period also involved the redefinition of what it is the state should actually be doing (Przeworski 1999), as well as the revival and concentration of the state's presence in those areas that have traditionally been regarded as crucial for defending the public good. These include, for example, the regulation of natural monopolies; the protection of property rights; the correction of externalities; and the more careful targeting of investments in education, health, and various other endeavors that directly promote human-capital development. In essence, deep institutional reforms were instrumental for bringing the state back to life, both quantitatively and qualitatively, and for instilling an ethos of constructive state action in a region where the state had long been regarded as a predatory intruder.

Having said all this, it is important to keep these gains in perspective. While the turn-of-the-century prognosis on the capabilities of the Latin American state is certainly more favorable than it was a decade ago, the bar has also been gradually raised on definitions of state effectiveness. In the initial stage of reform post-1982, public policy was considered a success if it met the formidable need for macroeconomic stabilization. This task having been accomplished by the end of the 1980s, the benchmark for effective intervention shifted to the state's ability to foster a sound economic recovery. As continued macroeconomic stability laid the groundwork for higher levels of growth and investment in the 1990s, measures of state effectiveness have come to focus increasingly on a number of unresolved microeconomic challenges in the areas of income distribution, efficiency, and competitiveness. In sum, although I have argued throughout this study that the Latin American state has largely reinvented itself over the past two decades, these lingering microeconomic weaknesses suggest that policy makers have been perhaps too literal in following neoliberal dictums for a minimalist state. The microeconomic data presented in table 18 confirm that rather than doing too much, the state still must do considerably more to rectify these microlevel problems.

The remainder of this chapter elaborates on these themes—first, by reviewing the more specific ways in which they have played out in the Peruvian case; and second, through a discussion of the kinds of direct and indirect policies that could enable state intervention to better supplement domestic markets. Again, the challenge now is not one of further minimalizing state intervention but rather of finding the proper interaction between state institutions and particular market situations. As Alice Amsden has observed from the East Asian setting, the lesson is to cultivate institutions "that use the impetus of the market but restrain its full impact. . . . [W]ithout institutional guidelines and vision, freer markets will only squelch the ability to compete, and at greater social cost."[1]

---

1. Alice H. Amsden, "An Asian Plan for East Europe," *New York Times*, Apr. 6, 1990, A35.

Peru in Retrospect

For a study of the dynamics and outcomes of state intervention in Latin America, the Peruvian case provides some rich insights. The five case-study chapters here were approached from the two perspectives mentioned earlier—focusing on the cluster of state-led problems that had crystallized in varying degrees across the region and on the kinds of institutional arrangements within the state and civil society that framed these trends. Having identified a general post–World War Two pattern in Latin America of state expansion based on external borrowing and weak institutional structures on the domestic front, the analysis drew out the ways in which Peru had con-

TABLE 18. Macro versus Micro Performance in Five Countries: 1990–2000

		Argentina	Brazil	Chile	Mexico	Peru
GDP (growth)	1991–2000	4.7	2.7	6.6	3.5	4.7
GDI (gdi/gdp)	1990–98	17.7	20.8	25.3	22.9	21.3
EXGDP (exp/gdp)	1990–2000	9.2	8.8	30.0	22.9	13.6
INF	2000	−0.9	7.0	3.8	9.5	3.8
RW	1990–2000	0.0	0.4	3.7	0.8	0.9
EMP	1990–99	1.3	1.7	2.1	3.0	2.9
LPRO	1990–95	4.1	−0.1	3.3	−2.2	2.2
URUN	1990–2000	12.2	5.8	7.7	3.5	8.7
EDGAP	1994	1.9[a]	4.7	1.5	3.1	2.6[a]
DIST: poorest 40%	1986	16.2	9.7	12.6	12.7[c]	14.1
DIST: poorest 40%	1990	14.9	9.6	13.4	11.7[b]	
DIST: poorest 40%	1994	13.9	11.8	13.3	10.8	14.1
DIST: poorest 40%	1998	14.9[d]	10.5[a]	13.4	10.8[d]	13.5[a]
DIST: richest 10%	1986	34.5	44.3	39.6	34.3[c]	35.4
DIST: richest 10%	1990	34.8	41.7	39.2	39.0[b]	
DIST: richest 10%	1994	34.2	42.5	40.3	41.2	34.3
DIST: richest 10%	1998	35.8[e]	44.3[a]	39.1	42.8[d]	35.4[a]

Source: GDP and INF: ECLAC Web site, 2001 <www.eclac.org>. GDI: World Bank, *World Tables, CD-ROM,* 2001. EXGDP: calculated from the "National Accounts" section of IMF 2001b. RW, EMP, LPRO, and URUN: ECLAC 2001. EDGAP: Behrman, Birdsall, and Szekely 1998. DIST: Data for Chile and Brazil are based on data for urban areas, and data for Argentina are based on data for Buenos Aires, all from ECLAC 1997b. Data for Mexico are from Pastor and Wise 2002. Data on national income distribution for Peru are from World Bank 1993b and 1996. The most recent distribution figures are from ECLAC 2001 and World Bank, *World Tables, CD-ROM,* 2001.

Note: GDP = gross domestic product; GDI = gross domestic investment as % of GDP; EXGDP = ratio of exports of goods and services to GDP; INF = percent change in consumer prices over previous year; RW = real wages, average annual growth rate; EMP = employment, average annual growth rate; LPRO = labor productivity, average annual growth rate; URUN = urban employment, average annual rate; EDGAP = average years behind in school for ages 15–18; DIST = % of national income accruing to groups.

[a]1996.
[b]1989.
[c]1984.
[d]1995.
[e]1997.

formed to this pattern. Peru's similarities with the other four countries in table 18 had to do with the poor management of macroeconomic policy and other indirect interventions, a luxury largely afforded by the government's easy access to foreign savings until 1983; the increasingly conflictual relationship between the state and the private sector; and the inability to effectively use state intervention to mitigate the country's highly skewed patterns of income distribution.

The difference between Peru and the other four countries is related to the later start with which the country embarked on the state-led path, the intensity with which the state expanded once the catch-up effort had gotten underway, and the near absence of much of the necessary bureaucratic machinery to back up the state's endeavors. The drawbacks of the Peruvian state-as-entrepreneur became acutely evident once the sources of external financing evaporated. On the one hand, a discussion of the subtext of the developmentalist era in Peru could easily be entitled "the limits to state action." On the other hand, this study revealed the extent to which these limits were largely self-imposed. In taking a step back from the details of the case study, what stands out is the paucity of hard decisions that were made up through the heterodox meltdown of the late 1980s and the lack of any follow-through on those steps that had been taken to strengthen the Peruvian state as a viable actor in the development process. In other words, the story up to 1990 is largely one of opportunities lost and paths not taken.

On this count, several critical junctures come to mind concerning the formation of the Peruvian state sector—its financing and the administrative and institutional evolution of the state. Concerning the financing of the state sector, of note is the passivity with which domestic policy makers approached the problem of shoring up the state's resources. The three main options for public revenue have traditionally been taxation, user fees, and borrowing. Since the early 1960s, when Peru's state-sponsored industrial strategy first got underway, the country saw just one serious tax overhaul. This occurred at political gunpoint in 1968, when it became clear that the state's severe fiscal crisis was a threat to the survival of civilian rule. Fiscal policy subsequently consisted of a long series of piecemeal indirect measures that, over time, gradually eroded what had started out as a comparatively diverse and progressive tax base in the 1950s.

Policy makers were more energetic about utilizing external debt to finance the state's undertakings but not so when it came to ensuring that those funds be put to productive use. The track record on managing the debt was poor. Throughout the 1963–90 period, the external debt had been successfully renegotiated in 1967–68 and in 1971. The very difficult 1977–78 debt crisis was "solved" by the 1979 mineral price boom, and the 1982–83 crisis was not fully dealt with until the finalization of Peru's Brady debt-restructuring deal more than a decade later. While the formal unilateral moratorium on debt payments declared by García in 1985 represented a legitimate attempt to strengthen the country's position vis-à-vis the international financial community, the prolongation of this policy and the failure to negotiate at all with foreign lenders ultimately placed the country in the weakest position possible. That is, a do-nothing stance on the debt front affected the flow of other crucial forms of development finance, like import financing, multilateral loans, and bilateral aid.

A good part of the case study was spent arguing that the passive policy stance stemmed largely from the country's weak administrative and institutional apparatus. Yet there were some attempts to reverse this situation, including the design of strategic pockets within the state bureaucracy where a fairly educated policy-making segment had been cultivated at one time or another. The period during the early 1970s, for example, saw the first massive administrative overhaul of the state, the creation of some new development institutions, and the strengthening of others like the INP. In retrospect, this stands out as a valiant effort at upgrading and modernizing the state apparatus. Some institutions, such as the BCRP, had developed highly professional recruiting and entry standards by this time and had brought together a large pool of technical and intellectual talent. In other words, in some measured ways, the state had begun to come into its own during this period.

The problem was one of continuity and of the inability to gather any lasting momentum in the direction of state reform. For the most part, and in contrast to Brazil, Chile, and Mexico, political and economic elites in Peru had not shown any sustained interest in building up the capacities of the state. The only other serious set of administrative changes, undertaken in 1978, went in the opposite direction. It took well into the 1990s for the central government to regain its footing from the massive layoffs of top public-sector personnel that took place at that time. Apart from a basic disregard for the importance of the inner workings of the state, elite executive policy makers shared a longstanding distrust of state agencies. The tendency had been to circumvent the considerable talent that had been gathered within major state institutions like the MEF and the BCRP and to rely heavily on patronage and the meager expertise of those who came up through the ranks of the political parties. Both the second Belaúnde administration and the García administration refined this practice to an art.

This brings us to the current period, analyzed in chapter 6, where hyperinflation and a full-blown civil war erupted against the backdrop of Peru's international financial isolation and its failure to stick to any stabilization plan at all. By 1990, the traditional political parties had collapsed, as had state finances, and large segments of the hinterland were governed de facto by guerrilla bands and drug traffickers (Webb 1991, 4). Longstanding entities like the BCRP and the MEF, overrun by domestic politics, had bungled monetary and fiscal policy so badly that both had lost all credibility. The 1990 dark-horse presidential victory of a little-known and inexperienced politician like Alberto Fujimori did not appear at the time to be a recipe for success. Yet hindsight shows that the crisis—surely the worst the country had faced in more than a century—had a paradoxical outcome. The demise of the ancien régime, and the loss of control over domestic politics and the state's resources by an entrenched *criollo* elite, paved the way for new actors who brought with them new approaches to the country's enormous backlog of problems.

The Fujimori administration has been rightfully criticized for relying too rigidly on the neoliberal mandates of the Washington Consensus (Kay 1997; Gonzáles 1998) and on an authoritarian political style to achieve its programmatic goals (Mauceri 1996; Maxwell Cameron 1997). But despite these negatives, Peru's economic turnaround in the 1990s has been such that it now ranks with the emerging-market countries in table 18, as opposed to the still-struggling Andean Community nations that remained the more appropriate point of comparison in 1990 (Vial and Sachs 2000). Rather than dismiss these economic gains out of hand because of their association with other less savory features of the reform effort, as some authors have, this study has instead sought to identify the sources of policy success. I attribute this success to a quiet process of state reconstruction and renovation that has underpinned the country's market transformation. Not only does Peru's macroeconomic performance in the 1990s reflect the biggest turnaround of any of the countries in table 18, but Peru is also the one case where the reform path was almost entirely state-centered through the decade.

In spite of the rhetoric of a minimalist state that prevailed under Fujimori (Boloña 1996), this study revealed an ongoing pattern of deep internal state reform that began at the outset of his administration (Ugarte 2000). Given that the renewal of blue-chip economic entities like the MEF and the BCRP was absolutely essential for purging the economy of hyperinflation and rebuilding international financial ties, both were restored to the super-agency status that they had historically occupied. Similarly, other mandatory tasks related to the modernization of state finances and the construction of a market-assuring regulatory framework required the creation or overhaul of an additional ring of state agencies. Under "normal" circumstances, the more common practice has been for executives to postpone the creation of autonomous public entities until the end of their terms, so as to avoid losing discretionary control over the policy process (Boylan 2000). In Peru of the early 1990s, with insurgencies proliferating and the military circling the presidential palace, the executive's time horizon was so uncertain that a slew of autonomous agencies was crafted at the start of Fujimori's first term in order to quicken the pace of stabilization and adjustment.

Thus, the flip side of the 1988–90 hyperinflationary crisis was the emergence of a broad consensus that major reforms could no longer be postponed. In turn, the growing social demand for reform fostered strong incentives for institutional renovation, as the very survival of the first Fujimori administration hinged on the ability of the state to deliver on the basic services and economic necessities that had been promised. In relying so strongly on state-centered reforms, the Peruvian case confirms that there is more than one route to economic recovery. Peru's experience does not, however, take away from those who have argued that the long-term success and sustainability of market reforms will also require that they be firmly grounded in cohesive political-party systems and coherent state-society relations (Haggard and Kaufman 1995; Mainwaring and Scully 1995; Bresser Pereira 1999). If anything, this last point is confirmed by the remarkable scandals that led to the unexpectedly quick unraveling of Peru's ruling coalition and to the calling of new presidential elections just months after Fujimori's contrived reelection to a third term in May 2000.

As Przeworski (1999, 16) reminds us, the task of state reform is "to equip the state with instruments for effective intervention and . . . to create incentives for public officials to act in the public interest. Some of these incentives can be generated by the internal organization of the government, but structure alone is not sufficient. If the government is to perform well, the bureaucracy must be controlled by elected politicians who, in turn, must be accountable to citizens." In Peru, the heavy reliance on structure alone allowed for the longevity of an incumbent president who had clearly lost sight of the public interest after a decade in office. As the faltering of Peru's civil-military alliance suddenly threatened the hard-fought victory of economic recovery, it became apparent that no amount of internal state reform could halt the damage to the credibility of the ruling coalition. At the very point when other state-centered reformers like Chile and Mexico faced this same dilemma, political elites effectively advanced the reform process by modernizing party systems and by more authentically incorporating citizen input into the reform agenda. While Fujimori's inclination had been to move in the opposite direction, the president and his military cronies were again reminded—by international actors, foreign investors, other political leaders in the region, and Peruvians themselves—that there is simply no sympathy or support for modern-day caudillos in Latin America.

As the country quickly regrouped with the 2001 election of President Alejandro Toledo, in a contest subject to strong OAS monitoring and hence the kinds of transparency and competitive rules that were completely lacking in the 2000 race, the next chapter in the evolution of the Peruvian political economy is already underway. Although too incipient to tackle at any length here, there is every indication that this next development phase will entail the revival of civil society and efforts to modernize state-society ties in ways that coincide with the reform trajectory of the other emerging-market countries considered here. A main purpose of this study has been to elaborate on how the Peruvian state, once an obstacle to such goals, has been reinvented to the extent that it is now capable of forging a productive partnership with civil society. The tasks of internal state reform are far from complete, but the state is no longer the missing actor in the formulation and implementation of sound development policies.

What tasks await the Toledo administration in terms of further promoting the reform of the Peruvian state? Given the inordinate role that the control of state resources and the manipulation of the country's legal apparatus played in prolonging Fujimori's incumbency, both problems require immediate attention. First, there is a need to install mechanisms that allow for greater oversight and accountability in the allocation of public expenditures and that reduce the considerable redundancy and overlap in state outlays, particularly in the social sectors. Equally important is the need to restore the rule of law—within congress, the courts, and the electoral system (García 2000; Mosquiera 2000). The capture and incarceration of Montesinos, and the disbanding of his sinister SIN in October 2000, represented important steps in this direction.[2] In the medium term, there are three interrelated challenges that the next generation of policy makers must grapple with in order to maximize on the state's potential for playing a constructive role in this transition.

First, the completion of internal state reform will require that the central government's line ministries be subjected to the same organizational overhaul and professionalization of personnel that has characterized the reform of the autonomous agencies discussed in chapter 6 (Ugarte 2000, 406–12). This mandate is now underway with the passing of a new state-modernization law by the Peruvian congress in January 2002, to be backed up by a US$150 million loan from the IDB.[3] Simultaneously, the autonomous agencies must be more firmly rooted in administrative law and integrated into the national budget, precautions that would render them a more permanent feature of the state regardless of who occupies congress or the executive office. Second, with Fujimori's undue emphasis on short-term social spending to secure political support, the country still lacks the kinds of targeted investments in human

---

2. Scott Wilson, "The Stakeout That Snared a Spy," *Washington Post,* June 26, 2001, A1.
3. "Congreso aprobó Ley de Modernización del Estado," *Gestíon* (Lima), Jan. 18, 2002, 28.

capital that are crucial for reducing inequality and enabling Peruvian workers to find their niche in the market economy. On the human-capital front, this tendency for microeconomic dynamism to lag behind the macroeconomic gains that have been realized is portrayed in table 18. In Peru, a main bottleneck has been the neglect of those social ministries like education and health that are ostensibly the main venues for promoting human capital. In the absence of a major modernization effort within these ministries, any further reallocation of expenditures toward these social categories would likely be offset by internal disarray.[4]

Finally, although Peru now ranks highly on specific competitiveness indicators related to government spending and domestic investment (Vial and Sachs 2000), it still trails in the bottom third of a developing-country sample (N = 62) in crucial areas like infrastructure, technology, and the overall quality of management. Throughout the region these low rankings in matters related to efficiency and competitiveness have increasingly become the focus of public policy. When viewed against the intractable patterns of income inequality that have prevailed in the wake of sweeping economic reforms, countries like Chile and Mexico have come to treat these tenacious trends as concrete instances of market failure. As such, state policy has risen to the occasion in designing compensatory incentives to bolster markets where they have faltered. In the following section I elaborate further on this competitiveness gap with a focus on the data in table 18. I then review where Peru stands with regard to formulating a set of macro- and microeconomic strategies that could more forcefully address these competitive challenges.

In Search of a Competitive Strategy

While the reform strategies of most Latin American countries conform closely to the neoliberal prescriptions of the Washington Consensus, table 19 also reflects the diversity of those policies that have been pursued under the banner of market reform. The "standard" approach depicted in the table signifies the basically hands-off management style that prevailed in Chile up until the 1982 debt shocks, in Mexico until the 1994 peso crisis, in Argentina until the meltdown of the Convertibility Plan in late 2001 (Pastor and Wise

---

4. Carlos Aramburu, executive director of Consorcio de Investigación Económica y Social, interview with the author, Lima, Jan 11, 2002; Carlos Salazar, general director of Secretaria de Cooperación Técnica Internacional, Presidencia del Consejo de Ministros, interview with the author, Lima, Jan. 18, 2002; Dr. Ariel Frischando, former executive directive of the Office for International Cooperation in Peru's Ministry of Health, interview with the author, London, Jan. 21, 2002.

TABLE 19. Standard versus Competitive Approaches to Economic Reform

	Trade		Exchange Rates		Finance		Fiscal		Human Capital		Institutions	
	Standard: Unilateral Liberalization	Competitive: Export Promotion, Indirect Incentives, Sectorally Neutral Trade Diversification Policies	Standard: Exchange Rate Fixed, Anti-inflation Anchor	Competitive: Exchange Rate Downwardly Flexible	Standard: Liberal Capital Account, Market Driven Interest Rates	Competitive: Regulations on Capital Flows, Interest Rates Driven by Productivity	Standard: Fiscal Overhaul	Competitive: Tax Incentives to Promote Exports, Non-traditionals, Higher Value Added	Standard: Flexible Labor Markets, Adjustment Assistance for Workers and Producers in Import-Competing Industries	Competitive: Technical Support for Smaller Firms, State Sponsored Programs for Employment Training	Standard: Policy-making by Executive Decree, Weak Business-Government Links	Competitive: Policy Grounded in Cohesive State Institutions, Strong Collaboration between Government and Business
Chile 1974–82	x		Until 1982		x		x		x		x	
Chile 1983–present	x	x		From 1983 on, pegged; 1999, float		x	x	x		x		x
Mexico 1985–95	x		Until 1994		x		x			x		x
Mexico 1996–present	x	x		From 1995 on, float	x		x	x		x		x
Brazil 1990–present	x	Partial	Until 01/99	From 01/99 on, float		Partial	x	x		x	Partial	Partial
Argentina 1989–present	x	Special trade regime for autos and sugar	1991–2001	From 01/02 on, float	x		x	x	Partial	Partial	x	
Peru 1990–present	x			"Dirty float"	x		x		x	Partial		x

2001), and that characterized Peru's policy framework until Fujimori's resignation. Under the standard or minimal approach, policy makers have purposefully assigned the task of economic development to comparative advantage while leaving microeconomic adjustment to market forces. The "competitive" strategy characterizes the more hands-on, market-supporting approach that Chilean policy makers adopted in the mid-1980s, that Mexico embraced in 1996, and that Brazil has applied sporadically since the onset of market reforms in the 1990s.[5] First, the competitive strategy recognizes a more active role for public policy in the face of adjustment stress or outright market failure; second, it actively embraces an export-led development model. In doing so, the competitive approach combines sound macroeconomic management with strategic institutional interventions and human-capital upgrading.

What accounts for the policy shifts that appear in table 19, whereby countries such as Chile and Mexico have been compelled to adopt a more proactive stance with regard to trade, monetary, fiscal, and social policy? Given the complexity of each case there are no simple answers to this question. However, a shorthand explanation would have to take into account the timing and magnitude of international shocks, as well as the interplay between external pressures and the different domestic institutional configurations discussed throughout this book. The political-economic forces that propelled Chile's policy shift are perhaps most relevant to Peru, because both are small, open, resource-based economies and because Peruvian economic policy makers expressed an affinity for the Chilean model (or at least their interpretation of it) at the outset of Fujimori's first term (Agenda 2000, 1991).[6] The Toledo administration, moreover, has revived this notion of emulating the best of the Chilean experience.

In the case of Chile, it was the hyperinflationary shocks of the early 1970s that triggered a military coup and hence a first wave of standard market reforms. When a second crisis of equal magnitude hit less than a decade later, this served as the catalyst for switching to a more hands-on approach to economic adjustment. Although the first wave of market restructuring had set the stage for a relatively quick turnaround in the 1980s, the policy reforms implemented in the mid-1980s helped to bolster this economic recovery while also correcting for past errors—all within the parameters of the market model. In brief, Chile's impressive turnaround since the mid-1980s has been

---

5. I borrow these "standard" and "competitive" categories from John Sheahan (1997, 9–11).

6. Iván Rivera, MEF economist and top advisor to the president, interview with the author, Lima, July 18, 1995.

based on a combination of internal state reform and the modernization of government-business relations. Together, these served as the springboard for a major macroeconomic overhaul and for the formulation of a microeconomic strategy proper (Bosworth, Dornbusch, and Labán 1994; Meller 1997; Schmidt-Hebbel 1999).

At the level of economic institutions, the most important changes concerned the professionalization of the state's regulatory activities and management practices; the consolidation of changes in tariff policy and budgeting procedures that helped limit the impact of special-interest lobbies; and the creation of an autonomous central bank (Velasco 1994; Boylan 2001). Against the backdrop of these institutional reforms, key macroeconomic adjustments were made—for example, in the shift from a fixed to a flexible exchange-rate regime, in the lowering of interest rates, and in the placing of new restrictions on short-term capital inflows (Sheahan 1997; Edwards and Lederman 1998). At the same time, policy makers declared an explicit commitment to a trade-led development strategy geared toward the promotion of nontraditional products that offered higher value-added returns to the economy (Meller 1997; Pastor and Wise 1999a), as it had long been recognized that this was the quickest way to boost a country's competitive position in world markets and to foster more dynamic patterns of job creation and wage gains (Edwards 1995; Sheahan 1999).

It was also during this period that a more clearly defined microeconomic strategy began to materialize, as the severe crisis context post-1982 opened up new avenues for broader private-sector input into the policy-making process. In fact, and in contrast to the 1970s, when the interests of the big conglomerates prevailed, government ministers actively sought the collaboration of wider segments of Chile's well-organized business community (Eduardo Silva 1996; Schneider 1998). By the time of the transition to civilian rule in 1990 a competitive strategy had become clearly defined, largely as a result of the combination of state reform, institutional innovation, and more cohesive interaction between the government and business groups.

Chile's microeconomic strategy included some of the following policies (Schurman 1996; Marcel 1999; Kurtz 2000): (1) well-designed incentives geared toward export promotion and diversification through the use of value-added tax exemptions, nontraditional-export subsidies, reduced-rate loan programs, marketing assistance, and a sharply devalued currency; (2) the investment of the state development corporation (CORFO) in research and human capital in the export sectors and the granting of special subsidies and credits to strengthen the market position of smaller producers of nontraditional (mainly industrial) exports; and (3) the maintenance of low labor costs through the use of repressive labor practices (Eduardo Silva 1996)—a trend that subsequent civilian policy makers have worked hard to reverse.[7]

By the late 1980s the "distributional moment" had arrived in Chile in terms of the glaring gap between macroeconomic recovery and distributional stress (Boylan, forthcoming, 2003). The long-run viability of market reforms came to depend, first, on the reincorporation of civil society into a management model that could no longer sustain itself through the disproportionate reliance on state coercion; and second, on more vigorous efforts to follow up this competitive export-led model with targeted social investments in such areas as primary education and health care. As table 18 shows, although these social policies have yet to fully pay off on the distributional front, they have delivered solid returns to the real economy (Schmidt-Hebbel 1999). Moreover, while never entirely free of patronage, the dispersal of social resources in Chile is handled through decentralized institutions that have risen above the fray of Fujimori-style opportunism. Societal demands for social capital are ever present, but increasingly these demands have been mediated through political parties and organized interest representation in Chile.

Where does Peru stand in comparison with this more competitive Chilean-style strategy? While Peru has advanced light years in the overhaul of frontline autonomous state agencies and the modernization of government-business relations, policy makers have still not gone the extra mile in articulating a competitive development model that can sustain high growth and income gains over the long term. Peru's tendency to stand by a hands-off management strategy based on traditional exports and comparative advantage can be attributed, first, to the ideological blinders worn by some within Fujimori's economic team, regardless of the failure of markets alone to infuse more dynamism into the microeconomy.[8] Moreover, an overly insulated leadership coalition, and the peculiar circumstances that led to the vetting of executive access by the military, have deterred debate about the proper role for public policy in facilitating innovation and microeconomic adjustment (Sagasti 1996).

---

7. Carlos Alvarez, Strategic Development Division head, CORFO, interview with the author, Santiago, July 8, 1996; Juan Morales, Director of Enterprise Development, Confederación Nacional de la Mediana y Pequeña Industria, Servicios, y Artesanado de Chile, interview with the author, Santiago, July 9, 1996.

8. In late 1998, when Peru was in the throes of adjusting to the Asian shocks and interest rates had skyrocketed, I asked a top policy official at the Ministry of Industry (MITINCI) in an off-the-record interview about the kinds of adjustment support available for smaller companies with burgeoning debt burdens. The response: "None . . . the private sector just doesn't get it, this is a generation that still clamors for protectionism. . . . [W]e are fully committed to relying on comparative advantage." Back in 1995, MEF policy advisor Iván Rivera had used the same argument to justify the lack of a development plan during the first Fujimori administration: "When markets are free, there is no need for planning." Iván Rivera, interview with the author, Lima, July 18, 1995.

Admittedly, the Peruvian economy went far in the 1990s under a purist market approach backed by deep institutional reform, and it did so despite an increasingly dysfunctional political backdrop. But to date, Peru's economic turnaround falls short of the kind of takeoff or breakthrough that Chile has registered from 1986 on. Prior to the political crisis that finally brought Montesinos down, and the president with him, the prospect of another five years of Fujimori meant, at best, that the political economy would continue to hover at the same turnaround point that appears in table 18. This is because the reform gaps that still need to be filled in such areas as human-capital investment, restructuring and modernization of small and medium-sized firms, export promotion, and further overhaul of the state had succumbed to a political gridlock that was not likely to dissipate with the prolongation of the Fujimori presidency. Now, quite unexpectedly, a new cohort of political and economic actors has been given a chance to put aside the authoritarian baggage of the Fujimori era and to articulate a competitive strategy that reflects critical thinking about the country's market failures, as well as the need for greater political accountability in initiating changes.

While Peru's takeoff is far from certain, the reform inroads that were made on multiple fronts over the past decade mean that the country is now better positioned than ever to break through those growth, trade, and investment barriers that define Chile's breakthrough as shown in tables 18 and 19.[9] But this will entail the shift to a competitive strategy, which now seems as much a matter of decision makers' vision and fortitude as it does the particular policies and expertise that are brought to bear on such a project. In the post-Fujimori era domestic-policy debates have centered on these very questions, and a rich base of local social-science research has emerged to inform public discourse concerning the future of the Peruvian political economy.[10] According to these diagnoses, a competitive strategy would entail a more dynamic role for public policy in at least three areas: (1) the completion of first-phase market reforms that are still pending; (2) the adoption of an explicit export-led development strategy; and (3) the depoliticization of social policy in favor of more targeted human-capital investments. Following I highlight the unfinished business within each of these categories.

Market-Completing Reforms

Apart from the remaining challenges concerning the reform of the state reviewed in the previous section, there are three other issues still left on the

9. This point is also argued convincingly by Eduardo Morón, "Crecer en medio de la crisis," *El Comercio* (Lima), Jan. 6, 2002, B4.

10. See, for example, Gonzáles 1998; Abusada, Du Bois, Morón, and Valderrama 2000b, vols. 1 and 2; Boza 2000; Parodi 2000; Portocarrero Súarez 2000; Vásquez 2000; and Webb 2000.

table from the first Fujimori administration. All have to do with the need to adjust policy approaches in ways that would render market reforms more dynamic. The first challenge lies in the macroeconomic realm. As table 19 shows, both Argentina and Peru have adhered to a standard policy approach with regard to trade, monetary, and fiscal policy. The result for both has been comparatively lower levels of trade as a percentage of GDP in the 1990s, a pattern underpinned by exchange-rate appreciation and unfavorable tax and credit incentives for domestic firms. Other problems related to these trends concern the higher levels of urban unemployment that each country has registered over the past decade, as in both cases the hands-off strategy has encouraged capital-intensive investments in nontradable services and natural resource development. It is interesting to note that this was the very plateau that Chile had reached in the mid-1980s when policy makers responded with the shift toward the competitive approaches detailed in table 19, and Peru would do well to follow suit. More ominously, this is the same critical juncture at which Argentina's currency board imploded, forcing a sloppy devaluation and President De la Rúa's resignation just two years into his term.

There is also considerable work left to do on the privatization front. Peru's track record in selling off the state's assets is considered to be one of the more transparent and professional in the region (Manzetti 1999). However, the impulse for privatization stalled midway into Fujimori's second term, placing in limbo earlier goals for further public-sector downsizing and the auctioning off of those state concessions (e.g., highways, seaports, airports, and sanitation services) that are essential for promoting greater competitiveness (Franco, Muñoz, Sánchez, and Zavala 2000). The delicacy with which privatization must be treated in the post-Fujimori era was made evident by the rioting and looting that occurred in June 2002 in the southern Andean town of Arequipa in response to the government's sale of two small electricity generators to a Belgian company.[11] Although a court mediator later ruled the US$167 million sale sound, the lesson for the Toledo administraiton with regard to further privatization was twofold.

First, such deals can no longer be made behind closed doors, as in the past. In hindsight, Peru's overall privatization program looks squeaky clean, especially when compared with Mexico's scandalous sell-off of the state banks or Argentina's blatant insider trading on any number of public assets. For Peruvians, the issue is how the privatization proceeds were disbursed, including some US$1.5 billion that went toward arms purchases under Montesinos and Fujimori, not to mention the millions in apparent kickbacks that have since

---

11. "Peru: A Popular Revolt Against Privatisation Spells Trouble for President Toledo's Government," <http://www.Economist.com>, June 20, 2002.

surfaced in foreign bank accounts tied to that administration. Hence, any future political luck with privatization will require the utmost of transparency, serious dialogue with the affected parties, and straight talk from the Toledo administration about its plans in this area. Second, the role of privatization in promoting the success of the export-led strategy must be made explicit. Obviously, in the case of electricity generation, this particular privatization could greatly enhance efficiency and productivity in this southern regional economy. However, it is up to the current team to connect these dots and to articulate how privatization can complement the country's development strategy in ways that outweigh the perceived costs.

On the question of further downsizing the state, Roberto Abusada and others (2000b, 48–52) have put forth the bold but plausible proposition that the central government should be streamlined to include just seven ministries and no more than twenty autonomous agencies. This would entail a cut of at least 25 percent of the public workforce in those productive-sector ministries (agriculture, mining, and industry) that find it harder to justify their existence under a market model. Other black boxes, such as the Ministry of the Presidency and the Ministry of Defense, could no doubt use a similar housecleaning. The lesson from the recent past, where reform opponents effectively deterred the president from forging ahead with the Program to Modernize the Public Administration, is that the Toledo administration should move quickly in completing these necessary tasks. In contrast with the earlier reform failures in the realm of public sector streamlining, this time around there is considerable multilateral support to finance state reform.[12]

The remaining reform gap in this category is the overlapping problem of stagnation in the rural sector and the age-old challenge of decentralization in Peru (Lizárraga 1985; Wilson and Wise 1986). Both are still common themes that unite all of the countries considered here. In Peru, however, the trauma of a twelve-year civil war fought largely in the more remote rural areas has compelled policy makers to tread lightly with reform implementation in the regions. To its credit, the Fujimori administration refrained from making the grandiose promises that every other government since 1963 had made concerning the decentralization of national resources, the modernization of agriculture, and the reduction of ancient patterns of rural poverty. It was, after all, the chronic failure to deliver on such promises that inspired the numerous guerrilla movements of the 1980s. Instead, by transferring unprecedented social resources to the country's twenty-four provinces via his powerful Ministry of the Presidency, Fujimori simultaneously provided poverty relief and

---

12. Author's interview, Vladimir Radovic, representative, Inter-American Development Bank, Lima, January 17, 2002.

won the support of regional voters. Especially after the dismal performance of the president's coalition in the various elections held in 1993, the link between regional social transfers and the president's political survival was solidified (Graham and Kane 1998).

Thus, whereas the multilaterals had touted decentralization in the 1990s as the route to greater efficiency, accountability, and transparency in the delivery of public goods (World Bank 1997; Peterson 1997), Peruvian-style decentralization in the 1990s offered just the reverse. Highly discretionary expenditures on local infrastructure (especially schools), social services, and municipal employment in the regions provided short-term relief but few institutionalized mechanisms to guarantee this support beyond the Fujimori administration (Palacios and Roca 2000). And in defiance of those political science theories that paint Latin American decentralization in the 1990s as "a political bargain involving presidents, legislators, and subnational politicians" (Willis, Garman, and Haggard 2000, 7), in Peru "decentralization" over the past decade has been a tenuous pact between the president and his mass of regional constituents (Roberts 1995; Kay 1997). Clearly, although the data show that they had little lasting distributional impact, these vertical ties and goodwill gestures created a sense of political inclusion for a group that had long been excluded from the national political economy (Seddon 1997).

However, Fujimori's early departure and the lack of fully institutionalized channels for the delivery of social resources to the regions create a precarious situation that the Toledo administration is currently seeking to address. The Chilean experience with decentralization over the past twenty years has shown that, despite the difficulties and pitfalls intrinsic to decentralization, the process can be greatly enhanced by the institutionalization of the flow of transfers from the central government such that the provincial managers can credibly supply the quality and quantity of services demanded; the design of organizational incentives that enable local communities to effectively convey their concerns to municipal authorities; and the democratic election of regional and municipal officials (Marcel 1999, 293–99). To its credit, the Toledo administration wasted no time in scheduling competitive nationwide municipal elections for late 2002, confirming that the reintroduction of decentralized institutional mechanisms and democratic checks is a priority for this next generation of state managers.

A Trade-Led Development Strategy

By definition, the sweeping liberalization that has occurred implies a commitment to an export-led strategy along Chilean or Mexican lines. This option for Peru is especially compelling in light of the country's proven success in promoting both traditional and nontraditional exports with higher value-added content during a brief period in the late 1970s (Schydlowsky 1986a, 1986b; Sheahan 1999). And although economists are known to disagree more often than not, one point of consensus is the crucial role that such higher value-added exports can play in spurring growth, productivity, jobs, and income gains (Edwards 1995; Londoño and Szekely 1997; Meller 1997). But for Peru such a strategy at this stage would require a more downwardly flexible exchange rate, not to mention an explicit set of incentives and planning guidelines to bring it to life. In the absence of such a strategy, Peru's exports as a percent of GDP have leveled off since 1990 (see table 18), as privatization incentives have pulled FDI into nontradable services (e.g., electricity and telecommunications). Moreover, while all five countries in table 18 continue to struggle against exchange-rate appreciation in the era of high capital mobility, the value of Peru's currency throughout the 1990s has not been particularly favorable to exports (Abugattas 1998).

In a recent ECLAC study published by Barbara Stallings and Wilson Peres (2000), Peru emerges as an aggressive reformer but a laggard performer with regard to the efficiency of investment, the dynamism of trade in relation to other market reformers, and the impact of both on employment and equity. Under the impulse of a standard approach to market reform, Peru's sectoral contribution to value-added followed a regional trend: a decline in manufacturing, a growth spurt in services, and a pattern of output in agriculture and mining that is more or less a continuation of prereform trends. Similar to its neighbors, the Peruvian economy also saw an increase in patterns of heterogeneity within these four main sectors during the 1990s, as economic liberalization ushered in new investors who brought with them first-best production practices (Carrillo and Hernández 2000; Shimizu 2000). Thus, the underside of market transformation for Peru and others has been the worsening plight of those smaller producers and less-skilled workers who have yet to reap the benefits of or integrate into international markets for investment and trade.

Where Peru stands out, according to Stallings and Peres (2000, 160–70), is in its disproportionate decline in investment in potentially dynamic manufacturing or semimanufacturing sectors (foodstuffs, metal products, pharmaceuticals, chemicals, pulp and paper) and in the exceptional growth of nonagricultural low-skilled rural employment in the 1990s (also see Escobal 2000). Meanwhile, in the urban setting, the bulk of employment creation came from those microenterprises and small firms operating in the largely informal service sector, while big capital-intensive firms have continued to dominate in their contribution to GDP. Outside of telecommunications, banking, and mining, Peru has also lagged in attracting investments that promote the greater application of technology to productive structures. This is not to take away from the productivity and wage gains that appear in table 18, or the trends in social mobility that have clearly occurred, but the fact is that the old dualist tendencies that have long plagued the Peruvian economy are still present.

Another point of consensus is that these shortcomings in the way of innovation and dynamism are amenable to public policy. Other countries have countered these trends by promoting higher value-added exports in both the traditional (mining, agriculture) and the nontraditional sectors of the economy (Hausmann and Rodrik 2002). Chile's strategies have already been addressed here. Other approaches include Mexico's incentives to promote business clusters and strengthen production chains for companies that have been weakened by trade liberalization (Pastor and Wise 1997); Brazil has similarly offered a range of tax and credit incentives to foster outward-oriented production (Stallings and Peres 2000). These efforts differ from the heavy-handed industrial policies of the past in that they are designed with an eye toward fostering horizontal cross-sectoral links and toward supporting firms in the market through training, support services, and access to know-how (Chudnovsky 1997). Whereas such interventions were unthinkable in Peru in 1990, particularly in light of the excesses of the García era, the magnitude of reform is now such that they are advisable for infusing greater dynamism into domestic markets.

The Human-Capital Frontier: Back to the Basics

Peru's continued lack of a cohesive social policy has been an overriding theme of this study. Contrary to the developmentalist era, when human-capital investments were promised but never sufficiently delivered, or the crisis-ridden 1980s, when policy makers groped in the dark for ways to stabilize the economy without further exacerbating poverty, the 1990s have produced an impressive body of data and research on both the sources of inequality and the most direct ways to address it.[13] This last statement holds for the policy community at large and for the impressive array of social-sector research that has been produced locally in Peru by think tanks and the academic community (e.g., Velarde and Rodríguez 1998; Abusada, Du Bois, Morón, and Valderrama 2000b; Parodi 2000; Portocarrero Súarez 2000; Vásquez 2000). The four main areas of research emphasis have been education, health care, pensions, and housing. The track record shows that Peru has made headway

---

13. See, for example, Birdsall and Londoño 1997; Londoño and Szekely 1997; Sheahan 1997; Stallings and Peres 2000; and World Bank 2000.

on the first three fronts, although education and health care stand out as the most progressive and direct means for alleviating poverty and bridging the equity gap that appears in table 18.

Although the struggle for greater upward social mobility is regionwide, Peru's social policy has been hampered in three ways. First, while the data show that social expenditures have increased by at least a third in the 1990s, such increases started from a very low base (Stallings and Peres 2000). Second, the siphoning off of the social-expenditure budget into the Ministry of the Presidency, and the executive's heavy reliance on social-capital expenditures to keep his incumbency alive through the 1990s, distracted from the more targeted human-capital investments that will be essential for sustaining poverty reduction in Peru (Vásquez 2000). Third, as a result of these first two trends, the will for reforming those frontline social ministries like education and health never gained momentum. Hence, education reform faltered very early on (Graham 1998; World Bank 1999), and health care has seen some isolated pockets of success, but nothing near the overhaul that current trends call for (Ewig 2000; Pollarolo 2000). Once the dust settles on the Fujimori era, hindsight will show that the failure to articulate a social policy that more directly linked human-capital investments with the new market model was a strong factor in the president's loss of popular support.

Again, contrary to the past, Peru's next generation of policy makers brings with it a high level of expertise and a whole arsenal of sound research to inform a revamped social policy. The success of such endeavors will depend on the modernization of those frontline ministries involved in the poverty-reduction effort, the clarification of responsibilities to be assumed by the various state agencies involved, and a much stronger coordination of policy making among entities. In retrospect, the failure to clear up the overlap and redundancy among public-sector institutions, or to harness the professional talent within the public sector to this larger set of social-policy goals, leads back to the authoritarian bottlenecks that built up around the office of the executive over the course of the 1990s.

Politics, Markets, and Competitive Strategies: Two Possible Transition Scenarios

Until the year 2000, the implementation of deep market reforms appeared to have laid the groundwork for economic recovery and the eventual transition to more competitive politics in all but the Peruvian case. As Peru now joins step with this trend, it helps to remember that these transitions have been anything but the smooth interplay between markets and democracy that had been hypothesized by an earlier generation of modernization thinkers (Shea-han 1987; Franko 1998). Under authoritarian regimes in Chile and Mexico, the lag between economic liberalization and authentic political opening was nearly twenty years. In Argentina and Brazil, chaotic political transitions in the early 1980s led eventually to hyperinflation, which in turn paved the way for new political actors with market-reform agendas in the 1990s (Cardoso 2000; Wise 2000). In both cases, the interaction between market reforms and domestic politics continues to challenge executive coalitions every step of the way—again, as witnessed by the December 2001 resignation of Argentine president Fernando De la Rúa just two years into his term and the political-economic chaos that ensued.

Peru has been the outlier here, in at least two respects. First, as in Argentina and Brazil, politics drove economics to the point of hyperinflation in the late 1980s, and market reforms thus became the only rational response to a highly irrational situation. Yet, in contrast to the situation in these two countries, the interplay between politics and economics in the Peru of the 1990s produced anything but democratic outcomes (Tanaka, forthcoming, 2003). Whereas economic recovery provided the potential for a more stable political opening in Peru, politics instead took an authoritarian turn. Second, in all four of the other cases, political parties were the key institutional cata-lysts for rendering market reforms and democratic transition more compati-ble. Certainly some party structures were more coherent and effective than others, but in all four countries parties were the locus for political-economic change in the era of market reform (Haggard and Kaufman 1995). In Peru, the complete collapse of traditional political parties by 1995, and the failure of new organized representative mechanisms to take their place, are unexpected departures from the reform trajectory of these other emerging-market coun-tries.

At the same time, a main theme of this study has been Peru's tendency to move forward at a slightly different pace than that of its neighbors. By regional standards, Peru's embracement of ISI came late, and a populist mil-itary experiment was launched at the very moment when highly dictatorial military regimes were touting neoconservative shock treatments in other parts of South America. Although all of those programs had gone up in flames by 1982, new civilian leaders in Peru would espouse the same neocon-servative strategy until it gave way to García's heterodox shock in 1985. In terms of economic strategy, Peru finally joined step with regional trends in the implementation of market reforms in the early 1990s. As Fujimori's eco-nomic advisors told it, they envisioned the Chilean path as the most viable option for Peru. But the Peruvian economy has yet to reach the development niche that Chile occupied in the mid-1980s. With regard to Chile, policy analysts are already pointing to the maturation of those export sectors linked to the processing of natural resources (e.g., mining, fishing, forestry, agroindustry) and to the need to generate a new business cycle based on more dynamic investments, higher levels of value-added, and the more sophisticated use of technology (Moguillansky 2000). Peru, again, has some considerable catching up to do.

A second theme of this study has been the quiet process of state reconstruction and renovation that has underpinned Peru's market transformation, and this constitutes another area in which Peru has caught up with the regional trend. That political-economic progress has been made over the past decade is indisputable, yet a third theme of this study has been the need to forge ahead with another round of state-sponsored reforms that offer more in the way of microeconomic dynamism and distributional equity. In the absence of a competitive strategy that assertively pursues these goals, it is doubtful that Peru's market-reform program will unravel or be reversed—there are now too many stakeholders to permit a massive reallocation of resources back toward protectionism and rampant statism. However, by sticking with the standard market strategy, Peruvian policy makers do risk settling for a more mediocre set of returns. Growth forecasts for the medium term still fall short of the annual 6 to 7 percent growth rates that are considered necessary for the expansion of employment and higher sustainable wage gains, and the same goes for gross investment projections.[14]

In Argentina, Chile, and Mexico, societal demands for more distributionally oriented policies have resulted in the election of proreform coalitions that built their entire platforms around such policies. This was the case with the 1999 victory of the Democratic Alliance in Argentina and the electoral successes of Chile's Coalition of Democratic Parties since 1990, as well as the oppositional triumph of Mexico's National Action Party in that country's July 2000 presidential contest. The previous chapter showed that, in Peru, the "distributional moment" has clearly arrived; regardless of incumbent Fujimori's generous social spending in the poorest districts of the country during his entire second term, the president's bid for reelection was challenged to the extent that he and his military cronies resorted to massive voting fraud in order to be assured a victory.

In other countries discussed here, the original architects of market reforms, for example, the PRI in Mexico or the Peronists in Argentina, proved incapable of generating second-phase follow-up reforms to correct for the failures and shortcomings of the first round. Despite the intention of each to stay in office indefinitely, hindsight shows that the inability of these

14. J. P. Morgan, *World Financial Markets*, Banco de J. P. Morgan, S.A., Apr. 14, 2000, 62.

parties to attend credibly to new kinds of distributional demands proved to be their ultimate undoing. In line with his wily pragmatism, Fujimori had already begun to promise the kinds of political reform and distributional policies that now characterize the economic program of President Vicente Fox of Mexico. To further bolster his sagging credibility, Fujimori had also rehired his popular former economics minister, Carlos Boloña, and stacked his new cabinet with an impressive lineup of technocrats, most of whom came from the private sector.

But too much damage had already been done, in terms of the violation of democratic procedures and the manipulation of public resources and the country's institutions of justice. The president and his military cronies finally fell prey to their own devices, and Toledo has secured yet another chance to liberalize politics and to restore the rule of law. This next generation of politicians and policy makers has also been given the opportunity to initiate another wave of economic reforms. In the event that they are unable to catalyze a coalition that can usher in the kinds of competitive adjustments discussed in the previous section, one medium-term scenario would be for Peru to simply hover at or slightly below the growth and investment rates that appear in table 18 (Abusada, Du Bois, Morón, Valderrama 2000b, 55–58). Again, while respectable, these figures are mediocre in the sense that they still fall short of the 6 to 7 percent annual growth rates that would signify a more dynamic takeoff (ECLAC 1997b). Thus, to stick with the same hands-off market strategy that has prevailed since 1990 is to relegate the Peruvian political economy to the same underachiever status that it occupied prior to 1990.

However, while mediocre economic returns once appeared to be almost structurally determined by the country's weak institutions and chaotic policy apparatus, this is no longer the case in contemporary Peru. The depth and breadth of the reforms that have been implemented in the 1990s constitute a necessary, although not entirely sufficient, condition for generating higher levels of growth, investment, and income gains. What's needed now is a more hands-on strategy that directly tackles the numerous reform gaps reviewed in this chapter, while also committing more firmly to an export-oriented development model that reaches beyond old-fashioned notions of comparative advantage based on primary exports.

Whereas the prospects for another wave of reform—within the state, the economy, and civil society—looked dim in the wake of the May 2000 election, the opposition has now been offered the same political opportunity structure that prompted the shift to a competitive strategy in Chile and Mexico. In chapter 6 I argued that, more than ever before, the institutional incentives in Peru are stacked in favor of policy success. Should this next generation of Peruvian decision makers seize the opportunities at hand, a second scenario could be Peru's successful shift to a competitive strategy, which, in these other countries, turned out to be a catalyst for greater societal participation and the transition to democratic rule. Even so, and keeping with the overriding theme of this book, there is no escaping the fact that "positive state activities have played quite a considerable part in the historical process of economic development" (Sen 1997, 4–5). Amartya Sen further reminds us that a complete turnaround for a country such as Peru will inevitably entail "deliberate patronage of particular types of economic activities," and the provision of "suitable social and economic preparation for the seizing of economic opportunities by the people."

Bibliography

Abugattas, Luis A. 1998. "Stabilisation, Structural Reform, and Industrial Performance." In *Fujimori's Peru: The Political Economy,* ed. John Crabtree and Jim Thomas. London: University of London, Institute of Latin American Studies.

Abusada, Roberto, Fritz Du Bois, Eduardo Morón, and José Valderrama. 2000a. "La reforma incompleta." In *La reforma incompleta,* vol. 1, ed. Roberto Abusada et al. Lima: Universidad del Pacífico and Instituto Peruano de Economía.

———, eds. 2000b. *La reforma incompleta,* 2 vols. Ed. Roberto Abusada, Fritz Du Bois, Eduardo Morón, and José Valderrama. Lima: Universidad del Pacífico and Instituto Peruano de Economía.

Agenda 2000. 1991. *Boloña/Buchi: Estrategias del cambio.* Lima: Agenda 2000 Editores.

Alvarez, Augusto. 1985. *Los objetivos de las empresas estatales.* Lima: Fundación Friedrich Ebert.

———. 1992. Empresas estatales y privatización. Lima: Editorial Apoyo.

Alvarez, Elena. 1998. "Economic Effects of the Illicit Drug Sector in Peru." In *Fujimori's Peru: The Political Economy,* ed. John Crabtree and Jim Thomas. London: University of London, Institute of Latin American Studies.

Ames, Barry. 1987. *Political Survival: Politicians and Public Policy in Latin America.* Berkeley and Los Angeles: University of California Press.

Amsden, Alice H. 1989. *Asia's Next Giant: South Korea and Late Industrialization.* New York: Oxford University Press.

Andean Development Corporation. 2000. "The Andean Community by Numbers: Basic Statistics." Database presented at the Annual Conference on Trade and Investment in the Americas, Washington, D.C., September 8.

Araoz, Mercedes, José Luiz Bonifaz, Carlos Casas, and Fernando González Vigil. 2001. *Factores limitantes de la inversión extranjera en el Perú.* Lima: Universidad del Pacífico.

Ardito-Barletta, Nicolás. 1994. "Managing Development and Transition." In *Managing the World Economy: Fifty Years after Bretton Woods,* ed. Peter B. Kenen. Washington, D.C.: Institute for International Economics.

Astiz, Carlos. 1969. *Pressure Groups and Power Elites in Peruvian Politics.* Ithaca: Cornell University Press.

Baca, Jorge. 2000. "El ancla fiscal: La reforma tributaria." In *La reforma incompleta,* vol. 1, ed. Roberto Abusada, Fritz Du Bois, Eduardo Morón, and José Valderrama. Lima: Universidad del Pacífico and Instituto Peruano de Economía.

Baer, Werner, and Adolfo Figueroa. 1981. "State Enterprise and the Distribution of Income: Brazil and Peru." In *Authoritarian Capitalism,* ed. Thomas Bruneau and Philippe Faucher. Boulder, Colo., and London: Westview Press.

Baer, Werner, and William Maloney. 1997. "Neoliberalism and Income Distribution in Latin America." *World Development* 25 (3): 311–27.

Balassa, Bela. 1981. *The Newly Industrializing Countries in the World Economy.* New York: Pergamon Press.

Balassa, Bela, Gerardo Bueno, Pedro-Pablo Kuczynski, and Mario Henrique Simonsen. 1986. *Toward Renewed Economic Growth in Latin America.* Washington, D.C.: Institute for International Economics.

Banco Central de Reserva del Perú (BCRP). 1962. "Plan nacional de desarrollo económico y social del Perú, 1962–1971." Lima: Banco Central de Reserva del Perú.

———. 1974. "Cuentas nacionales del Perú, 1960–1973." Lima: Banco Central de Reserva del Perú.

———. 1982. "La lucha contra inflación." Lima: Banco Central de Reserva del Perú.

———. 1984. "El proceso de renegociación de la deuda externa peruana: 1978–1983." Lima: Banco Central de Reserva del Perú.

———. 1985a. "Actividad empresarial del estado." Lima: Banco Central de Reserva del Perú.

———. 1985b. "Perú: Compendio estadístico del sector público no financiero, 1968–1984." Lima: Banco Central de Reserva del Perú.

———. 1986. "Evolución de precios de productos y servicios bajo control y regulación, 1981–1985." Lima: Banco Central de Reserva del Perú.

———. 1987. "Memoria 1986." Lima: Banco Central de Reserva del Perú.

Barak, Orbach. 2000. "Competition Policy in Transition: Lessons from Peru." In *The Role of the State in Competition and Intellectual Property Policy in Latin America,* ed. Beatriz Boza. Lima: National Institute for the Defense of Competition and the Protection of Intellectual Property Rights (INDECOPI).

Beaulne, Marie. 1975. *Industrialización por sustitución de importaciones: Perú, 1958–1969.* Lima: Escuela de Administración de Negocios para Graduados.

Behrman, Jere, Nancy Birdsall, and Miguel Szekely. 1998. "Data on Education Gap in Latin America." Paper presented at Workshop on Social Mobility, Brookings Institution, Washington, D.C. June 4-5.

Bennet, Douglas, and Kenneth Sharpe. 1980. "The State as Banker and Entrepreneur: The Last-Resort Character of the Mexican State's Economic Intervention, 1917–1976." *Comparative Politics* 12 (2): 165–89.

Birdsall, Nancy, and Juan Luis Londoño. 1997. "Asset Inequality Does Matter: Lessons from Latin America." *American Economic Review* 87 (May):32–38.

Birdsall, Nancy, and Augusto de la Torre. 2001. *Washington Contentious.* Washington, D.C.: Carnegie Endowment for International Peace and Inter-American Dialogue.

Bollinger, William. 1987. "Organized Labor in Peru: A Historical Overview." Occasional Paper Series, no. 10. Los Angeles: Interamerican Research Center.

Boloña, Carlos. 1996. "The Viability of Alberto Fujimori's Economic Strategy." In *The Peruvian Economy and Structural Adjustment,* ed. Efraín Gonzáles. Miami: North-South Center Press.

Boloña, Carlos, and Javier Illescas. 1997. *Políticas arancelarias en el Perú, 1980–1997.* Lima: Instituto de Economía de Libre Mercado and Universidad San Ignacio de Loyola.

Bosworth, Barry, Rudiger Dornbusch, and Raúl Labán, eds. 1994. *The Chilean Economy: Policy Lessons and Challenges.* Washington, D.C.: Brookings Institution.

Bouton, Lawrence, and Maariusz Sumlinski. 2001. "Trends in Private Investment in Developing Countries." Washington, D.C.: World Bank International Finance Corporation. June.

Bowen, Sally. 2000. *The Fujimori File: Peru and Its President, 1990–2000.* Lima: The Peru Monitor.

Boylan, Delia. 2000. "Bureaucratic Design in Comparative Perspective." Paper presented at the Twenty-third Congress of the Latin American Studies Association, Miami. March.

———. 2001. *Defusing Democracy: Central Bank Autonomy and the Transition from Authoritarian Rule*. Ann Arbor, MI: University of Michigan Press.

———, forthcoming, 2003. "Taking Concertación to Task: Second Stage Reforms and the 1999 Presidential Elections in Chile." In *Post-Stabilization Politics in Latin America: Competition, Transition, Collapse*, ed. Carol Wise and Riordan Roett. Washington, D.C.: Brookings Institution.

Boza, Beatriz, ed. 2000. *The Role of the State in Competition and Intellectual Property Policy in Latin America*. Lima: National Institute for the Defense of Competition and the Protection of Intellectual Property Rights (INDECOPI).

Branch, Brian. 1982. "Public Enterprises in Peru: The Perspectives for Reform." Austin: Institute of Latin Studies, University of Texas at Austin.

Bresser Pereira, Luiz Carlos. 1999. "Managerial Public Administration: Strategy and Structure for a New State." In *Reforming the State: Managerial Public Administration in Latin America*, ed. Luiz Carlos Bresser Pereira and Peter Spink. Boulder, Colo.: Lynne Rienner Publishers.

———. 2000. "State Reform in the 1990s: Logic and Control Mechanisms. " In *Institutions and the Role of the State*, ed. Leonardo Burlamaqui, Ana Celia Castro, and Ha-Joon Chang. Hants: Edward Elgar.

Brysk, Alison, and Carol Wise. 1997. "Liberalization and Ethnic Conflict in Latin America." *Studies in Comparative International Development* 32 (2): 76–104.

Bulmer-Thomas, Victor. 1987. *The Political Economy of Central America since 1920*. Cambridge: Cambridge University Press.

———. 1994. *The Economic History of Latin America since Independence*. Cambridge: Cambridge University Press.

Burki, Shahid, and Guillermo Perry. 1997. *The Long March: A Reform Agenda for Latin America and the Caribbean in the Next Decade*. Washington, D.C.: World Bank.

———. 1998. *Beyond the Washington Consensus: Institutions Matter*. Washington, D.C.: World Bank.

Cameron, David. 1978. "The Expansion of the Public Economy: A Comparative Analysis." *American Political Science Review* 72 (4): 1243–61.

Cameron, Maxwell. 1997. "Political and Economic Origins of Regime Change in Peru." In *The Peruvian Labyrinth*, ed. Maxwell Cameron and Philip Mauceri. University Park: The Pennsylvania State University Press.

Carbonetto, Daniel, ed. 1987. *Un modelo económico heterodoxo: El caso peruano*. Lima: Instituto Nacional de Planificacíon.

Cardoso, Eliana. 2000. "Brazil's Currency Crisis: The Shift from an Exchange Rate Anchor to a Flexible Exchange Rate Regime." In *Exchange Rate Politics in Latin America*, ed. Carol Wise and Riordan Roett. Washington, D.C.: Brookings Institution.

Carrillo, Carlos, and Manuel Hernández. 2000. "Economic Integration, Trade and Industrial Structure in the Andean Economies." In *Peru's New Perspectives on Trade and Development*, ed. Nobuaki Hamaguchi. Tokyo: Institute of Developing Economies.

Centeno, Miguel, and Patricio Silva, eds. 1998. *The Politics of Expertise in Latin America*. New York: St. Martin's Press.

Centro de Documentación Económico-Social. 1965. *Las empresas estatales en el Perú.* Lima: Centro de Documentación Económico-Social.

Chalmers, Douglas. 1977. "The Politicized State in Latin America." In *Authoritarianism and Corporatism in Latin America,* ed. James Malloy. Pittsburgh: University of Pittsburgh Press.

Chand, Vikram. 2001. *Mexico's Political Awakening.* Notre Dame: University of Notre Dame Press.

Chaudry, Shahid, Gary Reid, and Waleed Malik, eds. 1994. "Civil Service Reform in Latin America." World Bank Technical Paper no. 259. Washington, D.C.: The World Bank.

Chudnovsky, Daniel. 1997. "Beyond Macroeconomic Stability in Latin America." In *The New Globalism and Developing Countries,* ed. John H. Dunning and Khalil A. Hamdani. New York: United Nations University Press.

Cleaves, Peter, and Henry Pease. 1983. "State Autonomy and Military Policy Making." In *The Peruvian Experiment Reconsidered,* ed. Cynthia McClintock and Abraham F. Lowenthal. Princeton: Princeton University Press.

Cleaves, Peter, and Martin Scurrah. 1980. *Agriculture, Bureaucracy, and Military Government in Peru.* Ithaca: Cornell University Press.

Collier, David. 1993. "The Comparative Method." In *Political Science: The State of the Discipline II,* ed. Ada W. Finifter. Washington, D.C.: American Political Science Association.

Conaghan, Catherine M. 1988. "Capitalists, Technocrats, and Politicians: Economic Policy-Making and Democracy in the Central Andes." Working Paper, no. 109, Kellogg Institute for International Studies, University of Notre Dame.

———. 1995. "Polls, Political Discourse and the Public Sphere: The Spin on Peru's Fuji-golpe." In *Latin America in Comparative Perspective,* ed. Peter Smith. Boulder, Colo., and London: Westview Press.

———. 1998. "Stars of the Crisis: The Ascent of Economists in Peruvian Public Life." In *The Politics of Expertise in Latin America,* ed. Miguel Centeno and Patricio Silva. London: MacMillan.

Conaghan, Catherine, and James Malloy. 1994. *Unsettling Statecraft: Democracy and Neoliberalism in the Central Andes.* Pittsburgh: University of Pittsburgh Press.

Corden, Max. 2000. "Exchange Rate Regimes and Policies." In *Exchange Rate Politics in Latin America,* ed. Carol Wise and Riordan Roett. Washington, D.C.: Brookings Institution.

Cornejo, Roberto. 1985. "La planificación y el presupuesto en el Perú." Lima: Universidad del Pacífico, Proyecto de Gestión Pública.

Corrales, Javier. 2000a. "Presidents, Ruling Parties, and Party Rules: A Theory on the Politics of Economic Reform in Latin America." *Comparative Politics* 32 (2): 127–50.

———. 2000b. "Reform Lagging States and the Question of Devaluation: Venezuela's Response to the Exogenous Shocks of 1997–98." In *Exchange Rate Politics in Latin America,* ed. Carol Wise and Riordan Roett. Washington, D.C.: Brookings Institution.

Cotler, Julio. 1975. "The New Mode of Political Domination in Peru." In *The Peruvian Experiment: Continuity and Change under Military Rule,* ed. Abraham F. Lowenthal. Princeton: Princeton University Press.

———. 1995. "Political Parties and the Problems of Democratic Consolidation in

Peru." In *Building Democratic Institutions*, ed. Scott Mainwaring and Timothy Scully. Stanford: Stanford University Press.

Crabtree, John. 1992. *Peru under Garcia: An Opportunity Lost*. Pittsburgh: University of Pittsburgh Press.

———. 1998. "Neopopulism and the Fujimori Government." In *Fujimori's Peru: The Political Economy*, ed. John Crabtree and Jim Thomas. London: University of London, Institute of Latin American Studies.

Crabtree, John, and Jim Thomas, eds. 1998. *Fujimori's Peru: The Political Economy*. London: University of London, Institute of Latin American Studies.

Cruz Saco, Amparo. 1985. "El caso de la refinería de zinc de Cajamarquilla." Lima: Universidad del Pacífico, Proyecto de Gestión Pública.

Dancourt, Oscar. 1985. "Impacto macroeconómico del gasto de defensa." Lima: Universidad del Pacífico, Proyecto de Gestión Pública.

Degregori, Carlos Iván. 1999. "Sendero Luminoso: Los hondos y mortales desencentros, parte I." Documentos de Trabajo, Instituto de Estudios Peruanos, Lima, Peru.

De Soto, Hernando. 1989. *The Other Path: The Invisible Revolution in the Third World*. New York: Harper and Row.

Devlin, Robert. 1985. *Transnational Banks and the External Finance of Latin America: The Experience of Peru*. Santiago: Economic Commission for Latin America and the Caribbean (ECLAC).

Dominguez, Jorge, ed. 1997. *Technopols: Freeing Politics and Markets in Latin America in the 1990s*. University Park: The Pennsylvania State University Press.

Dornbusch, Rudiger. 1986. "International Economic Instability." In *Debt, Financial Stability, and Public Policy*, ed. Federal Reserve Bank of Kansas City. Kansas City: The Federal Reserve Bank of Kansas City.

Dornbusch, Rudiger, and Sebastian Edwards, eds. 1991. *Macroeconomic Populism in Latin America*. Chicago: University of Chicago Press.

Dresser, Denise. 1991. *Neopopulist Solutions to Neoliberal Problems: Mexico's National Solidarity Program*. La Jolla: Center for U.S.–Mexico Studies, University of California at San Diego.

Durand, Francisco. 1994. *Business and Politics in Peru: The State and the National Bourgeoisie*. Boulder, Colo., and London: Westview Press.

———. 1998. "Collective Action and the Empowerment of Peruvian Business." In *Organized Business, Economic Change, and Democracy in Latin America*, ed. Francisco Durand and Eduardo Silva. Miami: North-South Center Press.

Durand, Francisco, and Rosemary Thorp. 1998. "Tax Reform: The SUNAT Experience." In *Fujimori's Peru: The Political Economy*, ed. John Crabtree and Jim Thomas. London: University of London, Institute of Latin American Studies.

Echeverría, Rafael. 1985. *Empleo público en américa latina*. Geneva: International Labour Organization.

Economic Commission for Latin America and the Caribbean (ECLAC). 1992. *Social Equity and Changing Production Patterns*. Santiago: Economic Commission for Latin America and the Caribbean.

———. 1997a. *The Equity Gap*. Santiago: Economic Commission for Latin America and the Caribbean.

———. 1997b. "Insufficient Growth Limits Job Creation." *CEPAL News* 17 (6): 1–3.

———. 1997c. "Preliminary Overview of Latin America and the Caribbean, 1997." Santiago: Economic Commission for Latin America and the Caribbean.

———. 1998. *The Fiscal Covenant.* Santiago: Economic Commission for Latin America and the Caribbean.

Edwards, Sebastian. 1990. "The Sequencing of Economic Reform." *The World Economy* 13 (1): 1–13.

———. 1993. "Latin American Integration: A New Perspective or an Old Dream?" *The World Economy* 16 (3): 317–38.

———. 1995. *Crisis and Reform in Latin America: From Despair to Hope.* New York: Oxford University Press for the World Bank.

———. 1998. "The Andean Pact Reforms: How Much Progress? How Far to Go?" In *The Andean Community and the United States: Trade and Investment Relations in the 1990s*, ed. Miguel Rodríguez, Patricia Correa, and Barbara Kotschwar. Washington, D.C.: Organization of American States, Inter-American Dialogue, and the Andean Development Corporation.

Edwards, Sebastian, and Daniel Lederman. 1998. "The Political Economy of Unilateral Trade Liberalization: The Case of Chile." Working Paper, no. 6510, National Bureau of Economic Research, Cambridge, Mass.

Encinas del Pando, José A. 1983. "The Role of Military Expenditure in the Development Process, Peru: A Case Study, 1950–1980." *Ibero-American, Nordic Journal of Latin American Studies* 12 (1–2): 51–114.

Escobal, Javier. 2000. "El gran ausente: El agro." In *La reforma incompleta*, vol. 2, ed. Roberto Abusada, Fritz Du Bois, Eduardo Morón, and José Valderrama. Lima: Universidad del Pacífico and Instituto Peruano de Economía.

Escuela de Administración de Negocios para Graduados (ESAN). 1985. "El perfeccionamiento profesional del sector público: Diagnóstico y propuesta." Lima: Escuela de Administración de Negocios para Graduados, Proyecto de Gestión Pública.

———. 1986. "El rol y la gestión empresarial del estado: foro." Lima: Escuela de Administración de Negocios para Graduados, Proyecto de Gestión Pública.

Evans, Peter. 1979. *Dependent Development: The Alliance of Multinational, State, and Local Capital in Brazil.* Princeton: Princeton University Press.

———. 1989. "Predatory, Developmental, and other Apparatuses: A Comparative Political Economy Perspective on the Third World State." *Sociological Forum* 4 (4): 561–87.

———. 1995. *Embedded Autonomy: States and Industrial Transformation.* Princeton: Princeton University Press.

Evans, Peter, Dietrich Rueschemeyer, and Theda Skocpol, eds. 1985. *Bringing the State Back In.* New York: Cambridge University Press.

Ewig, Christina. 2000. "Democracia diferida: Un análisis del proceso e reformas en el sector salud." In *Políticas sociales en el Perú: Nuevos aportes*, ed. Felipe Portocarrero Súarez. Lima: Universidad del Pacífico.

Fishlow, Albert. 1985. "The State of Latin American Economics." In *Economic and Social Progress in Latin America.* Washington, D.C.: Inter-American Development Bank.

———. 1986. "Latin American Adjustment to the Oil Shocks of 1973 and 1979." In *Latin American Political Economy: Financial Crisis and Political Change*, ed. Jonathan Hartlyn and Samuel Morley. Boulder, Colo., and London: Westview Press.

———. 1990. "The Latin American State." *Journal of Economic Perspectives* 4 (3): 61–73.

Fitzgerald, E. V. K. 1976. *The State and Economic Development: Peru since 1968*. Cambridge: Cambridge University Press.

———. 1979. *The Political Economy of Peru, 1956–1978: Economic Development and the Restructuring of Capital*. Cambridge: Cambridge University Press.

Foxley, Alejandro. 1983. *Latin American Experiments in Neoconservative Economics*. Berkeley and Los Angeles: University of California Press.

Franco, Bruno, Italo Muñoz, Pedro Sánchez, and Verónica Zavala. 2000. "Las privatizaciones y concesiones." In *La reforma incompleta*, vol. 2, ed. Roberto Abusada et al. Lima: Universidad del Pacífico and Instituto Peruano de Economía.

Franko, Patrice. 1998. *The Puzzle of Latin American Economic Development*. New York: Rowman and Littlefield.

Frieden, Jeffry. 1991. *Debt, Development, and Democracy*. Princeton: Princeton University Press.

García, Mauricio. 2000. "La reforma de la administración de justicia." In *La reforma incompleta*, vol. 2, ed. Roberto Abusada, Fritz Du Bois, Eduardo Morón, and José Valderrama. Lima: Universidad del Pacífico and Instituto Peruano de Economía.

Geddes, Barbara. 1994. *Politician's Dilemma: Building State Capacity in Latin America*. Berkeley and Los Angeles: University of California Press.

George, Alexander. 1979. "Case Studies and Theory Development." In *Diplomacy: New Approaches in History, Theory, and Policy*, ed. Paul Gordon Lauren. New York: The Free Press.

Gereffi, Gary, and Peter Evans. 1981. "Transnational Corporations, Dependent Development, and State Policy in the Semi-Periphery: A Comparison of Brazil and Mexico." *Latin American Research Review* 16 (3): 31–65.

Ghio, José Maria. 1998. "The Politics of Administrative Reform in Argentina." Paper prepared for a conference on Building State Capacity in Developing Countries, Mexico City, June 2–6.

Giesecke, Alberto, ed. 1985. *Reporte de investigación: La organización del sector público*. Lima: Escuela de Administración de Negocios para Graduados, Proyecto de Gestión Pública.

Glade, William, ed. 1986. *State Shrinking: A Comparative Inquiry into Privatization*. Austin: University of Texas, Institute of Latin American Studies, Office of Public Sector Studies.

Glen, Jack D., and Mariusz Sumlinski. 1998. "Trends in Private Investment in Developing Countries." Washington, D.C.: World Bank International Finance Corporation. May.

Gonzáles, Efraín. 1987. "Crisis y democracia: El Perú en busca de un nuevo paradigma de desarrollo." Documentos de Trabajo, no. 21. Lima: Instituto de Estudios Peruanos.

———, ed. 1996. *The Peruvian Economy and Structural Adjustment: Past, Present, Future*. Miami: North-South Center Press.

———. 1998. *El neoliberalismo a la peruana*. Lima: Instituto de Estudios Peruanos.

Gorriti, Gustavo. 1999. *The Shining Path: A History of the Millenarian War in Peru*. Chapel Hill: University of North Carolina Press.

Graham, Carol. 1992. *Peru's APRA: Parties, Politics, and the Elusive Quest for Democracy*. Boulder, Colo.: Lynne Rienner Publishers.

———. 1994. *Safety Nets, Politics, and the Poor: Transitions to Market Economies*. Washington, D.C.: Brookings Institution.

———. 1998. *Private Markets for Public Goods.* Washington, D.C.: Brookings Institution.

———. 2000. "The Political Economy of Mobility: Perceptions and Objective Trends in Latin America." In *New Markets, New Opportunities,* ed. Nancy Birdsall and Carol Graham. Washington, D.C.: Brookings Institution.

Graham, Carol, and Cheik Kane. 1998. "Opportunistic Government or Sustaining Reform: Electoral Trends and Public Expenditure Patterns in Peru, 1990–95." *Latin American Research Review* 33 (1): 67–104.

Graham, Carol, and Moisés Naím. 1998. "The Political Economy of Institutional Reform." In *Beyond Tradeoffs: Market Reforms and Equitable Growth in Latin America,* ed. Nancy Birdsall, Carol Graham, and Richard Sabot. Washington, D.C.: Brookings Institution and the Inter-American Development Bank.

Grindle, Merilee. 1996. *Challenging the State: Crisis and Innovation in Latin America and Africa.* Cambridge: Cambridge University Press.

Guerra-García, Gustavo. 1999. *Reforma del Estado en el Perú: Pautas para reestructurar el Poder Ejecutivo.* Lima: Agenda Perú.

Haggard, Stephan. 1995. "Reform of the State in Latin America." In *Development in Latin America and the Caribbean,* ed. Shahid Burki, Sebastian Edwards, and Sri-Ram Aiyer. Washington, D.C.: World Bank.

Haggard, Stephan, and Robert Kaufman. 1989. "The Politics of Stabilization and Structural Adjustment." In *Debt and Economic Performance: Selected Issues,* ed. Jeffrey Sachs. Chicago: University of Chicago Press.

———. 1995. *The Political Economy of Democratic Transitions.* Princeton: Princeton University Press.

Hausmann, Ricardo, and Dani Rodrik. 2002. "Economic Development as Self-Discovery." Working Paper, no. 8952, National Bureau of Economic Research, Cambridge, Mass.

Haworth, Nigel. 1983. "Conflict or Incorporation: The Peruvian Working Class, 1968–79." In *Military Reformism and Social Classes: The Peruvian Experience, 1968–80,* ed. David Booth and Bernardo Sorj. New York: St. Martin's Press.

Heredia, Blanca, and Ben Ross Schneider. 1998. "The Political Economy of Administrative Reform: Building State Capacity in Developing Countries." Political Science Department, Northwestern University. Mimeograph.

Hirschman, Albert O. 1967. *Development Projects Observed.* Washington, D.C.: Brookings Institution.

———. 1968. "The Political Economy of Import-Substituting Industrialization in Latin America." *Quarterly Journal of Economics* 82 (1): 1–32.

Hopkins, Jack W. 1967. *The Government Executive of Modern Peru.* Gainesville: University of Florida Press.

Hunt, Shane. 1975. "Foreign Direct Investment in Peru: New Rules for an Old Game." In *The Peruvian Experiment,* ed. Abraham F. Lowenthal. Princeton: Princeton University Press.

Hunt, Shane, and Jaime Mezzera. 1983. *La promoción de exportaciones no tradicionales en el Perú: Una evaluación crítica.* Lima: Asociación de Exportadores del Perú.

Hunter, Wendy. 1997. "Civil-Military Relations in Argentina, Chile, Peru." *Political Science Quarterly* 112 (3): 453–75.

Hurtado, Isabel, and Marcos Robles. 1985. "Estadisticas de empleo en el sector público peruano." Lima: Escuela de Administración de Negocios para Graduados, Proyecto de Gestión Pública.

Ikenberry, G. John. 1988. "Conclusion: An Institutional Approach to American Foreign Economic Policy." *International Organization* 42 (1): 219–43.

Inter-American Development Bank (IDB). 1984. *External Debt and Economic Development in Latin America: Background and Prospects.* Washington, D.C.: Inter-American Development Bank.

———. 1985. *Economic and Social Progress in Latin America.* Washington, D.C.: Inter-American Development Bank.

———. 1986. *Economic and Social Progress in Latin America.* Washington, D.C.: Inter-American Development Bank.

———. 1988. *Economic and Social Progress in Latin America.* Washington, D.C.: Inter-American Development Bank.

International Monetary Fund (IMF). 1984. *International Financial Statistics Yearbook.* Washington, D.C.: International Monetary Fund.

———. 1994. *International Financial Statistics Yearbook.* Washington, D.C.: International Monetary Fund.

———. 1999. *International Financial Statistics Yearbook.* Washington, D.C.: International Monetary Fund.

———. 2001. *International Financial Statistics Yearbook.* Washington, D.C.: International Monetary Fund.

Iversen, Torben, and Thomas R. Cusack. 2000. "The Causes of Welfare State Expansion." *World Politics* 52 (2): 313–49.

Jaquette, Jane S. 1971. "The Politics of Development in Peru." Ph.D. diss., Cornell University.

Kahler, Miles. 1990. "Orthodoxy and Its Alternatives." In *Economic Crisis and Policy Choice,* ed. Joan Nelson. Princeton: Princeton University Press.

Kaufman, Robert, and Barbara Stallings. 1989. "Debt and Democracy in the 1980s: The Latin American Experience." In *Debt and Democracy in Latin America,* ed. Barbara Stallings and Robert Kaufman. Boulder, Colo., and London: Westview Press.

Kay, Bruce. 1997. "Fujipopulism and the Liberal State in Peru: 1990–1995." *Journal of Interamerican Studies and World Affairs* 38 (4): 55–98.

Keefer, Philip. 1995. "Reforming the State: The Sustainability and Replicability of Peruvian Reforms in Its Public Administration." Washington, D.C.: World Bank. Mimeograph.

Kessler, Timothy. 2000. "The Mexican Peso Crash: Causes, Consequences, Comeback." In *Exchange Rate Politics in Latin America,* ed. Carol Wise and Riordan Roett. Washington, D.C.: Brookings Institution.

Kim, Kwang. 1999. "Legal Base of Autonomous Agencies in Peru." Washington, D.C.: World Bank. Mimeograph.

———. 2000. "INDECOPI: A Case Study of Peruvian Autonomous Institutions." In *The Role of the State in Competition and Intellectual Property Policy in Latin America,* ed. Beatriz Boza. Lima: INDECOPI.

Kindleberger, Charles P. 1985. *Monetarism vs. Keynesianism and Other Essays in Financial History.* London: George Allen and Unwin.

Kisic, Drago. 1987. *De la corresponsabilidad a la moratoria: El caso de la deuda externa peruana, 1970–1986.* Lima: Fundación Friedrich Ebert and Centro Peruano de Estudios Internacionales.

―――. 1998. "Privatisation, Investment, and Sustainability." In *Fujimori's Peru: The Political Economy*, ed. John Crabtree and Jim Thomas. London: University of London, Institute of Latin American Studies.

Klarén, Peter. 2000. *Peru: Society and Nationhood in the Andes*. New York: Oxford University Press.

Klitgaard, Robert E. 1971. "Observations on the Peruvian National Plan for Development, 1971–1975." *Inter-American Economic Affairs* 25 (3): 3–22.

Knill, Christoph. 1999. "Explaining Cross-National Variance in Administrative Reform: Autonomous versus Instrumental Bureaucracies." *Journal of Public Policy* 19 (2): 113–39.

Krueger, Anne. 1990. "Government Failures in Development." *Journal of Economic Perspectives* 4 (3): 9–23.

Kuczynski, Pedro-Pablo. 1977. *Peruvian Democracy under Economic Stress: An Account of the Belaunde Administration, 1963–1968*. Princeton: Princeton University Press.

Kuczynski, Pedro-Pablo, and Felipe Ortíz de Zevallos. 2001. *El reto 2001: Competir y crear empleo*. Lima: Emprensa Editorial El Comercio.

Kurtz, Marcus. 2000. "State Developmentalism without a Developmental State: The Public Foundations of the 'Free Market Miracle' in Chile." *Latin American Politics and Society* 2 (1): 1–25.

Larkey, Patrick D., Chandler Stolp, and Mark Winer. 1981. "Theorizing about the Growth and Decline of Government: A Research Assessment." *Journal of Public Policy* 1 (2): 156–220.

Larraín, Felipe, and Jeffrey D. Sachs. 1991. "International Financial Relations." In *Peru's Path to Recovery: A Plan for Economic Stabilization and Growth*, ed. Carlos E. Paredes and Jeffrey D. Sachs. Washington, D.C.: Brookings Institution.

Larraín, Felipe, and Marcelo Selowsky, eds. 1991. *The Public Sector and the Latin American Crisis*. San Francisco: International Center for Economic Growth.

Lessard, Donald R., and John Williamson, eds. 1987. *Capital Flight and Third World Debt*. Washington, D.C.: Institute for International Economics.

Levinson, Jerome, and Juan de Onis. 1970. *The Alliance That Lost Its Way*. Chicago: Quadrangle Books.

Levy, Daniel, and Kathleen Bruhn. 2001. *Mexico: The Struggle for Democratic Development*. Berkeley and Los Angeles: University of California Press.

Lizárraga, Raúl. 1985. *Estrategias para la descentralización y el desarrollo regional*. Lima: Centro Peruano de Estudios para el Desarrollo Regional.

Londoño, Juan Luis, and Miguel Szekely. 1997. "Distributional Surprises after a Decade of Reforms: Latin America in the Nineties." Paper presented at the annual meeting of the Inter-American Development Bank, Barcelona. March.

Lowenthal, Abraham F., ed. 1975. *The Peruvian Experiment: Continuity and Change under Military Rule*. Princeton: Princeton University Press.

Mainwaring, Scott. 1995. "Brazil: Weak Parties, Feckless Democracy." In *Building Democratic Institutions*, ed. Scott Mainwaring and Timothy Scully. Stanford: Stanford University Press.

Mainwaring, Scott, and Timothy Scully. 1995. "Introduction: Party Systems in Latin America." In *Building Democratic Institutions: Party Systems in Latin America*, ed. Scott Mainwaring and Timothy Scully. Stanford: Stanford University Press.

Malloy, James M. 1982. "Peru's Troubled Return to Democratic Government." Hanover, N.H.: Universities Field Staff International.

Manzetti, Luigi. 1999. *Privatization South American Style*. New York: Oxford University Press.

Marcel, Mario. 1999. "Effectiveness of the State and Development Lessons from the Chilean Experience." In *Chile: Recent Policy Lessons and Emerging Challenges*, ed. Guillermo Perry and Danny Leipziger. Washington, D.C.: World Bank.

Marcenaro, Harold. 1996. "El ministerio de la presidencia y la reorganización del estado peruano." *Punto de Equilibrio* 5 (41): 1–3.

Marcus-Delgado, Jane. 1999. "The Logic of Presidential Legitimacy and Neoliberal Reform in Argentina and Peru." Ph.D. diss., Johns Hopkins University.

Matos Mar, José. 1984. *Desborde popular y crisis del estado*. Lima: Instituto de Estudios Peruanos.

Mauceri, Philip. 1996. *State under Siege: Development and Policy Making in Peru*. Boulder, Colo., and London: Westview Press.

McClintock, Cynthia. 1984. "Why Peasants Rebel: The Case of Peru's Sendero Luminoso." *World Politics* 37 (2): 48–84.

———. 1989. "The Prospects for Democratic Consolidation in a 'Least Likely' Case: Peru." *Comparative Politics* 21 (2): 127–48.

McClintock, Cynthia, and Abraham F. Lowenthal, eds. 1983. *The Peruvian Experiment Reconsidered*. Princeton: Princeton University Press.

Meller, Patricio. 1997. "An Overview of Chilean Trade Strategy." In *Integrating the Hemisphere*, ed. Ana Julia Jatar and Sidney Weintraub. Washington, D.C.: Inter-American Dialogue.

Moe, Terry. 1984. "The New Economics of Organization." *American Journal of Political Science* 28 (4): 739–77.

Moguillansky, Graciela. 2000. *Investment in Chile: The End of a Cycle of Expansion?* Santiago: Economic Commission for Latin America and the Caribbean.

Morley, Samuel, Roberto Machado, and Stefano Pettinato. 1999. "Indexes of Structural Reform in Latin America." Economic Reform Series, no. 12. Santiago: Economic Commission for Latin America and the Caribbean.

Mosquiera, Edgardo. 2000. "Las reformas institucionales para la creación de un sistema de derechos de propriedad." In *La reforma incompleta*, vol. 2, ed. Roberto Abusada, Fritz Du Bois, Eduardo Morón, and José Valderrama. Lima: Universidad del Pacífico and Instituto Peruano de Economía.

Naím, Moisés. 1994. "Latin America: The Second Stage of Reform." *Journal of Democracy* 5 (4): 32–48.

———. 1995. "Latin America's Journey to the Market: From Macroeconomic Shocks to Institutional Therapy." Occasional Papers, no. 62, International Center for Economic Growth, San Francisco.

North, Douglass. 1990. *Institutions, Institutional Change and Economic Performance*. New York: Cambridge University Press.

Nuñes, Edson de Oliveira, and Barbara Geddes. 1987. "Dilemmas of State-Led Modernization in Brazil." In *State and Society in Brazil: Continuity and Change*, ed. John D. Wirth, Edson de Oliveira Nuñes, and Thomas E. Bogenschild. Boulder, Colo., and London: Westview Press.

Obando, Enrique. 1998. "Fujimori and the Military." In *Fujimori's Peru: The Political Economy*, ed. John Crabtree and Jim Thomas. London: University of London, Institute of Latin American Studies.

Obando, Hugo M. 1977. "A Comparative Social Benefit-Cost Analysis of the Twelve

Principal Projects of Peru's Public Investment Program, 1968–1975." Ph.D. diss., Iowa State University.

O'Donnell, Guillermo. 1988. *Bureaucratic Authoritarianism: Argentina 1966–1973 in Comparative Perspective.* Berkeley and Los Angeles: University of California Press.

Olson, Mancur. 1968. *The Logic of Collective Action: Public Goods and the Theory of Groups.* New York: Schocken Books.

Ortíz de Zevallos, Felipe. 1986. "Peru: An Insider's View." In *State Shrinking: A Comparative Inquiry into Privatization,* ed. William P. Glade. Austin: University of Texas, Institute of Latin American Studies.

Palacios, Rosa María, and Leonie Roca. 2000. "El desafío de la descentralización." In *La reforma incompleta,* vol. 2, ed. Roberto Abusada, Fritz Du Bois, Eduardo Morón, and José Valderrama. Lima: Universidad del Pacífico and Instituto Peruano de Economía.

Panizza, Francisco. 2000. "Beyond 'Delegative Democracy': 'Old Politics' and 'New Economics' in Latin America." *Journal of Latin American Studies* 32 (3): 737–63.

Paredes, Carlos E. 1991. "Epilogue: In the Aftermath of Hyperinflation." In *Peru's Path to Recovery: A Plan for Economic Stabilization and Growth,* ed. Carlos E. Paredes and Jeffrey D. Sachs. Washington, D.C.: Brookings Institution.

Paredes, Carlos E., and Alberto Pascó-Font. 1987. "The Behavior of the Public Sector in Peru, 1970–1985." Washington, D.C.: World Bank.

Paredes, Carlos E., and Jeffrey D. Sachs, eds. 1991. *Peru's Path to Recovery: A Plan for Economic Stabilization and Growth.* Washington, D.C.: Brookings Institution.

Parodi, Carlos. 2000. *Peru, 1960–2000: Políticas económicas y sociales en entornos cambiantes.* Lima: Universidad del Pacífico.

Pastor, Manuel. 1990. "Capital Flight from Latin America." *World Development* 18 (1): 1–18.

———. 1991. "Private Investment and Debt Overhang in Latin America." Paper presented at the meeting of the Latin American Studies Association, Washington, D.C. September.

———. 1992. *Inflation, Stabilization, and Debt: Macroeconomic Experiments in Peru and Bolivia.* Boulder, Colo., and London: Westview Press.

Pastor, Manuel, and Carol Wise. 1992. "Peruvian Economic Policy in the 1980s: From Orthodoxy to Heterodoxy and Back." *Latin American Research Review* 27 (2): 83–117.

———. 1994. "The Origins and Sustainability of Mexico's Free Trade Policy." *International Organization* 48 (3): 459–89.

———. 1997. "State Policy, Distribution, and Neoliberal Reform in Mexico." *Journal of Latin American Studies* 29 (2): 419–56.

———. 1999a. "The Politics of Second-Generation Reform." *Journal of Democracy* 10 (3): 34–48.

———. 1999b. "Stabilization and Its Discontents: Argentina's Economic Restructuring in the 1990s." *World Development* 27 (3): 477–503.

———. 2001. "Argentina: From Poster Child to Basket Case." *Foreign Affairs* (October–November): 60–72.

———. 2002. "A Long View on the Mexican Political Economy." In *Mexican Politics and Society in Transition,* ed. Joseph Tulchin and Andrew Selee. Boulder, Colo.: Lynne Rienner Publishers.

Payne, James L. 1965. *Labor and Politics in Peru: The System of Political Bargaining.* New Haven: Yale University Press.

Pérez-Aleman, Paola. 1998. "Institutional Transformations and Economic Development: Learning, Inter-Firm Networks and the State in Chile." Rights vs. Efficiency Paper, no. 2, Institute for Latin American and Iberian Studies, Columbia University, New York.

Peterson, George. 1997. *Decentralization in Latin America: Learning through Experience.* Washington, D.C.: World Bank.

Pollarolo, Pierina. 2000. "La reforma del sector salud." In *La reforma incompleta,* vol. 2, ed. Roberto Abusada, Fritz Du Bois, Eduardo Morón, and José Valderrama. Lima: Universidad del Pacífico and Instituto Peruano de Economía.

Pollitt, Christopher. 1990. *Managerialism and the Public Service.* Oxford: Blackwell.

Portocarrero, Felipe Maisch. 1982. "The Peruvian Public Investment Programme, 1968–1978." *Journal of Latin American Studies* 14 (2): 433–54.

Portocarrero, Felipe Súarez, ed. 2000. *Políticas sociales en el Perú: Nuevos aportes.* Lima: Red para el Desarrollo de las Ciencias Sociales en el Perú.

Przeworski, Adam. 1999. "On the Design of the State: A Principal Agent Perspective." In *Reforming the State: Managerial Public Administration in Latin America,* ed. Luiz Carlos Bresser Pereira and Peter Spink. Boulder, Colo.: Lynne Rienner Publishers.

Przeworski, Adam, and Henry Teune. 1970. *The Logic of Comparative Social Inquiry.* New York: John Wiley.

Quijano, Anibal. 1971. *Nationalism and Capitalism in Peru: A Study in Neo-Imperialism.* New York: Monthly Review Press.

Ragin, Charles. 1987. *The Comparative Method: Moving beyond Qualitative and Quantitative Studies.* Berkeley and Los Angeles: University of California Press.

Ramos, Joseph. 1986. *Neoconservative Economics in the Southern Cone of Latin America, 1973–1983.* Baltimore: Johns Hopkins University Press.

———. 1987. "Planning and the Market during the Next Ten Years in Latin America." *Cepal Review* 31:145–52.

Rauch, James E., and Peter B. Evans. 2000. "Bureaucratic Structure and Bureaucratic Performance in Less Developed Countries." *Journal of Public Economics* 75:49–71.

Reid, Michael. 1985. *Peru: Paths to Poverty.* London: Latin American Bureau.

Remmer, Karen. 1990. "Democracy and Economic Crisis: The Latin American Experience." *World Politics* 42 (3): 315–35.

———, forthcoming, 2003. "Elections and Economics in Contemporary Latin America." In *Post-Stabilization Politics in Latin America: Competition, Transition, Collapse,* ed. Carol Wise and Riordan Roett. Washington, D.C.: Brookings Institution.

Rizo Patrón, Jorge. 1982. "Análisis de la estructura de la inversión pública." Lima: Ministry of Economy and Finance. Mimeograph.

Roberts, Kenneth. 1995. "Neoliberalism and the Transformation of Populism in Latin America: The Peruvian Case." *World Politics* 48 (1): 82–116.

Roberts, Kenneth, and Moisés Arce. 1998. "Neoliberalism and Lower-Class Voting Behavior in Peru." *Comparative Political Studies* 31 (2): 393–407.

Rodrik, Dani. 1998. "Why Do More Open Economies Have Bigger Governments?" *Journal of Political Economy* 16 (5): 997–1032.

Romero, Gustavo. 1985. "Proyecto Cerro Verde I: Problemática y gestión." Lima: Universidad del Pacífico, Proyecto de Gestión Pública.

Romero, Manuel. 1984. "Análisis de los casos de las centrales hidroeléctricas del Mantaro (I–III Etapas), Restitución y Charcani V." Lima: Universidad del Pacífico, Proyecto de Gestión Pública.

Rossini, Renzo, and Carlos E. Paredes. 1991. "Foreign Trade Policy." In *Peru's Path to Recovery: A Plan for Economic Stabilization and Growth,* ed. Carlos E. Paredes and Jeffrey D. Sachs. Washington, D.C.: Brookings Institution.

Rothrock, Van E. 1969. "The Autonomous Entities of the Peruvian government in Perspective." D.B.A. diss., University of Indiana.

Rudolph, James. 1992. *Peru: The Evolution of a Crisis.* Westport, Conn.: Praeger Publishers.

Rueschemeyer, Dietrich, and Peter Evans. 1985. "The State and Economic Transformation: Toward an Analysis of the Conditions Underlying Effective Intervention." In *Bringing the State Back In,* ed. Peter Evans, Dietrich Rueschemeyer, and Theda Skocpol. New York: Cambridge University Press.

Sachs, Jeffrey. 1989. Introduction to *Developing Country Debt and the World Economy,* ed. Jeffrey Sachs. Chicago: University of Chicago Press.

Sagasti, Francisco. 1996. "Hacía una reforma del estado peruano." *Estudios Internacionales* 24 (octubre–diciembre): 394–421.

Salinas, Patricia, José Garzón, and Carol Wise. 1983. *Problemática regional y política central en el Perú.* Lima: Universidad del Pacífico.

Sanborn, Cynthia. 1991. "The Democratic Left and the Persistence of Populism in Peru: 1975–1990." Ph.D. diss., Harvard University.

Sánchez, Fernando. 1984. "Política de desarrollo y empresas públicas en el Perú: 1970–1980." *Socialismo y Participación* 26 (junio): 31–65.

Saulniers, Alfred H. 1988. *Public Enterprises in Peru: Public Sector Growth and Reform.* Boulder, Colo., and London: Westview Press.

Schady, Norbert. 2000. "The Political Economy of Expenditures by the Peruvian Social Fund (FONCODES), 1991–1995." *American Political Science Review* 94 (2): 289–304.

Schmidt, Gregory. 1996. "Fujimori's Upset Victory in Peru: Electoral Rules, Contingencies and Adaptive Strategies." *Comparative Politics* 28 (3): 321–53.

———. 2000. "Delegative Democracy in Peru? Fujimori's 1995 Landslide and the Prospects for 2000." *Journal of Interamerican Studies and World Affairs* 42 (1): 99–132.

Schmidt-Hebbel, Klaus. 1999. "Chile's Takeoff: Facts, Challenges, Lessons." In *Chile: Recent Policy Lessons and Emerging Challenges,* ed. Guillermo Perry and Danny Leipziger. Washington, D.C.: World Bank.

Schmitter, Philippe C. 1971. *Interest, Conflict and Political Change in Brazil.* Stanford: Stanford University Press.

Schneider, Ben Ross. 1991. *Politics within the State: Elite Bureaucrats and Industrial Policy in Authoritarian Brazil.* Pittsburgh: University of Pittsburgh Press.

———. 1998. "The Material Bases of Technocracy: Investor Confidence and Neoliberalism in Latin America." In *The Politics of Expertise in Latin America,* ed. Miguel Centeno and Patricio Silva. New York: St. Martin's Press.

Schuldt, Jurgen. 1983. "Structural Reforms, Economic and Problem-Solving Policy of the Private Sector during the Military Regime, 1968–1980." Lima: Universidad del Pacífico. Mimeograph.

Schurman, Rachel. 1996. "Chile's New Entrepreneurs and the 'Economic Miracle': Invisible Hand or a Hand from the State?" *Studies in Comparative International Development* 31 (2): 83–109.

Schydlowsky, Daniel M., 1986a. "The Macroeconomic Effect of Nontraditional Exports in Peru." *Economic Development and Cultural Change* 34 (3): 491–509.

———. 1986b. "The Tragedy of Lost Opportunity in Peru." In *Latin American Political Economy: Financial Crisis and Political Change,* ed. Jonathan Hartlyn and Samuel A. Morley. Boulder, Colo., and London: Westview Press.

Scully, Timothy. 1995. "Reconstituting Party Politics in Chile." In *Building Democratic Institutions,* ed. Scott Mainwaring and Timothy Scully. Stanford: Stanford University Press.

Scurrah, Martin J. 1987. "El estado Latinoamericano y las políticas de austeridad: Perú, 1980–1985." *Apuntes* (primer semestre): 15–32.

Seddon, Jessica. 1997. "Puzzling Participation: Democracy and Neoliberalism in Fujimori's Peru." Senior thesis, Department of Government, Harvard University.

Sen, Amartya. 1997. "What's the Point of a Development Strategy?" DERP Working Paper, no. 3, London School of Economics, Development Economics Research Programme, London (April).

Sheahan, John. 1987. *Patterns of Development in Latin America: Poverty, Repression, and Economic Strategy.* Princeton: Princeton University Press.

———. 1994. "Peru's Return toward an Open Economy: Macroeconomic Complications and Structural Questions." *World Development* 22 (6): 911–23.

———. 1997. "Effects of Liberalization Programs on Poverty and Inequality: Chile, Mexico, and Peru." *Latin American Research Review* 32 (3): 7–37.

———. 1999. *Searching for a Better Society: The Peruvian Economy from 1950.* University Park: The Pennsylvania State University Press.

Shepherd, Geoffrey. 2000. "Policy Note: Peru's Public Administration and the Delivery of Public Services." Washington, D.C.: World Bank. Mimeograph.

Shimizu, Tatsuya. 2000. "The Diversification of Export Products: Expanding Non-Traditional Agricultural Exports (NTAEs)". In *Peru's New Perspectives on Trade and Development,* ed. Nobuaki Hamaguchi. Tokyo: Institute of Developing Economies.

Shugart, Matthew, and John Carey. 1992. *Presidents and Assemblies: Constitutional Designs and Electoral Dynamics.* New York: Cambridge University Press.

Sikkink, Kathryn. 1991. *Ideas and Institutions: Developmentalism in Brazil and Argentina.* Ithaca: Cornell University Press.

Silva, Eduardo. 1996. *The State and Capital in Chile: Business Elites, Technocrats, and Market Economics.* Boulder, Colo., and London: Westview Press.

Silva, Patricio. 1998. "Neoliberalism, Democratization, and the Rise of Technocrats." In *The Changing Role of the State in Latin America,* ed. Menno Vellinga. Boulder, Colo., and London: Westview Press.

Skocpol, Theda. 1985. "Bringing the State Back In: Strategies of Analysis in Current Research." In *Bringing the State Back In,* ed. Peter Evans, Dietrich Rueschemeyer, and Theda Skocpol. New York: Cambridge University Press.

Slemrod, Joel. 1995. "What Do Cross-Country Studies Teach about Government Involvement, Prosperity, and Economic Growth?" *Brookings Papers on Economic Activity* 2:373–415.

Smith, Peter. 1995. "The Changing Agenda for Social Science Research on Latin America." In *Latin America in Comparative Perspective,* ed. Peter Smith. Boulder, Colo., and London: Westview Press.

Stallings, Barbara. 1987. *Banker to the Third World: U.S. Portfolio Investment in Latin America, 1900–1986.* Berkeley and Los Angeles: University of California Press.

Stallings, Barbara, and Wilson Peres. 2000. *Growth, Employment, and Equity: The*

Impact of Economic Reforms in Latin America and the Caribbean. Santiago: Economic Commission for Latin America and the Caribbean.

Stepan, Alfred. 1978. *The State and Society: Peru in Comparative Perspective.* Princeton: Princeton University Press.

Stiglitz, Joseph. 1997. "More Instruments and Broader Goals: Moving Toward the Post-Washington Consensus." Helsinki: The 1998 WIDER Annual Lecture.

Stokes, Susan. 1991. "Politics and Latin America's Urban Poor: Reflections from a Lima Shantytown." *Latin American Research Review* 26 (2): 75–101.

———. 1996a. "Peru: The Rupture of Democratic Rule." In *Constructing Democratic Governance,* ed. Jorge Dominguez and Abraham Lowenthal. Baltimore: Johns Hopkins University Press.

———. 1996b. "Public Opinion and Market Reforms: The Limits of Economic Voting." *Comparative Political Studies* 29 (5): 499–519.

———. 1997. "Democratic Accountability and Policy Change: Economic Policy in Fujimori's Peru." *Comparative Politics* 29 (2): 209–26.

———. 1998. "Economic Reform and Public Opinion in Fujimori's Peru: The Limits to Intertemporal Politics." University of Chicago, Political Science Department. Mimeograph.

Sulmont, Denis. 1980. "El movimiento obrero peruano, 1890–1980: Reseña histórica." Lima: Tarea.

Tanaka, Martin. 1998. *Los espejismos de la democracia: el colapso del sistema de partidos en el Perú.* Lima: Instituto de Estudios Peruanos.

———, forthcoming, 2003. "The Political Limits to Market Reform in Peru." In *Post-Stabilization Politics in Latin America: Competition, Transition, Collapse,* ed. Carol Wise and Riordan Roett. Washington, D.C.: Brookings Institution.

Tanzi, Vito. 2000. "The Role of the State and the Quality of the Public Sector." *CEPAL Review* 71: 7–22.

Taylor, Milton C. 1967. "Taxation and Economic Development: A Case Study of Peru." *Inter-American Economic Affairs* 21 (3): 43–54.

Tendler, Judith. 1997. *Good Government in the Tropics.* Baltimore: Johns Hopkins University Press.

Thomas, Jim. 1998. "The Labour Market and Employment." In *Fujimori's Peru: The Political Economy,* ed. John Crabtree and Jim Thomas. London: University of London, Institute of Latin American Studies.

Thorp, Rosemary. 1967. "Inflation and Orthodox Economic Policy in Peru." *Bulletin of the Oxford University Institute of Economics and Statistics* 29 (3): 185–210.

———. 1977. "The Post-Import-Substitution Era: The Case of Peru." *World Development* 5 (1/2): 125–36.

———. 1987. "The APRA Alternative in Peru: Preliminary Evaluation of Garcia's Economic Policies." *The Peru Report* 1 (6): 5/1–5/23.

———. 1998. *Progress, Poverty, and Exclusion: An Economic History of Latin America in the Twentieth Century.* Washington, D.C.: Inter-American Development Bank.

Thorp, Rosemary, and Geoffrey Bertram. 1978. *Peru, 1890–1977: Growth and Policy in an Open Economy.* New York: Columbia University Press.

Tineo, Luis. 1997. "Competition Policy and Law in Latin America: From Distribution to Market Efficiency." Working Paper, no. 4, Center for Trade and Diplomacy, Monterey Institute for International Studies, Monterey, Calif.

Topik, Steven. 1987. *The Political Economy of the Brazilian State, 1989–1930.* Latin

American Monographs, no. 71. Austin: University of Texas, Institute of Latin American Studies.

Trebat, Thomas. 1983. *Brazil's State-Owned Enterprises: A Case Study of the State as Entrepreneur.* New York: Cambridge University Press.

Ugarte, Mayen. 2000. "La reforma del estado: Alcances y perspectivas." In *La reforma incompleta,* vol. 2, ed. Roberto Abusada, Fritz Du Bois, Eduardo Morón, and José Valderrama. Lima: Universidad del Pacífico and Instituto Peruano de Economía.

U.S. Department of Commerce. 1957. "Investment in Peru: Basic Information for United States Businessmen." Washington, D.C.: U.S. Government Printing Office.

Valdivia-Velarde, Eduardo A. 1978. "El sistema tributario peruano y su capacidad de captación de recursos, 1967–1977." Bachelor's thesis, Universidad del Pacífico.

Vallenas, Silvia, and Maria Emma Bolaños. 1985. "Empleo estatal y perfil de los renunciantes de la administración pública, 1978–1979." In *Reporte de investigación: La organización del sector público peruano,* ed. Alberto Giesecke. Lima: Escuela de Administración de Negocios para Graduados, Proyecto de Gestión Pública.

Vargas Llosa, Mario. 1994. *A Fish in the Water: A Memoir.* New York: Penguin Books.

Vásquez, Enrique. 2000. "La evaluación de la inversión social." In *Impacto de la inversión social en el Perú,* ed. Enrique Vásquez. Lima: Universidad del Pacífico.

Vega, Jorge G. 1997. "Foreign Trade Policy and Economic Integration in Peru." In *Integrating the Hemisphere,* ed. Ana Julia Jatar and Sidney Weintraub. Washington, D.C.: Inter-American Dialogue.

Velarde, Julio, and Martha Rodríguez. 1998. "Autonomia de tres instituciones públicas en el Perú." Serie de Documentos de Trabajo, R-342. Washington, D.C.: Inter-American Development Bank.

Velasco, Andrés. 1994. "The State and Economic Policy: Chile, 1952–92." In *Chilean Economic Policy: Lessons and Challenges,* ed. Barry Bosworth, Rudiger Dornbusch, and Raúl Labán. Washington, D.C.: Brookings Institution.

Vernon, Raymond. 1981. "State-Owned Enterprises in Latin American Exports." *Quarterly Review of Economics and Business* 21 (2): 98–114.

Vial, Joaquín, and Jeffrey Sachs. 2000. "Andean Competitiveness at a Glance." Paper prepared for the Annual Conference on Trade and Investment in the Americas, Washington, D.C., September 8.

Vigier, María Elena. 1986. "Ingresos y empleos en sectores urbanos de escasos recursos, el PAIT: Una experiencia heterodoxa." *Socialismo y Participación* 34 (junio): 37–47.

Wade, Robert. 1990. *Governing the Market: Economic Theory and the Role of Government in East Asian Industrialization.* Princeton: Princeton University Press.

Washington Office on Latin America. 1987. "Peru in Peril: The Economy and Human Rights, 1985–1987." Washington, D.C.: Washington Office on Latin America.

Webb, Richard. 1972. *Tax Policy and the Incidence of Taxation in Peru.* Discussion Paper, no. 27, Research Program in Economic Development, Woodrow Wilson School, Princeton University.

———. 1975. "Government Policy and the Distribution of Income in Peru, 1963–1973." In *The Peruvian Experiment: Continuity and Change under Military Rule,* ed. Abraham F. Lowenthal. Princeton: Princeton University Press.

———. 1987. "Stabilization Policy: Peru, 1980–1985." Lima: n.p. Mimeograph.

———. 1988. "Domestic Crisis and Foreign Debt in Peru." In *Development and External Debt in Latin America,* ed. Richard Feinberg and Ricardo French-Davis. Notre Dame: University of Notre Dame Press.

————. 1991. Prologue to *Peru's Path to Recovery: A Plan for Economic Stabilization and Growth*, ed. Carlos E. Paredes and Jeffrey D. Sachs. Washington, D.C.: Brookings Institution.

————. 2000. "Pilot Survey on Household Perceptions of Mobility: Peru, 1998." In *New Markets, New Opportunities*, ed. Nancy Birdsall and Carol Graham. Washington, D.C.: Brookings Institution.

Weyland, Kurt. 1999. "Economic Policy and Chile's New Democracy." *Journal of Interamerican Studies and World Affairs* 41 (3): 67–96.

Wilkins, John. 1999. "Improving Public Service Delivery through Semi-Autonomous Agencies." Washington, D.C.: World Bank. Mimeograph.

Williamson, John, ed. 1990. *Latin American Adjustment: How Much Has Happened?* Washington, D.C.: Institute for International Economics.

————. "The Washington Consensus Revisited." 1996. Paper presented at conference on Development Thinking and Practice, Inter-American Development Bank, Washington, D.C., September 3–5.

Williamson, Oliver. 1985. *The Economic Institutions of Capitalism.* New York: Free Press.

Willis, Eliza. 1986. "The State as Banker: The Expansion of the Public Sector in Brazil." Ph.D. diss., University of Texas, Austin.

Willis, Eliza, Christopher Garman, and Stephan Haggard. 2000. "The Politics of Decentralization in Latin America." *Latin American Research Review* 34 (1): 7–56.

Wilson, Patricia A., and Carol Wise. 1986. "The Regional Implications for Public Investment in Peru, 1968–1983." *Latin American Research Review* 21 (2): 93–116.

Wippman, Lawrence. 1983. "Blending Five Cultures in One Big Project." *International Management* (September): 29–34.

Wise, Carol. 1984. "Peru: Financiamiento externo, sector público, y formación de capital, 1970–1980." *Socialismo y Participación* 28 (setiembre): 59–81.

————. "Economía política del Perú: Rechazo a la receta ortodoxa." Documento de Trabajo, no. 15. Lima: Instituto de Estudios Peruanos.

————. 1989. "Democratization, Crisis and the APRA's Modernization Project in Peru." In *Debt and Democracy in Latin America*, ed. Barbara Stallings and Robert Kaufman. Boulder, Colo., and London: Westview Press.

————. 1994. "The Politics of Peruvian Economic Reform: Overcoming the Legacies of State-Led Development." *Journal of Interamerican Studies and World Affairs* 36 (1): 75–125.

————. 1997. "State Policy and Social Conflict in Peru." In *The Peruvian Labyrinth*, ed. Maxwell Cameron and Philip Mauceri. University Park: The Pennsylvania State University Press.

————. 1998. "The Trade Scenario for Other Latin Reformers in the NAFTA Era." In *The Post-NAFTA Political Economy*, ed. Carol Wise. University Park: The Pennsylvania State University Press.

————. 1999. "Latin American Trade Strategy at Century's End." *Business and Politics* 1 (2): 117–53.

————. 2000. "Argentina's Currency Board: The Ties That Bind?" In *Exchange Rate Politics in Latin America*, ed. Carol Wise and Riordan Roett. Washington, D.C.: Brookings Institution.

World Bank. 1982. *Peru: The Management and Sale of State-Owned Enterprises.* Washington, D.C.: World Bank.

———. 1983. *World Development Report.* New York: World Bank and Oxford University Press.

———. 1985. *Peru: Country Economic Memorandum.* Washington, D.C.: World Bank.

———. 1988. *World Development Report.* New York: World Bank and Oxford University Press.

———. 1989. *Peru: Policies to Stop Hyperinflation and Initiate Economic Recovery.* Washington, D.C.: World Bank.

———. 1993a. *The East Asian Miracle: Economic Growth and Public Policy.* New York: World Bank and Oxford University Press.

———. 1993b. *World Development Report.* New York: World Bank and Oxford University Press.

———. 1995. *Bureaucrats in Business.* New York: World Bank and Oxford University Press.

———. 1996. *World Development Report.* New York: World Bank and Oxford University Press.

———. 1997. *World Development Report.* New York: World Bank and Oxford University Press.

———. 1999. *Peru: Education at a Crossroads.* Washington, D.C.: World Bank.

———. 2000. *World Development Report.* New York: World Bank and Oxford University Press.

Woy-Hazleton, Sandra, and William A. Hazleton. 1987. "Sustaining Democracy in Peru: Dealing with Parliamentary and Revolutionary Changes." In *Liberalization and Redemocratization in Latin America,* ed. George A. Lopez and Michael Stohl. Westport, Conn.: Greenwood Press.

Yarrow, George. 1999. "A Theory of Privatization, or Why Bureaucrats are Still in Business." *World Development* 27 (1): 157–68.

Zysman, John. 1983. *Governments, Markets, and Growth: Financial Systems and the Politics of Industrial Change.* Ithaca: Cornell University Press.

Index